AMERICAN SLAVERY:
Privileges and Pleasures

VOLNEY GAY

IPBOOKS.net
International Psychoanalytic Books

International Psychoanalytic Books (IPBooks)
New York • http://www.IPBooks.net

International Psychoanalytic Books (IPBooks)
Queens, NY
Online at: www.IPBooks.net

Unless indicated otherwise, all scripture quotations are from the King James Version of the Bible.

Other scripture quotations are from the Holy Bible, New International Version®. NIV®. Copyright © 1973, 1978, 1984, 2011 by Biblica, Inc.™ All rights reserved worldwide. www.zondervan.com; and from the New American Standard Bible®, copyright © 1960, 1962, 1963, 1968, 1971, 1972, 1973, 1975, 1977, 1995 by The Lockman Foundation.

All web addresses were correct and operational at the time of publication.

Reproduction of The Abolition of the Slave Trade, by Isaac Cruikshank, 1792, by permission of the British Museum, England.

Illustration on page 231 is from Forrest Wilson, What It Feels Like to Be a Building (Washington, DC: Preservation Press, 1969), 17. Every effort has been made to obtain permission for the illustration. If any acknowledgments or rights have been overlooked, it is unintentional. Please notify the publisher of any omission, and it will be rectified in future editions.

Reproduction of Portrait of a Boy, by John Downman, 1815, by permission of the Birmingham Museums, England.

Cover design by Volney Gay and Kathy Kovacic of Blackthorn Studio
Interior book design by Maureen Cutajar

ISBN: 978-1-949093-94-0

*For my mother who when not impaired
by disease saw in every person a glimpse
of eternity*

Contents

Acknowledgments

I am grateful to colleagues and friends who read this book in various forms. Each helped me improve it. The flaws and errors that remain are mine, either through stubborn refusal to change something or through inadvertency. I thank William Brooks, Linda Faulkner, Don Fehr, Reid Finlayson, Evon Flesberg, Barbara Gay, Norm Nelson, and Joe Parsons. I also thank Louis Breger (psychoanalyst and author of *Freud: Darkness in the Midst of Vision*) and Barbara Breger (American historian) for their valuable comments.

I am grateful to Professor Alice Randall for reading the entire manuscript and for numerous vital conversations on these topics. I thank Christophe Ringer, Tony Brown, Lewis Baldwin, Stacy Floyd-Thomas, and Juan Floyd-Thomas for stimulating conversations on African American thought. I also thank Richard Chrisman, Laura Gay, Frank Gulley, Alan Mendelson, Sara Mendelson, Jim Rurak, Gene TeSelle, and John Wright who read sections of the book.

I thank Scott Zeman for citations from Immanuel Kant in his PhD dissertation, "A Critique of Modern Health Objectivity in Kant, Marx, and Psychoanalysis," at Vanderbilt University, July 2009. I also thank anonymous reviewers who forced me to clarify my presentation. I thank Dean Carolyn Dever and Professor Tony Stewart, College of Arts and Science, Vanderbilt University for supporting a research leave that facilitated the appearance of this book. I am grateful to the team at International Psychoanalytic Books as well: Arnold Richards, MD, and Tamar Schwartz have been a delight.

Foreword

In this book, I grapple with an awful truth: many people, including persons of undeniable greatness such as Washington and Jefferson found pleasure in owning persons. By facing this truth, we can better understand the contradictions of American slavery.

This book is rooted in forty years of psychoanalytic practice. I have studied how human beings enjoy domination, control, and psychic ownership of others. I apply my clinical knowledge to show how "freedom-loving" slave owners enjoyed those pleasures and then disguised that fact. They made continuous efforts to escape this awful truth. I scrutinize their efforts and refute them, one by one.

The cover of this book is taken from *The Washington Family*, a painting by Edward Savage, completed in 1796. These two panels represent the first president who, like numerous white Americans, extracted privileges and pleasures from enslaved persons.

George Washington, hero of the Revolution and the first US president, had just retired from his second term. He liked Savage's painting and bought four impressions of the print. I have shown only the painting's left side and its right side, omitting its center panel. The missing center panel displays a table facing an open window at Mount Vernon that looks out onto the Potomac River. Standing at the table is a granddaughter, Eleanor Parke Custis Lewis, who examines the new Federal City plans with her grandmother. (Photographs of the complete painting are in the public domain and available on the web.)

The left panel on this book's cover shows Washington and a grandson, George Washington Parke Custis. The right panel shows Martha Washington and an unnamed dark-skinned man. It is not difficult to read this painting's message: Washington is a great man, called by destiny, first in peace, first in war, of noble and calm visage. His military sword rests upon the table (it is not sheathed) and his right hand rests on the shoulder of his grandson, whose right hand rests upon a globe. In the boy's hand is a compass, an instrument needed to chart the way forward, with global consequences. Masonic and biblical references dominate the painting as they did Washington's hopes for the new nation.[1]

The (Almost) Invisible Black Man

I focus upon the unnamed Black man portrayed in the right-hand panel. Some 19th-century engravers omitted him in "versions designed for northern, potentially antislavery households."[2] Wishing to sell as many prints as possible, the engravers adjusted their product based on likely sentiments. But why was the Black man included in the *original*

---

1 Manca, Joseph (2011). A theology of architecture: Edward Savage's portrait of George Washington and his family. *Source: Notes in the History of Art*, 31:1, 29-36.

2 Casper , S. E. (1999). First First Family: Seventy Years with Edward Savage's The Washington Family. *Imprint*, 24 :2–15.

painting? And why was his image retained in prints sold to southern households?

I suggest that the original painting included the Black man because he represented something essential to Washington's sense of himself. Washington's sword, his uniform, his state papers, his Masonic symbols, the plans for the city that would bear his name, and his children demarcate his greatness, his demigod status as a founder, the Architect of the Nation. Washington's male slave, one of some 120 human beings he and Martha owned, does the same thing. The Black man reflects and augments Washington's luster. (It would be inelegant and cumbersome to portray all of Washington's human property.) In his fine livery, this almost invisible man symbolizes human beings who worked the plantations, especially those growing tobacco, who tended the gardens and the young children, ran the kitchen, and made Washington and his family rich.[3]

Slavery, a profound evil, preceded the Revolution by more than a century. It was shielded by the 1787 Constitution that rested uneasily upon the Declaration's affirmation of human equality. The Declaration itself derives from the Judeo-Christian axiom of the unity of human beings. According to Jewish and Christian scriptures, all human beings are created in the image of God (the *Imago Dei*).[4] They are therefore members of the same family. Slavery violates American and Christian ideals, yet many Christian Americans championed it.

The tyranny of slavery has a logic. It requires endless forms of violence and degradation of human beings. When tyranny is coddled

---

3 Morgan, P. D. (2005). "To Get Quit of Negroes": George Washington and Slavery. *Journal of American Studies, 39*(3), 403–429.

4 For example, 2 Corinthians 3:18: "But we all, with unveiled face, beholding as in a mirror the glory of the Lord, are being transformed into the same image from glory to glory, just as by the Spirit of the Lord." KJV.

within a constitutional republic, founded on Jewish and Christian affirmations, it festers. Tyranny deforms the minds and hearts of those who benefit from it. It poisons the minds and hearts of its victims. For example, superficial features of African appearance, skin color and such, gave slave owners a convenient depot for their poison: Africans were inherently inferior, they insisted. Africans were destined to be ruled by their racial superiors. Making them perpetual 'servants' was therefore fair, not a national sin.

It took continuous strife and a civil war, resulting in some 700,000 dead and the near-destruction of the American South, to amend the Constitution and make slavery illegal everywhere in the US for all time. To understand why white masters and mistresses felt wedded to an institution that violated their sacred beliefs requires our best efforts. I begin by reflecting on my own experiences of white privilege, the very thing graphically documented in *The Washington Family*.

Preface

This book is a study of the pleasures that slavery gives to owners. This is a demanding, if not an unfathomable topic that rests upon a simple, self-evident truth. The unfathomable part is because slavery seems remote from us now in the twentieth-first century as we struggle to imagine its workings from the sixteenth to the nineteenth centuries. The self-evident truth is that millions of Americans, over a span of nearly four centuries, owned slaves because they wished to. They actively chose and maintained a way of life which they felt merited protection and permanency. A small number of these people were sociopathic, most likely between 2 and 4 percent, the usual norm for large populations.[1] Most were not. Indeed, outstanding persons, among them undoubted geniuses like Thomas Jefferson, engaged in slavery all their lives. It is difficult to understand sociopathic persons, but the vast majority of owners were like you and me: normal. Great men who laid the foundations of American freedom defended to

---

[1] According to Craig S. Neumann, a respected researcher, "Among individuals from the general population, the prevalence of individuals with elevated levels of psychopathic features is estimated to be approximately 1–2%." R. D. Hare and C. S. Neumann,"Psychopathy As a Clinical and Empirical Construct."*Annual Review of Clinical Psychology* 4 (2008): 217–46, https://research.unt.edu/research -profiles/will-real-psychopath-please-stand.

their graves the institution of slavery. This book addresses three questions: What were these pleasures; how did freedom-loving, American Christians explain ownership to themselves; how did they defend themselves against this double contradiction?

These questions are not typical of those asked by historians. Historians discover and present the facts of history using methods that fit their task. While I cite many historians, this book is not a history in their sense of the term. It is an essay in applied empathy. It is based on the assumption that the better we understand slave owners, the better we understand our shared history. To do that we must conceive of ourselves in their circumstances, making their choices, using reasons and justifications that felt valid to them. Like us, they had rational and irrational thoughts, and they had visible and invisible feelings. Among the latter are their pleasures and their fears. I assume that like all persons our American ancestors, from North and South, at times were mysteries to themselves. For that reason they could not declare in direct speech and diary entries, which are the manifest data of historical documents, the totality of their motivations. However, we are removed from their circumstances and the emotional pressures that fell upon them. In that calmer mood we can try to grasp what they could not always see or when they saw it, denied it.

In his 1927 lectures at Cambridge University, the English novelist E. M. Forster made this precise point. He cited a French critic, Émile-Auguste Chartie, who noted that each person has a side that contains, "the pure passions, that is to say, the dreams, joys, sorrows and self-communings which politeness or shame prevents him from mentioning."[2] Forster took advantage of this idea when he wrote his great novels, including his dissection of English colonialism, *A Passage to*

---

[2] E. M. Forster, *Aspects of the Novel*, The Clark Lectures, sponsored by Trinity College of the University of Cambridge, https://d3jc3ahdjad7x7.cloudfront.net /bHl9Pl0voWl8xua UQDove2grx7KZGHFgtEWH2OB905qdfhjQ.pdf, 35. Forster says, "Paraphrased from *Système des Beaux Arts*, 314–315. I am indebted to M. André Maurois for introducing me to this stimulating essay." The author was Émile-Auguste Chartie (1868–1951).

India (1924). In that story, English masters, Hindu and Muslim sub-
jects, and their diverse traditions churn around a conflict between
Adela Quested, a young (white) Englishwoman and Dr. Aziz, a (dark)
Muslim physician.

Forster illuminated the clichéd racism of some of the English. For
example, Ronny, an English magistrate and Adela's intended, describes Dr. Aziz's clothing to his English friends: "Aziz was exquisitely
dressed, from tie-pin to spats, but he had forgotten his back collar-
stud, and there you have the Indian all over: inattention to detail; the
fundamental slackness that reveals the race."[3] One minor error of fastidious English style is sufficient to condemn two hundred million
people, "the entire race." Earlier, Ronny's explained his task as a magistrate, a lay judge, hearing minor disputes: "I'm here to work, mind,
to hold this wretched country by force. I'm not a missionary or a Labour Member or a vague sentimental sympathetic literary man."[4]
Forster also portrayed Dr. Aziz's naïveté, especially his romanticism.
Fond of passionate recitations of poetry to his friends, Aziz recites a
poem by the Indian poet, Mirza Ghalib (1797–1869). In response, his
friends "were overwhelmed by its pathos; pathos, they agreed, is the
highest quality in art; a poem should touch the hearer with a sense of
his own weakness, and should institute some comparison between
mankind and flowers."[5]

Pathos means sharing strong feelings; it emerges in sympathetic
union with others. When Aziz is emotionally overwhelmed by the
cliché that human life is similar to the life of flowers, his friends feel
overwhelmed too. They shared his romantic thrills and pleasures.
Empathy is not sharing strong feelings; it is recognizing strong feelings the way that we recognize the scent of food without eating it.
Forster showed an empathic sense toward all persons in his story,
both the victims and the victimizers. I pursue a similar mission. I
seek pathways to understand the minds of people who owned slaves.

---

[3] E. M. Forster, *A Passage to India*. (New York: Harcourt, 1924), 69.
[4] Ibid., 53.
[5] Ibid., 87.

We seek to discover what "self-communings" transpired within them and which were (and are) sources of shame if admitted. With benefit of hindsight we can see more clearly than they some of the reasons they—decent, non-sociopathic persons—pursued and defended the institution.

The title to this book might seem sensationalistic. The words *pleasures* and *slavery* evoke stories and images of violent, illicit sexual conquest. Those stories are thrilling, awful, and overwhelming; they belong either in sober studies or in dramas and novels that portray sexual crimes. Such conquests, violence, and every other version of human encounter occurred in the 350 years of American slavery. They deserve careful reflection. However, reflecting upon these crimes and upon the larger topic of American slavery is emotionally difficult. To portray these crimes, novelists of great skill must take us into the depths of these encounters but keep us from turning away, from dissociating or simply refusing to see these crimes in full.

In her discussion of slave narratives, Toni Morrison noted that ex-slaves faced a similar dilemma: they needed to describe their ordeals, but they feared overwhelming their readers with accounts of brutality and sexual violence. Some authors and editors found a way around this dilemma. Morrison names Lydia Maria Child (1802–1880), an abolitionist. Child feared that in publishing such accounts, many readers would accuse her of being indelicate. However, these stories needed to be and must be told. Morrison says that even these forth-right accounts lacked psychology: "But most importantly—at least for me—there was no mention of their interior life."[6] Imagining and narrating the interior lives of enslaved persons is among Morrison's missions. Imagining the interior lives of owners is ours.

Thinking about overt sexual crimes, even at a distance, as occurred in white abolitionist circles, may push one toward pornographic imagery and the illicit feelings that pornography can evoke. A history of

---

[6] Toni Morrison, "The Site of Memory," in *Inventing the Truth: The Art and Craft of Memoir*, ed. Russell Baker and William Zinsser (New York: Houghton Mifflin Harcourt, 1998), 91.

representations of slave auctions describes the mixed feelings that pictures of slave auctions roused in (white) viewers. In *Slaves Waiting for Sale: Abolitionist Art and the American Slave Trade*, Maurie D. McInnis discusses the multifaceted ways that English and American artists portrayed auctions in dozens of different formats. Marcus Wood, who reviewed the book, noted that "Particularly, impressive is the delicately nuanced discussion of the English imaginative obsession with the sentimentalised and all too frequently neo-pornographic subject of the slave auction."[7]

For example, provided here is an illustration of a well-known etching, *The Abolition of the Slave Trade, Or the inhumanity of dealers in human flesh exemplified in Captn. Kimber's treatment of a young Negro girl of 15 for her virjen [sic] modesty.*[8] Done by Isaac Cruikshank in 1792, the image of the naked, dangling girl roused indignant protestations. It also roused and rouses erotic suggestions: the girl's lithesome body is fully revealed in profile, her legs are parted but at an elegant angle, more like a dancer than a victim of an atrocity. A delicate, semitransparent garment barely covers her pubic region. The sailor who draws her up into the air is poised in an artful, even artistic, posture of strict proportion and counterweight: his sturdy arms tug at the rope, she hangs down, and together they create an equilateral triangle of bodies, ropes, and brown flesh contrasted with the sailor's white and red clothing. Captain Kimber, on the left, hugging a whip, is an unmistakable lout with a potbelly, sporting a lascivious smile and ruddy cheeks.

McInnis describes the mixed feelings that images like this evoked in opponents of the slave trade. To say that this was an English obsession, as does Marcus Wood, seems inaccurate, however. To motivate English citizens to oppose the lucrative English trade in Africans, abolitionists had to evoke strong feelings about the practice. Everyone

---

[7] Marcus Wood, "Slaves Waiting for Sale: Abolitionist Art and the American Slave Trade," *Slavery and Abolition* 34.1 (2013): 175.

[8] Source: Library of Congress, Prints and Photographs Division, British Cartoon Collection, LC-USZ62-6204. Originally published in London, April 10, 1792.

The ABOLITION of the SLAVE TRADE.

knew the abstract facts of slavery, but that knowledge had no purchase on their feelings, on their interior lives. Sentimentalized and eroticized images of naked men and women being punished (or saying good-bye to their children) did, but in complex ways. At various times, these images evoked fascination, revulsion, excitement, and indignation.

Not just English men and women were enthralled by such images. The scene of Captain Kimber and his captured maiden portrays a person whom we are taught to disavow even if we secretly intuit the lure of the sadistic pleasures he represents. Although social mores control the degree of sadism permitted in high culture, the lure of bondage, protest, struggle, and fascination with surrender to another's sexual wishes are permanent features of human appetites. Given this rootedness, the challenge is to acknowledge these all-too-human wishes, expose them to the light of day, and transform them into insight.

Ten years prior to the Kimber incident, a European composer, W. A. Mozart, put his hand to the same theme in his opera, *The Abduction from the Seraglio* (1782). A young (white) woman and her white maid-servant are taken from their ship and sold as slaves to a Turkish prince. Her Spanish (white) suitor and his (white) servant vow to rescue her and her maid, Blonde, from the (dark) Turks. Of paramount concern is that the two women have remained virginal, that is, unsullied by sexual contact with Turks. The nobleman asks indirectly, but his servant, Pedrillo, who is just about to rescue Blonde, asks her directly:

> Has Master Osmin never,
> As one might well believe,
> Exercised his lordly rights
> Upon you as your owner?
> That would [be] a poor bargain![9]

Capture, bondage, and sexual danger—the ingredients of sexual titillation—are treated in comic form, wrapped in gorgeous music. The opera assures us that although the white lady and her white maid were owned they were not raped, though the Turk had lordly rights. They did not experience the degradation visited upon the young black woman in the painting of Captain Kimber and his crew. For that matter, no one in the opera resembles Captain Kimber or his crew.

Overt sensational crimes like those ascribed to Captain Kimber occurred in American slavery, as did every other form of sexual coercion. However, these are not my topic. The pleasures I write about are everyday. They are far from, but not infinitely far, from sexual misuse. Among these everyday pleasures is the delight in being served by devoted servants. The sadistic leer plastered upon the captain's face would shock Southern gentry who owned persons. Kimber intends to use the young black woman in an unacceptable way; elite owners used black women and black men in acceptable ways, particularly within their homes. That the pleasures of domestic service and the financial benefits it afforded owners depended upon men like Kimber was an economic fact easily forgotten. When discovered and exposed, his kind could be sacrificed to political necessity. Owners of the slave ships, merchants, shipbuilders, and many others who profited by the

---

[9] operafolio.com/libretto.asp?n=Die_Entfuhrung_aus_dem_Serail&language =UK#Act2.

trade did not see themselves as anything less than honorable church-men, adamant protectors of Christian teaching.

Our task in this book is to achieve "empathy for the troubledness of the other," of our American ancestors who owned slaves. Empathy does not mean agreement and forgetting. Empathy begins by documenting differences, by remembering the harms done, and by observing the reasons—including the feelings—that drove the actors involved. Empathy is a first step, not a concluding judgment. To take this first step toward understanding slavery we must learn the basic facts of the institution, how it worked, and how valuable it was to owners. Then, with the facts in place, we can move forward. The benefit of abolitionist efforts was their political effect in rousing Northern states to action; the cost of these efforts, especially those that focused on atrocities, was that many owners easily distanced themselves from these terrible scenes. They felt secure in their Christian identities. They felt slandered by associating Kimber with them. They were correct in the narrow sense that most of them were not sadistic. They were wrong in the broader sense because they benefited from the institution and all found pleasures in it. They fervently believed that their pleasures, unlike Kimber's pleasures, were normal, indeed laudatory. Among those pleasures is the theme of domestic happiness in Southern homes.

The Book In Brief: *The Last Supper*

In *The Last Supper* (*La última cena*), Tomás Gutiérrez Alea, a Cuban film director, portrayed the naïveté of a "good" slave owner, a count, who owns a sugar plantation in eighteenth-century Cuba. In a fit of religious passion, the count decides to invite twelve of his slaves to an Easter meal that will replicate the Last Supper. Humans have long sacralized a shared meal; it predates the Passover Meal and the Last Supper, itself a Passover event.[10] In his reenactment, the count assigns

---

[10] Richard Wrangham and Rachel Carmody, "Human Adaptation to the Control of Fire," *Evolutionary Anthropology: Issues, News, and Reviews* 19.5 (2010): 187–199; Sidney W. Mintzand Christine M. Du Bois, "The Anthropology of Food and Eating," *Annual Review of Anthropology* (2002): 99–119.

the role of Jesus to himself. Alea illustrates the dozens of ways by which the owner luxuriates in his sense of Christian humility and virtue.[11] As he reenacts his version of Christ's last day on earth, the count washes the feet of his twelve slaves, murmuring words from scripture (although he gags when he smells their dirty feet). With care, Alea shows the count struggling to articulate the theological meaning of the Last Supper—of Christ's gift to all persons—to his stupefied slaves who scarf down unimaginable delicacies as he stumbles on. The count's self-understanding may appear ludicrous to us, but Alea does not portray him as a monster or as a fool.

The count embodies the contradictions and unconsciousness of slavery, but he is not a cartoon; his self-love and his grand gestures aim toward Christian consciousness even as he fails to grasp the core of his religion. The count wants both to own the labor of his slaves, and he wants them to view him as someone on par with Christ in humility and forgiveness. For that reason he invites Sebastian, a runaway slave whom he had disfigured earlier, to the reenactment. Sebastian's ear had been severed, a standard method used to punish disobedient slaves. Disfigurement warns other slaves, and it provides a ready means of identification should Sebastian run away again. When, during the supper, the count dramatizes his fantasy about Christ's suffering, the director cuts away to show Sebastian's damaged face, his actual suffering.[12] The count ecstatically proclaims his goodness, just like the Savior. Like Christ, he expects to be loved by his twelve disciples, men who were his slaves every day of the year except on Easter. The cost of the count's religious illusion and his self-contradiction emerges in the film's ending. The eleven slaves who did not see through the count's illusion and believed that they were truly

---

[11] 1976. The Cuban Institute of Cinematographic Art and Industry.

[12] Karen Jaehne, review of *The Last Supper*. *Film Quarterly* 33, no. 1 (Autumn, 1979): 48–53. "Happiness, as [the Count] defines it, is not only suffering but enjoying suffering and appreciating its purifying power. The Count's affectation of pain is a mannerist as eighteenth century crucifixes, but Alea's quick cut to Sebastian shows us true pain," 51.

raised up, pay with their lives. When they don't report for work the next day, Good Friday, the overseer is furious. The slaves revolt; in response they are slaughtered. (The twelfth slave, Sebastian, escapes.) Toward the film's end, we see eleven skulls arranged in a semicircle that mimics seventeenth-century paintings of the crucifixion of Christ and the two criminals on Golgotha, "the place of the skull."[13]

The count's dilemma—his wish to be both Christian and a slave owner—is the subject of this book. This dilemma cannot be resolved by theatrics and make-believe. Because slavery rests upon terror, it cannot persist if owners live their Christian faith every day of the year. To retain the luxuries and pleasures that slavery gave them, owners needed to find solutions to this contradiction. They needed to justify themselves as Christians and as good Americans, and at the same time retain hold of their slave property. Although legalized slavery, with its immense rewards, ended in 1865, there is no reason to conclude that the time-tested pleasures of "being white" have disappeared. As Derrick Bell put it, "Even those whites who lack wealth and power are sustained in their sense of racial superiority by policy decisions that sacrifice black rights. The subordination of blacks seems to reassure whites of an unspoken but no less certain property right in their whiteness."[14]

Bell is persuasive. White privilege persists because it provides benefits and diverse pleasures. As a "property right" white privilege provides a measure of comfort, of personal and emotional security. It does so at the expense of nonwhites. In a rough equation, the pleasure derived from micro-affirmations of white superiority depends upon the suffering microaggressions inflict upon nonwhite people. That equation, which is more complex than mere mathematics, is troublesome. I do not attempt

---

[13] Matthew 27:33 NIV, "They came to a place called Golgotha (which means 'the place of the skull')." The Latin translation is "*Calvariæ Locus.*"

[14] Derrick Bell, "Racism Is Here to Stay: Now What?" *Howard Law Journal* 35 (1991): 79, 85. Bell continues: "This [property] right is recognized and upheld by the courts and society, like all property rights under a government created and sustained primarily for that purpose."

to solve it. I take on a different project. I try to think about American slave owners and the pleasures that made slavery compelling and worthy of their defense. As an essay in applied empathy, this book has many limitations. It is not the last word on this subject, but it is among the first.

PART ONE

INTRODUCTION

Ownership and its Diverse Pleasures

Domestic pleasures, such as being served, do not appear in antislavery images used to rouse abolitionist fervor; they are not part of the antislavery literature of either England or the United States; they are not highlighted in influential antislavery books like *Uncle Tom's Cabin* (1852). On the contrary, these everyday pleasures appear in proslavery literature in the eighteenth and nineteenth centuries and in pro-Southern literature and movies in the twentieth century. Rather than hide the day-to-day pleasures of being served, literature about slaves in the South harped upon their service as instances of domestic order, simplicity, and gratification. These overt celebrations of everyday pleasures make it difficult to reflect upon this seemingly benign aspect of slavery. They are hidden in plain sight, offered as the best parts of Southern life.

Before the Civil War, numerous Southern preachers and other intellectual leaders celebrated the domestic benefits (and pleasures) of slavery. After the war, numerous writers offered identical celebrations of these aspects of slavery when they eulogized the civilization that slavery made possible.[1] A lost world of bounty and joy appears in the

---

[1] Lee Glazer and Susan Key, "Carry Me Back: Nostalgia for the Old South in

original words of Stephen Foster's 1852 song, "My Old Kentucky Home." Set to Foster's lovely music, the song's speaker is a slave sold from a Kentucky plantation to work in a sugar plantation, "By'n by hard times comes a knockin' at the door/Then my old Kentucky home, good-night!" Although some saw the song as antislavery it does not demand abolition, only mourning for the relative benefits of servitude in the mid-South compared to the deep South: "The head must bow and the back will have to bend/wherever the darky may go/A few more days and the trouble all will end/in the field where the sugar canes grow."

Uncounted Southern memoirs, histories, narratives, sermons, and novels portrayed a world of human sympathies, kindness, order, and civility. No sexual crimes and none of the ferocious weapons used to maintain slavery appear in these recollections. On the contrary, birds make music, the "darky" is happy, the corn is ripe and the world is in bloom. Postwar authors from both the North and the South wrote fond, loving portraits of the prewar South. By the early twentieth century, as one writer stated, "Nostalgic pages of flowery prose revealed a lavish Old South of immense wealth, self-sufficiency, honor, hospitality, happy master-slave relations, and, incredibly, the scents and sounds of innocent plantation upbringings remembered in old age."[2] With complete equanimity many white Southerners who remembered life before the Civil War eulogized for their children and their grandchildren the wonders of life during slavery. One woman wrote to her granddaughter about "the happy plantation days, the recollection of which causes my heart to throb again with youthful pleasure" against "the dreadful days, of war and fire and famine" that followed after the war's end in 1865.[3]

Nineteenth-Century Popular Culture," *Journal of American Studies* 30.01 (1996): 1–24.

[2] David Anderson, "Down Memory Lane: Nostalgia for the Old South in Post-Civil War Plantation Reminiscences," *The Journal of Southern History* (2005): 110.

[3] Ibid., 118.

Those everyday pleasures appear shamelessly in a cinematic classic, *Gone with the Wind* (1939), produced by David O. Selznick. For example, we find many entertaining scenes between Scarlett and her slaves, especially her Mammy, such as this one: "Her manners had been imposed upon her by her mother's gentle admonitions and the sterner discipline of her mammy; her eyes were her own."[4]

If pressed to explain why Mammy works at Tara, the O'Hara plantation, rather than raise her own family in her own house, we might dimly recall the murky laws of slavery in the United States. Those recollections are abstract; race laws do not appear on the screen; they are not exciting. Their effects and their extent—how they were reinforced—are in history books, except to African Americans who loudly protested the film when it was shown. For white audiences the film presents a masterful drama with luscious costumes, brilliant actors, vast sets, clever dialogue, and sensuous music. We might put ourselves in the shoes of those who protested the film if we learned how seemingly delightful moments between mistress and slave depend upon the permanent degradation of African-descended persons. In turn, that system depended upon the omnipresence of lethal force used by "low class" whites—like overseers and other hired hands. The latter did not attend cotillions and other delights. They were like Captain Kimber: marginal workers who did the bidding of elites but who were easily disowned when their actions became too public, that is, too difficult to ignore.

Nonsensational, everyday pleasures include, but are not limited to: being served, believing that one's family is superior, the thrill of investing in property that produces wealth and that will likely increase every fifteen to twenty years, the satisfaction of owning the talents, effort, and minds of people dedicated to your betterment, being treated like a lord, and feeling admired—even loved—by enslaved persons. In addition, European myths of racial superiority and the self-ascribed need to "raise up" lesser persons provide waves of self-esteem, indeed goodness. These quiet pleasures did not rouse abolitionists, and they

---

[4] Margaret Mitchell, *Gone with the Wind* (New York: Macmillan, 1936), 3.

do not arouse many of us who see versions of them in various media. Representations of these pleasures are not "neo-pornographic." When Mammy clucks her tongue about Scarlett's antics, we laugh; when Scarlett chastises Prissy for her silliness, we laugh also.

Uncounted Southern preachers added to this bounty of self-affirmation and pleasure. With a bit of adjustment to scripture, they offered solace to owners, to their families, and to others whose conscience might trouble them, even if momentarily. Adding to the domestic pleasures of ownership was the notion that genteel owners extended familial love to their black families, their slaves, and even included them in worship. Margaret Mitchell made this a centerpiece in her description of the O'Haras at prayer in the family's chapel,

> Their dark eyes gleamed expectantly, for praying with their white folks was one of the events of the day. The old and colorful phrases of the litany with its Oriental imagery meant little to them but it satisfied something in their hearts, and they always swayed when they chanted the responses: "Lord, have mercy on us," "Christ, have mercy on us."[5]

Although too simple to understand the meaning of scripture, the liturgy's rhythms satisfy an unsaid, unarticulated, something in the slaves. They get to pray with "their white folks" and savor a closer communion with them than at other times during the day. In the movie, the slaves form an outer circle, surrounding the white family and its matriarch, Ellen: she "closed her eyes and began praying, her voice rising and falling, lulling and soothing. Heads bowed in the circle of yellow light as Ellen thanked God for the health and happiness of her home, her family and her negroes."[6] In this gilded reverie, owners and those whom they own are united in prayer and solidarity; they are not equal, but they are joined in the way that a queen is joined to her subjects, that a general is joined to his adoring troops. Adding a sustained bass line to this scene is a subtext: this spiritual

---

[5] Ibid., 68.
[6] Ibid.

bounty was made possible by the patriarch, Gerald O'Hara, Scarlett's father. He had been "black" in the eyes of the English whose agent he killed in Ireland, but by becoming an American slave owner and marrying an aristocratic white woman, Ellen Robillard, he had earned his "whiteness."[7] He lived the dream that animated numerous people to seek the same kind of fortune.

Does the normalcy and ubiquity of these domestic pleasures make them trivial? No, it does not. It makes them almost invisible, however, to owners who lived within the system and to us who study it from afar. For being served, being esteemed, and feeling we are among the elite are pleasures that quickly become taken for granted. In addition, there was leisure and play, harmless enough pleasures it might seem. Margaret Mitchell ascribes to Scarlett the observation that her neighbors, "had money enough and slaves enough to give them time to play, and they liked to play. They seemed never too busy to drop work for a fish fry, a hunt or a horse race, and scarcely a week went by without its barbecue or ball."[8]

These quiet pleasures abound in slavery as they do in any vertiginous hierarchy: to enjoy the pleasures of domination and control one must have people to control. European colonization of Asia and Africa is a global example. After the collapse of European empires following World War II, scholars from almost every discipline, including psychiatry, examined the structures and costs of European colonialism. Frantz Fanon, discussed below, was an early, brilliant writer on this theme. He documented the methods used to subjugate entire nations and the psychic costs paid by the colonized, those who suffered under these imposed regimes.[9] I wish to add to this conversation. Using the

---

[7] Sinead Moynihan, "'Kissing the Rod that Chastised Me': Scarlett, Rhett and Miscegenation in Margaret Mitchell's *Gone with the Wind* (1936)," *Irish Journal of American Studies* (2004): 127.

[8] Mitchell, *Gone with the Wind*, 56.

[9] For example, see Warwick Anderson, Deborah Jenson, and Richard C. Keller, eds. *Unconscious Dominions: Psychoanalysis, Colonial Trauma, and Global Sovereignties.* (Durham: Duke University Press, 2011). On unconscious

test case of American slavery, I focus upon the quiet pleasures that ownership (and colonizing) brings to those in power.

From whom are these pleasures hidden? Slaves and their descendants knew it directly. Colonized subjects knew it directly. African American viewers of *Gone with the Wind* knew it. They are hidden from us, well-meaning whites who too easily enjoy a willful ignorance about American slavery. White historians know the full facts, of course; nothing I describe in this book is new to them (except, perhaps, my research in the Shaker archives in Kentucky). However, I've found no study that pushes us to reflect upon the palate of diverse pleasures that slavery afforded owners, pleasures that are strikingly similar to those enjoyed by colonial masters.

The importance of these pleasures is evident in the immense effort owners made to defend the institution. They are obscured, though, by equally strenuous efforts to deny them. A large part of these efforts were owners' strident appeals to Christian and American values. We see this in the consummation of the drama of the O'Hara family service as the matriarch concludes her devotions. After praying, Ellen O'Hara "clasped her white beads between long fingers and began the Rosary. Like the rushing of a soft wind, the responses from black throats and white throats rolled back: 'Holy Mary, Mother of

---

pleasure, see Freud's case history, "The Rat Man," in Sigmund Freud, "Notes Upon a Case of Obsessional Neurosis." *The Standard Edition of the Complete Psychological Works of Sigmund Freud,* vol. 10 (1909): Two Case Histories ("Little Hans" and "The Rat Man") and John D. Cash, "Sovereignty in Crisis" in Anderson, Jenson, and Keller, eds., *Unconscious Dominions: Psychoanalysis, Colonial Trauma, and Global Sovereignties,* 21–41. Supporting the eloquence of Fanon's insights are new efforts to map the biological costs of depression and other forms of psychological pain: "As pain becomes chronic, there is a tendency to be different—ones psychological state of being (and mind) is altered. Physical and emotional pain exists on the same continuum; with common brain networks involved with duplication and redundancy abounding." Laura E. Simons, Igor Elman, and David Borsook, "Psychological Processing in Chronic Pain: A Neural Systems Approach," *Neuroscience & Biobehavioral Reviews* 39 (2014): 62.

God, pray for us sinners, now, and at the hour of our death."[10] In this moment of merger, of family union, black throats and white throats utter passionate, or at least, dramatic prayers in unison, in one voice.

From within the film and for many viewers of the film (and the thirty million who bought the book), this crescendo of religious fervor validates the white-black arrangements celebrated in this union. The flow of pleasures that slavery gave to owners appears everywhere in the film, especially in its vivid scenes of beautiful people living in beautiful surroundings. Tara, the O'Hara plantation, is attractive but not as grand as others. Mitchell describes Scarlett's feeling about Twelve Oaks, her beloved Ashley's mansion:

> The white house reared its perfect symmetry before her, tall of columns, wide of verandas, flat of roof, beautiful as a woman is beautiful who is so sure of her charm that she can be generous and gracious to all. Scarlett loved Twelve Oaks even more than Tara, for it had a stately beauty, a mellowed dignity that Gerald's house [Tara] did not possess.[11]

For those outside this circle, these scenes are a barrage of sentimental illusion and disinformation.

White Privilege: Ordinary Unconsciousness and Pleasure

Growing up in a struggling family in Portland, Oregon I didn't feel privileged. When I was in grade school, I compared myself to kids whose families were not on welfare. In high school, I compared myself to kids whose fathers brought home new Chevrolets and helped their children plan for college. However, thanks to federal investments in secondary schools and universities in the 1960s, I received a free education in a good high school. That made it possible for me to attend a good college. While I earned admission to that institution, nothing external to me barred my way. I had absorbed stories about hard work and success; I took comfort in the mantra that character

---

[10] Mitchell, *Gone with the Wind*, 68.
[11] Ibid., 94.

and diligence counted above all. Heartened by those stories and their promises, I believed that I could secure my future. And I was correct. Saturdays at the Portland Public Library (free), with all the books and LPs I could desire, accrued day-by-day and book-by-book into a college, then a university career.

The Portland Library (known as the Multnomah County Library) opened in September 1913. Set in the park blocks in downtown Portland, a few blocks from the art museum and Portland State University, it's a handsome Georgian structure. Into that temple of learning I entered as a rightful citizen, co-owner of its treasures. Its photographs, portraits, books, statues, and resources seemed connected to me. In the words of Andrew Carnegie, whose autobiography I devoured, I belonged with the "girls and boys who have good within them and ability and ambition to develop it" for whom he built his three thousand public libraries. Carnegie described his boyhood delight when he was given access to a private library: "Every day's toil and even the long hours of night service were lightened by the book which I carried about with me and read in the intervals that could be snatched from duty. And the future was made bright by the thought that when Saturday came a new volume could be obtained."[12] I shared these hopes and benefited from the analgesia they afforded me. Discipline would pay off; I was building my future.

I moved from one temple of learning to another when I attended Reed College. Wandering in and out of those buildings I immersed myself in the study of Greek philosophers, Immanuel Kant, and other luminaries. In Reed's library, I found another surge of pleasure in merging with great authors and their traditions. While I knew that I would not be Kant's equal, I also believed that I was part of a tradition, even if my role was to be a caretaker and not a contributor. I was part of the cadre, the group that counted Kant (and similar authorities) as its legendary leader. I was not abandoned. I was not an exile, a stranger in a strange land. My youth and the surrounding culture

---

[12] Andrew Carnegie, *Autobiography of Andrew Carnegie* (London: Constable & Co. Limited, 1920), 46.

were on my side. I sometimes envied my rich friends their new stuff, but I did not envy them their futures.

A photograph of me at Reed shows a white young man. It took me a long time to recognize how that accidental feature of my life was an advantage. The shorthand for this advantage is "white privilege." My white privilege has at least four parts. The first is this bounty of union with others. Face-to-face with my (white) high school teachers (men and women), professors at Reed and the University of Chicago, and senior psychoanalysts in my postdoctoral studies, I felt at home. Those hundreds of linkages, of ties, of shared values and shared worlds were more powerful than my lower-class beginning. That disappeared when I wore better clothing and learned how to use cutlery, how to tip in restaurants, and how to take part in other niceties of middle-class life. As Andrew Carnegie promised, a plucky and industrious (white) kid can make good.

Each tie to these idealized predecessors, small in itself, combined to push me forward, like the undulations that propel a fish. Each added to my resilience in face of the usual challenges of life. In rare moments of friction with a professor, for example, I knew that my relationships with friends and with other professors were secure. Expectable difficulties did not signal to me imminent danger of discovery, of exposure and defeat. I felt that I could swim in the deep water as well as anyone else.

A second part of white privilege was the absence of malice toward me. Like most animals, I do not observe the absence of pain. I took my good health (and other advantages) for granted. For example, when I want to walk from room to room I don't marvel at my not-bad eyesight and my lack of arthritic pain. Should it occur that both activities become arduous, I will remember these good-old days with fondness. In the same way, I did not perceive the benefit of growing up in a culture that automatically validated my skin color and my gender. When I wore better clothing I was just like those around me and just like those whom I admired.

Naturally, groups in power prefer to replicate themselves (either by race or by class or by other markers of sameness). Living with academics and academics-in-training at a progressive college spared me the struggles of finding stature in a college that emphasized the right car, the right fraternity, and the right kind of career: banking, investments, or a grandfather's business. I learned to send and receive academic signals of rightness: verbal intelligence, a good memory, and tenacity. These cost nothing and so I gained entry. Those personal values would not have been sufficient at truly elite institutions, as Lauren Rivera observed. Working-class students invest their time in study and learning. They don't understand that interviewers look for subtle signs of class and polish.[13] An Ivy League degree in the United States, or a degree from Oxford or Cambridge in England, signals the right kinds of achievement to interviewers in prestigious institutions. It means either that the job applicant made it through the rigors of highly selective admissions or that the candidate comes from a family so well connected to the university that admission was all but guaranteed. A few questions about vacations, favorite sports, foreign languages, and such establishes a candidate's pedigree.[14]

The enslavement of Africans was facilitated by numerous markers of class and the indelible marker of skin color (and, of course, the long history of European racist ideologies). However, the need to make hierarchical comparisons, where one group is markedly better than another and so destined to rule, precedes European racism. Within groups of homogenous skin color, such as the United Kingdom until recently, the search for markers found much success by focusing upon speech. Those with "higher level" speech, so-called received pronunciation, are, it was said, better (in diverse ways) than those with nonstandard pronunciation.[15]

---

[13] Tett Gillian, "Why 'Pedigree' Students Get the Best Jobs." *Financial Times*, May 22, 2015, http://www.ft.com/intl/cms/s/0/39628abc-ff2d-11e4-84b2 -00144feabdc0.html?siteedition=intl.

[14] Anna Zimdars, "Fairness and Undergraduate Admission: A Qualitative Exploration of Admissions Choices at the University of Oxford." *Oxford Review of Education* 36.3 (2010): 307–23.

[15] Peter Roach, "British English: Received Pronunciation," *Journal of the International Phonetic Association* 34.02 (2004): 239–245. See also Lynda

Micro-affirmations and Microaggressions

Learning to send and receive signals of status is equivalent to gaining access to a constant source of micro-affirmations of privilege.[16] These shared signals seem as numerous as microaggressions against minority groups and others held to be marginal people. Through actions, speech, attitude, and unconscious assumptions, persons in authority (the elite) signal to nonelites their lesser value. Many studies suggest that the most damaging forms of denigrations are those subtle assumptions about the marginalized person from "well-intentioned individuals who are unaware that they have engaged in harmful conduct."[17] As D. W. Sue put it, "The power of microaggressions lies in their invisibility to perpetrators and oftentimes the recipients."[18] To be insulted a hundred times through invisible means is to absorb into one's self an internal conviction, an awful sureness that "this is me."

A similar power of micro-affirmation lies in their ability to confirm one's worth, one's standing, and one's goodness in the social world. These are all forms of pleasure. They consolidate over time into a conviction of interpersonal security. Joining the best fraternity or attending a prestigious college, and owning the best things are

---

Mugglestone, *Talking Proper: The Rise of Accent as Social Symbol* (Oxford: Oxford University Press, 2007).

[16] See also Lauren A. Rivera, "Hiring as Cultural Matching the Case of Elite Professional Service Firms," *American Sociological Review* 77.6 (2012): 999–1022. Also Lauren A. Rivera, "Status Distinctions in Interaction: Social selection and Exclusion at an Elite Nightclub," *Qualitative Sociology* 33.3 (2010): 229–255. Also Bourdieu Pierre, *Distinction: A Social Critique of the Judgment of Taste*, (Cambridge, MA: Harvard, 1984).

[17] Derald Wing Sue, ed. *Microaggressions and Marginality: Manifestation, Dynamics, and Impact* (Hoboken, NJ: John Wiley & Sons, 2010), 3.

[18] Ibid., 12. He cites Fred J. Hanna, William B. Talley, and Mary H. Guindon, "The Power of Perception: Toward a Model of Cultural Oppression and Liberation," *Journal of Counseling & Development* 78.4 (2000): 430–41, and Dacher Keltnerand Robert J. Robinson, "Extremism, Power, and the Imagined Basis of Social Conflict," *Current Directions in Psychological Science* (1996): 101–05.

pleasures for which people are willing to pay a great deal of money. Advertisers know this when they associate their products with famous people, with celebrities, and with the higher class. This is evident as far back as the 1890s when the Lydia E. Pinkham Medicine Company sold its goods to lower-class and working-class women using images of upper-class women.[19] A crucial element in these appeals is to exclusivity, emotionality, and scarcity (even if the product is pedestrian and widely available). This alluring aspect gives sellers of luxury and exclusive goods a problem when they wish to sell more stuff to more people. How can they solve this apparent contradiction? The answer is to create illusions of rarity since rarity signals expensive, hard-to-find metals like gold and silver, or gemstones, or when they were first introduced, electrical appliances. "Technorarity" is one such method, another is putting out limited editions, another is secrecy and rarified channels of advertisement.[20]

When people saw me one hundred feet away they did not leap to conclusions about my character, my morals, my intelligence. In short, I was not a young African American man in Oregon in the 1960s. I did not feel my classmates glance at me when we discussed "inner city crime" or Arthur Jensen's negative claims about blacks' IQs. Clerks, cops, and librarians did not pay special attention to imagined dangers I presented. I was not splattered with assumptions about my sexual appetites. Each of these embedded assumptions would have damaged the nurturing ties I had with those around me. I did not bear the cost of other people's projected disgust and self-doubts; I was not saddled with their phantoms alongside mine. On the contrary, my teachers and supervisors shared stories about their teachers, men and women whom they admired and whose books I read in college. The limitations, biases, and demerits of these admired forbears were milled away, lost in time, leaving only our shared values. These glowing lights of respect revealed

---

[19] Elizabeth V. Burt, "Class and Social Status in the Lydia Pinkham Illustrated Ads: 1890–1900," *American Journalism* 30.1 (2013): 87–111.

[20] Bernard Catry, "The Great Pretenders: The Magic of Luxury Goods," *Business Strategy Review* 14.3 (2003): 10–17.

timeless, ideal selves, like paintings in a museum.

A third part of my white privilege was the absence of shame for my ancestors and their histories. True, some of my great-great-grandparents lived in "Indian territory" and were no doubt complicit in attacks on Native Americans. However, the drama of those days, in which my side won battles against outnumbered and outgunned natives, was transformed in Western novels and movies about crimes on both sides. Without direct evidence of atrocities committed by my relatives, the Indian wars were interesting but not a source of shame. This brings us to the American Civil War. In grade school, I identified with Carnegie's best self (his discipline and optimism), not his worst self, the rapacious way he treated some of his employees. In high school when studying the American Civil War, I identified with Abraham Lincoln who was accounted an American saint, at least in Oregon. Other white Americans, especially those raised in the South, did not share this opinion of Lincoln; they identified with Robert E. Lee and other celebrated Confederate warriors.

Neither pro-Union nor pro-Confederate whites claimed spiritual unity with the four million enslaved persons enumerated in the 1860 census. I do not do so in the book. Why not? Because we are not black. That means that we do not bear the psychic costs of knowing that some (or all) of our ancestors were treated like property. How to articulate and how to ameliorate those costs are challenges facing those who live in that world. Numerous brilliant black writers have met and will continue to meet this challenge. That is not fair, of course. Being the recipient of another group's projections and its virulent hatred is unjust. Having to detoxify that hatred and to repair the generational damage it causes is also unfair. Ralph Ellison expressed both sides of this burden when his protagonist says, in *Invisible Man*, "I am not ashamed of my grandparents for having been slaves. I am only ashamed of myself for having at one time been ashamed."[21]

Distinguished black authors, like Langston Hughes, did not escape

---

[21] Ralph Ellison, *Invisible Man* (New York: Random, 1952), 15.

dealing with this burden of shame.[22] However, in numerous instances black Americans created ways to surmount these unfair burdens. Essential to these vehicles has been the Black Church. In his March 2008 speech in response to the Reverend Jeremiah Wright controversy, President Obama described his first experience in Wright's congregation, Trinity Church in Chicago. It was one of ecstatic relief:

> "People began to shout, to rise from their seats and clap and cry out, a forceful wind carrying the reverend's voice up into the rafters. . . . And in that single note—hope!—I heard something else." These black stories became universal, linked to all people, they "gave us a means to reclaim memories that we didn't need to feel shame about."[23]

This is a beautiful account of the rescue of self-worth and corporate worth through an institution, the Black Church that maintained so many African Americans and helped awaken thoughtful people in white churches as well.[24]

---

[22] "It is striking to note the frequency with which shame appears in writings of the period, even in the manifestos of the new. Langston Hughes ends his famous essay, 'The Negro Artist and the Racial Mountain' with the assertion that 'We younger Negro artists who create now intend to express our individual dark-skinned selves without fear of shame.'" Kenneth Chelst, *Exodus and Emancipation: Biblical and African-American Slavery* (Jerusalem, Israel: Urim Publications, 2009), 165.

[23] Citing his book, *Dreams From My Father: A Story of Race and Inheritance.* (New York: Three Rivers Press, 2004). T. Denean Sharpley-Whiting, *The Speech: Race and Barack Obama's "A More Perfect Union"* (New York: Bloomsbury Publishing, 2010), 241.

[24] See, for example, Juan Williams, *Eyes on the Prize: America's Civil Rights Years, 1954–1965* (New York: Penguin, 2013); Martin Luther King Jr., *The Essential Martin Luther King, Jr.: "I Have a Dream" and Other Great Writings* (Boston: Beacon Press, 2013); Clayborne Carson, *The Autobiography of Martin Luther King, Jr.* (New York: Grand Central Publishing, 2001); Nancy Joan Weiss, *Whitney M. Young, Jr., and the Struggle for Civil Rights* (Princeton, NJ: Princeton University Press, 2014).

A fourth aspect of white privilege is related to the *absence* of these national, psychic burdens. It is the sense of entitlement to whatever benefits and riches might come our way. In my story, as in many others, it took effort to overcome the psychic burdens of origins. However, once one settles those psychic debts, the way is open to find a place on the escalators of education and self-discipline, just as Carnegie promised. One of many benefits and riches that come to middle-class (and of course, richer) white people is the unmolested transfer of wealth from generation to generation. It goes without saying that these transfers are protected by law. In the same speech in Philadelphia, Barack Obama talked about the struggle to fulfill the promises made explicit in the Declaration of Independence and presumed in the Constitution. He also noted how systematic racism denuded many blacks of social and economic capital, especially home ownership.[25]

Owning a house has given millions of Americans the only thing of enduring monetary value that they could pass on to their children. On average, homeowners have between thirty and forty times the net worth of renters.[26] This is the story of my family. My paternal stepgrandmother owned a small farm in Idaho that she and her husband bought in 1930, when the Depression destroyed their small business in Spokane, Washington. My stepfather mustered out of the US Army in 1945, used the G. I. Bill to complete his education, and married my mother. They spent the then-large sum of $2,000 to make a down payment on our first house. Like many people of their generation, my parents moved from house to house. They retired in 1987, sold their large home, and retained a nest egg from the proceeds. Alongside my stepfather's social security payments, those were their retirement savings.

---

[25] Sharpley-Whiting, *The Speech: Race and Barack Obama's "A More Perfect Union,"* 243.

[26] http://economistsoutlook.blogs.realtor.org/2014/09/08/net-worth-of-home owners-vs- renters/. The US Census Table 1 for 2011 shows an even greater divergence: the net worth for average homeowners is $161,826 versus $2,066 for nonowners: a 78-fold difference, http://www.census.gov/people/wealth/.

It was enough. How did they manage this happy and dignified feat? My grandmother had credit with her Idaho bank, credit established in the 1930s. In 1958, she borrowed $2,000 against her farm. That was the source of my stepfather's down payment. To return to Obama's speech: a line of credit begun in Idaho in 1930 extended through Oregon into the 1950s and continued through my mother's death in 2010. Without credit on a forty-acre farm, my parents would have paid unending rent, built up no equity, and retired with marginal security. Some eighty years of financial stability rested on the decisions of a (white) bank official in Bonners Ferry, Idaho, in 1930 and another (or perhaps the same) bank official in the same town in 1958 to lend $2,000 against the family farm.

In addition to financial capital is social capital. A few years ago, a young African American physician, one of my students, shared with me his excitement and concerns about buying his first home. I understood his excitement but not his concern.[27] He explained that no one in his family—nor in his wife's family—had ever owned a house. His wife, also a physician, and he puzzled over the steps one takes to get a mortgage. My educated friend and his educated wife had passed their medical boards; they grasped the arithmetic of mortgage payments. Their income probably doubled mine. He and I looked at mortgage plans online. I explained how my wife and I got our first mortgage in 1978. I did not explain how we got money for the down payment because that wasn't an issue for him and his wife. It is relevant, though, to the story of Malcolm X, a brilliant African American thinker.

We recall that white terrorists murdered Malcolm X's father, Earl Little, in 1931, in Lansing, Michigan. Earl Little devoted himself to spreading the wisdom of Marcus Garvey's teaching about black independence and self-reliance. As Garvey said in 1923, "Chance has never yet satisfied the hope of a suffering people. Action, self-reliance, the vision of self and the future have been the only means by which the oppressed have seen and realized the light in their own

---

[27] From Volney Gay, "Meaningful Wealth: Obama's Speech on Race" Op Ed piece in *The Tennessean*, Nashville, Tennessee, March 2008.

freedom."[28] Honoring Garvey's teaching in the Universal Negro Improvement Association (UNIA), Earl Little had proudly paid for two life insurance policies; on his death the smaller one paid out, the larger one did not. That insurance company ruled his murder a suicide and refused to pay the amount due the family. This additional crime reduced Malcolm's family to penury and seven years later, his mother, Louise Little, collapsed and was committed to a mental hospital where she remained for twenty-four years. The connection between Malcolm X and me is that my wife and I made our down payment using funds left to her that derived from insurance payments made on her father's death in 1958. That his death was treated fairly meant that his family remained stable. My wife's mother had to budget, of course, and with fortitude she protected her two children. The death of her husband was distressing but it was not catastrophic; she did not collapse, she did not drown in sorrow and injustice. She did not enter a mental hospital; her children were not dispersed to strangers, bereft of their father and their mother.[29]

Awareness of white privilege seems to be helpful.[30] However, no matter the sincerity of one's wish to help ameliorate these attitudes, the embedded reality of American history is that the dominant actors, the centers of excellence, power, and authority are white. Electing an African American president, one out of forty-four, was remarkable and a hopeful sign. However, the swift reactions against President Obama and the upwelling of hatred against him and against his polices illustrate disdain for African Americans. President Bill

---

[28] Marcus Garvey, *The Philosophy and Opinions of Marcus Garvey, or, Africa for the Africans* (New York: Universal Publishing House, 1923), 1.

[29] Some evidence suggests that animosity against nonwhite is decreasing, generation-by-generation. Phyllis A. Katz, "The Acquisition of Racial Attitudes," in *Towards the Elimination of Racism*, ed. Phyllis A. Katz (Elmsford, NY: Pergamon Press, 1976).

[30] Tracie Stewart et al. "White Privilege Awareness and Efficacy to Reduce Racial Inequality Improve White Americans' Attitudes toward African Americans," *Journal of Social Issues* 68.1 (2012): 11–27.

Clinton was excoriated by many, but even he was spared intense, racialized hatred.[31] Like Bill Clinton, I am immersed in a world of privileges that have surrounded me since I entered preschool.[32] I do not see that fact until I am shaken out of my unconsciousness.

The Pleasure of Being "Loved" by Underlings

To be unconscious seems to be the fate of elite persons who occupy relatively high levels within a society. Many reasons account for this. One is that elites need not attend to obscure signals of distress from those below them unless mutiny or a similar upheaval seems imminent. The requirement to learn how to please others, how to predict their behaviors, and to discern subtle clues falls on those who serve, not on those who are served. Bamboozling elites is an ancient art, developed and mastered by slaves and servants for eons. It is as true of master concierges in elite country clubs today as much as it was of slaves in the US South. Which form of pleasure this gives to those in charge depends upon the circumstances and narrative that elites, such as colonial masters or slave owners, tell themselves. In country clubs and expensive restaurants, customers expect a high degree of friendly service: service with a smile. They expect to be liked and to be treated as if they deserve elaborate service.

In colonial domination and slavery there were few contractual and mutually beneficial relationships. There were numerous laws and regulations backed up by brute force. Feeling understood in this context means being obeyed. At the same time, being liked—that is, shown a smiling face—are required as is distortion of the colonized

---

[31] Michael Tesler, "The Spillover of Racialization into Health Care: How President Obama Polarized Public Opinion by Racial Attitudes and Race," *American Journal of Political Science* 56.3 (2012): 690–704.

[32] "Membership in active hate and extremist groups began to increase since 2008 and has seen steady growth during the Presidency of Obama." Wendy L. Hicks, and Bradley W. Hicks, "Polemic of Hate: How Mainstream Political Discourse Fueled the Growth in White Supremacy 2007–2012," *National Social Science* (2014): 39.

subject. Frantz Fanon noted that both during and after colonization, the dominant group insisted upon seeing native subjects as exotic, entertaining, frozen in time. Against the ideal of internal development, generated by themselves, Fanon states, "we find characteristics, curiosities, things, never a structure."[33]

A generation earlier than Fanon, E. M. Forster noted that the English in India would always "see India as a frieze, never as a spirit."[34] A frieze is carved into stone, immovable; a spirit moves like breath and wind. Distinctive foods, dances, and costumes of a region become selling points for tourists whose pleasures depends upon them finding what they had anticipated before they departed. During the colonial period, textbooks and every other vehicle of persuasion and training imparted the same message: the people of the dominant nation are benign, generous, thoughtful, and replete with heroic virtues. For example, in the *Royal Readers*, textbooks published in England and used throughout its empire, native subjects—the vast majority being brown or black skinned—read endless passages about (white) British leaders, battles, authors, and speeches. As Valerie Joseph put it, "The *Royal Readers* in subtle ways teach colonial students to embrace a romantic view in which racism does not exist, despite their oppression by it."[35] This romantic view imbues domination with a rosy glow and that rosy glow adds to the lustrous self-approval of the colonial masters.

Within American slavery, the demand upon subordinated people to like their masters often developed into the demand that they love

---

[33] Frantz Fanon, *Toward the African Revolution* (New York: Grove Press, 1967), 35, cited in Elizabeth A. Hoppe, "Tourism as Racism: Fanon and the Vestiges of Colonialism," in *Fanon and the Decolonization of Philosophy* (Lanham, MD: Lexington Books, 2010), 178.

[34] E. M. Forster, *A Passage to India* (New York: Harcourt), 48.

[35] Valerie Joseph, "How Thomas Nelson and Sons' Royal Readers Textbooks Helped Instill the Standards of Whiteness into Colonized Black Caribbean Subjects and Their Descendents," *Transforming Anthropology* 20.2 (2012): 150.

their masters. Many slave owners were convinced that their "black and white families" were united in affection. No doubt genuine affection occurred in both directions; however, we doubt that persons in bondage forgot who held the whip and who did not. On a different scale but under the same social rules, workers in contemporary corporations must also learn to discern their bosses' wishes, minds, and forms of feeling. Modern management experts affirm the need for employees to read their bosses with extra care and finesse. For example, two management experts describe a four-step campaign:

1. Select a framework for reading your boss.
2. Understand behaviour styles.
3. Determine your boss's behaviour style.
4. Decide how to work with your boss's style.[36]

These four steps amount to four rules that underlings should obey. They may be valuable suggestions. They also are demanding and arduous burdens placed on the employee. Indeed, the care and attention that employees must expend upon their boss's mind resembles an obsessive parent. Questions an employee must answer include: what is your boss's learning style, his or her thinking style, personality type—warm, confident, egotistical, dominant, etc. "Observe events over a period of several weeks to confirm your boss's behavior style."[37] The point of these exercises and fieldwork is to predict your boss's behavior; that improves your performance and allows you to get along better. By implication, if you fail to make these subtle discernments your job and possibly your career are in jeopardy. You will not be thrown into slavery; workers are not slaves, bosses are not slave owners. However, the requirement that those with little power focus on the minds of their bosses is identical in both circumstances. Of crucial importance is an unsaid fifth rule: do not let your boss

---

[36] Jay T. Knippen, and Thad B. Green, "Reading Your Boss," *Employee Counselling* Today 8.4 (1996): 15.
[37] Ibid., 17.

perceive your machinations. Feeling understood is a deep human pleasure. When it arises between lovers it cements their love; when it appears between caretakers and their clients it advances their shared work. When employed by clever underlings with bosses and other members of the hierarchy, it convinces them of one's value.

These four rules seem universal; persons who serve others and who have little defense against arbitrary actions must study the personality traits and learning styles of those whom they serve. By obeying these rules, which require one to present a false self, servants are in danger of sliding into self-deception. When the elites are from another culture with another language, which they idealize, native culture and native languages are automatically denigrated. Frantz Fanon put it directly, "Every colonized people—in other words, every people in whose soul an inferiority complex has been created by the death and burial of its local cultural originality—finds itself face to face with the language of the civilizing nation."[38] This insight seems both valid and tragic. Having achieved it, the colonized subject is also demoralized.

Variations on this theme occur worldwide. For example, courtesans in sixteenth-century China were elevated above mere prostitutes when they acquired the polish of women born in the upper classes. This required them to study hard and to affect the manners and education of upper-class women: "the true function of a courtesan (as opposed to a prostitute) was that of a "professional hostess" who was educated and cultivated in skills such as conversation, knowledge of classical literature, recitation of poetry, dancing, and musical performance."[39] By mastering these skills, a top-class courtesan brought more pleasure to her clients and so secured higher fees. From these fees some were able to save enough money to buy homes and gain

---

[38] Frantz Fanon, *Black Skin, White Masks* (1952, New York: Grove Press, 2008), 18.

[39] Harriet T. Zurndorfer, "Prostitutes and Courtesans in the Confucian Moral Universe of Late Ming China (1550–1644)," *International Review of Social History* 56.S19 (2011): 202.

financial security. Others who failed to please their clients were thrown into the streets.

The effect of these efforts to predict the wishes, pleasures, and needs of elites is to render the minds of sub-elites opaque to those in power. Servants, courtesans, and slaves presented "faces" that their masters wished to see. They hid their actual thoughts and feelings behind polite, friendly masks. These adaptations create a cognitive tilt against the elite. The boss, the mistress, and the master are often ignorant of what actually occurs in their houses and on their properties. Refined politeness, manners, and the cult of family devotion provides both servant and master a pleasant lie; it soothes the feelings of the master, and it safeguards the servant from harsh punishments for disobedience, surliness, and insubordination. These familial cults do nothing to protect those who serve when economic necessity requires decisive, harmful action against them.

The passage from *Invisible Man* cited earlier continues: the narrator describes his grandparents, newly freed slaves "told that they were free, united with others of our country in everything pertaining to the common good, and, in everything social, separate like the fingers of the hand. And they believed it. They exulted in it. They stayed in their place, worked hard, and brought up my father to do the same."[40] Just like the (white) kids who read how to get ahead books and planned a future secured by hard work alone, they raised their children to plan, to build a future. The phrase "separate like the fingers of the hand" refers to a famous speech by Booker T. Washington in 1895 in Atlanta. Sometimes called the "Atlanta Compromise Speech," Washington addressed his majority white audience directly. He assured them of racial harmony while preserving social differences between them and African Americans:

> We shall stand by you with a devotion that no foreigner can approach, ready to lay down our lives, if need be, in defense of yours, interlacing our industrial, commercial, civil, and religious life with yours in a way

---

[40] Ralph Ellison, *Invisible Man*, 15–16.

that shall make the interests of both races one. In all things that are purely social we can be as separate as the fingers, yet one as the hand in all things essential to mutual progress.[41]

Washington spoke only thirty years after the end of the Civil War. He faced a white audience in one of the South's strongholds. Many of them remembered Yankee attacks on their city, their lost loved ones, and their lost wealth. Washington's pleading was familial: African Americans had nursed their children, their parents, and mourned their deaths but always in humble ways. This was true. Washington played this card: former slaves and now their children would continue to shower on whites the pleasures of affection that they *alone* knew how to convey. African Americans would show "devotion that no foreigner can approach" because they had mastered those modalities for generations. In return for white persons' alliance, he pledged undying, but respectful, devotion to their defense. One of the acknowledged, often celebrated, pleasures of ownership—the respectful devotion of black servants—would persist in the post-slavery world. Washington's speech is a perfect instance of appeasement; for many reasons it roused passionate denunciations by other black leaders. Washington reported that whites rushed up to him to congratulate him on his words of conciliation; black audience members fell silent.[42]

Recalling this speech, the unnamed narrator's grandfather in *Invisible Man* announces on his deathbed that Washington's bargain was not kept. He had been wrong to imbibe Washington's dream. Black life with white bosses was not familial: it was a constant struggle, it was war he says:

"Son, after I'm gone I want you to keep up the good fight. I never told you, but our life is a war and I have been a traitor all my born days, a spy in the enemy's country ever since I give up my gun back in the Reconstruction.

---

[41] http://historymatters.gmu.edu/d/39/.

[42] Derrick Bell, "Racism Is Here to Stay: Now what? *Howard Law Journal* 35 (1991): 79, 81.

Live with your head in the lion's mouth. I want you to overcome 'em with yeses, undermine 'em with grins, agree 'em to death and destruction, let 'em swoller you till they vomit or bust wide open." They thought the old man had gone out of his mind. He had been the meekest of men.[43]

People in power think well of themselves—good things that come their way, from educational advantages to political power to social status, are their due. They earned these good things, even if sometimes that meant being born to them. Those that do not possess these good things have, it follows from this self-congratulatory logic, refused to apply themselves (or have been foolish or lazy). White privilege is unconscious because the narrative of discipline and investment, the American success story, seems sufficient to explain one's (white) triumph and to explain why others have failed to follow suit.

Like most people, elites wish to be admired by one and all. This includes their servants (or employees) in the twenty-first century, their slaves in the nineteenth century, and their concubines in every century. Masters respond well to praise and "warmth" from those who serve them. The grandfather had been the "meekest of men" because meekness helped him keep his job and provide for his family. He had had to swallow decades of "yes'm" to white masters and now he wants them to feel pain. To "agree 'em to death" is to supply as much fodder as they can handle. A "spy in the enemy's country" must be constantly on guard, alive to possible mistakes, dedicated to a double consciousness: divided against himself; counting the number of humiliations heaped on his head. As the grandfather dies he exhorts the narrator's father, "'Learn it to the younguns,' he whispered fiercely; then he died."

The Defense of Slavery and the Constitution

During the deliberations that issued in the US Constitution of 1787, proslavery forces won most of the battles over the institution. After

---

[43] Ralph Ellison, *Invisible Man*, 16.

1787, they mounted ferocious parliamentary campaigns to preserve it. Even when faced with a war they could not win, they defended slavery until utter defeat by the armies of the North. To ask a simple question: Why? To summarize this book's answer: because they enjoyed the institution, both its financial promises and its emotional pleasures. Slavery gave owners financial resources to build, to create, to master new territories. These are exciting and deeply satisfying ventures, as anyone can understand. It was thrilling to wring wealth from new, often hostile lands. The great houses and estates of owners, given grand names like Mount Vernon, Monticello, and The Hermitage, were beautiful. So-called slave walls in Kentucky and Tennessee, for example, remain beautiful today. True, many owners never made it to these luxurious heights. But every (white) man could dream that he and his children might join these elites.

God, the US Constitution, and the need to manage their slave property congealed in owners a conviction of their mission: to generate wealth for themselves and their successors. Essential to this wealth was the control of slave bodies, especially their sexual powers. By virtue of creating *chattel* slavery, American owners provided themselves a continuous windfall; they owned not just the bodies of their adult slaves but also the bodies of their slaves' offspring, in perpetuity.[44] Hence, all births to all slave women—no matter the father—increased the owner's wealth. If he or one of his sons were the father, the child might gain special favor but rarely freedom. By the early nineteenth century, owners in Virginia pursued the lucrative practice of selling excess slaves (generated by natural increase or through decreased need) to the western markets. This intra-national trade made expanding markets into new states mandatory. Owners with excess product needed federal guarantees that citizens in the new territories could legally import slaves. By entrenching federal laws that cosseted slavery— and by extending slavery into new, western states—their initial investments yielded fortunes beyond those afforded by agriculture.

---

[44] OED: movable property. "Middle English: from Old French chatel, from medieval Latin capitale, from Latin capitalis, from caput 'head'. Compare with capital and cattle."

One of the challenges to understanding American slavery is that it developed in a piecemeal, *ad hoc* fashion. Laws and "slave codes" were shaped by local needs for labor and by the annoying fact that sometimes slaves sought to disrupt the work their owners assigned them. For that reason historians of slave laws do not describe orderly, systematic reasoning about slavery. From the beginning, "colonial courts and legislatures addressed slavery frequently, in thousands of colonial statutes and cases relating to slaves, but the results were haphazard and inadequate for their tasks. Colonial slave law was incomplete, because the concern of local courts and legislatures was primarily with public law, the policing of slavery, while huge areas of daily concern to slaveowners, almost the entirety of private law, were not treated."[45] This absence of legal reasoning, and the English courts' silence upon American slave practices, left colonial legislatures free to create "codes." Owners had license to experiment with diverse doctrines. Jonathan Bush noted, "The quality of slave doctrine, however, was less significant than the fact that the colonists would dare to fashion such radically new doctrine."[46]

Depending upon their needs, American slave owners defined—and later, justified—slavery using assorted legal devices. These ranged from analogies to indentured servants, to "freehold" property analogous to serfs, and finally to chattel property. The latter was the most onerous for slaves and the most profitable for owners, for as one writer states: "Chattels were defined as the owner's personal belongings which he could

---

[45] Jonathan Bush, "Free to Enslave: The Foundations of Colonial American Slave Law," *Yale Journal of Law and the Humanities* 5, no. 2, article 7 (1993): 419.

[46] Ibid. "Colonial lawmakers learned, as jurists had recognized in slaveowning Rome and as American lawyers continued to realize in the nineteenth century, that the legal issues posed chattelized humans and thinking property could often not be accommodated within ordinary legal categories. But the response was slow, and slave law failed to develop any analytic apparatus until the last few years of the colonial period, long after Africans had been brought as slaves to the English colonies," 421–422.

dispose of as he pleased. In short, freehold slavery attached the slave to land, like a serf, while chattel slavery attached him to a master, a condition unknown in English law and a uniquely North American development."[47] This "uniquely North American development" was built upon the (white) European belief in the inferiority of Africans, that "slavery was the normal condition of Negroes."[48] Histories of the colonial period show owners and their supporters struggling to find the mix of legal niceties and punishments sufficient to control slaves. This fumbling continued until 1688 in South Carolina, "when the assembly enacted a law defining slaves as real estate, or freehold property. Four years later the assembly amended the law by making the slave a personal chattel in payment of his master's debts."[49] The peculiarity of slavery was evident from the beginning; how could one rationally and ethically make sense of "chattelized humans and thinking property"? Finding no systematic way to explain, much less justify, chattel slavery, Southern leaders fabricated rules and customs whose incoherence mirrored the incoherence of their minds. For that reason, exact speeches and texts are cited in this book. Those who championed slavery wrote in plain English; they explained themselves well. When they plotted to defend slavery using parliamentary devices, they wrote well too. When they sought to offer legal and ethical justifications for slavery they became incoherent. That incoherence stems from the hopelessness of their task: to make human beings into nonhuman beings.

Why Did Americans Own Slaves?

The incoherence that saturated slave codes in the seventeenth century saturated, as we well see, American justifications of slavery in the eighteenth and nineteenth century. Slave codes emerged in reaction to the efforts of "thinking property" to escape brutality; Southern justifications

---

[47] M. Eugene Sirmans, "The Legal Status of the Slave in South Carolina, 1670–1740," *The Journal of Southern History* 28, no. 4 (November 1962), 465.
[48] Ibid., 463.
[49] Ibid.

of slavery emerged as defenses of the economic and emotional benefits that slavery gave to owners. Although slavery had paltry legal standing and although it contradicted the high-flown rhetoric of (white) colonists' diatribes against the English Crown, Southern elites championed it with relentless energy. Using diverse legal stratagems, political control of every Southern statehouse, control of the US Senate and often the presidency, they defended the institution with everything available. They fought to protect a way of life that abolitionism in any form, from mere idea to outright legal fact, would destroy. Again, as we will see, they fought as if their lives depended upon the preservation of slavery.

They were correct: deprived of uncompensated slave labor and slave progeny, their private fortunes would evaporate. Southern defenders of slavery confronted two enemies, both rooted in human nature and both relentless. The first enemy was their shared ideal of universal human rights. It resided in their hearts even as it hovered over the Constitution and the Declaration, issued at America's political birth. Founders like George Washington, Thomas Jefferson, and Patrick Henry—slave owners—who demanded their rights from the English king understood the irony that they did so while they conspired to deprive others of theirs. In private letters and in public debates some of them acknowledged their anguish over this contradiction.

Their second enemy was their large slave population. From the owners' point of view, slaves were potential predators. Just as dangerous criminals require canny management and control, so too did slaves. Just as the criminal justice system must adapt to changes in inmates' behaviors, slave codes (and other forms of management) changed as circumstances dictated. Not accidently, this conviction that African Americans were predatory criminals animated anti-black novels, movies, and other propaganda that proliferated after the South lost the war. Owners struggled with these spiritual ironies of slavery for as long as slavery persisted; their legacy of systematic denigration of black Americans is still with us. When legal slavery disappeared, extralegal institutions and groups, such as the Klan, emerged to preserve and enforce the old rules.

The financial rewards of slavery were immense. However it is a mistake to explain the tenacity of slavery by wealth alone. After 1865, the United States no longer recognized the concept *slave* and the market value of slave property disappeared. That did not impede the machinery of vilification of blacks by both Southern and Northern institutions. At each juncture, those who operated this machinery found new ways to dominate African Americans. Before and after the war they made extraordinary efforts to humiliate and disenfranchise blacks. This was, of course, to preserve white control of political and financial resources. In addition, these relentless campaigns helped to preserve the real, though less visible, rewards of entitlement and superiority: disenfranchising some voters elevated those white men who enjoyed the elite status as citizens: "suffrage is a privilege only to the extent it is denied to others," as Pippa Holloway put it.[50] Southern political strategy after 1865 "developed into a larger effort to defame and thus disenfranchise the race—by associating African-Americans with criminality, degrading them through legal and extralegal violence, and denying the newly freed slaves the dignity traditionally associated with those deserving suffrage."[51] Infamy is a moral category; those who are punished by humiliating devices become infamous, tainted by their punishments. The more blacks were humiliated, by every means available, the less deserving they were of voting.

---

[50] Pippa Holloway, *Living in Infamy: Felon Disfranchisement and the History of American Citizenship* (New York: Oxford, 2013), 15.

[51] Ibid., 3. Holloway's brilliant book delineates the zeal with which white elites in the postwar period used a mix of legalisms and bizarre reasoning to malign African Americans and to associate them with criminals: "Degradation was believed to be characteristic of all African Americans, not just slaves," (ibid., 8). Since their forbears had enslaved millions of African Americans, and thus "degraded" them, their zeal to disenfranchise former slaves makes no legal sense. It does make emotional sense: they were immersed in the delusions of American racism and they could not bear to feel the depth of the national crime. In lieu of genuine remorse for having been beneficiaries of this system, they shouted louder, hated better, demeaned and terrorized blacks with more efficiency.

The goal of this book is to try to understand how slavery worked and how the victimizers, owners, and their advocates justified the institution. To do that we need to understand what they got from slavery and how they used every means possible to maintain ownership. The analogy between slave owners and wardens, and between plantations and prisons, is not trifling. Once we cross the gap that exists between owners and us, we understand that owners brought enemies into their homes and farms. While slavery is ethically criminal, it is not irrational. Owners, we recall, were the elites of their colonies and later their states: they made rules, laws, and codes that suited them. They had the powers of law, legislatures, courts, and religion on their side. Given those unchecked powers, owners' appetite for wealth and assorted luxuries met little external resistance.

Their internal struggle against their allegiance to ideals of freedom was quieted sufficiently by the convenience that Africans were marked as different and were "known" to be inferior. European racism provided a crucial rationale. It made empathy for slaves difficult, and it helped shore up the common delusion that slavery was "helping" blacks. The darker colors of Africans made them effectively pre-branded as not like us. Thus, they stood out against a Caucasian population that projected their disavowed selves upon them. From 1787 to 1865, owners, the police, and all white citizens in the South knew that any colored person was either a convict (that is, a person held in bondage) or an escaped convict (an escaped slave). Free blacks were non-slaves, a category that aggravated Southern authorities because it made it harder to police their blacks.

These beliefs (and the feelings tied to them) permeated debates about the text of the US Constitution. They mutated into national laws in the Constitution's three-fifths provision (article 1, section 2, clause 3), which gave the slaveocracy additional representation in Congress and in the fugitive slave clause (article 4, section 2, clause 3), which required citizens in all states to turn over escaped (or possibly escaped) slaves to "slave catchers." White prisoners who escaped could blend into the crowd by shunning their uniforms and chains used to mark them as dangerous; blacks could not escape their skin color.

With pernicious intelligence owners experimented with ways to extract the most value from slaves, people who had no allies and no resources in a country situated across the Atlantic from their homes. Africans stolen from their homes were devastated, traumatized by violence, and subjected to daily humiliations. Once on American soil, they could not escape without being hunted down according to the Constitution, American national law. True, some Southerners demurred from celebrating slavery, and many Northerners objected to it (as evident in the debates that preceded the ratification of the Constitution). However, the law of the land, for all US states, was written by and for owners.

Acting as near absolute rulers, owners and their underlings set plantation rules and used selected rewards and punishments as necessary. Often punishments included public whippings or maiming to clarify the futility and cost of disobedience. Sometimes punishment meant lethal force. Southern courts were reluctant to punish owners' use of lethal force against slaves except in unusually sadistic cases where public decency required a response. The reason for the judges' reluctance was that while slaves were recognized as human beings, they were dangerous human beings whose obedience created Southern wealth and whose disobedience threatened the lives of both owners and non-owners. In this latter sense owners made slaves into predators. Similar to other interactions between predator and prey, any advance by the predator (slaves) required a response from the prey (owners).

Slaves struggled naturally for their freedom. Given access to weapons and skilled leaders, African-descended persons, like Toussaint Louverture who led the Haitian Revolution of 1791–1801, made their intentions clear. In response to Louverture's victory over Haitian slave owners, Southern politicians demanded that President Jefferson not acknowledge Haitian slaves who had defeated their masters. The obvious danger was that American slaves might be inspired to emulate their Caribbean counterparts. Contrary to everything that he said about "natural rights," Jefferson bowed to the owners' demands: "he acquiesced in southern policy, the embargo of trade and nonrecognition, the defense of slavery internally and the denigration of Haiti abroad."[52] Jefferson did so because

---

[52] "Jefferson . . . was aware of the reaction of southern slaveholders against

slaveholders, like him, were terrified that slave uprisings would occur on American soil, as they had in the recent past.

Four Hundred Thousand American Slave-Owning Families

Few people were surprised when *12 Years a Slave* won three Academy Awards in 2014, including Best Picture to Steve McQueen, the first black director to win that award. A brilliant evocation of the cruelty of American slavery, the movie demonstrates immaculate injustice: a free man is kidnapped, wrenched from his family, abused, and tormented nearly to the breaking point. While the film is technically masterful, its theme—American slavery—elevated its importance. The film is not mere entertainment. It asks us to confront an awful question: Why in 1860 did some four hundred thousand American families own slaves? The simplest answer is also the most appalling: because they wanted to. They, white Americans, wished to expropriate the labor, luxuriate in the bodies, and dominate the minds of Africans and their descendants. When granted, each of these wishes yields pleasure. Expropriated labor turned worthless swamps into valuable farmland; black bodies became objects of sexual and physical pleasures and sources of new "product"; dominated minds generated tremors of narcissistic entitlement in the ruling classes. Using terror in all its forms and diverse bribes when needed, owners kept blacks as stupefied as possible. According to Southern leaders, every white person, no matter how vicious, was superior to every black person, no matter how noble. This clever adaptation of traditional European racism made it impossible for poor Southern whites to identify themselves and their dire straits with slaves and their worse straits. As

---

Saint Domingue-Haiti, especially the Great Fear in Virginia following the Gabriel slave conspiracy (1800) and subsequent Easter Plot (1802). Facing a Congress hostile to Haiti, he acquiesced in southern policy, the embargo of trade and nonrecognition, the defense of slavery internally and the denigration of Haiti abroad." Tim Matthewson, "Jefferson and the Nonrecognition of Haiti," *Proceedings of the American Philosophical Society* 140, no. 1 (March 1996), 22.

members of the so-called white trash put it, at least they weren't blacks. By instilling and nurturing this venom, Southern elites made it impossible for poor whites to align themselves with slaves. No union of slaves, who were easily identified as blacks in the South, and poor whites, who could gain access to guns, could emerge. Terrified owners shared a universal goal: to prevent the rise of an American Louverture.

We realize that the division between North and the South has persisted. Lincoln matters to us because the Civil War and the struggle over slavery and its roots in American racism matter to us. If we deny our potential to act and believe as Southerners did, as Lincoln put it, we deny our common bond with them. We also deny the immense wealth that slavery generated for both North and South. We cannot start to understand American slavery and the dogged ways that Southerners resisted abolition, emancipation, and civil rights for African Americans a hundred years after the Civil War. Their maniacal use of violence, before and after the war, becomes mysterious.

***

This book has three parts. In part 1, we examine the facts of slavery. In part 2, we review the history of the original US Constitution of 1787. It encapsulated the realities of slavery, a patchwork of penal codes, systematic propaganda, and police terror. Its authors did not know how to square the circle, the legal incoherence of "chattelized humans and thinking property." This conundrum, this contradiction was at the heart of the Constitution, the founders' master plan for the United States. In part 3, we examine four different resolutions to this contradiction arranged from the most harmful to the most valuable. The most harmful is splitting (as seen in Southern defenses of slavery before and after the war); the most valuable, though still incomplete, appears in the thought of Mother Ann, founder of the Shakers, and the speeches of Abraham Lincoln.

CHAPTER 1

Slavery for Profit, Reward, and Pleasure

Slaveholding and the Church

Bishop Leonidas Polk, a cousin of President James K. Polk, fought and died as a Confederate officer.[1] That he was a large slaveholder counted among his ecclesial virtues. His eulogist, the Right Reverend Stephen Eliot, explained: "The Church needed a large slaveholder, who might speak boldly and fearlessly to his peers, as being one of themselves, about their duty to their slaves, and might teach them, by his living example, what that duty was, and how to fulfil [sic] it; and she [the church] found it in this young disciple."[2] According to Reverend Eliot, if Polk were merely a small slaveholder he would not have had the experience necessary to understand the unique burdens placed upon owners with large holdings. Large slaveholders needed to instruct their slaves and hired hands in Christian obedience and deference to authority. This need was not driven by spiritual zeal to

---

[1] William Dusinberre, *Slavemaster President: The Double Career of James Polk* (New York: Oxford, 2003).

[2] St. Peter's Day, 1864, Funeral Solmenities [sic]. http://www.bencaudill.com/chaplain/polk_funeral.html.

champion Christianity among the less educated and so prepare them for heavenly eternity. It was another, temporal need: slave owners needed to use every resource available to corral, coerce, and contain slaves who might otherwise rebel, thus destroying their value as chattel. As Jefferson noted in the Declaration, tyrannical governance always evoked rebellion and rebellion was, by its nature, a catastrophe for those who held the chains of power.

Bishop Polk and Reverend Eliot were highly educated clergymen, yet they excised the Christian message of freedom whenever possible. English evangelists who wished to Christianize Native Americans and black slaves struggled with the same dilemma; while they recognized the unity of all persons as potential members of the church, their official body, the Society for the Propagation of the Gospel in Foreign Parts (SPG) did nothing to prohibit the slave trade nor slavery. On the contrary, as its mission program spread, the SPG grew more entangled with protecting slavery.[3] Anglican ministers in the Caribbean slave islands and in slaveholding regions on the continent moderated their beliefs about universal brotherhood according to the dictates of the SPG. Because the SPG controlled funding and local fees, "Prudent clergy in the colonies learned quickly the importance to their own well-being of understanding local culture and personalities," according to one writer.[4] In a similar way, colonial owners and their clergy replaced public religious rituals of marriage and baptism with private, domestic rituals for themselves and their kin. This decision created

---

[3] Travis Glasson, *Mastering Christianity: Missionary Anglicanism and Slavery in the Atlantic World* (New York: Oxford, 2011). "Paradoxically, while part of its missionary program was inspired by the commitment to the unity of mankind and by a desire to reform enslaved people, master, and slavery itself, the SPG's ideological and material investment in slaveholding deepened across the eighteenth century" (ibid., 6). He adds: "from the 1760s through the 1830s, a number of SPG figures emerged as proslavery spokespeople and the Society's history was used to defend slaveholding" (ibid., 11).

[4] Nicholas Beasley, *Christian Ritual and the Creation of British Slave Societies, 1650–1780.* (Athens, GA: University of Georgia Press, 2009), 5.

additional forms of segregation. It served to diminish dangerous ideas of commonality between blacks and whites; it strengthened the sense of difference between blacks and whites, between slaves and owners. What had been a shared form of worship and civic engagement, a public event, became exclusive and hierarchical.[5]

Rewards of Transporting, Selling, and Owning Slaves: North and South

Until economic historians investigated the financial rewards of slavery, we had incomplete knowledge of the immense profits that slavery brought to ship captains, clerks, builders, and thousands of other unknown persons. These unknown persons are never portrayed in the grand narratives and movies about the Civil War. No one grows misty-eyed over the humdrum work of bankers and clerks. A century before the Civil War, New England colonists gladly engaged in the diverse and lucrative trades that made up slavery.[6] Just before the American Revolution, New York City had twenty thousand slaves "making it the largest slave population north of Maryland."[7] This is surprising if one has learned to see the Civil War and American race issues as primarily a Southern problem. Looking back at slavery through the Civil War, it seems impossible to believe that New York and many other Yankee cities could have this history. Steven Deyle and dozens of other historians reveal a naked truth: many colonial governments sought to regulate slavery by taxing it. They did so to raise revenue, to address their debts, and to prevent slave revolts, said Deyle, "Never did the colonies enact duties for humanitarian reasons."[8]

If we see American slavery as primarily an economic issue—with

---

[5] Ibid., 11. See also 135–36.

[6] Steven Deyle, "'By Farr the Most Profitable Trade': Slave Trading in British Colonial North America," *Slavery & Abolition* 10 (September 1989), 107–25: "It is hard to overemphasize the prevalence of slave-trading in colonial American society" (ibid., 107).

[7] Ibid., 109.

[8] Ibid., 110.

fortunes to be made—many of the oddities of slavery disappear. However, those economic benefits were not sufficient to obliterate threads of empathy toward slaves as fellow human beings. Those threads tied owners to their property and provoked the constant need to explain slavery to themselves. For example, at various times Virginia planters favored preserving the importation of slaves, then they opposed importation; sometimes they wished to preserve the Union, at other times they sought to secede. Some owners disliked keeping young children with their slave mothers; at other times owners wished to keep mothers and children together. The unifying factor that explains these apparent contradictions is alterations in the market for slave property. Virginia politicians came to support the ban on importation when they realized that they had a surplus of domestic slaves. By banning imports, the value of their stock of surplus slaves increased. Using the same reasoning, Virginians supported the expansion of slavery into the West because that maintained a steady market for their goods: between 1790 and 1860 East Coast slave owners transported more than a million slaves to Southern and Western regions.[9]

When owners felt there were too many slaves they sought ways to profit by selling them in Western markets where slavery was not prohibited by federal law. When that seemed infeasible, primarily because of fierce Northern resistance to expanding slavery, they turned their minds to entrepreneurial gambits—never to emancipation. In an 1852 unsigned article, "Excessive Slave Population—the Remedy," the authors note with regret that the limits of the slave territory are fixed. Yet they have excess slaves. To preserve slavery (which is their aim) they argue that owners should lease out slaves to industry and so bring manufacturing to

---

[9] Steven Deyle, "An 'Abominable' New Trade: The Closing of the African Slave Trade and the Changing Patterns of U.S. Political Power, 1808-60." *William and Mary Quarterly*, 66 (October 2009), 832–49. "From 1790 to 1860, Americans transported more than 1 million African slaves from the Upper South [Virginia, North Carolina] to the Lower South [Alabama, Georgia, South Carolina, Louisiana, Mississippi, Florida, Texas]," (ibid., 839).

Southern states. This would decrease the number of field hands, which, in turn, would diminish the size of the cotton crop (and so improve prices). As one authority put it, they must "seek out and find new fields for slave labor, whenever it ceases to be profitable in agriculture."[10]

The Puzzle of Slavery

Southern apologists who demanded that the Civil War be viewed as a matter of states' rights generated confusion about the economic, social, and aesthetic pleasures of ownership. Instead of understanding slavery—and the South—we are shocked and then pass on by. We ascribe slavery's rewards and pleasures to monstrous "others" who are unlike us.

One remedy to this confusion is to pursue Abraham Lincoln's insight: that if we had lived in the South in 1861 we might have acted and believed as they did. This awful truth generates discomfort. To eliminate that discomfort we may be drawn to the Civil War itself, which is dramatic, but not to its origins and to its consequences. Grant, Lee, and Lincoln of the war period are fascinating; but the prewar and postwar periods are perplexing.

Before the attack on Fort Sumter on April 12, 1861, the puzzle of American slavery appears nakedly in writings and speeches. After the war ended in 1865, industrious persons rewrote the rationale for the war. Such rewriting and vociferous defense of the South, by both Northern and Southern elites, obscured what was clear earlier. When we examine the history of American slavery, a secret emerges like a submarine coming to the sea's surface. That secret, hidden behind sermons and sentimentality and 150 years of denials, is the multidimensional pleasures and rewards of owning human beings.

In popular imagination "ownership of persons" evokes images of sexual conquest and control. Sexual slavery is a common human fantasy. Erotic fiction trades on this theme. It pervades Western notions of sexual conquest. When directed toward others, sexual slavery generates fantasies of conquest and surrender: the other becomes our sexual slave.

---

[10] *De Bow's Review* 12, no. 2, 182–85.

(When directed toward oneself, it animates laments about one's power-lessness to resist sexual urges.) These, however, are metaphors people use to describe moments of life when one feels powerless to resist an erotic urge. At other moments, we are in control and our enslavement has disappeared. Actual slaves had no such reprieve—once a slave, always a slave. According to the rules of American slavery, neither could they expect reprieve for their children or for their grandchildren.[11]

American slave owners had no need for—and no use for—metaphors. The realities of slavery, of owning other persons' bodies, included using those bodies for sexual pleasure. That sexual activity occurred between owners and slaves and between other whites and slaves over a long period of time is undeniable. Recent studies of the genetic makeup of African-descended persons in ten different American locations, ranging from Jamaica to Detroit, showed that "European genetic ancestry ranged from 6.8 percent (Jamaica) to 22.5 percent (New Orleans)."[12] In a similar study done in South Carolina, researchers found that European genetic ancestry in African Americans living in the Gullah Sea Islands, on the Atlantic Coast, showed a 3.5 percent admixture of European and African genes. Moving inland, the proportion of European admixture increased to 10 to 14 percent in the Low Country and to 17.7 percent in Columbia, the state capital.[13] More so, genetic studies also show that the preponderance of European partners in these sexual encounters were men.

---

[11] For example, regarding Thomas Jefferson, see Annette Gordon-Reed, *The Hemingses of Monticello: An American Family* (New York: Norton, 2008) and *Thomas Jefferson and Sally Hemings: An American Controversy* (Charlottesville, VA: University Press of Virginia, 1997). Regarding sexual conquest, see Edward Ball and E. G. Ballard, *Slaves in the Family* (New York: Farrar, Straus and Giroux, 1998).

[12] E. J. Parra et al., "Estimating African American Admixture Proportions by Use of Population-Specific Alleles," *American Journal of Human Genetics* 63(6) (December 1998): 1839–51.

[13] E. J. Parra et al., "Ancestral Proportions and Admixture Dynamics in Geographically Defined African Americans Living in South Carolina," *American Journal of Physical Anthropology* 114(1) (January 2001), 18–29.

The larger range of rewards and pleasures tied to ownership include pride, display, companionship, and status. For example, Dolly Madison, an esteemed First Lady and an outstanding person in many respects, owned slaves her entire life. After her husband, James Madison, died in 1836 she did not free her slaves, even though she was penniless and her husband had requested she do so. She refused. It is doubtful that at age seventy-eight Mrs. Madison found her slaves sexually exciting. More likely is that she and her slaves, to some degree, felt bound by genuine affection to each other. Rather than free them and let them choose to stay or go, she retained ownership and thus control over their decisions.[14]

Numerous sexual crimes were committed against enslaved persons. But not every Southern supporter of slavery took part in those crimes. They and their descendants can hotly deny complicity in sexual crimes. They cannot deny their complicity in ownership.

If we deny our capacity for the nonsexual pleasures of ownership, slavery and the agonizing ways that the South has responded to it remain puzzling. In *Slaves in the Family*, an account of being the descendant of South Carolina slave owners, Edward Ball described his boyhood in the late twentieth century when his family no longer enjoyed the prestige it had commanded since the early eighteenth century. Although his family's wealth had disappeared, something else of value remained:

> Inwardly the plantations lived on. In childhood, I remember feeling an intangible sense of worth that might be linked to the old days. Part of the feeling came from the normal encouragements of parents who wanted

---

[14] She sold Paul Jennings, her husband's body slave, late in her life. Jennings extended her pocket money when he could. See Dorothy Schneider, "Carl J. Schneider" (2009). *First Ladies: a Biographical Dictionary* (New York: Info Base Publishing,), 32. See also "A Colored Man's Reminiscences of James Madison," electronic ed. Paul Jennings, b. 1799. http://docsouth.unc.edu/neh/jennings/jennings.html. See also Clarence Lusane, *The Black History of the White House* (San Francisco: City Lights. 2011), 132–36.

their children to rise. An equal part came from an awareness that long ago our family had lived like lords, and the world could still be divided into the pedigreed and the rootless.[15]

As Ball notes, descendants of slaves had the inverse inheritance. Their "intangible sense" of self was contaminated by the degradation of their ancestors wrought at the hands of his ancestors.

The European and American abolition crusades were crucial to the defeat of slavery. An unintended consequence of the campaign, however, was that it became difficult to see the aesthetic and emotional rewards of ownership. They circulated images of brutalized bodies and sexual atrocities against Africans. In doing so they rallied sentiment against slavery and helped galvanize England and the North to oppose the South. The rightness and effectiveness of their campaign are unquestionable. But they also contributed to making images of Africans shocking, taboo, and distressing.

Slavery as Normal Business

Part of our collective error has been to vilify slave overseers and to distinguish them from slave owners, many of whom, we are told, wished to ameliorate the worst parts of the system. William Scarborough reviewed records of 1,500 slave overseers in seventeen counties in the South. Dedicated to writing a fair account of overseers, whom he sees as demeaned by planters and antislavery activists, Scarborough documented the management techniques overseers used to control slaves. He reprinted "rules of government" for the Green Valley plantation in the Yazoo-Mississippi Delta around 1840. Among its seventeen rules, six govern the handling of slaves. Thus, rule 11 and 14:

The negroes must be Kept [*sic*] as much as possible out of the rain. It is much better to lose some time than to run the risk of Sickness & death."

"The [negro] children must be very particularly attended to, for rearing

---

[15] Ball, *Slaves in the Family*, 13.

them is not only a Duty, but also *the most profitable part of plantation business.* They must be kept clean, dry & warm, & wellfed.[16]

Some authorities estimate that up to one-half (or more) of Southern wealth was slave property. These solicitous rules for the treatment of slaves are identical to those for the treatment of valuable livestock. The overseer's tasks were demanding: extract maximum work from slaves without killing or alienating them, protect the owner's investment in slaves—the most profitable part of plantation business—and when possible increase the number of slaves through reproduction. These values are clear and their authors are unashamed. The trouble is that slaves are human beings and as such resist tyranny. Maintaining a slave workforce required access to a wide range of devices, without which slavery would have disappeared: "Slave discipline was clearly the decisive factor in the success or failure of an overseer."[17]

Indeed, at least one writer has found there are uncanny parallels between the techniques used by slave managers and ideas advanced by F. W. Taylor and his school of scientific management: "The administration of [slave] labor was carefully studied by the slaveowners, whose achievements in this regard anticipate those by Taylor himself."[18] To keep their slaves busy and forestall bad habits, some planters avoided laborsaving devices, such as the improved plow, because while such devices enhanced productivity in one domain, they threatened to diminish the master's ability to extract maximum effort during crucial periods. Within the world of slavery it made sense to keep the workforce occupied throughout the year. To minimize the cost of overt control, including punishment and other forms of coercion, owners demanded

---

[16] William Kauffman Scarborough, *The Overseer: Plantation Management in the Old South* (Baton Rouge, LA: Louisiana State University, 1966), 69. (My emphasis.)

[17] Ibid., 93. See also William E. Wiethoff, *Crafting the Overseer's Image* (Columbia, SC: University of South Carolina Press, 2006).

[18] R. Keith Aufhauser, "Slavery and Scientific Management." *The Journal of Economic History* 33, no. 4 (Dec., 1973), 812.

that slaves work before and after their daily chores. That way they could grow their own food and so decrease the owner's costs. In addition, small favors, gifts, and other goods placated the laborers.[19] Even petty theft and pilfering, if not excessive, helped enhance loyalty and keep the workforce docile. Clever owners and their overseers learned that by using these small rewards they could placate slaves and decrease friction.

Imperfect Creatures: More Alike than Different

Every group—from a tiny Amazon village to the People's Republic of China—affirms a paradoxical truth. We affirm both (1) that our way of life (our culture, rules, language, and so forth) is arbitrarily different from our neighbor's, and (2) it is also, somehow, sacred and *not* arbitrary. To imagine changing our sacred rules is to contemplate the end of the known world, which will soon be gone with the wind. Facing a similar catastrophe, Pope Gregory (540–604) described the invasion of Italy by the Lombards in 568 as not just the end of the Roman Empire, but as the end of the world, "Beasts possess the regions where before many men had their dwellings."[20] For American slave owners, every hint of abolition carried with it the threat to end their world.

Slavery is an evil, but the slave owners were not, on the whole, evil persons. As Lincoln noted, many learned lawyers and statesmen, including the majority of early presidents of the United States, defended slavery. This means that they received something from ownership that non-slaveholders did not receive. This something includes substantial wealth, a fact well documented by exhaustive accounts of the

---

[19] "Many planters sought to promote contentment, loyalty and zeal by gifts and rewards, and by sanctioning the keeping of poultry and pigs and the cultivation of little fields in off times with the privilege of selling any produce." Ulrich B. Phillips, *Life and Labor in the Old South* (Boston: Little Brown, 1963), 200.

[20] Dialogues <on the Lombard Invasion>. http://www.ewtn.com/library/MARY/GREGORY.HTM

financial realities of slavery. It also includes a profound, deeply distressing pleasure: that as a slave owner, one controls the body, spirit, and actions of another human being. Here we should disallow the common assertion that owners saw their slaves as subhumans, as little more than animals. This cliché obscures an important truth. The value of slavery and its pleasures stem from the fact that slaves are just like us: human beings. They have, therefore, much more value than animals.

The three US presidents from Tennessee, Andrew Jackson, James K. Polk, and Andrew Johnson, were remarkable men. They were not brutes; neither were they sadistic perverts who enjoyed inflicting harm. On the contrary, each said that he regretted the need to "discipline" slaves who worked too little or threatened to flee their bondage. This brings us back to the puzzle of slavery: If these outstanding persons could own slaves—and defend the institution— what good did it afford them that we, from our vantage point, do not perceive? And how did otherwise normal people justify an unjust institution to themselves?

We are sure of our values now, having imbibed them over a lifetime of education and reflection in post–civil rights America. Would we possess those values if we were transported back to Thomas Jefferson's estate in the late eighteenth century? The majority of whites of Jefferson's milieu found ways to justify the institution. Since most people are "average," the odds are we would occupy the middle ground of Southerners. That the majority no longer defends slavery signifies the heroic efforts required to challenge it and its aftermath. Like all Americans we are the beneficiaries of these heroes.

Only the Finest

A simple example of the pleasure of ownership is to reflect upon owning a fine horse. The handsomer the animal, the more pleasure; the better trained the animal, the more pleasure; the more responsive, the more skilled and immediate in tandem performance, the more pleasure it affords us. Show jumping is an exciting event to do and to watch because we seem to glimpse moments of perfect working harmony between the rider (who commands) and the horse (which obeys). Millions of people thrill to see the harmony exhibited between the Lipizzaner stallions and their lifelong masters and riders. American historian Robert Vincent Remini recounts how Andrew Jackson became famous for his skills at riding and judging superb horses.[21]

Even prize horses and cattle may fail to reproduce sufficiently to recoup their initial costs. More so, prize horses and cattle are rare, expensive, and available only to the rich who can afford to lose. But slaves can reproduce. They do earn their masters a living. They do increase one's net worth. They do respond (usually) to the master's commandments; they do afford the owner both the pleasure of command and the happy prospect of increased wealth in perpetuity. Each owner enjoys the luxury of being acknowledged as superior to all slaves. Generations of Southern authorities proclaimed that any white man—no matter his skills or attainment—is superior to any black man. This is not an abstract point of law. It is a concrete form of pleasure, a title like that afforded the English nobility, or members of the House of Lords. Ownership is a badge of superiority, refinement, and stature. It is like the "silks" worn by the Queen's Council, English barristers whom the profession has chosen to honor by giving them distinctive silk gowns worn in the courtroom. Given these pleasures and the financial advantages of slave ownership, it is not surprising that slaveholders would find ways to defend the institution. That they professed to be Christians presented some difficulties; these difficulties were resolved by the authority of ministers like Reverend Polk, by the learned men of the times, and by the mystic language of tradition.

That great men—like Washington, Jefferson, Madison, Jackson, and Polk—championed, though professed to dislike, slavery gives it the status of a conundrum. Slavery was a puzzle they could not solve. If all Southern proponents of slavery were like Simon Legree, the villain

---

[21] Robert Vincent Remini, *Andrew Jackson and the Course of American Empire* (New York: Harper & Row), 1977. Reprinted as vol. 1 of his three-volume work, *Andrew Jackson and the Course of American Empire, 1767–1821* (Baltimore: Johns Hopkins Press, 1998), 41.

of *Uncle Tom's Cabin*, it would be easier to see through the proslavery and pro-Confederacy propaganda generated for the past 150 years. However, US presidents and similar persons of great ability defended slavery. After Reconstruction, equally refined and educated persons defended Jim Crow laws and even lynching.

Added to an illustrious group of men were feminists like Rebecca Latimer Felton (1835–1930). Felton championed women's suffrage and became famous for her progressive views regarding women's rights. She also came to share a demonic view of black men. Born in Georgia, Felton was a tireless advocate for reform, women's rights and eventually suffrage, and temperance. She criticized politicians who used alcohol to cajole black male voters. "She claimed [that] they put white women at risk of assault."[22] Because the customary punishment for black on white rape was lynching, Felton urged authorities to control the alcohol that she believed fueled sexual crimes. However, in the same speech she said that the biggest problem facing women on the farm was the danger of black rapists. "If it takes lynching to protect women's dearest possession from drunken, ravening beasts," she said, "then I say lynch a thousand a week."[23] Lynching as penalty for black on white rape was, she said, the "unwritten law of the state [Georgia]."[24]

Missing the Signals: the Cost of a Divided Mind

Idealizing the slaveholder presidents, accepting their narratives, and ignoring the self-evident pleasures and rewards of ownership—while we abhor slavery—requires us to divide our minds. Some might say that this national program of forgetting the facts of slavery and the actual causes of the Civil War was necessary to prevent a second attempt at secession. In his charming narrative to Ken Burns's Civil War documentary, Shelby Foote says that after the surrender at Appomattox,

---

[22] Estelle B. Freedman (2013). *Redefining Rape: Sexual Violence in the Era of Suffrage and Segregation* (Cambridge, MA: Harvard University Press, 2013), 98.
[23] Ibid.
[24] Ibid.

the North agreed to proclaim itself the winner and to let the South proclaim itself the better at soldiering. This compromise may have occurred, and it may have calmed the South and helped to pacify it. However, it is another defensive maneuver. It cannot be true as a general statement. On both sides, valorous men fought and died; both sides had talented generals and foolish generals; both sides showed instances of epic heroism and abject cowardice. No one can propose an objective way to assess the claim that Southern men were "better at soldiering" than Northern men. Like many legends told about the War Between the States, this is another instance of idealization and defense against historical realities.

This and other defensive maneuvers prevent mental distress, but they cost us mental clarity. We cannot gain a better sense of American history if we refuse to confront the disunity that idealization, sentimentality, and similar defenses induce in us. However much satisfaction they afford in the present, these maneuvers make genuine reconciliation impossible. Elaborate movies, clever TV shows, and other media portray the valor and drama of the Civil War. We feel moved by poignant scenes of the Boys in Blue and the Boys in Grey; we may feel—as Americans—that the war was fought nobly and out of it came a united country. If we must agree, in perpetuity, to the South's self-portrait that it had the better generals and better soldiers, we cannot bridge the intellectual gulf that such a compromise requires. We must continue to idealize Robert E. Lee, for example. Ernest B. Furgurson, an American author, describes his boyhood in Virginia in the 1950s: "I grew up on Lee Street in Danville, Virginia, the last capital of the Confederacy, and I attended Lee Street Baptist Church and Robert E. Lee School, where I played the role of General Lee in our fifth-grade pageant much more convincingly than Martin Sheen did in the film *Gettysburg*."[25]

---

[25] Ernest B. Furguson, "Danville, Virginia: Hallowed Ground," *Smithsonian Magazine*, January 2011, http://www.smithsonianmag.com/travel/Danville-Virginia-Hallowed-Ground.html.

The Argument against Slavery: Empathy

The argument against slavery is short and conclusive. It turns on empathy or the Golden Rule. Lincoln used it in various ways in his numerous speeches against slavery. He reasoned along these lines:

1. We would not wish our children or ourselves to be slaves.
2. Under what circumstances should persons be consigned to slavery?
3. Only if they (not their parents) were found guilty of terrible crimes.
4. Did the majority of American slaves commit such crimes?
5. No. Then American slavery is unjust and should be abolished.

The arguments for slavery are lengthy, convoluted, diffuse, and replete with confabulations. Because they turn upon the conundrum of seeing persons as things, as property, legal codes that condone slavery struggled with irresolvable contradictions.

"Helpless, tongueless, defenseless Africans"

The account of the Spanish schooner *La Amistad* shows that the oddities of American slavery appeared throughout the nineteenth century. In late June 1839, *La Amistad* left Havana with forty-nine African slaves and headed toward the Cuban port Puerto Principe. During the voyage, one of the enslaved Africans, Cinque, secured a file, freed himself, and with his fellow slaves took command of the ship. They killed the Spanish captain but kept two Spaniards alive, forcing them to sail back to Africa. The Spaniards secretly sailed toward the United States not toward Africa. In late August, the ship approached Long Island, New York. Lt. Thomas R. Gedney, commanding an American cutter, discovered some of the crew on land and investigated their origins. He arrested the Africans, freed the Spaniards, and sailed *La Amistad* to Connecticut where he hoped to claim both the vessel and the slaves on board as salvage. Contesting Gedney's claim, two other men claimed salvage rights. The two Spaniards filed claims to regain control of the ship, its cargo, and the slave property.

Supported by Northern abolitionists, the Africans filed suit denying that they could be construed as property. The US Attorney for
Connecticut sided with the Spanish government that supported the
Spaniards. The District Court found for the Africans and awarded the
ship and salvaged goods to Gedney. President Van Buren disliked this
outcome and forced the US Attorney for Connecticut to appeal the
verdict.

The US Supreme Court heard the case in January 1841. On March 9,
the court found for the Africans and freed them. Arguing for the Africans was John Quincy Adams, twelve years after he had left the
presidency. The son of John Adams, the second US president, he was
immersed in the history of the Constitution and its compromises with
slavery. Although the authors of the Constitution tolerated slavery, they
never denied that slaves were persons. The Constitution, Adams said,
"recognizes the slaves, held within some of the States of the Union, only
in their capacity of persons." By excluding the words *slave* and *slavery,*
the authors used circumlocutions that "are the fig-leaves under which
these parts of the body politic are decently concealed."[26]

In his forty-four-thousand-word defense of the Africans, Adams
dissected the demands of the Spanish government. It had asked the
United States to return the Africans to Spanish authorities to be tried for
murder and piracy. The Spanish government also sought indemnifica-
tion for the loss of value that the slaves, as property, represented. Adams
responded by noting the "confusion of ideas and a contradiction of positions from confounding together the two capacities in which these
people are attempted to be held. One moment they are viewed as
merchandise, and the next as persons." On the one hand, the slaves
were actors whom the Spanish wished to try as persons guilty of capital crimes. On the other hand, they were chattels, objects of value that

---

[26] For a chronology and archive of contemporary accounts, the trial records, and
contemporary scholarship, see http://law2.umkc.edu/faculty/projects/ftrials/
amistad/AMISTD.htm. The case—also known as *United States v. The Amistad,*
40 U.S. 15 Pet. 518 (1841)—is here: http://supreme.justia.com/us/40/518/
case.html.

various people wished to retain as property: "These demands are utterly inconsistent."

Adams thundered that according to the Spanish, the slaves were both robbers who stole goods from the rightful owners—and they were the stolen goods: "the merchandise were the robbers, and the robbers were the merchandise." Because both Spain and the United States had outlawed the slave trade, those who captured the Africans, took them across the Atlantic, and sold them were, Adams said, acting illegally. They robbed the Africans of their natural liberty and transported them against international law. If the captain, crew, and Spanish slave traders had sailed into New York with the Africans as chattel slaves on board, they would have been tried for capital offenses and possibly hanged.

Adams explained the psychology of the American officials and politicians who sided with the two Spanish slave traders. They were, Adams said, acting out of sympathy with the plight of all slaveholders, not with consideration for slavery's victims nor grasp of the logical contradictions of their position: "The sympathy of the Executive government, and as it were of the nation, in favor of the slave traders, and against these poor, unfortunate, helpless, tongueless, defenseless Africans, was the cause and foundation and motive of all these proceedings."[27]

President Van Buren opposed the annexation of Texas, which would have added a slave state to the Union, but defended the institution of slavery within the District of Columbia where it had always existed. As the head of the executive branch, Van Buren struggled to find compromises between proslavery and antislavery factions without which disunion was likely. Facing the same conflicts with the slave powers that confronted Washington, and every president after

---

[27] Argument of John Quincy Adams Before the Supreme Court of the United States in the case of the *United States, Appellants, v. Cinque, and others, Africans, captured in the schooner Amistad, by Lieut. Gedney,* Delivered on the 24th of February and 1st of March 1841. [Originally published in 1841 by S. W. Benedict.], http://www.historycentral.com/amistad/amistad.html.

him, Van Buren temporized. Adams is somewhat unfair to Van Buren; his "sympathy" was not per se with the slave traders, it was with the founders whose Constitution had concretized their fragile compromises with slavery—and its rewards.

In addition, Van Buren confronted Southern factions who might, if their interests seemed imperiled, turn against him and thwart his programs even if those programs had nothing to do with slavery. Until 1820, Southern politicians supported national funding to build roads, canals, and other construction projects. This genial support ended in the 1820s and 1830s.

The Missouri Debate of January and February 1820 focused national attention on the expansion of slavery into the new states. Ferocious Northern resistance to this proposal and passionate denunciations of slavery by Northern leaders spurred Southern anxieties that if the institution of slavery were not defended everywhere it would become insecure in Southern states as well. Because that was intolerable, they shifted from accommodating national improvements toward inhibiting them. A Congress strong enough to carry out massive new building projects, erect bridges, build canals, strengthen the national bank, and increase tariffs would have dangerous powers to challenge slavery, even in the South. As Nathaniel Macon, the Speaker of the House from North Carolina, and a slave owner, put it, "If Congress can make canals they can more properly emancipate [our slaves]."[28]

What Caused the Civil War? Slavery in Retrospect

Robert Durden, a distinguished historian, notes that "After the Civil War ended, a cardinal element in southern apologia . . . was the emphatic denial that the South's primary aim in fighting was the preservation of slavery."[29] This denial isn't found in Southern speeches made before the

---

[28] Daniel M. Mulcare, "Restricted Authority: Slavery Politics, Internal Improvements, and the Limitation of National Administrative Capacity." *Political Research Quarterly* 61, no. 4 (December 2008): 676.

[29] Robert F. Durden, *The Gray and the Black: the Confederate Debate on Emancipation* (Baton Rouge: Louisiana State University Press, 1972), 3.

war. Durden's study of postwar apologia appeared forty years ago, but the mystification continues. In April 2011, on the 150th anniversary of the beginning of the Civil War, the Pew Research Center found that 48 percent of Americans believed that the main cause of the war was states' rights; 38 percent said that the main cause was slavery; another 9 percent said that both were equally important. A majority (56 percent) felt that the Civil War was still relevant to American political life.

Somehow slavery and the battle over states' rights were offered as separate issues. Slavery, most now admit, was an admitted evil. States' rights and limited government seem to be different matters of intellectual and political discourse that are independent of slavery. Yet the notion of states' rights was, effectively, the right to preserve the compromises on slavery written into the US Constitution of 1787. Those compromises protected slavery, made the fugitive slave law nationwide, and preserved the institution against encroachment by abolitionists and other antagonists.

If these two allegedly separate reasons for the war do not reinforce one another, then secession becomes mystical and confusing. More so, US history from 1787 to 1861 (if not later) becomes incoherent. The compromises that led to ratification of the Constitution, the battles over the slave trade, the legislative struggles of the 1830s and 1840s, the Mexican War in 1846, the annexation of Florida and Texas, and the South's resistance to admitting free states into the Union make sense if one sees them as part of a whole: the continuous effort by generations of elite Southerners to preserve slavery and their status as owners.

Before 1860, Southern authors were clear: slaves were valuable property; they cultivated the land at low costs and generated fortunes. With those fortunes came status and power. Slave owners dominated political discourse, shaped religious sentiments, and controlled intellectual life in the antebellum South for at least 140 years. These are sufficient reasons to account for the war fever that possessed Southern leaders when Lincoln won the presidency in 1860. However, these facts do not account for the pall of forgetfulness that descended upon public education after 1865, when the South was defeated. Nor does it account for the widespread denial of Southern culpability among Southern church leaders after 1865. When they sought to explain why the South lost a war—which, according to Southern preachers, it ought to have won—many leading churchmen explained it as the lack of sufficient religious zeal (not the existence of slavery).[30]

Prior to and during the war, Southern religious leaders championed secession, defended slavery, and urged on the Southern Cause. For example, Benjamin Morgan Palmer, a Presbyterian minister in New Orleans, spoke on Thanksgiving Day, November 29, 1860, three weeks after the election of Abraham Lincoln. With Lincoln's election the nation was in peril, he said, because the cords that had kept the North and South united were broken. According to Daniel Stowell, "Sectional divisions, a jealousy of rival interests, the lust of political power, a bastard ambition ... a reckless radicalism, which seeks the subversion of all that is ancient and stable, and a furious fanaticism" create a portentous crisis.[31] Palmer explained that Southern wealth consisted of land and servants (slaves), that "our products can only be cultivated by labor which must be controlled in order to be certain." Slavery is necessary to the South, sanctioned by the Bible; it has "determined all our habits of thought and feeling and moulded the very type of our [southern] civilization."[32] After he repeated well-worn arguments for slavery and its capacity to elevate Africans entrusted to white Christians, Palmer urged the Louisiana legislature to secede.[33]

---

[30] "Civil War at 150: Still Relevant, Still Divisive," Pew Research Center, April 8, 2011, http://pewresearch.org/pubs/1958/civil-war-still-relevant-and-divisive-praise-confederate-leaders-flag.

[31] "Religious southerners upheld the Confederacy both in victory and in defeat. Few, if any, groups could surpass Confederate clergymen in their devotion to the southern cause." Daniel Stowell, *Rebuilding Zion: The Religious Reconstruction of the South, 1863–1877* (New York: Oxford University Press, 1998), 33.

[32] B. M. Palmer, *Thanksgiving Sermon: Delivered at the First Presbyterian Church, New Orleans, on Thursday, December 29, 1860* [*sic* November] (New York: George F. Nesbitt & Co), 5.

[33] Ibid., both citations from p. 8.

Palmer reprinted his twenty-page pamphlet many times throughout the South. He was quite clear about both the cause of strife between North and South—the institution of slavery—and what all true Christians and Southerners should do—defeat President Lincoln whose party had vowed to prohibit the extension of slavery. If this required secession and war, so be it: "Though war be the aggregation of all evils, should the madness of the hour appeal to the arbitration of the sword, we will not shrink even from the baptisms of fire."[34] Palmer is lucid and emphatic: the crucial issue is perpetuation of slavery through the United States and forever. He does not justify secession by the defense of Southern women nor to states' rights both of which, after the war, were regularly invoked to explain secession and the war. Palmer's plain speech and his rationale—like many other preachers' words about the continuance of slavery—were forgotten.

To explain that forgetfulness we must ponder the visible and invisible pleasures that owners enjoyed. Among the visible ones was the vast wealth that slavery promised (but did not always deliver.) Like all those who touted the "Southern way of life," secessionist preachers proclaimed that without African slave labor, Southern agriculture would languish. Among the invisible pleasures were the unacknowledged thrill of domination and the social stature that ownership brought with it. As Edward Ball said, knowing that one's ancestors lived like lords gives one a sense of self and substance not otherwise available. One cannot be a genuine lord without hordes of peasant, servants, and when available, slaves over whom one rules. This form of pleasure and reward runs contrary to American values and the American story of basic equality. To acknowledge it sparks painful doubts about oneself, about the Lost Cause, and about the cost in lives and Southern treasure. For example, some Southern seminaries invested their endowments in bonds of the Confederate States of America (CSA) that soon became worthless. A few Southern Christians acknowledged the ethical crisis that slavery presented; most did

---

[34] God had "'providently committed to the South the duty' to conserve and perpetuate the institution domestic slavery as now existing."

not. Rather than mourn the ethical morass of the Cause, the majority erected a barrier between the North and themselves, and, I suggest, within themselves. As one author put it in 1866, "If we cannot gain our *political*, let us establish at least our *mental* independence."[35]

Rather than acknowledge these hidden pleasures and suffer guilt and shame for them, most spokesmen for the South mounted vociferous defenses against the mental pain that guilt and shame induces. Among these defenses were denial (the overt attack on historical fact); forgetfulness (an automatic mechanism that blots out memory); idealization (casting a glow of wonder and nobility upon past actions); and splitting (affirming an idea in one moment, denying it in the next).

I focus first upon denial and splitting. Denial is a general mechanism of defense; splitting helps account for our national fascination with the Civil War and our confusion about its origins. We may feel that our minds and beliefs are unities. Often enough that is not so. For example, many—if not most—cultured Christians of the prewar South could affirm both Jesus's teaching of human equality and, at the same time, defend their ownership of persons. What they affirmed on Sunday, they contradicted Monday through Saturday. They managed to live with this contradiction by splitting their minds into separate regions, and their religion and its preachers helped them maintain these splits. Another defense is idealization. It is perhaps the most insidious defense. Even intelligence and learning prove ineffective against it. A writer as subtle as Robert Penn Warren, for example, can succumb to idealization. Reflecting upon his grandfather, who served in the Confederate Army, and upon Jefferson Davis, the first and last president of the Confederacy, Warren says that Davis "holds eternal franchise in that shadowy, ages-ago-established, rarely remembered nation of men and women who in their brief lives learned

---

[35] Stowell, *Rebuilding Zion*, 44. Southern Methodists, for example, affirmed that they would not merge their churches with Northern Methodist bodies that have "incorporated social dogmas and political tests into their church creeds" (ibid., 45).

the true definition of honor, far beyond the triviality of the code duello once defended by the young Davis."[36]

This sentence is eloquent and nostalgic. Warren portrays a golden period when Southern men and women held their destiny in their hands. In a brief four years, from 1861 to 1865, a civilization that defined "true honor" rose and fell to overwhelming force. While Warren does not defend slavery, he feels the call of blood to defend Southern soldiers like his grandfather and Jefferson Davis who lived by fixed codes. The *code duello* refers to a late eighteenth century document that lays out the rules for dueling and points of honor among British, Continental, and American elites.[37] Like similar codes in the ancient world, it emerged in military contexts in which personal courage was essential to success on the battlefield. To be a leader of men willing to kill or be killed required that one exemplify personal heroism in defense of honor. For honor presumes hierarchy and rank: to be a man whose word was his bond and a man who could command others to risk their lives, the true gentleman/warrior had to be willing to risk his own.

In the Anglo-Irish version of the code, we find twenty-five rules that lay out procedures for addressing insults to one's character or to certain women. For example, Rule 10 states "Any insult to a lady under a gentleman's care or protection to be considered as, by one degree, a greater offense than if given to the gentleman personally, and to be regulated accordingly." These rules provide the script for duels portrayed in hundreds of novels and films. The code defines the nature of offenses, their rank by gravity, and the roles of the seconds and the surgeons who attended the participants. In these ritualized dramas, personal honor, one's standing as a gentleman superior to non-gentlemen, supersedes all other concerns, especially personal

---

[36] Robert Penn Warren, *Jefferson Davis Gets His Citizenship Back* (Lexington, KY: University of Kentucky Press, 1980), 112.

[37] Hamilton Cochran, "Code Duello: The Rules of Dueling" in *American Duels and Hostile Encounters* (Philadelphia: Chilton Books, 1963), at http://www.pbs.org/wgbh/amex/duel/sfeature/rulesofdueling.html

safety. For that reason, rule 13 declares: "No dumb shooting or firing in the air is admissible in any case." Shooting into the air makes dueling trivial; it becomes a game with no real consequences.

Rule 13 defends the honor of the code itself. To pretend to duel and then fire into the air destroys the element of danger and therefore makes courage under fire impossible. It is childish and disgraceful. In the same vein, Rule 14 requires "Seconds to be of equal rank in society with the principals they attend, inasmuch as a second may either choose or chance to become a principal, and equality is indispensible." Other rules enforce this value, noting that men who avoid a duel forfeit the honor of being counted as gentlemen. In such cases, their cowardice is "posted," that is advertised, and dishonor follows them everywhere.[38]

Warren captured this martial spirit, these antique virtues as he called them, when he described Jefferson Davis's combat experiences in the Battle of Buena Vista during the Mexican War. Davis "even had the glory of a wound—in the foot, with blood welling in the boot as he continued to command."[39] The glory of a wound is that it demonstrates to others and to oneself that one has passed a test of manliness and leadership under fire. Like dueling scars, wounds inflicted by the enemy evoke special recognition and praise. That Davis continued to lead while wounded was a model of proper manly spirit. In a similar

---

[38] Bertram Wyatt-Brown, *Southern Honor: Ethics and Behavior in the Old South*, 2nd ed. (New York: Oxford University Press, 2007). "Above all else, white Southerners adhered to a moral code that may be summarized as the rule of honor. Today we would not define as an ethical scheme a code of morality that could legitimate injustice— racial or class. Yet so it was defined in the Old South. The sources of that ethic lay deep in mythology, literature, history, and civilization. It long preceded the slave system in America. Since the earliest times, honor was inseparable from hierarchy and entitlement, defense of family blood and community needs. All these exigencies required the rejection of the lowly, the alien, and the shamed. Such unhappy creatures belonged outside the circle of honor. Fate had so decreed" (ibid., 46-47).

[39] Warren, *Jefferson Davis Gets His Citizenship Back*, 58–59.

way, Warren spoke for generations of Southern boys (if not girls) who celebrated the courage of CSA generals, especially Nathan Bedford Forrest who led his troops into battle, fighting in hand-to-hand combat. Forrest "slew twenty-nine adversaries in his lifetime, and had thirty horses shot from under him—three at Fort Pillow alone," Warren writes.[40]

Forrest's exploits lose some of their luster when we look at this battle, conducted on April 12, 1864, on the Mississippi River just north of Memphis. Some historians call it "the massacre at Fort Pillow." By this point in the war, Union armies included black soldiers. At Fort Pillow, Forrest commanded some two thousand men facing six hundred Union soldiers, half of them black, half of them white. His troops overwhelmed the fort and then, according to eyewitnesses, killed Union troops who had offered surrender, focusing their attack upon black soldiers many felt were slaughtered. Five days after the battle, General Grant ordered his staff to negotiate thenceforth exchange of black and white Union soldiers on equal footing, that is, as equals. This demand for equal treatment of blacks infuriated the Confederate secretary of war, James Alexander Seddon, who refused to accommodate it. He pled, "I doubt, however, whether the exchange of negroes at all for our soldiers would be tolerated. As to the white [Union] officers serving with negro troops, we ought never to be inconvenienced with such prisoners."[41]

Seddon's refusal illustrates the ideology that caused the war, and it illustrates the contradictions of slavery. If, indeed, blacks were fit only for slavery, then, by definition, black soldiers were inferior to white soldiers. Proslavery propagandists had argued that slavery was a form of benign recognition of racial differences—that slavery was, on the

---

[40] Ibid., 64.

[41] U. S. Grant, Memoires, 1048, quoted in Richard Fuchs, *An Unerring Fire: The Massacre at Fort Pillow* (London: Fairleigh Dickinson University Press, 1994), 144. "Non-acquiescence by the Confederate Authorities . . . will be regarded as a refusal on their part to agree to the further exchange of prisoners, and will be so treated by us."

whole a positive good. Because blacks, they said, could not match whites in intellect, courage, and other virtues, they required permanent white governance. The "benevolent control" exercised by white owners of black bodies and black minds was required by this structural inferiority. In rebuke of this premise were Confederate debates in late 1864 through spring 1865. Once the South started to lose the war, Southern leaders debated proposals to bring slaves into their armies, even to arm them for battle against the North. By November 1864, Jefferson Davis proposed a radical plan to offer emancipation to Southern slaves if they would fight for the South. To do this would require that Southerners see slaves not merely *as property* that could be pressed into service (like mules or other livestock), but also *as persons* who could act independently as soldiers and then, after the South had won, become free.

Davis's proposal addressed the South's severe manpower shortages while it also exposed the contradiction upon which slavery rests— that one can have property in persons. In April 1864, according to Southern leaders, black Union prisoners did not deserve to be treated with the respect afforded white prisoners. Yet in November, four months later, the president of the Confederacy urged the CSA to arm slaves—an idea which, up to that point, would have been treasonous. "Arming slaves" was what John Brown proposed in 1859 when he murdered whites at Harpers Ferry and tried to foment rebellion. Images of armed blacks had long terrified Southern whites. In reaction to Davis's proposal, Representative Howell Cobb of Georgia asserted, "If slaves will make good soldiers, our whole theory of slavery is wrong."[42] An editor for the Richmond *Examiner* excoriated Davis: "[this] is totally inconsistent with our political aim and with our social as well as political systems. We surrender our position whenever we introduce the negro to arms."[43]

Some one hundred years ago, Thomas Hay, an American historian,

---

[42] Thomas Robson Hay, "The South and the Arming of the Slaves," *The Mississippi Valley Historical Review* 6, no. 1 (June 1919), 63.

[43] Robert Franklin Durden, *The Gray and the Black: the Confederate Debate on Emancipation* (Baton Rouge: Louisiana State University Press, 1972), 108.

documented the extent of Confederate opinions on this idea; some, like Davis, came to it reluctantly, others, like General Patrick Ronayne Cleburne, who had seen black Union soldiers fight were enthusiastic: "If they can be made to face and fight bravely against their former masters, how much more probable is it that with the allurement of a higher reward [emancipation], and led by those masters, they would submit to discipline and face dangers?"[44] Most, however, could not share this sentiment. An Irishman, Cleburne took seriously the rhetoric that the war was about Southern independence; he was not prepared when his idea was soundly rejected. In January and February 1865, suffering yet more defeats and facing imminent collapse, the CSA Congress passed separate resolutions condemning the use of Negro soldiers.[45] Cleburne did not understand that his rational proposal, to find more soldiers with which to fight the North, ran aground upon the irrationality of Southern slavery. Because the war was fought to suppress and exploit black bodies, it made no sense to free those bodies and then arm them. Freed blacks roaming the South with weapons, learned in the arts of war, was the stuff of nightmares for owners

Reconciling Opposites

Robert Penn Warren, a distinguished poet and novelist, grasped the contradiction that Cleburne failed to appreciate. Raised in the South, Warren was associated with the Southern Agrarians, among them distinguished Vanderbilt University professors of English, including Donald Davidson. In response to Northern criticism, these poets, historians, and philosophers defended Southern values, especially agrarian values against the anonymity of industry and mass culture and the loss of traditional relationships. They published their political/literary manifesto, *I'll Take My Stand*, in 1930.[46]

---

[44] Hay, "The South and the Arming of the Slaves," 44. See also Craig L. Symonds, *Stonewall of the West: Patrick Cleburne and the Civil War* (Lawrence, KA: University Press of Kansas, 1997).

[45] Hay, "The South and the Arming of the Slaves," 55–56, 63.

[46] Paul Murphy notes that its authors "evoked the mythology of the Lost

Warren and many of his fellow Agrarian writers had heard stories about the Civil War from grandparents who witnessed it. Aware that with the death of these witnesses, no living memory of the war would be preserved, so Warren and other passionate young people sought ways back to the Old South.

David W. Griffith, the director of *The Birth of a Nation* and author of its notorious celebration of the Ku Klux Klan, had a similar fascination with the war. Born in 1875 in Kentucky, Griffith heard stories of the war from his father, Jacob Wark Griffith, who served as a colonel in the CSA. Griffith told his official biographer that a CSA sword he possessed came from his father: he "remembered him donning his old uniform and taking up the saber to thrust and parry with imagined enemies for the amusement of his children."[47] Griffith's film *The Birth of a Nation* tells the story of the Klan's origins in heroic defense of white women, just as Jefferson Davis had said fifty years earlier. By modern standards, the film is tedious, but it is essential viewing, especially with the addition of a recorded interview of Griffith by Walter Huston; in a great library, both men in tuxedos, Griffith handles a CSA cavalry sword and remembers warm conversations with his father about the war.

In *The Birth of a Nation* after setting up his narrative device—to follow the war by following the destinies of a Pennsylvania family (the Stonemans) and a South Carolina family (the Camerons)—Griffith has us meet the main characters, charming young (white) men and (white) women. Griffith makes clear that their bonds of family (and race) are natural, strong, and spontaneous. When the young male Stonemans visit the Camerons in South Carolina he tells us in a title card: "Chums—the

---

Cause; the anthology was consciously underwritten by an explicit appeal to southern nationalism. To be southern and of the Agrarians' generation was, in some ways, to feel as inheritors of a noble but failed tradition." Paul V. Murphy, *The Rebuke of History: The Southern Agrarians and American Conservative Thought* (Chapel Hill, NC: University of North Carolina Press, 2001), introduction.

[47] Richard Schickel, *D. W. Griffith: An American Life* (New York: Simon and Schuster, 1984), 15.

younger sons, North and South." This seems heavy-handed now, but in 1915 its redundancy was useful for it told the viewers that the war could be understood as an error that white solidarity would repair. After light-hearted moments of horseplay and camaraderie, we see "the darkies at play." A title card tells us that with the election of Lincoln, the stability won by defeating the English in 1781 had ended. We see Charles Sumner, the South Carolinian who led the Senate, confer with Austin Stoneman, the Pennsylvanian patriarch. A radical congressman modeled on Thaddeus Stevens, Austin is so enamored with Lydia, his dark-skinned mistress (his "great weakness" as the subtitle put it) that he dismisses his noble Southern colleague. The title card informs us: "The mulatto aroused from ambitious dreamings by Sumner's curt orders." (Whom she spits at as he leaves Stoneman's office.)

Using brilliant artistry, Griffith conveys the nobility of the Lost Cause and the criminal consequences of Reconstruction. He used 232 title cards to make his case; each tells us who is good and who is bad and precisely what to feel. For example, rather than be raped by a black man, an innocent white woman jumps to her death. In response to this crime and its tragic ending, the Klan rises up; its leader shouts:

> 194. "Brethren, this flag bears the red stain of the life of a Southern woman, a priceless sacrifice on the altar of an outraged civilization."
> 195. "Here I raise the ancient symbol of an unconquered race of men, the fiery cross of old Scotland's hills. . . . I quench its flames in the sweetest blood that ever stained the sands of Time!"

Later, another lovely and innocent white girl, Elsie (Lillian Gish) seeks help from Lynch, a mulatto politician who lusts after her: "Her father failing to return, and ignorant of Lynch's designs on her, Elsie goes to the mulatto leader for help" (No. 211). She refuses his advances and Lynch declares his intentions: "See! My people fill the streets. With them I will build a Black Empire and you as a Queen shall sit by my side" (No. 214).[48] The catastrophic danger in the film are free blacks and mixed race

---

[48] All titles from http://intertitleorama.webs.com/birthofanation.html.

men (mulattoes) who lust to defile white women. *The Birth of Nation* embodied Jefferson Davis's post-war explanation for the conflict—the war was fought in the defense of Southern (white) women. To unify Northern whites with Southern whites, Griffith brilliantly portrays the fantasy of a common enemy, African Americans and the white criminals who empowered them. And lest we misunderstand, we see Northern and Southern white men unite to defend women, as the title card put it, "The former enemies of North and South are united again in common defence [*sic*] of their Aryan birthright." (No. 210)

Sharing the same wish to recapture the passionate feelings he had experienced when his grandfather described the war, Warren said that his book on Jefferson Davis was "symbolic memory." Thoughts engendered by Davis's name came with such force that the feelings and images of his beloved grandfather, who spoke about Jeff Davis, emerged and time itself was reversed. With sufficient imagination, Warren travels back to 1865, forty years before he was born and contemplates Davis as if he were with him. Through the power of his prose Warren evoked Davis's emotional life. Using the new technology of film, Griffith drew upon his artistic mastery to animate his boyhood dreams about the war and the postwar South.

These evocations are the province of novelists and artists; their analysis is the province of historians and scholars. The Agrarians' literary skill and their persuasiveness helped them cast Southern history in a glowing, nostalgic light. Nostalgia is a mixture of pain, loss, and yearning for better times, of "gone are the days," when men were iron and ships were wood. Nostalgia is a mood; it disconnects past complexities and faults from us in the present. It makes collective forgetfulness mandatory. Griffith answered our wish to identify with Lincoln's timeless virtues and not with the rewards and pleasures of slavery. He managed this slight-of-hand with his usual artistry. Griffith first shows us the murder of the president, then portrays the assassination of Lincoln as a Southern tragedy:

110. "The news is received in the South."

111. "Our best friend is gone. What is to become of us now!"

That Lincoln's assassin, John Wilkes Booth, was a Southern patriot who exacted revenge on the Great Liberator, is deleted. Through this masterpiece Griffith helped maintain the splitting, idealization, and denial that make the history of American slavery obscure.

Few slave owners were monsters even as they took part in a monstrous system; most possessed the strengths and weaknesses that we display. Slavery promised them future wealth; it gave them immediate pleasures of control, mastery, stature, and domination over others. To enjoy these benefits and to pass them on to their progeny—another form of pleasure—owners had to explain themselves to themselves. As we will see, two centuries prior to the Civil War they did this by using diverse rationalizations and defenses of the "need" for slavery. For a century and a half after the Civil War, those who defend the South adopted these rationalizations and added new ones. Chief among these later additions was idealization of the Lost Cause, of its heroes in grey, and of their gallant legacy. These devices were persuasive, brilliant, and dazzling.

CHAPTER 2

Owning Slaves

Our sense of American slavery has been shaped by movies, TV, and the efforts by passionate defenders of the South to portray slavery as a distant cause of the Civil War. While they acknowledge that slavery was unfortunate, these defenders imply that only a very few wealthy families owned slaves. The truth is otherwise.

The United States census of 1860 lets us calculate the percent of white families owning slaves, by state. Going from the highest percentage to the lowest, they are:

Mississippi 49%	Louisiana 29%	Kentucky 23%
S. Carolina 46%	Texas 28%	Arkansas 20%
Georgia 37%	N. Carolina 28%	Missouri 13%
Alabama 35%	Virginia 26%	Maryland 12%
Florida 34%	Tennessee 25%	Delaware 3%

These are not trivial numbers.

The majority of powerful families and their leaders, all white men, were slaveholders. They, not white laborers and farmers, controlled the printing press, the statehouse, the pulpit, the legal and medical professions, the police, the sheriffs' offices and the militias, the colleges and universities, and every other organ of power and communication at local, state, and federal levels. Alongside these powerful families, were less wealthy families who owned as many slaves as they could.

When abolitionists threatened the institution of slavery and when Lincoln threatened its expanse, white owners, both large and small, had universal control of the legal machinery necessary to resist.

Who Fought for the South?

However, even such a high percentage of slave owners doesn't explain why hundreds of thousands of soldiers of the Confederate States of America (CSA) would fight to secure an institution that did not benefit them—why did those not in the wealthy brackets fight in favor of slavery?

Even though large numbers of CSA soldiers owned slaves, it was never more than 50 percent. In that context, it would follow that the spirit that animated the other 50 percent was not the defense of slavery but something else. While it is true that enlisted men tended not to own slaves, such was a measure of their relative wealth, not their sentiments about slavery. Those sentiments were shaped by the vast educational and propaganda efforts exerted by elites on behalf of the institution.

Since many wealthier families did own slaves, all forms of abolitionism threatened a central pillar of their worth, namely, their property in human beings. These wealthier families had long dominated every aspect of governance, power, and control in the slaveholding regions. Over many decades they perfected arguments for slavery and propagandized their ideas for it in every available venue, from the pulpit to the printing press, to popular culture. The brilliance and comprehensiveness of this propaganda extended immediately after the war. We see it vividly in a famous song that appears to speak from the hearts of uneducated enlisted men who loved the South and refused to aid Reconstruction: "Oh, I'm a good old Rebel soldier, now that's just what I am" and ends with "And the lying, thieving Yankees, I hates 'em wuss and wuss!"[1]

---

[1] http://www.civilwarpoetry.org/confederate/songs/rebel.html.

Written with poor grammar and in rural dialect, the song seems to emerge from the Boys in Grey who gladly joined Master Robert E. Lee, "Marse Robert." It begins with "I followed old Marse Robert for four years, near about" and ends with "But I killed a chance o' Yankees, and I'd like to kill some mo'!" It seems to represent Southern whites of modest means who gladly joined Robert E. Lee and other slaveholding gentry to fight against the North. This is false. The song was written by Major Innes Randolph, a scion of the famous Randolph family of Virginia. Beginning with the Revolutionary period, the Randolphs of Virginia included a president of the Continental Congress (Peyton Randolph), an attorney general (Edmund Randolph), a governor of Virginia (Thomas Mann Randolph), the secretary of war for the CSA (George Wythe Randolph), and "the cultivated man of letters and poet, the late Major Innes Randolph, C. S. A."[2] A cultivated man of letters fabricated the accent of the common soldier in order to perpetuate misinformation about Southern feelings about their legacy.

Who Were Slaveholders?

In the Lower South a large number of white families owned slaves. By 1850, some economists argue, slave owners controlled up to 95 percent of agricultural wealth.[3] Large and small slaveholding families had similar economic concerns. Secession and similar efforts to preserve slavery echoed the concerns of both large and small slaveholders alike. Indeed, Gavin Wright notes that, "Property rights in human beings shaped the investment strategies, the economic geography, and the political economy of the South. As compared to the American North, the incentives of slave property tended to disperse population across the land, reduce investments in transportation and in cities, and limit the exploration of southern natural resources."[4] Wright supports many of the points that

---

[2] *The House Beautiful*, December 1900, vol. 9–10. These citations come from an article on the Randolphs' mansion, "Tuckahoe," twenty miles from Richmond, 37.

[3] Gavin Wright, *The Political Economy of the Cotton South* (New York: Norton, 1978), 34–35.

[4] Gavin Wright. *Old South, New South: Revolutions in the Southern Economy*

Hinton Rowan Helper made in 1857: because of slavery and the resources invested in the purchase of slaves, the South "was reluctant to invest heavily in schooling and education."[5]

"Subjects of your undisputed will and pleasure"

Numerous persons perceived the conflict between the Declaration's claims to universal liberty and the Constitution's preservation of slavery. Many offered explanations for the continuation of slavery well past the founding of the Republic. But none appear to take up what Francis Daniel Pastorius, a German-American Quaker wrote in 1688, that owning slaves is sometimes lucrative but always pleasurable.[6] In Pastorius's terms, to own a slave is to control a person who is subject to one's undisputed will and pleasure.

An honest account of some of those pleasures appears in an 1815 book, *Journal of a West-India Proprietor, Kept during a Residence in the Island of Jamaica*, written by an Englishman, Matthew Gregory Lewis (1775–1818).[7] Having inherited a sugar estate in Jamaica, Lewis journeyed there and surveyed his new property. Among his slaves was a young mixed-race woman, Mary Wiggins: "I really think that her form and features were the most *statue-like* that I have every met: her complexion . . . was an ash-dove colour; her teeth were admirable, both for colour and shape; her eyes equally mild and bright; and her face merely broad enough to give it all possible softness and grandness of contours." She was more beautiful, he said, than Josephina Grassini, a famous soprano and lover to Napoleon,

---

Since the Civil War (New York: Basic Books, 1984), 11. See also Susan B. Carter et al., ed. *Historical Statistics of the United States,* Millennial ed. University of California Project on the Historical Statistics of the United States, September 2003. On the history of US slavery, see http://hsus.cambridge.org/HSUSWeb/search/searchessaypath.do?id=Bb.ESS.01.

[5] Hinton Rowan Helper, *The Impending Crisis of South: How to Meet It* (New York: A. B. Burdick, 1859, rpr. 2011, 2015), 14.

[6] Marion Dexter Learned, Samuel Whitaker Pennypacker, *The Life of Francis Daniel Pastorius, the Founder of Germantown* (Philadelphia: W. J. Campbell, 1908), 261.

[7] Elibron Classics. www.elibron.com. Also Adamant Media Corporation.

who appeared in the opera, *La Virgine del Sole*.[8]

Lewis was an educated Englishman given to quoting Romantic poets. He does not indicate that he sexually exploited his lovely slave. The large number of "mulattoes" proved to him that other white owners had fewer reservations. Lewis affirms his Christian values even as he laments the alleged necessity of slavery. He proclaims that persons of humanity would not wish to create the systems of slavery and would wish for its disappearance. Yet, it is so important to the economies of Jamaica and Great Britain that cessation would be "an absolute impossibility, without the certainty of producing worse mischiefs than the one which we annihilate." We find numerous versions of this lament in those who defended slavery as necessary to Southern prosperity.[9]

A telling instance of the pleasures of ownership appears in an anecdote about young Thomas Jefferson, who at seventeen attended the College of William and Mary with a body servant, a slave named Jupiter. Determined that his horse's coat should shine "as faultlessly as a mirror," Jefferson assessed Jupiter's work by draping a white handkerchief "lightly over the animal's withers."[10] If any dirt showed on the cloth, Jefferson required Jupiter to groom the horse again.

Jefferson and other owners gave slaves names of their own fancy the way that some name a favorite dog or horse. The winner of the 1862 Kentucky Derby was named Apollo, for example. *The Afro-Louisiana History, 1719–1829* database of slaves lists 170 instances of

---

[8] http://en.wikipedia.org/wiki/Giuseppina_Grassini.

[9] Legislators in Southern states struggled to define *mulatto* and related terms, as well as legal consequences to white woman who bore mixed-race children. By 1785, many Southern states adopted Virginia's rule: "every person who shall have one fourth part or more of negro blood, shall . . . be deemed mulatto." Thomas D. Morris, *Southern Slavery and the Law, 1619–1860* (Charlotte, NC: University of North Carolina Press, 1999), 23. White, upper-class landowners rarely suffered consequences for fathering children with their female slaves.

[10] Alan Pell Crawford. *Twilight at Monticello: the Final Years of Thomas Jefferson* (New York: Random House, 2008), 33.

the name "Jupiter" in Louisiana, one of the smaller slaveholding states.[11] Riding a beautiful horse with a beautifully manicured coat must have been marvelous. That pleasure was made possible by the labor of Jupiter and other slaves.

The Logic of Ownership: Naming Slaves in the US Census

The contradiction inherent in American slavery—that persons were treated as chattel—reappeared in the Senate and House debates on the census for 1850 and 1860. Of particular concern regarding the 1850 census was whether or not to record the names and birthplaces of slaves: logic argued for recording both items, but Southern politicians were anxious to depersonalize slavery and give no ammunition to abolitionists who regularly besieged Congress. They realized that abolitionists could use facts about slaves' mortality, slave children's health, "the migration patterns imposed by the internal slave trade, the illegal importation of African slaves (as would be suggested by a place of birth in Africa after 1808), and the results—and future implications—of racial amalgamation," says David Paterson.[12]

Paterson notes that some Southern senators, among them William R. King (Alabama) argued *both* that slave owners could not be expected to know the names and origins of their slaves *and* that for sure, all slaves born after 1808 (the cessation of the international slave trade) "were 'known' to be born within the slave South." In addition, as Paterson affirmed, because slaves constituted at least half of the

---

[11] Similar names and their frequency: Venus 171; Mars 56; Nero 25; Castor 25; Hercules 22; Bacchus 19; Cupid 6; Caeser 4; Apollo 3; Lucifer 2; Plato 1; Night 1; Orestes 1. Maintained by Dr. Gwendolyn Hall, Professor Emerita of History, Rutgers University, http://www.ibiblio.org/laslave/fields.php.

[12] See David E. Paterson, "The 1850 and 1860 Census, Schedule 2, Slave Inhabitants." Unpaged. http://www.afrigeneas.com/library/slave_schedule2.html. "One Southern gentleman wanted to test a pet theory that mulattoes were less fertile than blacks of 'pure blood.'" Accessed 8/26/09/. See also Walter Johnson, ed., *The Chattel Principle: Internal Slave Trades in the Americas* (New Haven, CT: Yale University Press, 2004).

total wealth of the average slaveholder, it is unlikely that owners would not know the ages, names, and status of their human property.

Senator Arthur P. Butler (South Carolina) argued that because some plantations had hundreds of slaves the owner could not know the names of the many hundreds of slave children begotten on their lands.[13] More so, he asserted, slave mothers themselves did not know how many children they had had or their names. Senator William H. Seward (New York) challenged these claims about the ability of slave women to forget their own children: "There is no woman... who can have forgotten the number of children that she had borne. If it be true, as it is said, that there are women who do not know whether their children be living or dead, and even how many they have borne, I should like to ascertain the number of such that there are of all races.... I wish to know how rapid that progress is. I believe it cannot be possible that there are any women, even in Africa, who have forgotten the number of children they have borne."

As Paterson says, Seward's question exposed the incoherence of the Southern refusal to enumerate and name enslaved persons. White people got names; slaves (who were either black or mulatto) got numbers.[14]

The Logic of Ownership

Once the contradictory equation of slaves with property was made, honest persons had to struggle with its consequences. To defend

---

[13] The US government resource is: http://memory.loc.gov/ammem/amlaw/lwcglink.html#anchor31.

[14] Paterson, "The 1850 and 1860 Census," Census workers in 1860 were instructed to use a separate census form (no. 2) to enumerate slaves: "Under heading 2, entitled 'Number of slaves,' insert, in regular numerical order, the number of all the slaves, of both sexes, and of every age, belonging to the owner whose name you have recorded. In the case of slaves, numbers are to be substituted for names. The description of every slave, as numbered, is to be recorded, and you are to enumerate such slaves as may be temporarily absent, provided they are usually held to service in your subdivision."

themselves against abolitionists some Southern speakers painted slavery as benign, as did John C. Calhoun in his speech "Slavery a Positive Good."[15] In another speech that month, "Foreign Aggression upon American Slave Property," Calhoun lambasted British officials who had freed slaves when an American vessel was forced by bad weather to land in Bermuda. This action was an attack, said Calhoun, upon "American Slave Property" and was "one of the greatest outrages ever committed on the rights of individuals by a civilized Power."[16] Once the Confederate States of America became an organized nation, its Congress reaffirmed that the basis of Southern wealth was slavery and that slaves constituted property. On February 10, 1863, Representative Benjamin L. Hodge noted that the North was enlisting Negroes as soldiers in the US army. This was unacceptable because "both of the Confederate States and the United States, recognize Africans and their descendants as property; and Whereas we can not consent to any change in their political status and condition: Therefore, *Resolved,* That the Committee on the Judiciary be instructed to inquire into the expediency of bringing in a bill providing the proper forms for the disposition of all negroes or mulattoes who may be captured from the enemy in such manner that those of them who are fugitives from their masters may be restored to their rightful owners, and those for whom no masters can be found shall be sold into perpetual bondage for the purpose of raising a fund to reimburse citizens of this Confederacy who have lost their slave property."[17]

---

[15] For lengthy excerpts of proslavery arguments that defend it as a "positive good," see Drew Gilpin Faust, ed., *The Ideology of Slavery: The Proslavery Argument in the Old South, 1830-1860* (Baton Rouge, LA: Louisiana State University Press, 1981). February 6, 1837, on the Senate Floor: As Calhoun saw it, "Abolition and the Union cannot coexist," 710–12. http://memory.loc.gov/cgi-bin/ampage?collId=llrd&fileName=026/llrd026.db&recNum=358.

[16] See Register of Debates, Senate, 24th Congress, 2nd Session, 725–26.

[17] Journal of the Congress of the Confederate States of America, 1861-1865 TUESDAY, February 10, 1863.http://memory.loc.gov/cgi-bin/ampage?collId=llcc&filename=006/llcc006.db&recNum=91&itemLink=r?ammem/hlaw:@field%28DOCID+@lit%28cc0064%29%29:%230060007&linkText=1.

William Rives (Virginia), a relatively moderate Southern senator, could both disown Calhoun's benign portrait of slavery and affirm that slavery was protected in the US Constitution. After citing Washington, Jefferson, Madison, and Marshall who lamented the fact of slavery, Rives added: "It never entered into their minds, while laying the foundation of the great and glorious fabric of free Government, to contend that domestic slavery was a positive good—a great good." However, while slavery is evil, "it is now indissolubly interwoven with the whole frame of our society; and, if remedy there be for it, that *remedy can come from the hand of Omnipotence only.* In the mean time, it is inviolably protected by the sanctuary of the constitution itself."[18] (My emphasis.)

George Washington and Tom, a Negro

Fritz Hirschfield, a Washington biographer, says that it is distressing to realize that Washington was a careful buyer and seller of persons. Washington, Hirschfield says, "treated his slaves as well as was necessary in order to keep them disciplined and productive, but he was not concerned with their personal happiness."[19] Washington used euphemisms such as "my people" and "my family" to refer to his slaves. However, he sometimes needed access to harsher and more threatening punishments to control his property. Hirschfield reprints a letter from Washington to Thomas Swift, a captain of a schooner, dated July 2, 1766. Washington asks Thompson to take on board "a Negro (Tom) which I beg the favour of you to sell, in any of the islands you may go to, for whatever he will fetch, & bring me in return for him."[20] He then lists goods from the West Indies that he wants in exchange

---

[18]http://memory.loc.gov/cgi-bin/ampage?collId=llcc&fileName=006/llcc006.db &recNum=91&itemLink=r?ammem/hlaw:@field%28DOCID+@lit%28cc0064%2 9%29:%230060007&linkText=1. http://memory.loc.gov/cgi-bin/ampage?collId =llrd&fileName=026/llrd026.db&recNum=364.

[19] Fritz Hirschfield, *George Washington and Slavery* (Columbia, MO: University of Missouri Press, 1997), 52.

[20] Ibid., 186–87.

for Tom. To retrieve some of his expenses, to punish Tom, to prevent him from rebelling and thus portending freedom to other slaves, Washington chose to make an example of him. He sent Tom to the dreaded West Indies. There "few slaves survived for very long the tropical climate, the endemic diseases, and the cruel and inhumane treatment that they received at the hands of the overseers on the sugar plantations."[21]

Similar realism emerged when Washington drew up his will in 1799. To his wife, Martha, he allocated the 124 slaves he had acquired and the 153 "Dower slaves" she had brought with her to the marriage. (Attached to his will, Washington named 317 slaves making him an unusually wealthy man.) Within a year of Washington's death Martha had manumitted most of them. This was not out of sympathy but from anxiety that since her slaves would be freed upon her death, they might hasten her death with that incentive.[22] She gave Elish, one of her mulatto men, to her grandson, Washington Parke Custis.[23]

Andrew Jackson and the Runaway

We find similar thoroughness—and defensive sentimentality—in another American president, Andrew Jackson. In the 1830s, a male slave escaped from Jackson's plantation.[24] Jackson and thousands of others seeking to capture runaways asserted their property rights.[25] He paid to have an advertisement placed in local papers. It included these inducements:

---

[21] Ibid., 67–68.

[22] Helen Bryan. *Martha Washington: First Lady of Liberty* (Hoboken, NJ: John Wiley and Sons, 2002), 377–78.

[23] Hirschfield, *George Washington and Slavery*, 219.

[24] For a comprehensive review of escaped slaves, see John Hope Franklin and Loren Schweninger, *Runaway Slaves: Rebels on the Plantation, 1790-1860* (New York and London: Oxford University Press, 2000). See chap. 10, "Managing Human Property," especially 234–62.

[25] For as sampling of announcements in Maryland, see http://teachingamerican historymd.net/000001/000000/000096/html/t96.html.

> $50 reward for the capture of the slave.
> $10 bonus for every hundred lashes the slave is
> given, up to 300 lashes.

Why did Jackson encourage the would-be slave catcher to lash his slave up to three hundred times? How would Jackson, a fanatical business man, *know* that the slave catcher had administered the number of strokes claimed and was therefore entitled to extra funds? Jackson authorized this force in order to encourage the capture of his slave and to demonstrate to other slaves their fate should they attempt to emulate the escapee.[26]

James Parton, an admiring nineteenth-century biographer, called Jackson an ideal slave owner, though Jackson was thorough and exacting in his treatment of his human property: "Near death, he was said to have gazed on his servants 'with tender solicitude,' expressing in his final breaths the hope of a reunion in Heaven with both white and black."[27]

If Jackson was an ideal, he was ideal in the way a dictator can be kind, namely by denoting the precise rules: do it this way and you'll not be beaten; do it another way and you will be damaged. Subordination will elicit leniency; resistance will elicit punishment. Jackson's defense of slavery and his absolute rights to dominate his property appear throughout his life. A few citations from Robert Vincent Remini's biography of Jackson give the Jacksonian flavor:[28]

---

[26] See also Jon Meacham, *American Lion: Andrew Jackson in the White House* (New York: Random, 2007).

[27] James Parton, *The Life of Andrew Jackson. In Three Volumes.* (New York: Mason Brothers, 1860; repr. New York: Houghton, Mifflin and company, 1888), vol. 3: 677, quoted in Andrew Burstein, *The Passions of Andrew Jackson* (New York: Alfred A. Knopf, 2003), 24. It doesn't sound happy for his slaves; having served Jackson in life, they get to spend eternity serving him in heaven.

[28] Robert Vincent Remini, *Andrew Jackson and the Course of American Empire* (New York: Harper & Row, 1977). Repr. as vol. 1 of his three-volume work, *Andrew Jackson and the Course of American Empire, 1767-1821* (Baltimore:

1820: "The Missouri question so called, has agitated the public mind, . . . [it] will be the entering wedge to separate the union. It is even more wicked, it will excite those who is [*sic*] the subject of discussion (i.e. slaves) to insurrection and massacre. . . . I hope I may not live to see the evils that must grow out of this wicked design of demagogues, who talk about humanity, but whose sole object is self agrandisement regardless of the happiness of the nation." (Remini, 391)

1835: Regarding abolitionist materials mailed to southern citizens: "I have read with sorrow and regret that such men live in our country—I might have said monsters—as to be guilty of the attempt to stir up amongst the South the horrors of a servile war—Could they be reached, they ought to be made to atone for this wicked attempt, with their lives. But we are the instruments of, and executors of the law; we have no power to prohibit anything from being transported in the mail that is authorized by the law... (The postmaster should) deliver to no person those inflammatory papers, but those who are really subscribers for them. . . . The postmaster ought to take the names down, and have them exposed thro the public journals as subscribers to this wicked plan of exciting the negroes to insurrection and to massacre." (Jackson, *Papers*, vol. 5, 360–1).

The Persistence of Slavery

From one perspective, to ignore the immorality of American slavery is deny a primary ethical fact.[29] Yet, as Lincoln noted, slavery persisted for 250 years among people who proclaimed themselves dedicated to liberty and Christian charity. To understand that conundrum empathically we must visualize ourselves born—as were Washington, Jefferson, and Jackson—in a world centered upon Negro servitude. The gravity of the crime of slavery must coincide, roughly, with the intrinsic values it afforded slaveholders.

Johns Hopkins Press, 1998). Some of these citations appear in http://www.nas.com /~lopresti/ps7.htm.

[29] John Rawls, *A Theory of Justice* (Harvard University Press, 2009), 26–28.

That value was that without slavery white gentry who proclaimed themselves of royal class would lose the wealth and power they enjoyed. While Washington, Jefferson, Patrick Henry, and James Madison could speak eloquently about (white) liberty, they steadfastly defended the alleged need for slavery in the South. Because they were lawyers and accomplished orators, authors, and soldiers, and because they controlled the telling of colonial history, their self-narratives and their laments about slavery may appear persuasive.

If these were honest laments, why not free the enslaved Africans? Jefferson did not do so even when another great man sought to purchase their freedom. Jefferson's allegiance to slavery reappeared when he broke his sacred vow to the Polish Revolutionary War hero, Tadeusz Kościuszko. In his emotional last testament, Kościuszko had pledged his substantial American fortune, given in recognition of his contribution in the war, to Jefferson. He asked Jefferson to use the funds to free Jefferson's own slaves (that is, to pay himself for their freedom). He stated: "I hereby authorize my friend Thomas Jefferson to employ the whole thereof in purchasing Negroes from among his own or any others." After Kościuszko's death in 1817, Jefferson refused to honor his vow to his friend and he did not purchase freedom for any of his slaves.[30] If we wish to see Jefferson as he presented himself—an enemy to despots everywhere—we will find this fact shocking and needing explanation.

However, if we understand Jefferson's values—and those of similar slaveholders—his failure to honor a promise to a beloved friend is consistent with his lifelong defense of slavery. Having inherited slaves and three thousand acres from his father and another 135 slaves from his father-in-law, Jefferson could assert that he was the paterfamilias

---

[30] From Gary B. Nash and Graham Russell Gao Hodges, "Why We Should All Regret Jefferson's Broken Promise to Kościuszko," History News Network, http://hnn.us/articles/48794.html. See Gary B. Nash and Graham Russell Gao Hodges. *Friends of Liberty: A Tale of Three Patriots, Two Revolutions, and the Betrayal that Divided a Nation: Thomas Jefferson, Thaddeus Kosciuszko, and Agrippa Hull* (New York: Basic Books, 2008).

for a dependent people. Having been torn from their native lands, language, religion, and dignity and then brutalized for one, two, or three generations, Virginian Negroes, to use Jefferson's term, did not appear capable of running their own lives. Though a man of uncommon intellect, Jefferson did not use his gifts to construct a long-term solution to the catastrophes inflicted on his slaves.[31]

A trip to Monticello, Jefferson's luscious five-thousand-acre estate in Virginia, tells us why. Monticello let him become a master of natural sciences, the mechanical arts, philosophy, agriculture, and the lord of a great estate where he could conduct his various experiments. Jefferson's handwritten manuscripts, including his farm and garden journals, document those experiments and observations. He records costs, disbursements, and financial dealings of Monticello down to the penny. For example here is page 77 of his Farm Book:

Labourers.

build the Negro houses near together that the fewer nurses may serve & that the children may be more easily attended to by the super-annuated women.

children till 10. years old to serve as nurses.

from 10. to 16. the boys make nails, the girls spin.

at 16. go into the ground or learn trades.

a barrel of flour yields 17. pecks of flour, & the labourers prefer recieving [*sic*] 1. peck of flour to 1 1/2 peck of Indian meal.[32]

---

[31] For a conservative defense of Jefferson's self-understanding, see William J. Bennett, "The Greatest Revolution" in *America: The Last Best Hope (Volume I): From the Age of Discovery to a World at War* (Nashville: Thomas Nelson, 2006), 99. See also Matthew Mason, *Slavery and Politics in the Early American Republic* (Chapel Hill, NC: University of North Carolina Press, 2006), 99–101. On his inheritance, see http://www.monticello.org/jefferson/dayinlife/plantation/dig.html.

[32] Thomas Jefferson, Farm Book, 1774–1824. From the collections of the Massachusetts Historical Society, Boston, Massachusetts. http://www.masshist.org/thomasjeffersonpapers/farm/index.html.

Jefferson was not unthinking. He had scruples about selling slaves; for example, his "infrequent purchases were usually made to fulfill needs of the moment and selling was primarily a reluctant reaction to financial demands."[33] On his marriage Jefferson acquired 135 slaves which, when added to the 52 slaves he possessed made him the second largest slaveholder in Albemarle County. He held around two hundred slaves throughout his life. Following his death on July 4, 1826, massive debts forced his heirs to sell some 130 slaves. Within three years the house and land were put up for sale.

As the *paterfamilias,* Jefferson wished his slaves to marry other slaves on his property and "stay at home." As he said to one of his overseers, "They are worth a great deal more in that case than when they have husbands and wives abroad."[34] Committed to watching his costs and accounts, Jefferson noted when slaves shortchanged him. One of his slaves, Dick, had delivered a load of soap that weighed "thirty-eight pounds rather than, as should have been the case, forty-five; 'and the barrel of apples [he brought] is a little more than half full.'"[35] With the same attention, Jefferson was quick to correct overseers who drove slaves too hard: "The deaths of five slave children in the last four years made Jefferson wonder whether the white men in his employ were allowing the mothers sufficient time to care for their infants." Slave women were valuable—even more valuable than field hands—because their progeny contributed to the estate's labor force: "A child raised every 2 years is of more profit than the crop of the best laboring man." Coinciding with this valuable (and therefore pleasing) fact was that both the mother-infant pair and the master prospered under this rule. Here Jefferson noted that "providence had made our interests & our duties coincide perfectly."[36]

---

[33] Lucia Stanton, *Slavery at Monticello* (Charlottesville, VA: University of Virginia, 1993), 14.

[34] Edwin Morris Betts, ed., *Thomas Jefferson's Garden Book* (Philadelphia, PA: American Philosophical Society, 1944), 540.

[35] Alan Peal Crawford, *Twilight at Monticello: The Final Years of Thomas Jefferson* (New York: Random House, 2008), xv–xvi.

[36] Latter three citations from Crawford, *Twilight at Monticello*, xvi.

A Slave Owner's Wealth

Without slavery, Southern oligarchs argued, the South would sink into swampland and penury. Slavery was, according to this prediction, a necessary wrong that made a greater good—the development of the Southern United States—possible. Images of their beloved lands at risk from abolitionists appear throughout speeches in defense of slavery by the South's leading men. Slavery was a certain kind of wealth and with wealth came the possibility of advancement and civilization for some white citizens. Thus, slaves constituted Southern wealth.[37]

Slavery made human beings property that, in some climates, increased the value of marginal land. It also gratified slaveholders. Of additional importance, slaves reproduced, and thanks to the law of perpetual servitude, slave owners saw their human property increase in value, generation by generation as Jefferson said. Many owners claimed the children that they sired with female slaves as additions to their slaveholdings. As writers have noted, even natural feelings towards one's own children failed to undo the attraction of ownership.

Defenders of slavery had to argue that slaves were, as property, *identical* to cattle or other beasts of burden. Yet, human beings are not cattle. Slaves have language. They speak, they communicate ideas and feelings, they can plan (or, from the point of view of owners, they can conspire). They are subject to attraction and repulsion from other human beings. Most obviously, slaves understood their state as unjust and wretched. In other words, not wishing to remain enslaved, they conspire to escape. (Horses and cattle do not conspire and they do not conceive of alternative futures.)

To surmount the moral contradictions of slavery, some owners

---

[37] On slaves as property, see also Morris, *Southern Slavery and the Law 1619–1860*, 61–84. "In Virginia from 1705 to 1792 slaves were defined as real estate for some purposes. South Carolina tried to characterize slaves as real estate in 1690, when it followed the Barbadian code, but this was disallowed by the English Privy Council. In Louisiana slaves were designated as 'immoveables,' although sometimes the phrase 'real estate' was used" (ibid., 64).

told stories about the "good plantation." In addition, citing fragments from the Old and New Testaments, they argued that God warranted slavery as part of the divine plan. More honest Southerners rejected these arguments and instead articulated the legal consequences of ownership. These jurists traced the unhappy outcomes that chattel slavery produced: namely, that to enslave men and women permanently one must deny them *any* human attributes. A clear instance is an opinion delivered by North Carolina judge Daniel Ruffin.

State v. John Mann

In 1829, Judge Ruffin adjudicated an appeal in which a white man, John Mann, was found guilty of assault and battery upon a female slave, Lydia, whom he had leased from Elizabeth Jones. (Like many owners, including Thomas Jefferson, Jones rented her slaves for extra income.)[38] During the course of the lease, Lydia offended Mann; he berated her, she ran away, "whereupon the Defendant called upon her to stop, which being refused, he shot at and wounded her."[39] Mann lost the initial case and was convicted because he was not the slave's owner.[40] Mann appealed and Judge Ruffin found for him because, he said, the trial judge had incorrectly proposed that "the Defendant had but a special [limited] property" in Lydia. However,

> Our laws uniformly treat the master or other person having the possession and command of the slave, as entitled to the same extent of authority. The object is the same—the services of the slave; and the same powers must be confided. In a criminal proceeding, and indeed in reference to all other

---

[38] In the famous case of Dred Scott, heard by the US Supreme Court in 1856/1857, Scott had been leased out by a widow, Mrs. Irene Emerson. See http://digital.wustl.edu/d/dre/index.html.

[39] All direct citations are from *State v. John Mann*. 13 N.C. 263 (1829). See http://plaza.ufl.edu/edale/Mann.htm.

[40] Regarding the *State v. Mann* and the conflict between natural law of equal liberty and positive law, see Robert M. Cover, *Justice Accused: Antislavery and the Judicial Process* (New Haven, CT: Yale University Press, 1984), 77–79.

persons but the general owner, the hirer and possessor of a slave, in relation to both rights and duties, is, for the time being, the owner.

It follows that Mann had all the rights afforded any legal owner. Hence, the question becomes whether any owner, the original owner or one who leases a slave, "is answerable *criminaliter* [criminally], for a battery upon his own slave." Judge Ruffin responds to his question in the negative: "There have been no prosecutions of the sort." Judge Ruffin acknowledged the brutality of his conclusion: "The struggle, too, in the Judge's own breast between the feelings of the man, and the duty of the magistrate is a severe one, presenting strong temptation to put aside such questions, if it be possible." Human feelings that resist tolerating murder must be put aside to support the laws and customs of the institution.

To his credit, Judge Ruffin articulates the logical consequence of perpetual ownership: the ordinary rules of human conduct cannot apply. Many slave owners shared Washington's and Jefferson's euphemism and viewed their slaves as part of their extended family. However, they were wrong. In parallel instances of the exercise of authority within a family, the master over the pupil, or the father over the child, the goal is to better the child's future life. But with regard to slaves Judge Ruffin opined: "There is no likeness between the cases. They are in opposition to each other, and there is an impassable gulf between them.—The difference is that which exists between freedom and slavery—and a greater cannot be imagined," (*State v. John Mann*. 13 N.C. 263 [1829]).

The aim of slavery is to extract labor, to constrain, to intimidate, and to take from slaves the fruit of their work and ingenuity in perpetuity. To secure this, the master must have access to every form of coercion necessary. As Judge Ruffin explained:

"The power of the master must be absolute, to render the submission of the slave perfect." Judge Ruffin pursued this logic and deduced the inescapable consequence of slavery: "This discipline belongs to the state of slavery. They cannot be disunited, without abrogating at once the rights of the master, and absolving the slave from his subjection. It constitutes the curse of slavery to both the bond and free portions of our population. But it is inherent in the relation of master and slave" (*State v. John Mann*. 13 N.C. 263 [1829]).

Presidents Washington, Jefferson, and Jackson wished to appear to be kind and temperate owners. But behind these appearances loomed the authority to employ coercive acts that increased in severity and included the power to inflict death. Judge Ruffin, himself a large slave owner, articulated the need for such authority.[41] The conundrum facing Christian slave owners reappears: they described their use of slaves as benign yet they needed to assure those very persons that resistance and escape would provoke massive retaliation. Because they struggled with the contradiction of "Christian" slavery, they struggled continuously to find the balance between too much charity and too much tyranny. In the same way, while owners wanted their slaves to be Christians, they did not fancy them absorbing the radical egalitarianism of Jesus or doctrines that affirmed the transcendental unity of humankind. Similarly, slaves would be more useful if they could read, but only the right kinds of documents, not Thomas Paine's essays on American freedom, for example.

Judge Ruffin acknowledged that there were no doubt horrible actions done by masters to slaves, actions that offended ordinary sensibilities and that might spur some magistrates to indict an owner for excess. However, even in these circumstances the logic of slavery conflicted with one's ordinary sentiments. For legal reasoning requires us to pursue the structural effects of the institution of slavery, the judge said, we cannot,

enter upon a train of general reasoning on the subject. We cannot allow the right of the master to be brought into discussion in the Courts of Justice. The slave, to remain a slave, must be made sensible, that there is no

---

[41] Timothy C. Meyer. "Slavery Jurisprudence on the Supreme Court of North Carolina, 1828–1858: William Gaston and Thomas Ruffin," *Campbell Law Review* 33 (2010), 313–14.

appeal from his master; that his power is in no instance, usurped; but is conferred by the laws of man at least, if not by the law of God" (*State v. John Mann.* 13 N.C. 263 [1829]).

Until the state makes new laws regarding slavery or offers explicit guidelines regarding acceptable degrees of punishment and constraint, "it will be the imperative duty of the Judges to recognize the full dominion of the owner over the slave." Judge Ruffin concluded by expressing his hopes for amelioration over time. Like the majority of Southern commentators on slavery, he rejected calls for emancipation, a "fanatical philanthropy, seeking to redress an acknowledged evil, by means still more wicked and appalling than even that evil."

Other jurists in North Carolina did not engage Judge Ruffin's systematic reflection. However, all struggled with the implications of the "first law of North Carolina" regarding slavery. "That law was a clause in the Fundamental Constitutions and ran as follows: 'Every freeman of North Carolina shall have absolute power and authority over negro slaves of what opinion and religion soever [*sic*].'"[42]

Examining the history of the North Carolina Supreme Court, Bryce R. Holt in *The Supreme Court of North Carolina and Slavery* found large variations in both how slaves charged with crimes and how owners charged with harming slaves were treated.[43] Beginning as early as 1699, the North Carolina legislature crafted laws dealing with runaway slaves and the arraignment of slaves for trial: "If the offense were of a serious nature the slave was to be tried before any three justices of the peace and three additional freeholders who were also slaveholders" (ibid., 7). By 1740, the rules were liberalized so that

---

[42] Bryce R. Holt, *The Supreme Court of North Carolina and Slavery.* Historical Papers published by the Trinity College Historical Society. Series XVII. (Durham, North Carolina: Duke University Press, 1927), 12, citing Colonial Records, I. 204. http://www.archive.org/stream/historicalpapers17trin/historicalpapers17trin_djv u.txt. For the text of the Fundamental Constitutions of Carolina (March 1, 1669), para. 110, http://avalon.law.yale.edu/17th_century/nc05.asp.

[43] Holt, *The Supreme Court of North Carolina and Slavery.*

slaves charged with capital offenses were given a trial, sometimes by a jury of twelve slaveholders in open court. Of special concern in these trials was harm done to the owner of the indicted slave: if the slave were imprisoned, or killed while resisting arrest, or executed, the law (sometimes) made provision to compensate the owner for the loss of his property.

Some courts found white owners who had killed a slave guilty of murder; other courts found similar defendants guilty of manslaughter: "These [latter] decisions, rendered at the time when pro-slavery sentiment was in the flush of victory . . . tend to show that the right of the slave as a human being would receive the protection of the judiciary" (ibid., 10). Various judges strove to find a balance wavering between full recognition of slaves as human beings and as mere property. In a case involving a white owner who killed a slave who was said to be "turbulent, insolent, and impudent," Chief Justice Taylor announced: "many acts will extenuate the homicide of a slave, which would not constitute a legal provocation if done by a white person" (ibid., 15). Judge Ruffin and other jurists found the absolute power given to slave owners, or in some cases, any white man, over the lives of slaves offensive to their Christian consciences. However, slavery requires the exercise of gradations of force in order to preserve the institution and, many asserted, public safety. There were, it appears, no general rules governing the treatment of slaves; each case was decided on its own merits.

The struggle to ground legal reasoning upon the quicksand of slavery appears in an appeal by a slave who had killed a white man in an altercation and was found guilty of murder. The white man had drawn a knife on the slave; the slave had defended himself with a stick. The appellate court reversed the murder conviction. Justice Gaston, usually thought to be less rigid than Justice Ruffin, explained the difference.[44]

---

[44] "Ruffin based his slavery jurisprudence on rigid logic and narrow assumptions. He consistently sought to strengthen the rights of slaveholders and, more generally, to fortify the institution of slavery against perceived threats

Homicide through passion and homicide through malice was to hold as much in the trial of a slave as in the trial of a white man; but that the same matters which would be deemed a sufficient provocation for whites would not be such for slaves. Some words of a slave might be so aggravating as to arouse the temporary anger which destroys the charge of malice, and the rule would hold good regardless of the personal merits or demerits of a white man. The insolence of a slave would justify a white man in giving him moderate chastisement at the moment, but would not be a cause for excessive battery.[45]

In other words, the court affirmed any white man's rights to chastise any slave for insolence. If the slave's life is threatened by excessive chastisement, the slave may defend himself though he may not intend to kill the white assailant.

In another famous North Carolina case, *State v. Negro Will* (1834), the Supreme Court heard an appeal by Will, a slave owned by James S. Battle, convicted of murdering Battle's overseer, a man named Richard Baxter. On the fateful day Baxter had felt that Will was disobedient. He grabbed a gun, snuck up on the slave, and shot him in the back. Though wounded, Will ran off. Baxter followed with a group of slaves; they caught up with Will, scuffled, and in the battle, Will slashed Baxter with his knife. Baxter bled to death soon after. Will fled but then returned. He was arrested, tried, and convicted of murder with the sentence of death.

Will's owner hired "two leading members of the bar, Bartholomew F. Moore and George Washington Mordecai, to represent him; to Moore, Battle paid the extraordinary fee of $1,000. Moore and Mordecai took

---

ranging from abolitionists to slave revolts. The result was increasingly to define slaves solely as chattel, with an almost total de-emphasis on their humanity-and their legal rights. By contrast, Gaston took a more moderate view and sought to balance a greater variety of interests." Meyer, "Slavery Jurisprudence on the Supreme Court of North Carolina," 318.

[45] Holt, *The Supreme Court of North Carolina and Slavery*, 25.

Will's appeal to the state supreme court."[46] In his 8,340-word statement, Moore argued that while Justice Ruffin had earlier shown the necessity of force to maintain slavery, owners did not have complete, king-like authority over their slave property. While owners enjoyed wide latitude over the use of physical force, they did not have unfettered discretion: "Uncontrolled authority over the [slave's] body, is uncontrolled authority over the life; and authority, to be uncontrolled, can be subject to no question."[47]

Christian conscience and the fact that slaves are human beings require us to draw a line at killing: "It is here alone that the slave, in the eye of the law, ascends from the level of mere property and takes an humble stand amid his species" (ibid., 6).

In circumstances where free men or apprentices might find cause to defend themselves legally—such as being excessively punished by a master, or insulted—and then inadvertently kill their assailant, they are not guilty of murder. However, unless they are threatened with death or great bodily harm, slaves have no such defense. The laws of black servitude require them to squelch the universal instinct of self-preservation: "The law demands it as a duty that we should tame our passions to suit the condition which it has assigned to us" (ibid., 8).

Within the tortured logic of slavery, slaves were *both* inferior *and* superior to all who are not slaves. According to the law, slaves are inferior to apprentices and free men for the latter can legally and rightfully defend themselves and slaves cannot. They are also superior to apprentices and free men in the discipline of self-constraint. Free men need not tame their deepest passions, slaves must. Indeed, slaves should not experience slights and insults that would drive most men to violence. Because he found that the deceased had used excessive and unjustified violence

---

[46] Martin H. Brinkley, "*State v. Negro Will.*" *Encyclopedia of North Carolina.* ed. William S. Powell (Chapel Hill, NC: University of North Carolina Press, 2006). http://ncpedia.org/state-v-negro-will

[47] *State v. Will*, 18 N.C. 121, 1 Dev. & Bat. Law 121, 1834 N.C. LEXIS 30 (1834), 4. Holt, *The Supreme Court of North Carolina and Slavery*, 26.

against the slave, Justice Gaston sided with the defendant and found Will guilty of manslaughter, not murder.

This peculiar and impossible burden upon slaves—to ascertain that precise moment when humiliating punishment becomes deadly assault—is matched by a peculiar burden upon the courts and legislatures where slavery was legal. Courts cannot offer definitive judgments:

> No question can be more delicate, or attended with so many bad consequences if settled in error. It would be next to impossible for the judiciary to adjust this relation adversely to any strong and deliberate opinion entertained by the public mind. The momentum of this feeling, acting through the juries of the country and the spirit of the legislature, would be too powerful, successfully to be encountered by the Courts (ibid., 10).

We recall that late seventeenth-century colonial courts reasoned in a similar vein. Because slavery had no substantial legal standing (and could gain none under English jurisprudence), American jurists were left to cobble together assorted justifications for rulings that varied, depending upon how the judge understood the "strong and deliberate opinion" of the public mind.

In a similar case in 1849, this contradictory psychology—denying what slaves do feel and ascribing to them what they ought to feel— reappears. Two white men on slave patrol (a civic duty for white men in North Carolina) got drunk, then found Dick and Caesar, two slaves, in a field. The white men gave each slave two or three light licks. Dick laughed, which infuriated the white men. Charles, a third slave, overheard and joined them. Caesar resisted the beating and smacked one of the white men with a rail, which killed him. Caesar was convicted of murder; he appealed seeking to reduce his conviction to manslaughter. The majority denied his appeal on racial grounds and on the logic of slavery: if all parties had been white, "it would have been manslaughter; but a provocation which would "dethrone reason for a time," if given by one white man to another, should not do so when given to a slave by a white man." The difference is that according to law, slaves cannot feel resentment and degradation, thus they cannot suffer the same as whites: "between two white men there is a sense of degradation, while in the case of the slave only bodily pain is suffered."[48] Here, again, we struggle to understand this bit of reasoning: it cannot be true that slaves suffer only physical pain, never psychic pain. Rather, the laws, customs, and rituals of slavery require us to accede to a delusional belief.

As Chief Justice Ruffin explained it, using the same reasoning he employed in *State v. Mann*, the law cannot permit slaves (who were of African descent) the same defense as whites. Hence, the slave must have killed the other man from malice. Judge Ruffin knew, of course, that African-descended persons could feel embarrassment, resentment, and other "wounded sensibilities." He was a jurist who attempted to make the laws that governed slavery systematic. In these slavery cases he was not citing facts about Caesar the man; he was affirming the core delusion of slavery proponents about Caesar the slave. Because slaves were not fully realized persons Caesar could not cite wounded pride in his defense. If advocates of slavery did not affirm this falsehood, they might see the moral chasm opened at their feet. This was not going to occur. Hence, Judge Ruffin held that because Caesar was a slave, he could not claim self-defense. Nor could he claim wounded sensibilities that a white man would have suffered under the same circumstances. "Such a conclusion he held to be necessary in order to protect the white race. 'It is not a question,' he said, 'of whether these things are naturally right, and proper to exist (meaning the conditions of slavery). They do exist actually and legally.'"[49]

In an article published in 1851, Col. H. W. Walter, of Mississippi, described punishment dealt to slaves for various crimes. For all offenses other than capital the punishment was whipping; "except in cases of perjury, in which cases the penalty is both whipping and cutting off of the ear."[50] Crimes, in addition to murder, that merited

---

[48] Ibid., 27.

[49] Ibid.

[50] "Slave Laws of the Southern States: Mississippi." *De Bow's Review* 11, no.

execution included attempts to poison, raping a white woman, arson, conspiracy to rebel or to not report rebellion, and attempts to kill a white person.[51] The moral equivalence of these alleged crimes is puzzling until we see that conspiracy to rebel, for example, threatens white domination and white security. In the same way, teaching slaves to read was an act not far from treason. Some slaves were taught to read scripture until abolitionists sent their literature to them. Selected passages from scripture were tolerable; abolitionist tracts that cited Christian teachings of equality and freedom were not. For that reason reading among other "ameliorating privileges have been lost to the slave from the same causes."[52]

The Logic of Ownership—Black Masters

The urge to make skin color a defining feature of persons animates both the powerful and the dispossessed. The extent and depth of American "race" laws, which are color laws, is well known and well documented. When extended to American slavery, skin color seems to predict the owners (whites) and the owned (blacks). That black persons owned slaves in the prewar South may come as a surprise. Given the brutality of slavery and its dependence upon violence against black bodies and minds, we might expect former slaves and other persons of African descent to reject ownership.

But this did not occur. On the contrary, American historian Larry Koger points out that the 1830 federal census revealed that hundreds

---

6, (1851), 617–21.

[51] The author describes a rebellion by slaves on the German coast, above New Orleans, that began on January 5, 1811 and ended on January 15th when a white court condemned twenty slaves to die: "The military carried out the sentences, shooting the condemned and decapitating their corpses while silent crowds watched." Edward Baptist, *The Half Has Never Been Told: Slavery and the Making of American Capitalism* (New York: Basic Books, 2014), 63. Wise to the ways of terror, the enslavers mounted the heads of their victims for all to see. It demonstrated the swift punishment of any who wished to emulate them.

[52] Ibid.

of blacks in South Carolina, for example, owned collectively thousands of slaves.[53] Confronting this apparent anomaly, Carter G. Woodson, an African-American historian, argued in 1924 that, "the majority of Negro owners of slaves were such from the point of view of philanthropy."[54] In other words, according to Woodson, "Negro" owners used the formalities of slave law to protect family and friends from being sold and taken away.

This might be true of some families. However, the pleasure of ownership is characteristic of human beings (black and white; male and female). We should not be surprised that blacks who won the economic race took for themselves the spoils and rewards of a slave economy.

Koger examined this philanthropic interpretation of black masters in detail. According to his research, black owners acted like white owners: some were benevolent and kind; most acted according to the dictates of property. The majority of black owners used slaves as chattel, bought and sold them, used them as collateral, and retained them as long as they could. "Black masters continued to own slaves even when the Union army was preparing to invade South Carolina in 1864."[55]

Like white owners, black masters sold slaves when they needed funds or when they were dissatisfied with their slaves' behavior (ibid., 93); they punished them when they needed to control them (ibid., 92). Koger claims that 92 percent of black owners exploited their slaves as property, the remaining 8 percent "acquired just relatives and friends" (ibid., 101). Like white owners, black slave masters feared emancipation and were dismayed by Union victories. When the Twenty-First US Colored Troops invaded and secured Charleston, South Carolina, in

---

[53] See Larry Koger, *Black Slaveowners: Free Black Slave Masters in South Carolina, 1790–1860* (London: McFarland & Company, 1985).

[54] Carter Woodson, "Free Negro Owners of Slaves in the United States in 1830," *Journal of Negro History* 9 (January 1924): 42, cited in Koger, *Black Slaveowners*, 80.

[55] Koger, *Black Slaveowners*, 85.

fall 1864, slaves rejoiced. However, according to one writer, "the colored masters of Charleston perceived the invasion as apocalyptic destruction rather than salvation."[56]

Most black owners were of mixed African and European ancestry: "83.1% of the Negro masters were mulattoes, while nearly 90% of their slaves were of dark skin."[57] We can understand this as the effect of nineteenth-century American racism. According to this ideology, being more white than black moved a person up the ladders of value and merit. In addition, "mulattoes," the first generation offspring of a white parent and black parent, received special attention from the one white parent. This gave mixed-race children added security, support, and incentive to enter white society and take part in the larger economy. By owning slaves, black masters eased the anxieties of elite whites. The latter perceived that their fellow owners would defend slavery with an enthusiasm equal to their own. To this degree, the pleasures of ownership and its rewards emerge in these stories of black masters.[58]

This transient solidarity between white masters and black masters did not dissolve the depth of American racism, however. The European

---

[56] Joel Williamson, *After Slavery: The Negro in South Carolina During Reconstruction 1861-1877* (New York: Norton, 1976), 30–35, cited in Koger, *Black Slaveowners*, 192.

[57] Koger, *Black Slaveowners*, xiii.

[58] A parallel story occurred in North Carolina in the 1830s where Thomas Day, a successful cabinet maker and businessman, owned slaves and enjoyed political support from white slaveowners who threatened to curtail activities by all free blacks. Of mixed racial heritage, Day owned up to fourteen slaves. White officials, among them Romulus Mitchell Saunders, the attorney general of North Carolina, endorsed Day whom he said whites should not fear. Day would not conspire against the institution "as he is the owner of Slaves [*sic*] as well as of real estate." Cited in Patricia Phillips Marshall and Jo Ramsay Leimenstoll, *Thomas Day: Master Craftsman and Free Man of Color* (Chapel Hill, NC: The University of North Carolina Press, 2010), 22. See also William. S. Powell, *North Carolina Through Four Centuries* (Chapel Hill, NC: University of North Carolina Press, 1989).

American compulsion to idealize white skin and white heritage permeates American history and dominates our collective account of the Civil War. Before the war Southern elites trumpeted the enslavement of black bodies; after the war they smothered themselves in nostalgia about a Christian civilization gone with the wind.

CHAPTER 3

Ownership and the Political Defense of Slavery

Many still hold that on the whole, in spite of the Three-fifths Compromise and the fugitive slave clauses, the 1787 Constitution was neutral regarding slavery. This suggests a common wish to see the beginnings of our country as wholly benign, as wholly sanctioned, as built upon moral foundations. This wish to see one's country and one's heroes as flawless stems from the first-person possessive pronoun: *my* unarticulated belief that what is great and lovable could not begin in compromise and venality. And this belief rests upon the denial of the duality of human beings, that noble persons can also be venal and self-serving. Were Americans not to become altogether different than Europeans, a new order of persons for a "New World Order"?

However, the wish to find unity in great persons yields irrational and unsolvable conundrums. We revisit the puzzle that Jefferson could write *A Summary View of the Rights of British America* (1774) and the Declaration of Independence (1776) and yet keep his own children as slaves on his grand estate. We might assume that Jefferson's brilliance and eloquence would make him better able to discern right from wrong, to reason about morality, to derive just and valid conclusions. The facts do not support this assumption.

In contrast to Jefferson's muddle, the clearest ethical reasoning about slavery appeared in the Quaker admonitions: Jesus said do unto others as you would have them do unto you. Lincoln said that as he would not be a slave, neither would he be a slave owner. Frederick Douglass said listen to the songs of enslaved persons and you will be changed. Each insight derives from an empathic sense of the other: Quakers could imagine themselves in the status of perpetual slave; Lincoln shuddered with the memory of seeing slaves chained together on a boat; Douglass drew upon memories of being enslaved. These intuitions drove them to denounce slavery as inherently wrong, antagonistic to Christianity and to democratic government. Because slavery destroys personal liberty, they argued that slavery is antithetical to a nation dedicated to individual freedoms. In Lincoln's words, the nation could not persist part free, part enslaved, divided against itself.

However, many men more learned than Lincoln or Frederick Douglass defended slavery. Chief among them were distinguished congressmen and senators who mounted vigorous political defenses of slavery. Their elaborate and often erudite speeches dominated senate debates about slavery and its expansion. Each proponent of slavery drew upon clauses in the 1787 Constitution that protected slavery as a historic and necessary institution for the founding of the United States. And each offered lengthy historical recitations of the benefits of slavery to other great nations, among them the Roman Republic. By direct and indirect means each argued that to diminish or eliminate slavery would be to diminish the United States itself.

As we have seen, proponents of secession identified slavery as the central purpose of the Confederacy. In a speech on March 21, 1861, in Savannah, Alexander H. Stephens, later vice president of the Confederate States of America (CSA), asserted:

> The new [CSA] constitution has put at rest, *forever*, all the agitating questions relating to our peculiar institution—African slavery as it exists

amongst us—the proper *status* of the negro in our form of civilization. This was the immediate cause of the late rupture and present revolution.[1] (His emphasis.)

In opposition to Lincoln and to the Republican insistence upon the universality of political rights for African as well as European Americans, Stephens proclaimed:

> Our new government is founded upon exactly the opposite idea; its foundations are laid, its corner-stone rests, upon the great truth, that the negro is not equal to the white man; that slavery—subordination to the superior race—is his natural and normal condition.[2]

Stephens makes his theology and his politics clear: the transcendental claims of the Declaration and Lincoln's adherence to them are outmoded; slavery is based upon scientific, objective grounds. Slavery is therefore normal and natural—and perpetual. After the war, Stephens altered his tone and denied his principle claims:

> As for my Savannah speech, about which so much has been said and in regard to which I am represented as setting forth "slavery" as the "corner-stone" of the Confederacy, it is proper for me to state that that speech was extemporaneous, the reporter's notes, which were very imperfect, were hastily corrected by me; and were published without further revision and with several glaring errors.[3]

---

[1] Henry Cleveland, *Alexander H. Stephens, in Public and Private: With Letters and Speeches, Before, During, and Since the War* (Philadelphia: National Publishing Co., 1886), 721.

[2] Ibid.

[3] Myrta Lockett Avary, ed., Recollections of Alexander H. Stephens (Sunny South Publishing Company and Doubleday, Page & Company, 1910; Baton Rouge, LA: Louisiana State University Press, 1998), 173–75. Citations refer to 1998 edition.

We cannot be persuaded that an errant reporter inserted the words *slavery* and *cornerstone* into a speech that was about slavery as the cornerstone of the Confederacy. Stephens's frail excuse—a stupid scribe got it backward—prefigures the amnesia that affected Jefferson Davis and numerous others after the South was crushed on the field of battle. Both are efforts to deny the facts of slavery, the craven features of the 1787 Constitution, the origins of the Civil War, and the guilt secessionist leaders incurred for starting the bloodshed.

Perhaps wishing to see the founders as morally correct, we can understand the Sons of Confederate Veterans, the United Daughters of the Confederacy, and other defenders of Dixie. Their argumentative histories of the Civil War shelter and foster their identification with an idealized past. That their revisions appeared so quickly and were done with such enthusiasm suggests the shock that defeat brought to the South. Having lost the war, Southern elites vowed to win the peace by an epic effort at restoration and nostalgia. The North sanctified Abraham Lincoln, shot on Good Friday, martyred at 7:22 a.m. on Holy Saturday; the South idealized Robert E. Lee and Stonewall Jackson as heroic officers, first serving the Confederacy, and after the war, the nation.

A set of remembrances of General Stonewall Jackson, who died in 1863, begins:

> Thomas Jonathan Jackson was a product of the American people. His fadeless renown is the legacy of all America. The family quarrel is over. It has strengthened the bonds of Union. All martial deeds and prowess exhibited in that mighty contest, belong to every patriotic citizen. The preservation of the wonderful annals of Stonewall Jackson's achievements is a sacred duty to the South, the Union and to all mankind.[4]

One must admire how these authors separate Stonewall Jackson from his defense of a secessionist movement, which was dedicated to

---

[4] *"Stonewall Jackson" A Thesaurus of Anecdotes and Incidents In The Life of Lieut-General Thomas Jonathan Jackson, C. S. A.* (Annapolis, MD: Riley's Historic Series 1920), v.

preserving slavery, and elevate him to become an exemplar for the entire United States and nations beyond it.

The only mention of the words *slave* or *slavery* in the book's 203 pages appears in an anecdote about Jackson teaching the Bible to black children:

> And his voice seemed to tremble as he prayed for a special blessing on his little charge—the negro children of the town whom he had gathered together in a Sunday School. It was the days of slavery, and their neglected condition excited his sympathy, and a sense of duty impelled him to make an effort to rid them from the slavery of sin.[5]

At the center of this story are the "dusky children," the general's sympathy for them, and his trembling voice. According to this story, another, perhaps worse, kind of slavery is to be ignorant of Christian teachings. General Jackson found himself accommodating to the realities of (mere) physical slavery, but he championed a higher, better kind of freedom from sin (spiritual slavery). To his natural children and to his slave children he showed the road to eternal salvation.

General Jackson was admired by the South, but Robert E. Lee and his horse received even grander praise. A poem by Stephen Vincent Benét about Traveller portrays the gray horse carrying the man leading the Lost Cause. In Benét's 1928 poem, "Army of Northern Virginia," Lee's face and Traveller's visage are matched:

> He too, is iron-grey,
> Though the thick hair and thick, blunt-pointed beard
> Have frost in them.[6]

Much later in 1988, in the novel *Traveller*, author Richard Adams cites Benét's lines in his poem narrated by the gray horse:

---

[5] Ibid., 141.
[6] Stephen Vincent Benét, "Army of Northern Virginia." 1930, lines 125–31.

You're weeping! What, then? What more did you see?
A gray man on a gray horse rode by.[7]

Lee became the heroic figure that the South required. He represented the best of the old tradition, leading his men against great
odds, exemplifying duty. Lee emerged as the central figure of the past.
He was, says Roger D. Abrahams, "a figure who embodies the past in
all its glory, a representative figure somehow left behind on the land-
scape in spite of more recent historical forces. Such a figure
epitomizes the sad feelings that arise from the notion of lost lands
and lost inheritances intrinsic to acts of displacement."[8]

Visitors to Georgia's Stone Mountain, sixteen miles east of Atlanta, see a
gigantic stone carving that shows Lee, Stonewall Jackson, and Jefferson
Davis in monumental profile. Thanks to the efforts of the United Daughters of the Confederacy and enthusiastic support from the Ku Klux Klan,
the rights to the huge outcrop were secured by 1912 and planning had begun to immortalize these three leaders of the Confederacy.[9]

Helen C. Plane, then president of the UDC, pushed to fund a massive
carving on the dome with images of Davis, Lee, Jackson and members of
the KKK because the KKK "had saved us from Negro domination and
carpetbagger rule."[10] Plane's wish to honor the Klan was sincere and historically accurate since the site had witnessed the rebirth of a new Klan
group, "The Knights of Mary Phagan."[11] Although no images of the KKK

---

[7] Richard Adams. *Traveller* (New York: Knopf, 1988), ii.

[8] Roger D. Abrahams. "Phantoms of Romantic Nationalism in Folkloristics."
The Journal of American Folklore 106:419 (1993): 9.

[9] The carving "measures three acres, larger than a football field. The carving of
the three men towers 400 feet above the ground, measures 90 by 190 feet, and is
recessed 42 feet into the mountain. The deepest point of the carving is at Lee's
elbow, which is 12 feet to the mountain's surface." http://www.stonemountain
park.com/faq/.

[10] Carole Blair and Neil Michel in "The Rushmore Effect: Ethos and National
Collective Identity," ed. Michael J. Hyde, *The Ethos of Rhetoric* (University of
South Carolina Press, 2004), 161.

[11] "Phagan, a young white factory worker, had been murdered in Atlanta

were used in the display, the Klan provided the initial inspiration and continuous support for the monument.

Despite their efforts, support for this gigantic project faded until the Supreme Court ruling in *Brown v. Board of Education* on May 17, 1954. That landmark decision obliterated the South's legal claim that its doctrine of "separate but equal" schools for black and white students was constitutionally justified. In the language of the unanimous decision, "We conclude that in the field of public education the doctrine of "separate but equal" has no place. Separate educational facilities are inherently unequal. Therefore, we hold that the plaintiffs and other similarly situated . . . are . . . deprived of the equal protection of the laws guaranteed by the Fourteenth Amendment."[12]

The ruling triggered a surge in racist ideology and enthusiasm for all things Confederate. It also triggered the formation of so-called Citizens Councils in Mississippi and elsewhere. By 1955 a newspaper, the *Citizens' Council*, appeared. Its editors excoriated civil rights leaders, predicting that their mission would lead to riots, orgies, arson, looting, mutiny, witchcraft, murder, and rape because "the Negro is utterly incapable of governing himself much less anyone else."[13] In

---

two years earlier. Leo Frank, a Jewish industrialist, was (erroneously) convicted of the crime. In August 1915, a band of whites took him from prison and hanged him. Spurred by their success and inspired by the recently released film Birth of a Nation, which told a tale of purported Reconstruction horrors, the men, some of whom had participated in lynching Frank, meet on top of Stone Mountain to form the second national Klan." James W. Loewen, *Lies Across America: What Our Historic Sites Get Wrong* (New York: Simon and Schuster, 2007), 242.

[12] History of *Brown v. Board of Education.* http://www.uscourts.gov /EducationalResources/ConstitutionResources/LegalLandmarks/HistoryOf BrownVBoardOfEducation.aspx. See also http://www.streetlaw.org/en/Page/ 519/Key_Excerpts_from_the_Majority_Opinion_Brown_I_1954.

[13] Eaun Hague and Edward H. Sebesta, "Neo-Confederacy and Its Conservative Ancestry." in *Neo-Confederacy: A Critical Introduction*, Euan Hague, Heidi Beirich, Edward H. Sebesta (Austin: University of Texas Press, 2008), 24. They cite Citizens' Council, 5:10 (1960) 2.

1958, the state of Georgia purchased Stone Mountain and used public funds to help complete the memorial to the leaders of the Confederate States of America. On its massive face would be displayed images of its leaders and their horses: President Jefferson Davis, General Robert E. Lee, General Thomas J. "Stonewall" Jackson, and their horses, "Blackjack," "Traveller," and "Little Sorrel."

In his historical study of Stone Mountain, David Freeman recounts the original grandiose plans by Gutzon Borglum that included relief carvings of Confederate armies on the surface of the rock, an arcade of thirteen columns, and a room 60 feet by 40 feet by 320 feet carved *into* the mountain. In the center of this massive hall would be a seated figure of a "Southern woman entitled *Memory*, which would be as large as the figure being carved for the Lincoln Memorial in the nation's capital."[14] While Borglum made an impassioned speech that thrilled Helen Plane, she was not able to raise the two million dollars needed to fulfill his vision. Borglum scaled back his plans, but World War I intervened, and he shut down operations. The war ended, Borglum began again, raised more money, overcame many obstacles, and through the early 1920s used public relations techniques to inflame interest. For example, on "Virginia Day," as Borglum called it, large crowds assembled to hear E. Lee Trinkle, the governor of Virginia, deliver the keynote address. Trinkle hammered home the claim that the "Southern War," while lost, was noble. Borglum's carved portraits of the Confederacy's great men would outlast everything human made and, we note, all attempts to counter the narrative enshrined on the mountain:

> We shall have erected a monument which will outlive the centuries and which will carry the history of our Southern War to a future so distant that the mind of man is not gifted to grasp it. . . . Centuries will be born to die—age will follow age down the unending pathway of the years; cities, government, people will change and perish—while yet, our heroes

---

[14] David Freeman, *Carved in Stone: the History of Stone Mountain* (Macon, GA: Mercer University Press), 60.

carved in stone, will stand on guard—the custodians of imperishable glory, the sentinels of time.[15]

While most CSA foot soldiers did not own slaves, they could hope to own some (and thus enjoy the wealth slavery entailed).[16] More importantly, they shared the planters' belief that the entire structure of the South, including sexual mores, depended upon white supremacy. Gunnar Myrdal, a Swedish social scientist famous for his midcentury analysis of American racism, described the same caste structure eighty-five years later. White police, he noted, stood for the law and for white supremacy: "a break of caste rules against one white person is conceived of as an aggression against white society and, indeed, as a potential threat to every other white individual."[17] Minor transgressions became in this way major transgressions and were punished accordingly.

States' Rights and Other Forms of Camouflage

John C. Calhoun, senator from South Carolina and the seventh US vice president, was the chief architect of the so-called states' rights argument justifying secession. In a famous senate speech delivered on June 27, 1848, Calhoun pursued four lines of thought. He argued on legal, historical, sociological, and philosophic grounds. The legal arguments derive from his reading of the US Constitution and its origins. His historical arguments derive from his review of the history of the Constitutional Convention. His sociological arguments derive from his observations of the differences between white and black persons, which meant, of course, white owners and black slaves. His philosophic arguments derive from his theory of government.

---

[15] Ibid., 70. Freeman cites "Address by Governor E. Lee Trinkle, 18 June 1923," Mary Carter Winter Collection, Georgia State Department of Archives.

[16] Chandra Manning, *What This Cruel War Was Over: Soldiers, Slavery, and the Civil War* (New York: Norton, 2007).

[17] Gunnar Myrdal, *An American Dilemma: the Negro Problem and Modern Democracy*, vol. 2 (New York: Harper & Row, 1944), 535.

In twelve thousand words Calhoun explained why he and other Southern senators opposed the Oregon Bill (which passed on August 14, 1848, six weeks after Calhoun's speech.) If Congress passed the bill it would ratify the actions of citizens in the Oregon territory who had voted to exclude slavery. In effect the Oregon Bill granted to Oregon citizens power to exclude other American citizens who legally owned slaves in other states from entering Oregon with their property, which included their slaves. The Oregon Bill gave to Oregon, a mere territory, the power to contravene the United States Constitution since, as Calhoun shows, the latter explicitly defended the institutions of slavery. While Calhoun is cited as a champion of "states' rights," here he argued that no state (or territory) could legally draft laws that contradicted the language of the Constitution whose slavery provisions were hard won. Northern and Southern states were constituent parts of the Federal Union. They were equals in all relevant respects. In addition to this legal argument, Calhoun recounted the history of the lengthy debates that preceded the Constitution and were repeated during its drafting. Calhoun summarized how he, the primary champion of slavery in the US Senate, understood the institution:

> Slavery existed in the South when the constitution was framed, fully to the extent, in proportion to the population, that it does at this time. *It is the only property recognized by it*; the only one that entered into its formation as a political element, both in the adjustment of the relative weight of the States in the Government, and the apportionment of direct taxes; and the only one that is put under the express guaranty of the constitution.[18]

Calhoun asked if the Northern states have constitutional power to prevent Southern people from emigrating freely, with their property, which includes their slaves.[19] Referring again to the formation of the

---

[18] "On the Oregon Bill" in *The Works of John C. Calhoun*, vol. 4 (New York: D. Appleton & Company, 1883), 482.
[19] Ibid., 483.

United States and the history of the Constitution, Calhoun's lengthy answer is that they do not. Southern states had equal share in the Constitution and slave owners enjoyed national protection. That many Northerners openly disobeyed this national law, including the Constitution's defense of owners seeking to reclaim their escaped slave property, does not mean that the South abdicated its claims under Federal law. Northern states had not stopped agents from "enticing and seducing the slaves to leave their masters, and to run them into Canada beyond the reach of our laws—in open violation, not only of the stipulations of the ordinance, but of the constitution itself."[20] Just as the Constitution trumps state and territorial law, it trumps laws inherited from formerly Mexican states where slavery had been outlawed. Those Mexican states also outlawed the Protestant religion. Calhoun argued that as Americans would not countenance that legal oddity neither should they countenance Mexican law overriding the US Constitution: "All we demand is to stand on the same level with yourselves, and to participate equally in what belongs to all. Less we cannot take."[21]

Calhoun then turned to sociology and cited what he felt were the essential natures of white and black persons, underscoring the alleged supremacy of whites. This supremacy of white over black, he argued, was a fact of nature. His argument turns on the core idea of white solidarity and the odd claim that all whites are "upper class" while all blacks are "lower class." It is a remarkable expression of a divided and absolutistic mind. Calhoun begins with a sociological comment about Southern customs:

> With us the two great divisions of society are not the rich and the poor, but white and black; and all the former, the poor as well as the rich, belong to the upper class, and are respected and treated as equals, if honest and industrious; and hence have a position and pride of character of which neither poverty nor misfortune can deprive them.[22]

---

[20] Ibid., 489.

[21] Ibid., 503.

[22] For a thoughtful discussion of this speech, see Harry V. Jaffa, *A New Birth of Freedom* (Lanham, MD: Rowman & Littlefield, 2000), 283ff.

Calhoun was noted for his legal acumen and the thoroughness of his presentation. He wrote precisely what he meant to say. If we read the 1787 Constitution the way he did, his argument against the Oregon Bill appears valid. The South could compromise as it had before, as he notes, but this new affront to slave owners prefigured the rise of a national consensus that could, over time, revise Constitutional law. That would not only restrict the growth of slavery in new territories and states, it could also reach into Southern states where it had been legal since before the Republic.

Calhoun concluded his sociological analysis by rejecting Jefferson (whom he had praised earlier) and then offered a philosophic argument about the nature of political liberty. When Jefferson penned the Declaration of Independence his infatuation with the abstract idea of human equality got the better of him, Calhoun said. By focusing on the individual, Jefferson overlooked the true nature of political life and the defense of liberty. In brief, Jefferson's error lay in his focus on individuals as the locus of liberty.[23] This hypothetical truism ignores human realities:

> "Every man would be his own master, and might do just as he pleased. But it is equally clear, that man cannot exist in such a state; that he is by nature social, and that society is necessary, not only to the proper development of all his faculties, moral and intellectual, but to the very existence of his race" (ibid., 536).

> Since no persons can persist and flourish independently of others, we need society and with it forms of government. For that reason, individual freedoms and rights "must be subordinate to whatever power may be necessary to protect society against anarchy within or destruction from without" (ibid.).

Persons who are ignorant, stupid, or of unequal gifts cannot wield political power.

[When] "people rise in the scale of intelligence, virtue, and patriotism,

---

[23] "On the Oregon Bill" in *The Works of John C. Calhoun*, 479–512.

and the more perfectly they become acquainted with the nature of government, the ends for which it was ordered, and how it ought to be administered, and the less the tendency to violence and disorder within, and danger from abroad, the power necessary for government becomes less and less, and individual liberty greater and greater" (ibid., 536–37).

Thus, political freedoms are merited; they are won by intelligence, courage: "they are high prizes to be won, and are in their most perfect state, not only the highest reward that can be bestowed on our race, but the most difficult to be won—and when won, the most difficult to be preserved" (ibid., 537).

Jefferson's grand pronouncement in the Declaration "that all men are born free and equal" was a poisonous idea, Calhoun said. Any attempt to realize this pronouncement was dangerous, erroneous, and bound to fail. It has "done more to retard the cause of liberty and civilization, and is doing more at present, than all other causes combined" (ibid., 537). While earlier in his speech Calhoun offered Northern senators a compromise that "would fix the line between the slaveholding and non-slaveholding States in about 36° 30" (ibid., 532), he would not abandon his principle defense of slavery as legal and perpetual. To defend that principle he, like many slavery proponents, rejected Jefferson's tragically divided response to slavery. The dormant ideal of equality so possessed Jefferson, Calhoun concluded, that Jefferson did great harm to the United States. Jefferson, Calhoun said, took "an utterly false view of the subordinate relation of the black to the white race in the South; and to hold, in consequence, that the former, though utterly unqualified to possess liberty, were as fully entitled to both liberty and equality as the latter; and that to deprive them of it was unjust and immoral" (ibid., 538).

Safely ensconced in the upper-class realms of Southern power, Calhoun denied that poor white folk are of the lower classes. Poor whites would likely have found this amusing since "white trash" was a name used by rich whites to categorize poor Caucasians.[24] Some historians

---

[24] See Matt Wray, *Not Quite White: White Trash and the Boundaries of*

argue that because manual labor was allocated only to black persons, the social position of whites grew worse. Writing in 1902, John Fiske noted that slaves belonged to "the grand establishment of a powerful or wealthy master, and from this point of view society might be said to have a place for him, even though he possessed no legal rights. There was no such haven of security for the mean whites."[25]

Calhoun wished to be seen as a gentle master and it is unlikely that he whipped his slaves; he didn't have to. That dreadful task he, Washington, Jefferson, and other elites assigned to poor whites. In postwar interviews about their conditions, some former slaves noted that upper-class whites rarely manned slave patrols or brutalized slaves. As Mia Bay, a professor of American history, observes, this was for a simple reason: the rich hired lower class white men to do it for them.[26] It is false to say that rich landowners and slavers respected and treated poor whites as equals. Lincoln noted that the slave overseer and other whites who broke slaves had no welcome in the front parlors of white gentry.

In Calhoun's world, blacks could not be upper class. Yet many free persons of color owned businesses, farms, and small industries in Louisiana. In Calhoun's native state of South Carolina, dominated by the planter class, few free persons of color owned substantial property. Those that owned even small parcels of land, given to them upon

---

Whiteness (Durham, NC: Duke University Press, 2006), chap. 2, "Imagining Poor Whites in the Antebellum South: Abolitionist and Pro-Slavery Fictions." "Rather than viewing class inequalities as an impediment to democracy, southern apologists tended to view them as important boundaries that gave order and discipline to what would otherwise be chaotic mob rule" (ibid. 49).

[25] "There can be little doubt that the white freed-men of degraded type were the progenitors of a considerable portion of what is often called the 'white trash' of the South." John Fiske, *Old Virginia and Her Neighbors* vol. 2. (New York: Houghton, Mifflin & Co, 1902), 219–20.

[26] Mia Bay, *The White Image in the Black Mind: African-American Ideas about White People, 1830–1925* (New York: Oxford University Press, 2000), 155–56.

manumission by grateful owners, were subject to legal assaults from aggrieved white heirs. One slave named Peter, owned by William Hallum who lived in the Pendelton District of South Carolina, was freed in 1803 and given land, money, and a gun to protect himself. Upon the death of Hallum's widow, Peter assumed control of the land given him. He was challenged in court by white heirs who said that "a black man could not own land, which Pendleton Judge John Harris confirmed in 1827."[27]

The alleged pride that all whites feel, rich and poor alike, of which they cannot be deprived, must be the fact that they are not black. Yet the accidental feature of one's skin color cannot be a matter of "character" since character is the sum total of one's actions. If Calhoun was correct, then the most feeble-minded white person, "if honest and industrious," is superior to the most able and substantial black person.

Some economic historians of the Old South argued that antebellum economic life was dominated by the planter class in ways that made non-slave-owning whites poorer than their Northern counterparts. The diverse names assigned to low-income whites ("poor white trash" and "crackers") refer to caste differences in the Southern economy.[28] Poor whites in the plantation areas were forced largely to compete with slave labor on land since the handicraft work through which the poor whites might otherwise have escaped stagnation tended more and more to be done by slaves. The large planters owned their smiths and shoemakers. These were often hired out at rates so low that theoretically free men could never hope to learn the arts.[29]

---

[27] W. J. Megginson. *African American Life in South Carolina's Upper Piedmont, 1780-1900* (Columbia, SC: University of South Carolina, 2006), 53. Regarding Calhoun's slaves and his financial dealings, see 149–52.

[28] See Mamie Meredith, "Variants of 'Poor White Trash'" *American Speech* 6, no. 4 (April 1931), 311. In upstate New York, around 1905, poor whites were called "Clappers," "honies," and "slouters."

[29] James M. Reinhardt and William van Royen, "The 'Glamour' of the Old South," review of *De Landelijke Arme Blanken in Het Zuiden der Vereenigde Staten,* by A. N. J. den Hollander, *Social Forces* 14, no. 3 (March 1936): 441–44.

As Derrick Bell noted one hundred years later, although illiterate and dispossessed, being white amounted to a property right, a right that black equality would destroy.

It partly explains their ready participation in the war. They feared the consequences of emancipation more than they despised the existing economic system.[30]

Among the postwar defenses of the CSA was the notion that the South fought to maintain a distinctly rural, egalitarian (for whites) society based on ancient traditions of land, gentry, and limited government. John D. Majewski, an economic historian, exposed this distortion in a detailed study of the CSA's actual governance and its leaders' hopes for a centralized, modern economy controlled by a militaristic state. In other words, fascism.[31] Because the South lost the Civil War it could not achieve full-fledged statehood and thus full-fledged fascistic controls. On the contrary, immediately after the surrender to Ulysses S. Grant, Southern leaders shifted their intense militaristic values from the South to the nation as a whole. So, when European fascists were enamored of Jim Crow laws and other post–Civil War legalisms erected by Southern politicians, the Southerners did not return the compliment. Hitler, for example, was enthralled by the movie version of *Gone with the Wind* (*Vom Winde verweht*) and the military values he saw championed in that film. While he may have mused about how similar Nazi values were to those of the American South, Hitler did not enthrall Southern politicians. According to David Runciman, "Despite their endless misgivings about federal government and Northern aggrandisement, Southerners also saw themselves as patriots. They were sensitive to any slights to national honour."[32]

---

[30] Ibid., 443.

[31] John Majewski, *Modernizing a Slave Economy: The Economic Vision of the Confederate Nation: The Economic Vision of the Confederate Nation* (Chapel Hill, NC: University of North Carolina Press, 2009).

[32] David Runciman, "Destiny v. Democracy," review of *Fear Itself: The New Deal and the Origins of Our Time* by Ira Katznelson, *London Review of Books*

Given access to a modern economy with additional wealth and enhanced policing powers, the CSA could, as a nation, protect slavery far better than individual states might. "States' rights" rhetoric was secondary, Majewski argues, to the fact that "In the antebellum period, southerners routinely supported various forms of police action— including local slave patrols, statewide censorship of mails and newspapers, and national fugitive slave laws—to ensure the safety of slavery."[33] Majewski cites Armistead Burt, a South Carolinian, who said: "Property in slaves, of all other property, can least endure aggression, and most needs the arm of government."[34]

The arms of a racist government were long indeed. It needed policing powers that extended in every location where abolitionism might flourish. To the degree that normal sentiments favor freedom and that Christianity and Judaism dictate the equality of all persons as children of God, these locations included the hearts, minds, and souls of Southerners. The CSA, founded in 1861, could not live by the rules of an open society just as the apartheid government of South Africa, elected in 1948, could not tolerate open democratic institutions. Each became a centralized state using its police powers to keep emancipation (in the South) and democratic representation (in South Africa) from spreading. For example, echoing many Southern leaders, Andrew Jackson favored seizing and destroying US mail and newspapers that championed emancipation. Though pledged to defend the United States Constitution, including the First Amendment, Southern congressmen and senators had no difficulty imposing gag rules upon both the House and Senate chambers regarding debates over slavery.[35] We find that the same impulses to suppress speech that criticized slavery flourished in the CSA's empire.

35, no. 8 (2013): 13–16, http://www.lrb.co.uk/v35/n08/david-runciman/destiny-v-democracy.

[33] Majewski, *Modernizing a Slave Economy*, 8.

[34] Armistead Burt to Thomas Byrd et al., in *Columbus (Georgia) Enquirer*, June 3, 1851, p. 8.

[35] See Garry Wills, *"Negro President": Jefferson and the Slave Power* (New York: Houghton Mifflin Harcourt, 2003), 217–22.

Luxury and the Pleasures of Being Served

Abraham Lincoln was not raised in luxury. Joining other poor whites, he labored to eke out a minimal living. Though such work was identical to that done by slaves, he could have joined the poor whites who despised Negroes. That Lincoln did not share this bit of pleasurable superiority is among the puzzles of his ethical development. We know that he early intuited his intellectual abilities and that his mother, Nancy Hanks Lincoln, doted upon him, recognizing how unusual her son was. In his generous study of Lincoln's ethical development, William Lee Miller helps us follow Lincoln's growing ability to distinguish moralizing from reasoning based on moral principles: the first is a common reactivity of judgment, to condemn what bothers us or impedes us. That which reduces my profits is bad; what increases them is good. What diminishes my pride is bad; what enhances it is good. The second, reasoning based upon moral principles, is the hard-won product of reflection upon values that might, if implemented, work against our self-interest.[36] In this way moral reasoning resembles legal reasoning and scientific reasoning; all three procedures require one to tolerate the possibility that we might be wrong. Ethicists, jurists, and scientists must learn to temper their wishes and emotions (which impel us to actions) by the rules of evidence pertinent to their disciplines. Training in these disciplines turns on this demand for self-restraint, modesty, and radical honesty.

Miller calls Lincoln's speech of October 4, 1854, in Springfield, Illinois, in which Lincoln argued the case against slavery and against repeal of the Missouri Compromise, the first great speech of his life. Though that October 4 speech is now lost to us, Lincoln repeated the bulk of it on October 16, 1854. Repeal of the Missouri Compromise, he argued, meant that slavery could spread into new states and federal territories and, in principle, into all the states. Worse, repeal meant that the transcendental vision of the Declaration, that men (and eventually all persons) are of equal dignity, was shredded, "insisting there

---

[36] William Lee Miller, *Lincoln's Virtues: an Ethical Biography* (New York: Alfred A. Knopf, 2002).

is no right principle of action but self-interest."[37] Lincoln was especially agitated by comments of John Pettit,[38] a senator from Indiana who argued on the Senate floor in February 1854 on behalf of the Kansas-Nebraska Act of 1854, which repealed the Missouri Compromise of 1820. The Missouri Compromise, crafted by Henry Clay of Kentucky, was the complicated deal struck between Northern states and Southern states that permitted new states to enter the Union if the balance of proslavery and antislavery states remained. In the compromise Congress admitted Missouri as a slave state and admitted Maine (carved out of upper Massachusetts) as a free state. In addition:

> all that territory ceded by France to the United States, under the name of Louisiana, which lies north of thirty-six degrees and thirty minutes north latitude, not included within the limits of the state, contemplated by this act, slavery and involuntary servitude, otherwise than in the punishment of crimes, whereof the parties shall have been duly convicted, shall be, and is hereby, forever prohibited.[39]

In line with the 1787 Constitution, the Kansas-Nebraska Act of 1854 reaffirmed the rights of slave owners to pursue runaways everywhere in the United States:

---

[37] Abraham Lincoln, October 16,1854. Speech at Peoria, Illinois, In Reply To Senator Douglas, *Abraham Lincoln: Complete Works: Comprising his Speeches, Letters, State Papers, and Miscellaneous Writings,* vol. 1., ed. John Hay and John George Nicolay, 180–209. See also Roy P. Basler, ed., *The Collected Works of Abraham Lincoln,* vol. 2 (October 16, 1854), 275.

[38] Pettit was well connected. He ran for reelection to the Senate in 1854, was defeated and then was appointed chief justice of the United States courts in the Territory of Kansas from 1859 to 1861. After that he became judge of the supreme court of Indiana, from 1870 to 1877. The Senate Historical Office, http://bioguide.congress.gov/scripts/biodisplay.pl?index=P000277.

[39] Conference committee report on the Missouri Compromise, March 1, 1820; Joint Committee of Conference on the Missouri Bill, 03/01/1820 -03/06/1820; Record Group 128l; Records of Joint Committees of Congress, 1789–1989; National Archives.

That any person escaping into the same, from whom labour or service is
lawfully claimed, in any state or territory of the United States, such fugitive may be lawfully reclaimed and conveyed to the person claiming his
or her labour or service as aforesaid.

The Missouri Compromise postponed the momentous question of
slavery and its protection in the Constitution. The Kansas-Nebraska Act
of 1854 repealed that compromise and allowed voters in new territories
to include or to exclude slavery. In his lengthy comments on the Kansas-
Nebraska Act on the senate floor, Pettit complained that antislavery zeal-
ots had misrepresented Jefferson's phrase in the Declaration that "We
hold these truths to be self evident, that all men are created equal." Of
this proposition, Pettit said, "I hold it to be a self-evident lie. There is no
such thing."[40] Pettit repeated the standard argument that anthropologi-
cally speaking, persons differed dramatically in their intellectual talents,
skills, endowments, and so on: "You may, *per* force of human laws, make
political equality; but *per* force of no human laws can you make social
equality." Since God did not make us all identical to one another, Petit
argued that Jefferson's affirmation was "false in form, and false in fact."
Indeed, Pettit argued that fairness requires that slavery opponents respect the feelings of those for whom slavery is a way of life. He offered a
novel argument:

Let us reverse our positions, and see how we should stand. Suppose that
the South had the numerical powers in the Senate and in the House . . .
and should say that no State should hereafter come into this Union, unless with a slave constitution; would we, I ask, as freemen, demanding an
equality of political rights in this Union, submit to it?[41]

[40] U.S. Congressional Documents and Debates, 1774–1875. Congressional
Globe, Senate, 33rd Congress, 1st Session: In the Senate, February 20, 1854,
http://memory.loc.gov/cgibin/ampage?collId=llcg&fileName=036/llcg036.d
b&recNum=219.
[41] Ibid.

This peculiar argument leaves out the principal subjects of slavery, slaves, and their thoughts and feelings about their state of bondage. Lincoln objected to this dismissal of the Declaration and to Pettit's (and Calhoun's) reading of American history with regard to the compromises that shaped the original Constitution. As he would do many times, Lincoln in his speech recited the history of the slavery provisions. He emphasized feelings of shared moral intuition. These feelings are prior to reflection; they are as immediate as sensations of pain:

> The great majority South, as well as North, have human sympathies, of which they can no more divest themselves than they can of their sensibility to physical pain. These sympathies in the bosoms of the Southern people manifest, in many ways, their sense of the wrong of slavery, and their consciousness that, after all, there is humanity in the negro.[42]

The incoherence of slavery reappears when Lincoln says that by agreeing to outlaw the international slave trade and to employ capital punishment as a deterrent, Southerners acknowledged that slaves were more than animals. If black people were animals, then we would not prosecute men for "bringing wild negroes from Africa to such as would buy them. But you never thought of hanging men for catching and selling wild horses, wild buffaloes, or wild bears" (ibid.). Lincoln marches through the history of the 1787 Constitution's fugitive slave clause, the three-fifths clause, and the imbalance the latter created in national governance. As always, he defers to the standing law and does not reject these infamous provisions: "Now all this is manifestly unfair; yet I do not mention it to complain of it, in so far as it is already settled. It is in the Constitution, and I do not for that cause, or any other cause, propose to destroy, or alter, or disregard the Constitution. I stand to it, fairly, fully, and firmly" (ibid., 198).

Lincoln challenged his opponent, (former judge) Stephen Douglas,

---

[42] Abraham Lincoln, October 16, 1854. Speech at Peoria, Illinois, In Reply To Senator Douglas, *Abraham Lincoln: Complete Works*, 194.

who argued that the Missouri Compromise was not directed to re-stricting the number of new slave states:

> A word now as to the judge's desperate assumption that the compromises
> of 1850 had no connection with one another; that Illinois came into the
> Union as a slave State, and some other similar ones. This is no other
> than a bold denial of the history of the country. If we do not know that
> the compromises of 1850 were dependent on each other; if we do not
> know that Illinois came into the Union as a free State,—we do not know
> anything (ibid., 208).

He harkens back to the illogicality of denying the role of the Dec-laration in organizing how future Americans were to understand the Union: "To deny these things is to deny our national axioms,—or dogmas, at least,—and it puts an end to all argument. If a man will stand up and assert, and repeat and reassert, that two and two do not make four, I know nothing in the power of argument that can stop him" (ibid., 209).

After summarizing the history of federal efforts to constrain slav-ery, Lincoln acknowledges the duality of human thinking. As he sees it, human beings are selfish and can enjoy owning slaves, but in their deeper feelings they recognize that such ownership is wrong:

> Slavery is founded in the selfishness of man's nature—opposition to it in
> his love of justice. These principles are an eternal antagonism, and when
> brought into collision so fiercely as slavery extension brings them,
> shocks and throes and convulsions must ceaselessly follow. Repeal the
> Missouri Compromise, repeal all compromises, repeal the Declaration
> of Independence, repeal all past history, you still cannot repeal human
> nature. It still will be the abundance of man's heart that slavery extension
> is wrong, and out of the abundance of his heart his mouth will continue
> to speak (ibid., 199).

Prior to the war, Lincoln was not an abolitionist nor did he have a modern sensibility about race nor did he anticipate the readiness of

African Americans to assume full citizenship.[43] On August 14, 1862, Lincoln addressed a group of free men of color urging them to emigrate either to Liberia or to an unnamed Central American region:

> Go where you are treated the best [in the United States] and the ban is still upon you. I do not propose to discuss this, but to present it as a fact with which we have to deal. I cannot alter it if I would. It is a fact about which we all think and feel alike, I and you. We look to our condition. Owing to the existence of the two races on this continent, I need not recount to you the effects upon white men, growing out of the institution of slavery.[44]

Lincoln exhorts the free black men to recall the sacrifices of Washington and others who risked their comfort to help forge a new nation. He asks for an initial vanguard: "Could I get a hundred tolerably intelligent men, with their wives and children, and able to 'cut their own fodder,' so to speak? Can I have fifty? If I could find twenty-five able-bodied men, with a mixture of women and children,—good things in the family relation, I think,— I could make a successful commencement."[45] (As I visualize this scene, the president sees that his cajoling has failed and confronting the resistance of the men, he bargains down from one hundred to twenty-five settlers.)

---

[43] Ibid., 201–02. Hence, Lincoln says (in 1854), "Stand with anybody that stands right. Stand with him while he is right, and part with him when he goes wrong. Stand with the Abolitionist in restoring the Missouri Compromise, and stand against him when he attempts to repeal the fugitive-slave law. In the latter case you stand with the Southern disunionist. What of that? You are still right. In both cases you are right. In both cases you expose the dangerous extremes. In both you stand on middle ground, and hold the ship level and steady. In both you are national, and nothing less than national. This is the good old Whig ground."

[44] Abraham Lincoln, *Complete Works, Comprising His Speeches, State Papers, and Miscellaneous Writings*, vol. 2, ed. John G. Nicolay and John Hay (New York: Century, 1920), 223–24.

[45] Ibid.

As the war progressed and black troops fought for their freedom, Lincoln came to see how retrograde his earlier opinions had been. Having examined hundreds of letters from Union and Confederate soldiers, Chandra Manning, a contemporary American historian, argues that by 1864, Union soldiers loved Lincoln because they witnessed the terrors of slavery and they had fought alongside freed slaves. These ordinary soldiers helped reinforce Lincoln's belief that the Union's cause was emancipation, a belief not shared by everyone at home.[46]

Lincoln's racialist understanding, which appears to have been nearly universal in his time among whites, did not preclude his asserting the transcendental claim of human equality—given by a Creator or by Nature's God as Jefferson put it—that only government derived from assent was legitimate. He cites the Declaration, that to secure "these rights, governments are instituted among men, deriving their just powers from the consent of the governed." Slaves cannot give assent: "The master not only governs the slave without his consent, but he governs him by a set of rules altogether different from those which he prescribes for himself."

From this early speech we can derive four decisive claims. (1) Lincoln's anthropology, we might call it, holds that human beings are both selfish (susceptible to the pleasures of slave ownership) and capable of sympathetic identification with victims of injustice, including slaves; (2) all persons are of equal dignity and deserving of basic rights—a categorical truth recognized in Jefferson's preamble; (3) laws should be reciprocal—by definition, law is beyond personalities and what is fair for me must be fair for others; and (4) a just government derives its powers from the assent of the governed, or else it is tyranny. As Lincoln put it, "Allow all the governed an equal voice in the government, and that, and that only, is self-government."[47]

---

[46] Chandra Manning, *What This Cruel War Was Over: Soldiers, Slavery, and the Civil War* (New York: Random House, 2007), 13–14.

[47] Abraham Lincoln, *Complete Works, Comprising His Speeches, State Papers, and Miscellaneous Writings*, vol. 2. All citations on p. 196. See also

Slavery violates all four claims and for that reason the US founders aimed for its eventual extinction.

Lincoln, Empathy, and Being Hungry

By retelling the story of the founding of the Republic, Lincoln put his ethical stamp upon American history. Although he wishes to show that the founders of the United States shared this ethical vision, he does not offer an exact, scientific historical account of the many currents and opinions that swirled around these matters sufficient to prove this claim. Instead, Lincoln offers an emotional reading of the founder's internal experiences. He imagines their dreams, joys, sorrows, and self-communings, as E. M. Forster put it, through his empathic imagination. Empathy requires a dual registration, a dual mindedness.

Empathy is based in the body. To ignore one's bodily experiences, one's feelings, or the bodily experience of others is to forgo the possibility of understanding them. It is tempting to believe that Lincoln's empathy was instilled from his mother, Nancy Hanks, his "Angel Mother," and after her death when he was nine, from his stepmother, Sarah Bush Johnston. For the immediacy of Lincoln's moral intuition never wavered. It was not deduced; it was based on perception, not argumentation. When he shuddered at the sight of manacled slaves, he must have felt in his muscles and bones the bite of those chains. That tactile immediacy preceded and trumped all learned disquisitions on the naturalness and rightness of slavery. As Lincoln said of his mental processes, though he was slow to learn new subjects, once mastered their imprint was engraved as if on steel. The same was true of his moral sensibilities. When he reacted against the Dred Scott decision in 1857, Lincoln drew upon his tactile, empathic sense of the body of the slave. That decision to deny full personhood to four million enslaved Americans was a conspiracy to bind their collective

---

Harry V. Jaffa, *A New Birth of Freedom* (Lanham, MD: Rowman and Littlefield, 2004). He entitled his third chapter, "The Divided American Mind on the Eve of Conflict."

bodies, "a Gulliver tied down, stretched out on a continent that was now to be one giant whipping-machine," as Edward Baptist put it.[48]

Later, Lincoln mounted detailed arguments against slavery, but those speeches, as great as they are, clarified his primary intuition: if slavery is not wrong, nothing is wrong. To be empathic is to grasp the ways another person experiences the world of visual, sensory, and values. Folk wisdom has long recognized that to understand (and therefore predict) persons' actions we must walk in their shoes, to see things from their point of view and similar notions of grasping another person's perspective.

Lincoln looked at slavery and saw a crime. John C. Calhoun looked at slavery and saw whites (the upper class) elevating blacks (the lower class) into a higher state of civilization. One difference between the two men and their formulations on the slavery question is that Lincoln began his thinking with the body of the slave. He recognized the experience of exhausting labor, of being confined to a miserable piece of land; he was able to empathize with being enchained and being hungry. Using stories supplied by upper-class schooling and planter ideology, Calhoun began with images of "degraded life in Africa" from which slavery provided rescue. Wishing to be seen as a kind master and a good Christian, Calhoun assumed that his wishes denoted facts. As Calhoun saw it, white gentlemen gave to Africans, who are lesser beings, a chance to elevate themselves. Calhoun's selective inattention to the reality of slavery—its origins in terror and violence, the crushing humiliation of perpetual bondage, the endless brutalization—meant that, in his mind, no such reality obtained.

In his many comments on slavery, Lincoln typically refers to earning and eating one's daily bread. The phrase comes from his assiduous reading of the King James Version of Genesis 3:19: "In the sweat of thy face shalt thou eat bread, till thou return unto the ground; for out of it wast thou taken: for dust thou art, and unto dust shalt thou return." Some

---

[48] Edward Baptist, *The Half Has Never Been Told: Slavery and the Making of American Capitalism* (New York: Basic Books, 2014), 379.

writers and many preachers cited this passage as a metaphor for the fall from Eden into earthly life, the life of the body. Lincoln does not cite this passage as a metaphor; it is a literal description of earning one's bread. He means that having been forced to do the least esteemed jobs, as menial laborers and body servants, black slaves raised, cooked, and served the foods eaten by their owners.[49] This echoes one of Lincoln's persistent themes: that those who raise the food own it and ought to eat it. Because slavery steals the labor of the slave, it denies a fundamental element of human beings: that we ought to be masters of ourselves. This simple dictum appears throughout Lincoln's notes to himself. On (October–December, 1858):

> Suppose it is true, that the negro is inferior to the white, in the gifts of nature; is it not the exact reverse justice that the white should, for that reason, take from the negro, any part of the little which has been given him? 'Give to him that is needy' is the Christian rule of charity; but 'Take from him that is needy' is the rule of slavery." He adds, that slavery is a peculiar good in that "it is the only good thing which no man ever seeks the good of, for himself. Nonsense! Wolves devouring lambs, not because it is good for their own greedy maws, but because it is good for the lambs!!![50]

Lincoln articulated his religious views in a letter to the American Baptist Home Mission Society on May 30, 1864. It foreshadows the theological language at the end of the Second Inaugural delivered in

---

[49] Calhoun says that whites do not and ought not perform the least prestigious jobs: "There is no part of the world where agricultural, mechanical, and other descriptions of labor are more respected than in the South, with the exception of two descriptions of employment—that of menial and body servants. No Southern man—not the poorest or the lowest—will, under any circumstance, submit to perform either of them. He has too much pride for that, and I rejoice that he has. They are unsuited to the spirit of a freeman." *The Works of John C. Calhoun*, vol. 4 (New York: Appleton, 1854), 505.

[50] http://teachingamericanhistory.org/library/index.asp?document=783.

March 1865. Concerning the help the Home Mission gave to the Northern cause, Lincoln notes: "It is difficult to conceive how it could be otherwise with any one professing Christianity, or even having ordinary perceptions of right and wrong. To read in the Bible, as the word of God himself, that 'In the sweat of *thy* face shalt thou eat bread,' and to preach therefrom that, 'In the sweat of *other men's* faces shalt thou eat bread,' to my mind can scarcely be reconciled with honest sincerity.[51]

He cites the Golden Rule and its paramount place in Christian teaching: "When, a year or two ago, those professedly holy men of the South met in the semblance of prayer and devotion, and, in the name of him who said, "As ye would all men should do unto you, do ye even so unto them," appealed to the Christian world to aid them in doing to a whole race of men as they would have no man do unto themselves, to my thinking they contemned [despised] and insulted God."[52]

When Southern preachers begged the world to support secession they were begging them to support slavery, a condition that no persons would wish for themselves or their children. Lincoln's homely comment about the sweat of labor is, again, not a metaphor. It speaks directly to the structure of slavery: that owners appropriated their slaves' labor for themselves, granting, as compensation, the slaves' lives back to them. Honest proponents of slavery could not sidestep this moral truth, try as they might. It appears continuously in their efforts to confront the contradictions of slavery.

---

[51] "May 30, 1864.—Letter To Dr. Ide And Others." *Abraham Lincoln; Complete Works, Comprising His Speeches, State Papers, and Miscellaneous Writings*, vol. 2, ed. John Hay and John G. Nicolay (New York: Century, 1920), 526. (His emphasis.)

[52] Ibid., "May 30, 1864.—Letter To Dr. Ide And Others," 526. The quotation is from Luke 6:31.

PART TWO

CHAPTER 4

The Original Contradiction: Property in Human Being

Many Americans of the past century were educated to scorn slave-holders and to idealize George Washington, Thomas Jefferson, Patrick Henry, and Andrew Jackson. That each great man owned slaves seemed secondary. Thanks to eloquent narratives about these men, and in the case of Jefferson, his own writings, we may view their ties to slavery as regrettable, but understandable, lapses for persons of their time.[1] Sharing a sense of American exceptionalism, that the nation was blessed in unusual ways, many believe that the Constitution

---

[1] In 1785, Jefferson wrote to Dr. Price, an English philanthropist, regarding an antislavery treatise: "Southward of the Chesapeake it will find but few readers concurring with it in sentiment, on the subject of slavery. From the mouth to the head of the Chesapeake, the bulk of the people will approve it in theory, and it will find a respectable minority ready to adopt it in practice; a minority, which, for weight and worth of character, preponderates against the greater number, who have not the courage to divest their families of a property, which, however, keeps their consciences unquiet. Northward of the Chesapeake, you may find here and there an opponent to your doctrine as you may find here and there a robber and murderer; but in no greater number." Jefferson, *Writings*, I, 376–78.

was dedicated to liberty and that the founders wished to see slavery eradicated.

In its most naked form, American exceptionalism is the belief that the United States is uniquely blessed, founded on Christian principles, whose people affirm "In God We Trust" unlike any other modern society. For example, Seymour Lipset, a noted American social scientist, writes, "The saga of American history puts into sharp relief the controversies about the role of individual greatness in history. But however one comes to this debate, there can be little question that the hand of providence has been on a nation which finds a Washington, a Lincoln, or a Roosevelt when it needs him."[2] The "hand of providence" means that God took special pains to bless the United States above all other nations. During the Civil War, both Northern and Southern preachers—and politicians—exhorted their followers to affirm this pious story of America's destiny. Like preachers before them, they peppered their sermons with references to the Chosen People, the Jews who were blessed when they were faithful to God. They asserted that America and Americans were also divinely chosen—and could remain chosen with the proper devotion and piety. Among relevant texts from the Hebrew Bible is God's promise to the faithful: "Thou shalt be blessed above all people: there shall not be male or female barren among you, or among your cattle" (Deuteronomy 7:14).[3]

---

[2] Seymour Lipset, *American Exceptionalism: A Double Edged Sword* (New York: Norton, 1996). In sharp contrast to Lipset, Andrew J. Bacevich argued that this doctrine can blind American policy makers, a blindness that helped make the success of the attacks of Septembers 11, 2001, more likely. See *The Limits of Power: The End of American Exceptionalism* (New York: Holt, 2008), 1–4.

[3] Mormon theologians made these parallels explicit: "Mormon theology still holds to the doctrine that America is a choice land, protected by and ordained by God, yet this is always tempered by a belief that the land will be protected only so long as its people are righteous." Brett Lunceford, "One Nation Under God: Mormon Theology and the American Continent," in *The Rhetoric of American Exceptionalism: Critical Essays*, ed. Jason A. Edwards (Jefferson, NC: McFarland & Co., 2011), 59.

George Washington and other founders lamented the evils of slavery that were present from the beginning. Washington declared: "I can only say that no man living wishes more sincerely than I do to see the abolition of (slavery)."[4] In a famous passage written around 1782, Jefferson said slavery had made many Americans coarse and unjust. The "whole commerce between master and slave is a perpetual exercise of the most boisterous passions, the most unremitting despotism on the one part, and degrading submissions on the other. . . . Indeed I tremble for my country when I reflect that God is just."[5]

We were taught that the Declaration of Independence (penned by Jefferson in 1776) and the Constitution drafted in 1787 were dedicated to liberty. However, deep compromises run through the Constitution of 1787. How to square the belief of the founders' dedication to American liberty with the language of the Constitution, such as the three-fifths provision (article 1, section 2, clause 3), which grants the slaveocracy additional representation in Congress, and the fugitive slave clause (article 4, section 2, clause 3), which requires citizens in free states to turn over escaped slaves to "slave catchers," is a task many of us postponed. We learned both that the foundations of the nation were morally sound and that those foundations rested upon slavery, protected in the Virginia territory of Washington, DC, and locked into the Constitution.[6]

---

[4] The next sentence reads: "But when slaves who are happy & content to remain with their present masters, are tampered with & seduced to leave them . . . it introduces more evils than it can cure." Fritz Hirschfield, George Washington and Slavery (Columbia, MO: University of Missouri Press, 1997), 187.

[5] *Notes on the State of Virginia* [1787] 9th ed. (Boston: H. Sprague and Co., 1802), 223–24.

[6] Article 1, section 2, clause 3: Representatives and direct Taxes shall be apportioned among the several States which may be included within this Union, according to their respective Numbers, which shall be determined by adding to the whole Number of free Persons, including those bound to Service for a Term of Years, and excluding Indians not taxed, three fifths of all other Persons. (Modified by the 14th Amendment on July 9,1868.) Article 4, section 2, clause 3: No Person held to Service or Labour in one State, under the

Many of us were taught that it was unfair to judge eighteenth- and nineteenth-century persons against contemporary values, that these issues are so complex that we cannot assess that period without a lifetime immersed in scholarship. We were impressed by the eloquence and charm of Shelby Foote, Walker Percy, and other distinguished Southern writers. As Foote—himself committed to equal rights—explained it, the Civil War was a struggle between the states, not about slavery per se, but about Southern independence.[7] We also believed, informed it seems by *Gone with the Wind* and similar films, that few Southerners owned slaves; hence the Civil War was fought for reasons other than slavery. These teachings are wrong on all counts.

Washington, Madison, and Jefferson, and Robert E. Lee and Andrew Jackson—each an outstanding man—lived divided lives. By admiring them uncritically we absorb those divisions into ourselves. Having raised them to the level of secular saints (Washington, Jefferson, Madison) and national heroes (Robert E. Lee, Andrew Jackson), we believe them when they said that they disliked slavery but that somehow it was necessary. Because they were men of great talent, and

---

Laws thereof, escaping into another, shall, in Consequence of any Law or Regulation therein, be discharged from such Service or Labour, but shall be delivered up on Claim of the Party to whom such Service or Labour may be due. (Superseded by the 13th Amendment on December 6, 1865.)

[7] Foote was the passionate commentator with a deep Mississippi accent who appeared throughout Ken Burn's PBS epic, "The Civil War," first shown in 1993 on PBS, 690 minutes. See also William C. Carter, ed., *Conversations with Shelby Foote* (Jackson, MS: University Press of Mississippi, 1989), 21–55. Interviewed by John Carr: "CARR: Do you think that the [Lincoln] Administration inserted the moral issue of slavery into the war as a kind of public relations gesture? FOOTE: The question was handled by Lincoln in a political, and, above all, a diplomatic way. It was Lincoln's Emancipation Proclamation which absolutely insured that the one thing the North had most to fear was not going to happen: that England might come into the war [on the Southern side]." Foote cites a monument at home: "To the Memory of the Confederacy, the only nation which lived and died without a sin on its record" (ibid., 35).

because many of us yearn to identify with greatness, to share it symbolically, we are sympathetic to their self-portraits.

Even Erik Erikson, a distinguished psychoanalyst and himself a victim of European fascism, found ways to ameliorate Jefferson's slaveholding. In a lengthy essay, he cited Jefferson's laments about slavery. Erikson added that Jefferson faced an ancient question about the nature of human beings: Were they essentially the same? "Why God had created all men equal and had then let climate and geography discriminate against some, was a question at once theological, scientific, and ideological."[8] This is too sympathetic to Jefferson. It accepts Jefferson's laments at face value, and it locates Jefferson's struggles in intellectual spheres, the sciences, theology, and ideology. Jefferson's actions do not merit this overly generous portrait. The whole point of slavery is to improve one's financial and social lot and those of one's (white) children. Jefferson achieved his goals: to live like a lord among slaves and workers and upon their backs build a great estate. The struggle over slavery was never a matter of intellectual niceties. It was internal, within the hearts and minds of owners who knew that their choices were wrong, and external, between themselves and those whom they enslaved.

Erikson's praise also presupposes that no one of that period could solve this alleged conundrum.[9] Erikson's and our yearning to idealize the founders and their work leads us astray.

---

[8] Erik H. Erikson, *Dimensions of a New Identity: Jefferson Lectures 1973* (New York: Norton, 1974), 25.

[9] A similar error occurs when Erikson describes Jefferson's "natural aristocracy" and adds "The antagonism between the Southern Athens and the Northern Sparta" deepened to the point of civil war (ibid., 76). Northern universities were as "Athenian," and more numerous and superior compared to Southern institutions. Of the ten earliest American institutions, nine were in the North: Harvard, Cambridge, MA, founded in 1636; Yale, New Haven, CT, 1701; Princeton, Princeton, N.J. 1746; Columbia, New York City, 1754; Univ. of Pennsylvania, 1757; Brown, Providence, R.I., 1764; Rutgers, New Brunswick, N.J., 1766; Dartmouth College, Hanover, N.H., 1769. The only commensurate Southern school was College of William & Mary, Williamsburg, VA, founded in 1693, at which Jefferson matriculated in 1760.

Quakers in the North and South

The clearest moral sense appears in the Philadelphia Quakers beginning in the seventeenth century through John Wright, a Unitarian
minister, in the early nineteenth century. Francis Daniel Pastorius,
(noted in chap. 2), a German-American Quaker wrote, with three
others, "Germantown Protest Against Slavery" in 1688. When he
wrote that to own a slave is to control a person who is subject to one's
undisputed will and pleasure, Pastorius condemned the slave trade
and asserted the dominance of the Golden Rule: "These are the reasons why we are against the traffick of men Body, as followeth: Is
there any that would be done or handled at this manner? viz., to be
sold or made a slave for all the time of his life?" The simplicity of this
criticism and its roots in Jewish-Christian teachings obviate efforts to
establish which races are better than others. A transcendental insight—the spiritual unity of human kind—supersedes the cataloguing
of accidental differences. As Pastorius notes, "There is a saying, that
we shall doe to all men, licke as we will be done our selves; making no
difference of what generation, descent or Colour they are."[10]

Some Northern Quakers early criticized slavery in all its forms;
their Southern colleagues took longer to reach the same conclusions.[11] However, by 1739 some Quakers in North Carolina refused to
hold slaves, to become overseers, to take part in slave patrols, and to
have any dealings with slavery in the state.[12] Confronting legal and

---

[10] Learned and Pennypacker, *The Life of Francis Daniel Pastorius, the
Founder of Germantown,* 261.

[11] Slave trading and dealing did not disappear in Pennsylvania quickly:
"Slavery expanded in Philadelphia to a greater extent during the first two
decades of the eighteenth century than at any later time." Gary B. Nash and
Jean R. Soderlund, *Freedom by Degrees: Emancipation in Pennsylvania and
Its Aftermath* (New York: Oxford University Press, 1991), 45. It took another sixty years for the majority of Philadelphia Quakers to reject slave trading
and slave holding (ibid., 41–64).

[12] Stephen Beauregard Weeks. *Southern Quakers and Slavery: A Study in Institutional History* (Baltimore, MD: The Johns Hopkins Press, 1896), 200–201.

political resistance to manumission, Southern Quakers carefully documented the emancipation of slaves under their control. For example, in 1784, Joseph Jordan, a North Carolinian Quaker, crafted emancipation papers for his slaves. (Without such papers, freed persons of color might be captured and enslaved.) It is valuable to read his will in his original words. He said that

> being *desirous to fulfill the injunction of our Lord and Saviour Jesus Christ, by doing to others as I would be done by,* [I] do therefore declare, that having under my care a number of negroes named and aged as follows [the names and ages are here inserted] I do for myself my heirs Executors and administrators, hereby release unto so many of them as are come of age, men twenty one, and women eighteen, all my right interest and claim or pretensions of claim whatsoever.[13]

Antislavery societies existed in the South as well as in the North.[14] In other words, everyone knew the moral facts; the problem was that slaves made their masters money, and during labor shortages and other inconveniences, slaves kept merchants in business.[15]

A similar bifurcation appears in Southern planters, most of whom were devout Christians. They had heard the arguments against slavery advanced during the previous one hunded years. George Washington owned a copy of a famous antislavery pamphlet, written by John Dickinson, a Quaker, former president of Delaware, and a member of

---

[13] Ibid., 222n1. (My emphasis.)

[14] Ibid., 241n1. "Poole, *Anti-Slavery Opinion before* 1800 (p. 72), [reports] . . . that in 1827 there were 130 abolition societies in the United States, of which 106 were in the slave States. There were eight in Virginia, twenty-five in Tennessee with a membership of one thousand, fifty in North Carolina with three thousand members. See William Frederick Poole. *Anti-slavery Opinions Before the Year 1800* (Cincinnati, OH: Robert Clarke & Co., 1873).

[15] See Mary Stoughton Locke. *Anti-Slavery in America: from the Introduction of African Slaves to the Prohibition of the Slave Trade (1619–1808)* Radcliffe College Monographs, vol. 11–14. (Boston: Ginn and Co., 1901.)

the Continental Congress. Dickinson's pamphlet, *A Serious Address to the Rulers of America*, published in 1783, proclaims:

> "Ye rulers of America beware!' Let it appear to future ages, from the records of this day, that you not only professed to be advocates for freedom, but really were inspired by the love of mankind, and wished to secure the invaluable blessing to all; that, as you disdained to submit to the unlimited control of others, you equally abhorred the crying crime of holding your fellow men, as much entitled to freedom as yourselves, the subjects of your undisputed will and pleasure.[16]

The same bifurcation appeared in the letters of Kentucky Shakers. Their carefully composed letters reveal their struggle to oppose slavery while living among neighbors who held slaves and who doubted the Shakers' adherence to the laws defending the institution.

The Shakers: "A dollar obtained for human flesh"

The Shakers who resided in Kentucky wrote numerous letters to fellow Shakers explaining their circumstances and their struggles. In the archives at Pleasant Hill, Kentucky, one of two Shaker villages in that state, these letters are preserved. Among them is a letter from Benjamin Joseph and Molly Mercy, written on May 1,1813, explaining why they rejected selling slaves given to them as legal property by a wealthy convert:

---

[16] Ibid., 61. "A copy of [Dickinson's] pamphlet, which belonged to George Washington's library, is now in the possession of the Boston Athenaeum" (ibid., 61n1). In a review of antislavery arguments advanced from 1783 to 1808, Mary Stoughton Locke noted "little that is new, since the fundamental principles had already been established. The inconsistency of slavery with the teachings of Scripture is still urged though much less conspicuously than its inconsistency with the principles and professions of the American Revolution. The moral argument of the degrading effects of slavery on both master and slave is often repeated on the same lines as in the earlier period." (ibid., 178.)

Some might think it is too much to throw away $25,000 to $30,000 by which a poor people might be greatly benefited, and that a dollar obtained for human flesh is nothing different from any other dollar—but we have our thoughts about it, and in living in a slave country, we are compelled to have many feelings about it which we would willingly exchange for feelings produced by a better cause.[17]

Benjamin Joseph and Molly Mercy were elder and elderess in the Shaker community of South Union, Kentucky. They wrote frequently to their spiritual advisers in Mount Lebanon, New York, twenty-four miles southeast of Albany, on the border with Massachusetts. Mount Lebanon was the largest Shaker community in North America. Benjamin and Molly's letters illustrate the day-to-day realities of slavery in the United States.

Willie Jones, an affluent convert to the church, had given all his property to the Kentucky community, as did all who joined the group. Among items Willie owned were 107 "Blacks," that is, slaves. The Kentucky group pondered how best to handle this part of his bequest. Willie wished his slaves to join the Kentucky Shaker community with him, but the elders worried about bringing that many freed blacks into the center of Kentucky, a slaveholding state. Instead of keeping the "Blacks" as slaves or selling them as legal property, they freed them. Shaker religious teaching compelled them to do so; their social realism compelled them to measure the cost of their religious convictions, about $30,000. (Equivalent to about $6 million in today's dollar).[18] They reported that, "four of his Black people were sent to this country [area] and the rest were disposed of in Carolina, without price, as it was not our faith that they should be sold and the money

---

[17] From South Union, Kentucky, Benjamin Joseph and Molly Mercy, to the Elders at Mt. Lebanon, New York. Shaker Manuscript Collection of the Western Reserve Historical Society (WRHS). Section IV—Correspondence; Part A—Items: Folder-South Union, KY.: 1801–1920.

[18] It is $445,000 using the CPI; $6,130,000 in unskilled wages. http://www.measuringworth.com/index.php.

made use of among the Believers, as it was Willie's faith."[19]

When slave owners became Shakers they offered their slaves the choice to stay and live as equals or to leave as freed persons. In both cases, owners drafted emancipation documents that affirmed their slaves' freedom (and, in the latter, cautioned those not remaining with the Shakers to move to non-slaveholding states). For example, one emancipation document reads:

> Absalom Chisholm and Samuel Whyte, by bill of sale from James Joskins of the 24th of September 1816 became owners of a certain Woman of Color named Lucy. This will therefore make it known that by the Said Absalom Chisholm do this day and forever hereafter Emancipate, release, and set free from servitude, to us and our heirs, the Said Lucy from conscientious and religious motives and in consideration of the regard we have and to bear to the moral conduct and natural rights of the Said Lucy and allow the Said Lucy hereafter to trade, bargain and do so for herself as a free woman. October 9, 1830.[20]

Another emancipation document stipulated that the freed slaves must leave Kentucky, "and fix their residence in either the state of Ohio, Indiana, or Illinois."[21]

In many letters, elders lamented the challenges that Shakers faced living in a region, or "country" as they put it, where slavery was practiced. In a letter written on August 1, 1813, John Rankin described their struggles to establish the new community and to manage gifts of land, livestock, and slaves whom they freed but who then became burdensome. In a lengthy postscript he reported that many potential white converts who hailed from Kentucky and similar regions failed to uphold the community's rules. They have shown "so much disrespect & disobedience to some." The reason for this is, "Some have

---

[19] (WRHS). Section I: Covenants, Laws, and Legal and Land Records. Part A—Items. Folder 15—South Union, KY.

[20] Ibid.

[21] Ibid.

been long acquainted with the sense of Master and Slave, that has spread its influence more or less amongst the generality in this country." This long acquaintance with slavery, Rankin explained, had made it difficult for some to give and receive requests for they perceived all such encounters as "something unfriendly." Rankin added that while all the converts recognized the rules of the community, some could not shake off their immersion in the mores of slavery. Even "those persons will acknowledge the one to be as good a man as the other," at one time, at others they refused to comply with the community's needs.[22]

Their Kentucky neighbors recognized that Shakers rejected slavery and they monitored them closely. Some accused them of fomenting abolitionism and other ideas that created unrest among slaves. In a report to the *Russellville Herald* dated August, 1835, a newspaper published near the South Union Shaker community, a Mr. U. E. Johns gave a firsthand account of a recent meeting held between members of the Shaker community and leading citizens from surrounding counties. The purpose of the meeting was for "consulting and taking such steps as they might think proper to counteract the abolition influences supposed by some to be improperly exercised in this community. All feeling an interest were invited to attend."[23] Dr. John Patterson produced a large packet of papers, having been commissioned to do so at a previous meeting, which pertained to the Shakers. Although "there were no specific charges, they seemed to be aimed at the whole community of Shakers." Among the complaints were that Shakers exerted "an improper influence with the neighborhood slaves" and some Shakers had helped "slaves make their escape, giving free papers." Among the six resolutions endorsed by the meeting, by the Shakers as well as local citizens, was this, the fifth: "That we are a law-abiding community and cannot consent that the laws of

---

[22] (WRHS). Section IV—Correspondence. Part A—'Items: Folder—South Union, KY: 1801–1920. WRHS, IV:A-60.

[23] (WRHS). Section I: Covenants, Laws, and Legal and Land Records. Part A—Items. Folder 15—South Union, KY.

our land shall be disregarded and trampled under foot, even in vindication of a supposed violation of rights."[24]

A Countrywide Dilemma

This town-hall meeting illuminates, in miniature, the dilemma of numerous Americans. As citizens of Kentucky and the United States, each was honor-bound to obey "the laws of our land." At the highest level of law, the US Constitution, slavery was acknowledged and protected with strict language that stated the extent of its influence—everywhere—and its duration—forever. Even those who acted out of humanitarian and religious concerns for the "supposed violation of rights" of enslaved persons were compelled to support the institution. The Shakers' public disapproval of slavery, their radical doctrines of male and female equality as well as racial equality, and their refusal to engage the slave trade made them suspicious actors in the United States prior to 1865.

Sentiments similar to the Shaker rejection of slavery appear in the writings of John Wright, a Unitarian minister. In his 1820 pamphlet, *Refutation of Sophisms*, Wright confronted a Virginia author who claims moral superiority for agreeing to stop the international trade.[25]

Wright criticized Southerners who claimed that the United States was morally superior to England, which had, they said, forced the colonies to accept the international slave trade. The issue Wright noted was the *internal slave trade*: "Do not *droves* of *manicled* [*sic*] slaves pass . . . the White House, and even the Capitol itself?"[26]

By idealizing Washington and Jefferson, we imbibe their defensive efforts; we share their divided minds; and we agree too readily with

---

[24] All citations from (WRHS). Section I: Covenants, Laws, and Legal and Land Records. Part A- Items. Folder 15—South Union, KY.

[25] *A Refutation of the Sophisms, Gross Misrepresentations, and Erroneous Quotations Contained In an American's "Letter to the Edinburgh Reviewers"* (Washington, DC: Privately Printed, 1820). http://www.archive.org/stream/refutationofsoph02wrig/refutationofsoph02wrig_djvu.txt.

[26] Ibid.

their self-diagnosis and self-assessments. Doing so we defer thinking about the emotional pleasures associated with slavery: the thrill of dominance and the sense of hierarchy and aristocracy that racism in its most virulent form brings to those in power. Washington's and Jefferson's plaintive comments on slavery disguise the fact that fascism and slavery are fascinating to those who rule nations or smaller domains, like Mount Vernon and Monticello. Both men were supremely respected, assured of American immortality, and affluent and protected from the harshness of working-class life. Yet they could not forgo owning slaves, and even in the light of Jefferson's intellect, not act upon their moral centers.

George Washington and the Problems of Ownership

The search for the legal and ethical justification for slavery required owners to affirm transcendental truths, such as God made some people slaves and some free, and affirm self-understanding, such as "I am a good and generous Master" or, as in Washington's case, "My slaves are like my children; all are part of my family." The latter is illogical. Slaves were chattel property; wealthy (white) children inherited slaves as part of their estate. Slaves were disciplined and threatened with terrible punishment (imprisonment, torture, separation from their loved ones, deportation to the sugar islands); owners' white children were disciplined to train them to assume the status (or higher) of their parents. Mixed-raced children of the master were themselves chattel property and had no legal protection; white children of the master were protected by state and national laws. Senator Calhoun and other Southern notables tried to align Southern slavery with the laws and customs of the Roman Republic. However, with regard to children, Roman law offered protections of slaves never envisioned by American masters: "There was no limit to the amount of property a slave could acquire, nor were there limits on the kind of property."[27] Slaves could become educated, could earn substantial incomes, and

---

[27] Thomas D. Morris, *Southern Slavery and the Law, 1619–1860* (Charlotte, NC: University of North Carolina Press, 1996), 47.

could own slaves themselves. Many American slaves were adults or became adults; they were not permanent children. The claim of "family"
was designed to obscure its opposite.

Strict hierarchies, rigid class lines, gender lines, color lines, and so
on reinforce the psychological phenomenon of splitting: the divided
external world mirrors our divided internal world. Many a slave owner
might wish to free his slaves, but because his slaves were uneducated
(having been brutalized and traumatized from birth) he also worried
that once freed, the slave part of his family might perish. As many
owners argued, because slavery appeared to be permanent, it was best
to make it work as well as possible. The effect of living a contradiction stopped reflection and made it impossible to think coherently. In
Jefferson and similarly refined people, splitting produced more refined effects, such as idealization, romanticism, mystification, and
sentimentality.

Recasting the Civil War as the Second American Revolution

All these devices appeared in assiduous efforts to recast the Civil War as
the Second American Revolution, to deny the facts of slavery, to dispar-
age Abraham Lincoln, to aggrandize the Southern fighting man, to deify
Robert E. Lee and Stonewall Jackson, and to manufacture a picture of the
antebellum South as cultured, as an Athens to the Northern Sparta.[28]
Among those leading this effort were Jefferson Davis—who was never
tried for treason—and groups such as The Ladies Hermitage Association,

---

[28] Founded in 1896, the web page of the Sons of Confederate Veterans proclaims: "The citizen-soldiers who fought for the Confederacy personified the
best qualities of America. The preservation of liberty and freedom was the moti-
vating factor in the South's decision to fight the *Second American Revolution*."
(Their emphasis.) http://www.scv.org/. A similar wish animates the Military
Order Stars & Bars, "comprised of Descendants of the Confederate Government, Officer Corps, and Civil Officials" founded in 1938. Members must be
males above the age of twelve who can prove lineage linking them to men in the
Confederate Officer Corps, members of the Confederate Congress, or any elected or appointed member of the Executive Branch of the Confederate
Government. http://www.mosbihq.org/History_and_Purpose.htm.

United Daughters of the Confederacy, and Sons of Confederate Veterans. In consort, by the 1890s they had crafted portraits of the South centered upon manly courage, chivalry, and the timeless grandeur of plantation life. With that focus it became easier to bring the South back into the Union. The original reasons for the war disappeared. In their stead were endless accounts of Southern valor and heroism. As valid as those accounts may have been, these revised histories overlooked the immensity of the crimes of slavery.[29]

The Proslavery Constitution of 1787

The debate over the slavery clauses found in the 1787 US Constitution was loud and rancorous. Luther Martin, a founder and anti-Federalist from Maryland, argued that the fugitive slave clause was unfair, exaggerated Southern influence, and encouraged the slave trade:

> It involved the absurdity of increasing the power of a State in making laws for free men in proportion as that State violated the rights of freedom—That it might be proper to take slaves into consideration, when taxes were to be apportioned, because it [high taxes] had a tendency to discourage slavery; but to take them into account in giving representation tended to encourage the slave trade, and to make it the interest of the States to continue that infamous traffic.[30]

More so, the three-fifths ratio disenfranchised Northern citizens.

---

[29] On the postwar task of amalgamating two very different ideologies that helped produce the war, see John R. Neff, *Honoring the Civil War Dead: Commemoration and the Problem of Reconciliation* (Lawrence, KS: University Press of Kansas, 2005). The UDC was founded in part to honor Jefferson Davis's daughter—although she married a Yankee (ibid., 175–76). On the intellectual and ideological tasks of welding two nations into one in post-Civil War America, see Drew Gilpin Faust, *The Creation of Confederate Nationalism: Ideology and Identity in the Civil War South* (Baton Rouge, LA: Louisiana State University Press, 1989).

[30] 1788 Storing 2.4.14--15, 16, 28--34, 45, http://press-pubs.uchicago.edu/founders/documents/a1_2_3s9.html.

He predicted accurately that this imbalance would give Virginia and other Southern states the power to hinder decisive federal action.[31]

Some forty-five years later, Joseph Story, an American jurist and legal scholar, reassessed the 1787 debates and noted:

> The real (and it was a very exciting) controversy was in regard to slaves, whether they should be included in the enumeration, or not. On the one hand, it was contended, that slaves were treated in the states, which tolerated slavery, as property, and not as persons. They were bought and sold, devised, used as collateral, and transferred through inheritance. They had no civil rights, or political privileges. They had no will of their own; but were bound to absolute obedience to their masters.[32]

Southern states treated slaves as both mere property (in the legal definition of slave) and as persons whom the Congress should count in some manner: "Thus, five thousand free persons, in a slave-state, might possess the same power to choose a representative, as thirty thousand free persons in a non-slave-holding state."[33]

Story concluded that the final compromise giving slave states additional representation was "a necessary sacrifice to that spirit of conciliation, which was indispensable to the union of states having a great diversity of interests, and physical condition, and political institutions." In a similar way, Don E. Fehrenbacher, holds that

> The three-fifths, slave-trade, and fugitive-slave clauses, together with the double lock put on the slave-trade clause, were the only parts of the Constitution written with slavery primarily in mind, and one of them

---

[31] See also: Herbert J. Storing ,"Moral Foundations of the Republic" in *Slavery and its Consequences: the Constitution, Equality, and Race,* ed. Robert A. Goldwin and Art Kaufman (Washington, DC: American Enterprise Institute, 1988), 43–63.

[32] Joseph Story, *Commentaries on the Constitution of the United States.* 3 vols. (Boston, 1833), http://press-pubs.uchicago.edu/founders/documents/a1_2_3s22.html.

[33] Ibid.

called the institution by its name. *Without a doubt*, the three-fifths clause, or some equivalent, was essential for the success of the Constitution as we know it.[34] (My emphasis.)

Favoring this reading are opinions from conservative authors who argue that the Constitution was not proslavery:

Furthermore, understood in context, the apportionment rule was not proslavery. Even though slaves were property under the laws of the Southern states, the Constitution itself acknowledged that they were persons. In addition, by tying both representation and direct taxation to apportionment, the Framers removed any sectional benefit, and thus any proslavery taint, from the special counting rule.[35]

This is a mistaken way to read the minds of the Southern founders, all of whom were deeply committed to slavery and its perpetuation. Joseph Story noted that while slaveholders traded the three-fifths clause for a direct tax on their holdings, this was hardly a compromise: "The principle of representation is constant, and uniform; the levy of direct taxes is occasional, and rare. In the course of forty years no more than three direct taxes have been levied; and those only under very extraordinary and pressing circumstances."[36] Southern states gained

---

[34] Don E. Fehrenbacher, "Slavery, the Framers, and the Living Constitution" in *Slavery and its Consequences: the Constitution, Equality, and Race,* ed. Robert A. Goldwin and Art Kaufman, 12. Fehrenbacher won the 1979 Pulitzer Prize for his book on the Dred Scott decision, *The Dred Scott Case: Its Significance in American Law and Politics* (New York: Oxford University Press, 1978).

[35] Eric M. Jensen, "Three-Fifths Clause," in *The Heritage Guide to the Constitution,* ed. Edwin Meese, David F. Forte, and Matthew Spalding (Washington, D.C.: Regnery Publishing, 2006), 55. See also Herbert J. Storing, "Slavery and the Moral Foundations of the Republic," in *The Moral Foundations of the American Republic,* ed. Robert H. Horwitz (Charlottesville, VA: University Press of Virginia,1986), 313–32.

[36] http://press-pubs.uchicago.edu/founders/documents/a1_2_3s22.html.

advantage from the three-fifths clause; at every election and in the day-to-day operation of the federal government, they were able to shape, if not control, federal legislation that might impinge on slavery. More so, a systematic study of the intricacies of taxation before, during, and after the 1787 Convention shows that the tax portion of the clause had little effect on either the slave trade or the spread of slavery.[37]

One reason that the proslavery Constitution was adopted and persisted emerges when we consider the number of US presidents and other high federal officers who owned slaves or who encouraged slave ownership. Twelve US presidents owned slaves at sometime in their lives; eight owned slaves while serving as president. By one count, during the first sixty years of the Republic, slaveholders were president for fifty.[38]

In his 1857 denunciation of slavery, *The Impending Crisis of the South: How to Meet It,* Hinton Rowan Helper made the identical point. Helper uses 413 pages to review the history of federal officers who held slaves or were friendly to slavery. While dominating the presidency, slaveholders and their sympathizers also dominated the major posts of secretaries of state, navy, war [Defense], and attorney general.[39] In addition, thanks to the three-fifths rule and Southern solidarity, slavery proponents often controlled the Supreme Court (five of the nine positions) and leadership in the House and in the

---

[37] See Robin L. Einhorn, *American Taxation, American Slavery* (Chicago: University of Chicago Press, 2006).

[38] http://hauensteincenter.org/slaveholding/. (Accessed January 15, 2016.) See also Hinton Rowan Helper, *The Impending Crisis of the South: How to Meet It* (n.p. 1859), 160. http://docsouth.unc.edu/nc/helper/helper.html.

[39] Helper (ibid., 316) cites a South Carolinian, William Henry Hurlbut, who counted Southern politicians and other defenders of slavery:

Presidents 11 of 16

Judges–Supreme Court 17 of 28

Attorneys–General 14 of 19

Presidents of the Senate 61 of 77

Speakers of the House 21 of 33

Foreign Ministers 80 of 134

Senate. Garry Wills notes that even John Quincy Adams, an opponent of slavery, "had to settle for a southern cabinet, led by the slaveholding [Henry] Clay" whom he made secretary of state.[40]

Helper also used the 1850 census to compare Southern versus Northern economies, beginning with a survey of the comparative advantages of Virginia versus New York, of North Carolina (his home state) versus Massachusetts.[41] For example, Virginia began with economic and population advantages that had disappeared by 1856: "The real and personal estate assessed in the City of New-York amounted in valuation to $511,740,491, showing that New York City alone is worth far more than the whole of the State of Virginia" (ibid., 13). In 1856, Helper noted that Boston could "buy the whole State of North Carolina" (ibid., 16). Using Southern claims of value of slaves (ibid., 83–84) and evidence from the 1850 census, he argued: "the value of all the property in the slave States, real and personal, *including* slaves, was, in 1850, only $2,936,090,713."[42] If we agree with some estimates that slaves were worth $1.6 billion, then subtracting "slave property" from the estimate of Southern states leaves "the True Wealth of the slave States" as $1.3 billion, while the free states were worth $4.1 Billion. This made the North about three times as rich as the South.[43]

---

[40] Garry Wills, *"Negro President": Jefferson and the Slave Power* (New York: Houghton Mifflin Harcourt, 2003), 7. Clay held national prominence before the age of thirty until his death forty-five years later.

[41] Helper's vociferous attack on slavery coincided with his own strident racism. Speaking of Chinese in California, Helper said, "No inferior race of men can exist in these United States without becoming subordinate to the will of the Anglo-Americans." Quoted by George M. Fredrickson, *The Arrogance of Race: Historical Perspectives on Slavery, Racism, and Social Inequality* (Middletown, CT: Wesleyan University Press, 1988), 36.

[42] Helper, *The Impending Crisis of the South: How to Meet It*, 83

[43] In the Virginia House of Delegates, Jan. 30, 1832, Charles James Faulkner compared the productivity of Ohio vs. Kentucky: "*They seem to have been purposely and providentially designed to exhibit in their future histories the difference which necessarily results from a country free from, and a country*

Before the War: the Defense of Property; after the War, the Defense of Liberty

A mix of piety, illusion, and ethnic solidarity animates postwar efforts to explain the causes of the Civil War. Among the devices is the imaginary defense of "womanhood"—white, middle- and upper-class Southern women—for whom, we learn, the Civil War was fought. This sentimentalized refrain—brought to the screen in *The Birth of a Nation*—appears on the masthead of the United Daughters of the Confederacy:

> I am a Daughter of the Confederacy because I have an obligation to perform. Like the man in the Bible, I was given a talent and it is my duty to do something about it. That is why I've joined a group of ladies whose birthright is the same as mine . . . an organization which has for its purpose the continuance and furtherance of the true history of the South and the ideals of southern womanhood as embodied in its Constitution.[44]

The same emotions appeared in Jefferson Davis's lengthy dedication of his memoirs, published in 1881. It is instructive to cite the dedication in full and to highlight each metaphor and its appeal. Each line recasts the reasons for the war, its origins, and its meaning for future generations. Added together they illustrate Davis's defense for the accused, a defense that numerous Southern defenders took up after him. Like an attorney litigating a weak case, Davis shifts the tone of the debate and the subject of the dispute. The tone is lamentation; the subject is that the war was not about slavery.

(The original dedication is in small caps, centered, and takes up nearly a full page of his book.)

---

afflicted with, the curse of slavery." (Quoted in Helper, *The Impending Crisis of the South*), 100. (His emphasis.)

[44] "Written by Mary Nowlin Moon (Mrs. John), a member of Kirkwood Otey Chapter 10, Lynchburg, Virginia. First read at a Chapter meeting on June 2, 1915." http://www.hqudc.org/. This mission, now approaching one hundred years, is to recast the history of the Civil War.

To the Women of the Confederacy,
Whose Pious Ministrations to Our Wounded Soldiers

Southern women (not Southern men who made the war and profited by it) become the central actors in this story. They are pious, devout, ministers of Christian mercy to dying men. Dying men are not dangerous; the most ardent Yankee would applaud a mother or wife who sought to comfort her dying loved one.

Soothed the Last Hours of Those Who Died Far from the
Objects of Their Tenderest Loves

Davis paints a scene of dying heroes, most of them unvisited by their kin. They are surrounded by women who care for strangers hoping that other Southern women are doing the same for their men if their husband, brother, or father is wounded or dying.

Whose Domestic Labors
Contributed Much to Supply the Wants of
Our Defenders in the Field;

It is true that numerous Southern women sent goods and food to men in the field, as did numerous Northern women who supported their men. Southern soldiers, however, were not defenders until Davis and others had made them offenders when the South attacked Union forces at Fort Sumter. The fact that the South initiated the war, in reaction to the democratic process that brought Abraham Lincoln to the White House, is obliterated. In its stead is a scene of warriors who gave everything to protect home and family from invaders.

Whose Zealous Faith in Our Cause
Shone a Guiding Star Undimmed by the
Darkest Clouds of War

That Southern women wished to protect their loved ones during times of danger is undeniable. It is a truism that applies to all women for all time in all wars. It is misleading, though, to call this wish to protect their men a "zealous faith in our cause." Davis's cause was not to defend Southern women against Northern aggressors but to defend and perpetuate slavery. That cause gave rise to the war and the war gave rise to, among other things, thousands of dead and wounded Southern men whom Southern families mourned. The metaphor of the "guiding star" comes from Christian scripture and Christian preachers.[45] They cited the Hebrew Bible (King James Version), such as Numbers 24:17, "I shall see him, but not now; I shall behold him, but not nigh: there shall come a Star out of Jacob, and a Scepter out of Israel," and Isaiah 9:2, "The people that walked in darkness have seen a great light; they that dwell in the land of the shadow of death, upon them hath the light shined." From these well-known and well-loved texts it is a short distance to the New Testament account of the Star of Bethlehem in Matthew 2:1-2, "Now when Jesus was born in Bethlehem of Judaea in the days of Herod the king, behold, there came wise men from the east to Jerusalem, Saying, Where is he that is born King of the Jews? for we have seen his star in the east, and are come to worship him." Davis was well educated and like thousands of others who defended the South and its traditions, he cited Christian scriptures and the US Constitution when he castigated outside agitators who criticized slavery. In an earlier, lengthy address in Boston, in 1858, he demanded to know from abolitionists upon what authorities they drew: "Not the Constitution; the Constitution recognizes the property in slaves in many forms, and imposes obligations in connection with

---

[45] For example, in 1851 Louisa Payson Hopkins published *The Guiding Star*, a popular book that showed parents and teachers how to persuade children of the truths of Christianity. Hopkins followed a long tradition of rereading Hebrew scripture, which preceded the New Testament, as if it foretold the birth of Jesus. If one grants this claim—which is miraculous—then Hebrew poems about a guiding star written hundreds of years before the birth of Jesus foretold and validate Christian teachings.

that recognition. Not the Bible; that justifies it. Not the good of society; for, if they go where it exists, they find that society recognizes it as good. What, then, is their standard?"[46] It cannot be Christian values, he argued, for slavery has brought Christian salvation to Africans and their descendants: "Is there, in the cause of Christianity, a motive for the prohibition of the system which is the only agency through which Christianity has reached that inferior race, the only means by which they have been civilized and elevated?"[47]

WHOSE FORTITUDE
SUSTAINED THEM UNDER ALL THE PRIVATIONS TO WHICH THEY
WERE SUBJECTED;

Southern women did suffer when the war came to their cities, towns, and homes. Many showed great fortitude, no doubt, as did many Northern women. The source of their "privations" is what matters to us. Davis's lament for a lost civilization is a dirge to the greatness that might have been. He sounds notes of sorrow for the rise and fall of a nation that struggled to defend itself against great odds. Davis's lamentation subsumes Southern women into the South's mission and its war aims and asserts that that mission sustained them—mothers, wives, sisters—who had lost loved ones. By this peculiar tactic, Davis "feminizes" the war. A war that he and other men began to defend their right to property in human beings (men, women, children) is recast as a struggle to defend Southern women. Because they could not hold office, no Southern women voiced opinions in any statehouses or in any courts or in any military councils. It is erroneous to proclaim that Southern women shared the aims of the men who created the war. No one, including Davis, knows what Southern women believed as an aggregate. It seems likely that some women did

---

[46] "Address of Jefferson Davis, at Faneuil Hall, Boston, October 12, 1858." Jefferson Davis, *The Rise and Fall of the Confederate Government*, appendix E, n.p.
[47] Ibid.

not share Davis's unbridled passion for the war when so many beloved men failed to come home and when Southern cities lay in ruin.

WHOSE ANNUAL TRIBUTE
EXPRESSES THEIR ENDURING GRIEF, LOVE, AND REVERENCE

By slight of hand Davis merges genuine grief and love for men lost
with a "reverence" for the war and its mission. We do not doubt that
grieving family and friends suffered enduring sorrow and did their
best to remain linked to those they had lost. That does not mean that
they also revered the war or its authors, including Jefferson Davis.

FOR OUR SACRED DEAD;

Lincoln and other Northern statesmen freely evoked imagery
from Christian scripture when they spoke of the Union dead. We do
not doubt that Southern families suffered as deeply as their Northern
counterparts. It would be unfair to criticize Davis for ascribing these
sentiments to his Southern readers. However, his rhetoric lends itself
to exaggeration. In a much-cited poem, Henry Timrod, a Southern
writer offered a similar refrain about the Southern dead:

> Sleep sweetly in your humble graves,
> Sleep, martyrs of a fallen cause;
> Though yet no marble column craves
> The pilgrim here to pause.[48]

Timrod declares what Davis implied; that the Southern dead were
martyrs to a great, though fallen, cause. Like Davis, Timrod's readers
were Southern Christians steeped in the language of evangelical Christianity. Its central theme was the blood sacrifice of Jesus who in perfect

---

[48] Henry Timrod, http://en.wikisource.org/wiki/Ode:_Sung_on_the_Occasion_
of_Decorating_the_Graves_of_the_Confederate_Dead_at_Magnolia_Cemetery,
_Charleston,_S.C.,_1867.

innocence knowingly chose death in order that the guilty, all of us, might through his perfect atonement receive everlasting life. Timrod's readers resonated with these scriptural passages, which they knew by heart.

They had heard innumerable sermons on the nature of Christ's sacrifice: "Whom God hath set forth to be a propitiation through faith in his blood, to declare his righteousness for the remission of sins that are past, through the forbearance of God" (Romans 3:25).[49] Paul, the author of the Letter to the Romans, dominated discourse about Christ's sacrifice: death through Adam, life through Christ sums up his message. Christians understood their ideal selves; under the right circumstances, they would rise up to the demands of Christian witness illustrated in the lives of the saints and the martyrs of the early church.

When Timrod used the word *martyr* he signified that the Southern dead (killed by Northern troops) had risen to that idealized level.[50] They were identical to those heroic Christians who voluntarily chose death at the hands of beasts and men rather than forsake their Christian faith. The life, death, and resurrection of Jesus is, of course,

---

[49] Other texts include: "For when we were yet without strength, in due time Christ died for the ungodly. For scarcely for a righteous man will one die: yet peradventure for a good man some would even dare to die. But God commendeth his love toward us, in that, while we were yet sinners, Christ died for us. Much more then, being now justified by his blood, we shall be saved from wrath through him. For if, when we were enemies, we were reconciled to God by the death of his Son, much more, being reconciled, we shall be saved by his life. And not only so, but we also joy in God through our Lord Jesus Christ, by whom we have now received the atonement" (Romans 5:6–11); "Therefore as by the offence of one judgment came upon all men to condemnation; even so by the righteousness of one the free gift came upon all men unto justification of life. For as by one man's disobedience many were made sinners, so by the obedience of one shall many be made righteous" (Romans 5:18–19).

[50] Northern writers used the term to describe the death of Abraham Lincoln who was known as the Martyr President. "martyr, n." *OED* Online. March 2013. Oxford University Press.

the crux of Christian faith. The author of the Acts account makes these parallels between the two deaths explicit.[51]

In Timrod's poem, the narrator stops and ponders Southern graves which, through his art and vision, will gain added meaning for future generations:

> In seeds of laurel in the earth
> The blossom of your fame is blown,
> And somewhere, waiting for its birth,
> The shaft is in the stone!

Laurel is an evergreen. Its leaves made up the crown of laurels that graced the brows of Greek athletes who were made immortal by Greek poets. Winners of those contests become laureates—well-remembered heroes. Although Southern soldiers lost the war—through no fault of their own—they might win another kind of victory, Timrod implies. Shifting the metaphor a bit, he says that the blossoms from their laurels will fly through the air, ready to alight in new soil and be reborn. In that way Southern heroism and the Southern Cause will become immortal. Martyrs and poets see visions of a future not yet born: the martyr's life and the poet's verses link past greatness, intense human passions, and a future, wished-for victory.[52]

By transforming a defeat into victory, martyrs transform history. Through their courage their mortality becomes immortality. Their

---

[51] "Both are tried before the Council [of Jewish elders] . . . Both die a martyr's death . . . 'Lord Jesus, receive my spirit,' [uttered by Stephen] echoes Luke 23:46, 'Father, into thy hands I commit my spirit.' . . . Both stories contain a Son of Man saying: Luke 22:69 ('But from this time on the Son of Man will be seated at the right hand of the power of God') and Acts 7:56 ('Behold, I see the heavens opened and the Son of Man standing at the right hand of God')." Charles H. Talbert, *Reading Acts: A Literary and Theological Commentary on the Acts of the Apostles* (Macon, GA: Smith & Helwys, 2005), 66–67.

[52] Talbert, *Reading Acts*, 64. "It is part and parcel of the literature of martyrdom that martyrs see visions."

graves became cultic sites at which the devout could pray, commune with the martyr, and seek the martyr's blessing.[53] Naturally, where crowds existed and passions ran high, politicians and merchants found ways to exploit the events.[54] Timrod and Davis exploited the same theme when they merged their defense of the war with this ancient Christian tradition. Both authors help nourish the cult of the Southern dead and through that cult the perpetuation of the South's war aims.

AND

WHOSE PATRIOTISM

WILL TEACH THEIR CHILDREN

TO EMULATE THE DEEDS OF OUR REVOLUTIONARY SIRE[55]

The words *Revolutionary sires* refer to both the founders, the patriots of 1776 who won their freedom from English tyranny, and to the leaders of the Confederate States of America who fashioned themselves members of the Second Revolution who sought freedom from Northern tyranny. This last line of Davis's dedication provides the cornerstone in the myth of the Lost Cause. By aligning himself with Washington, Jefferson, and other great Southern men of 1776, Davis transformed the history of the Civil War: the Cause was about expanding freedom, not about slavery. That the South lost this cause is the source of Davis's lamentation.

Throughout his memoirs, Davis argued that the war was about sectional strife (which he calls "sectional aggrandizement"), not slavery.[56] The debate between "freedom" and "slavery" was specious, he

---

[53] Pauline Allen et al., *"Let Us Die That We May Live"*: *Greek Homilies on Christian Martyrs from Asia Minor, Palestine, and Syria c.350–450* (London: Routledge, 2003), 3–38.

[54] Ibid., 19–20.

[55] Jefferson Davis. *The Rise and Fall of the Confederate Government*, vol. 1 (New York: D. Appleton and Co., 1881), iii.

[56] Regarding the personhood of slaves, Davis approvingly cites the majority

proclaimed. Rather it was simply a matter of fairness: "The question was merely whether the slaveholder should be permitted to go, with his slaves, into territory (the common property of all) into which the non-slaveholder could go with *his* property of any sort."[57] (Emphasis in original.) Echoing Thomas Jefferson and John C. Calhoun before him, Davis asserted that spreading slavery into new states would dilute the unfortunate effects of slavery by dispersing a fixed number of slaves over a wider territory. This claim fails to reflect that, by law, slaveholders owned the children of their slaves. Thus their slaveholdings tended to increase, even without new importation.[58]

The Confederate States of America (CSA) Constitution, adopted on March 11, 1861, was dedicated to protecting slavery, not Southern womanhood as asserted in Davis's dedication.[59] As we have seen, the latter was vividly illustrated in D. W. Griffith's film, *The Birth of a Nation* (1915), and again in Victor Fleming's *Gone with the Wind* (1936). Each film evokes frightening images of marauding black men threatening the virginity of white women. However, on examining the CSA Constitution, the words *woman* and *women* appear nowhere. The words *slave* and *slaveholding* appear ten times; the words *negro* and

---

opinion in Dred Scott that repeatedly describes slaves as *property*. See *The Rise and Fall of the Confederate Government*, 581–83.

[57] Davis, *The Rise and Fall of the Confederate Government*, 7.

[58] Indeed, thanks to natural increase, Virginian slave owners, Jefferson among them, favored female over male slaves. Facing a surplus of slave labor in over-farmed areas, they realized new profits by selling slaves to more westerly states: "Virginia was the state most interested in exploiting the cut-off in foreign slave trade, since it was the leading seller of slaves in the domestic market." Wills, *Negro President*, 121.

[59] See Karen L. Cox. *Dixie's Daughters: The United Daughters of the Confederacy and the Preservation of Confederate Culture* (Gainesville: University Press of Florida, 2003). From her book: "The UDC perpetuated the values of the Old South through monument building, caring for needy Confederate men and women, and ensuring that the next generation of white southerners would imbibe traditional Confederate values." Traditional Confederate values rest upon the denigration of dark-skinned peoples.

negroes appear four times. To say that the CSA's Constitution was designed to protect "women" and not to safeguard slavery is to misrepresent the document and those who drafted it.

A modest survey of the history of antislavery agitation, beginning with the 1787 debates on the US Constitution through the Dred Scott decision of 1857 to the election of Abraham Lincoln in 1860, reveals that the drafters of the CSA document sought to defeat, whenever possible, challenges to slavery. The CSA Constitution continued this campaign. It replicated the Bill of Rights of the USA Constitution and added explicit language preserving the right to own slaves: (article 1, section 9, clause 4): "No bill of attainder, ex post facto law, or law denying or impairing the right of property in negro slaves shall be passed."[60]

Knowing that Lincoln and others argued that the US Constitution refused to use the term *slave* because the founders rejected the idea of property in man, the CSA corrected that oversight. There was nothing ambiguous in its version of the three-fifths clause:

> Representatives and direct taxes shall be apportioned among the several States which may be included within this Confederacy, according to their respective numbers, which shall be determined by adding to the whole number of free persons, including those bound to service for a term of years, and excluding Indians not taxed, three fifths of all slaves. (article 1, section 2, clause 3)

Bitterly aware of the resistance to the expansion of slavery into new Federal territories, the CSA drafters protected the right of owners to move their slave property anywhere they wished.

> The citizens of each State shall be entitled to all the privileges and immunities of citizens in the several States; and shall have the right of transit and sojourn in any State of this Confederacy, with their slaves and other property; and the right of property in said slaves shall not be thereby impaired. (article 4, section 2, clause 1)

---

[60] http://avalon.law.yale.edu/19th_century/csa_csa.asp.

The CSA's version of the fugitive slave clause minced no words. The murky language of the 1787 US Constitution regarding "other persons in service" was replaced with the unambiguous term *slave*:

> No slave or other person held to service or labor in any State or Territory of the Confederate States, under the laws thereof, escaping or lawfully carried into another, shall, in consequence of any law or regulation therein, be discharged from such service or labor; but shall be delivered up on claim of the party to whom such slave belongs, or to whom such service or labor may be due. (article 4, section 2, clause 3)

Regarding the right to slaves as property, the CSA Constitution was emphatic. The Dred Scott ruling that supported this claim was to hold for all new CSA territories and states:

> In all such [new] territory the institution of negro slavery, as it now exists in the Confederate States, shall be recognized and protected by Congress and by the Territorial government; and the inhabitants of the several Confederate States and Territories shall have the right to take to such Territory any slaves lawfully held by them in any of the States or Territories of the Confederate States. (article 4, section 3, clause 3)

The CSA Constitution forbids the reintroduction of the international slave trade:

> The importation of negroes of the African race from any foreign country other than the slaveholding States or Territories of the United States of America, is hereby forbidden; and Congress is required to pass such laws as shall effectually prevent the same. (article 1, section 9, clause 1)

Yet, Confederate leaders also instructed CSA ambassadors to inform European powers that individual states might, at their choice, reintroduce trading in slaves.[61] Once the slave trade was scheduled for

---

[61] See W. E. B. DuBois, *The Suppression of the African Slave Trade to the*

curtailment (in 1808), owners could profess moral superiority to those who took part in the international trade. Yet, another contradiction emerged for domestic slaveholders, as pointed out by Adam Rothman: "the distinction between the two evaded a basic reality of slavery—that slaveholding required slave trading—legislative restrictions failed to regulate or curtail the internal trade."[62]

With the election of Abraham Lincoln in November 1860, Southern elites prepared articles of secession. Some states issued terse legal documents of separation; others were loquacious. Those legislators who explain their reasons for leaving the Union declared that as president, Lincoln would curtail slavery. While they presuppose the lengthy and well-articulated concept of states' rights, these articles of secession were not abstract defenses of abstract theories; there were adamant proclamations of the right to own, sell, and transport slave "property."[63] More so, at least one state (Georgia) announced the value of this property in the aggregate: they estimated the value at $3 billion in 1860. If secession could occur without war, as many Southerners predicted, that property would remain secure.[64] The logic and reasoning these legislators employed are nakedly expressed in their declarations. We consider four declarations below.[65]

United States of America 1638–1870. (Lenox MA: Hard Press, 2006), 189-91.

[62] Adam Rothman, "The Domestication of the Slave Trade in the United States" in *The Chattel Principle: Internal Slave Trades in the Americas,* ed. Walter Johnson (New Haven, CT: Yale University Press, 2004), 33.

[63] "Because national policy was on the verge of becoming hostile to southern interests, southern decision-makers began to seek a different course of action to ameliorate their grievances." Lawrence M. Anderson, "The Institutional Basis of Secessionist Politics: Federalism and Secession in the United States." *Publius* 34, no. 2 (Spring, 2004): 1–18.

[64] Gavin Wright argues that "Secessionist convention debate revealed widespread acceptance of the idea that the North could not possibly risk war on cotton, and, if she did, England would have to intervene on the side of the South." *The Political Economy of the Cotton South* (New York: W. W. Norton, 1978), 146–47.

[65] All citations of declarations of secession come from http://www.civilwar.org /education/history/primarysources/declarationofcauses.html?referrer=https:// www.google.com/.

Four Declarations

The South Carolina Declaration of Secession[66]

Having threatened to secede in 1852, legislators in South Carolina finally did so on December 20, 1860. They cited the fugitive slave clause of the Constitution and noted: "For many years these laws were executed. But an increasing hostility on the part of the non-slaveholding States to the institution of slavery, has led to a disregard of their obligations, and the laws of the General Government have ceased to effect the objects of the Constitution." Many Northern states have curtailed enforcing the clause; worse, some states have actively resisted: "In the State of New York even the right of transit for a slave has been denied by her tribunals; and the States of Ohio and Iowa have refused to surrender to justice fugitives charged with murder, and with inciting servile insurrection in the State of Virginia."

The compromises of 1787 should remain in force, they asserted: "The right of property in slaves was recognized by giving to free persons distinct political rights, by giving them the right to represent, and burthening [*sic*] them with direct taxes for three-fifths of their slaves; by authorizing the importation of slaves for twenty years; and by stipulating for the rendition of fugitives from labor." Antislavery activists have criticized the South, and

> have denounced as sinful the institution of slavery; they have permitted open establishment among them of societies, whose avowed object is to disturb the peace and to eloign the property of the citizens of other States. They have encouraged and assisted thousands of our slaves to leave their homes; and those who remain, have been incited by emissaries, books and pictures to servile insurrection.

---

[66] The authors make themselves clear. They explicitly cite religious objections to slavery: "Sectional interest and animosity will deepen the irritation, and all hope of remedy is rendered vain, by the fact that public opinion at the North has invested a great political error with the sanction of more erroneous religious belief."

President-elect Lincoln is a man "whose opinions and purposes are hostile to slavery. He is to be entrusted with the administration of the common Government, because he has declared that that Government cannot endure permanently half slave, half free, and that the public mind must rest in the belief that slavery is in the course of ultimate extinction." This is an accurate assessment of Lincoln's expressed intentions: he wished to see slavery extinguished through legal, democratic means. No poetic murmurings about Southern women appear in this or any other declarations. The central goal is to preserve the right to own slaves, to own their labor, and to own their offspring in perpetuity.

The Mississippi Declaration of Secession

On January 9, 1861, the Mississippi legislature met and passed a secessionist declaration. In that declaration the supporters of secession explained their reasoning. They were straightforward:

> Our position is thoroughly identified with the institution of slavery—the greatest material interest of the world. Its labor supplies the product which constitutes by far the largest and most important portions of commerce of the earth. These products are peculiar to the climate verging on the tropical regions, and by an imperious law of nature, none but the black race can bear exposure to the tropical sun. These products have become necessities of the world, and a blow at slavery is a blow at commerce and civilization.

The authors review the history of the antislavery sentiments that produced the Ordinance of 1787, the Missouri Compromise, and other efforts made for more than eighty years to curtail the spread of slavery. Northern hostility to slavery, they announced,

> denies the right of property in slaves, and refuses protection to that right on the high seas, in the Territories, and wherever the government of the United States had jurisdiction. It refuses the admission of new slave States into the Union, and seeks to extinguish it by confining it within its present limits, denying the power of expansion.

Of special concern to the authors was the effect antislavery sentiments had upon slaves themselves. These sentiments are pernicious
and harmful: they have created a doctrine that

> nullified the Fugitive Slave Law in almost every free State in the Union,
> and has utterly broken the compact which our fathers pledged their faith
> to maintain. It advocates negro equality, socially and politically, and
> promotes insurrection and incendiarism in our midst. It has enlisted its
> press, its pulpit and its schools against us, until the whole popular mind
> of the North is excited and inflamed with prejudice. It has made combi-
> nations and formed associations to carry out its schemes of
> emancipation in the States and wherever else slavery exists.

This is a well-founded fear based upon an accurate reading of the antislavery agitation sponsored by Northerners. The Mississippi delegation
does not exaggerate the extent of these agitations nor does it misrepresent the goals of abolitionists: to emancipate slaves wherever and
whenever possible. The central question for these authors was not an
abstract puzzle of states' rights versus federal power. It was tangible
threats to Southern wealth, Southern political power, and the vast rewards—economic and narcissistic—that slavery gave to owners.

The Texas Declaration of Secession

On February 1, 1861, the Texas legislature declared that Texas had
joined the United States assuming

> that she should enjoy these blessings. She was received as a common-
> wealth holding, maintaining and protecting the institution known as
> negro slavery—the servitude of the African to the white race within
> her limits—a relation that had existed from the first settlement of her
> wilderness by the white race, and *which her people intended should exist
> in all future time.* (My emphasis.)

With the election of Lincoln, Texans feared that slavery would be
prohibited in new territories and that subsequently the North would

use its new congressional majorities "as a means of destroying the institutions of Texas and her sister slaveholding States." More so, "When we advert to the course of individual non-slave-holding States, and that a majority of their citizens, our grievances assume far greater magnitude." Northerners often refused to honor the fugitive slave clause, "a provision founded in justice and wisdom, and without the enforcement of which the compact [Constitution] fails to accomplish the object of its creation." Like all Southerners who defended slavery, the authors of the Texas declaration welded themselves to the 1787 Constitution because it defended and promoted slavery. Their fury at Northerners who challenged slavery found a natural redoubt, a fortress of civic devotion, in this historical fact. *They*, not abolitionists, were faithful to the Constitution and its sacred principles. *They* were the true patriots defending the founders and their founding document against those who trampled on justice and wisdom.

Worse, they said, Lincoln's party showed "an unnatural feeling of hostility to these Southern States and their beneficent and patriarchal system of African slavery, proclaiming the debasing doctrine of equality of all men, irrespective of race or color—a doctrine at war with nature, in opposition to the experience of mankind, and in violation of the plainest revelations of Divine Law." Their defense of slavery and the concomitant denigration of people of African descent is clear:

> We hold as undeniable truths that the governments of the various States, and of the confederacy itself, were established exclusively by the white race, for themselves and their posterity; that the African race had no agency in their establishment; that they were rightfully held and regarded as an inferior and dependent race, and in that condition only could their existence in this country be rendered beneficial or tolerable.

The United States was founded, as Stephen Douglas said in his debates with Lincoln, for "all white men [who] are and of right ought to be entitled to equal civil and political rights" and that "the servitude of the African race, as existing in these States, is mutually beneficial to both bond and free, and is abundantly authorized and justified by the experience of mankind, and the revealed will of the Almighty Creator." As with the Mississippi authors, the Texas delegation had no tolerance for any scheme of gradual emancipation, no matter how arrived at. Lincoln's philosophy—the moral equivalence of white persons and black persons—was abhorrent now and forever. Only whites had the superior mental and ethical development necessary to found the United States; these truths are grounded in nature and affirmed by God. They will not change over time. Thus any scheme, no matter how pursued over how lengthy a period of time, affronts natural law and God's law. (We note, again, no Southern women appear in these arguments.)

The Georgia Declaration of Secession

On January 19, 1861, the Georgia legislature met and declared that "The people of Georgia having dissolved their political connection with the Government of the United States of America, present to their confederates and the world the causes which have led to the separation." That reason was that

> For the last ten years we have had numerous and serious causes of complaint against our non-slave-holding confederate States with reference to the subject of African slavery. They have endeavored to weaken our security, to disturb our domestic peace and tranquility, and persistently refused to comply with their express constitutional obligations to us in reference to that property, and by the use of their power in the Federal Government have striven to deprive us of an equal enjoyment of the common Territories of the Republic.

With the election of Abraham Lincoln, an antislavery party gained control of the federal government:

> The party of Lincoln, called the Republican party, under its present name and organization, is of recent origin. It is admitted to be an anti-slavery party. While it attracts to itself by its creed the scattered advocates of exploded political heresies, of condemned theories in political economy, the

advocates of commercial restrictions, of protection, of special privileges, of waste and corruption in the administration of Government, anti-slavery is its mission and its purpose. By anti-slavery it is made a power in the state.

As in other documents of secession, these authors write with clarity and force: Lincoln ran on a platform of eventual emancipation and the curtailment of slavery wherever the laws permitted. When Lincoln won the presidency in November 1860, the odds of that platform being pursued increased and the odds of retaining the compromises of 1787 decreased.

Although the "question of slavery was the great difficulty in the way of the formation of the Constitution" with sufficient compromise and Southern control of either the presidency or the House or both, no federal authority existed to overthrow slavery in the South. By preserving a hold on federal power, slaveholders could block and defeat numerous foes who attacked the institution. "A distinct abolition party was not formed in the United States for more than half a century after the Government went into operation. The main reason was that the North, even if united, could not control both branches of the Legislature during any portion of that time." In addition, they argued, Northern industries benefited mightily from tariffs that protected nascent manufacturing but which added costs to Southern consumers. The authors held that Northern interests merely used antislavery sentiment to harm the South and to protect Northern interests:

> The antislavery sentiment of the North offered the best chance for success. An anti-slavery party must necessarily look to the North alone for support, but a united North was now strong enough to control the government in all of its departments, and a sectional party was therefore determined upon. Time and issues upon slavery were necessary to its completion and final triumph.

This complaint turns on the fact that the South demanded the extension of slavery into new territories including lands taken from Mexico (where slavery had been outlawed) by conquest.

We had acquired a large territory by successful war with Mexico; Congress had to govern it; how, in relation to slavery, was the question then demanding solution. This state of facts gave form and shape to the anti-slavery sentiment throughout the North and the conflict began. Northern anti-slavery men of all parties asserted the right to exclude slavery from the territory by Congressional legislation and demanded the prompt and efficient exercise of this power to that end. This insulting and unconstitutional demand was met with great moderation and firmness by the South.

The Georgians were furious that the Missouri Compromise led to the prohibition of slavery in new states formed from the conquered lands of Mexico. James Madison and Thomas Jefferson (both slavery advocates) "predicted that it would result in the dissolution of the Union." Antislavery politicians from the North (no antislavery Southerner could win national office) revealed their "purpose to limit, restrain, and finally abolish slavery in the States where it exists. The South with great unanimity declared her purpose to resist the principle of prohibition to the last extremity." The rise of the Republican Party and the nomination of Abraham Lincoln made it clear that "the prohibition of slavery in the Territories is the cardinal principle of this organization." Citing the 1787 Constitution's tolerance of slavery, and the Dred Scott ruling, they grieved the loss of their ability to pursue escaped slaves unencumbered:

> for above twenty years the non-slave-holding States generally have wholly refused to deliver up to us persons charged with crimes affecting slave property. Our confederates, with punic [treacherous] faith, shield and give sanctuary to all criminals who seek to deprive us of this property or who use it to destroy us.

As they read the history of the 1787 debates, without the fugitive slave provision and similar guarantees, "it is historically true that we would have rejected the Constitution."

Antislavery sentiments were also dismaying: "a citizen cannot travel the highway with his servant who may voluntarily accompany him, without being declared by law a felon and being subjected to infamous punishments." Similar to many Southerners who traveled to Northern cities, the authors feared that their slaves (not servants) who must accompany them (slaves have no "voluntary" action) might be seduced into escaping and yet they, the rightful masters, were criticized. The Georgians did not hide their largest complaint; it was economic, not abstract. Antislavery agitation was a threat to *"$3,000,000,000 of our property* in the common territories of the Union." Depending upon how one measures the value of an 1860 dollar, this amounts to a current worth of between $830 billion and $10.04 trillion.[67] The 2011 US GDP was approximately $15 trillion.[68]

In 2011 dollars, the relative worth of $3 billion in slave property in 1860 was:

$83,700,000,000	using the Consumer Price Index
$64,300,000,000	using the GDP deflator
$511,000,000,000	using the unskilled wage
$1,050,000,000,000	using the Production Worker Compensation
$1,050,000,000,000	using the nominal GDP per capita
$10,400,000,000,000	using the relative share of GDP[69]

---

[67] This is a realistic estimate figuring four million slaves valued at $750 each = $3 billion. See http://www2.census.gov/prod2/decennial/documents/1860a-02.pdf. Total slave population: 3,953,760; total Free Colored Persons: 487,970; approx. number of "mulattoes": 591,776. *Preliminary Report on the Eighth Census*, 131. US Government Printing Office: http://www2.census.gov/ prod2/decennial/ documents/1860e-05.pdf. The average ownership throughout the slave states was 26%.

[68] http://www.measuringworth.com/calculators/uscompare/result.php for 2011.

[69] Calculations from "Measuring Worth." http://www.measuringworth.com/ index.php. For a valuable discussion see "Measuring Slavery in 2011 Dollars" by S. H. Williamson and L. P. Cain, http://www.measuringworth.com/ slavery.php.

Slaves and the Return on Investment

How one assesses the productive value of slaves held in 1860 determines which of these adjusted figures one uses. Of course, if abolitionism prevailed all these values fell to zero. With the election of Abraham Lincoln in fall 1860, slave owners confronted that grave danger. In 1819, forty years prior to the Georgia secession declaration, James Madison, fourth US president, attempted to calculate the value of American slaves. At that time, he estimated there were about 1.5 million slaves, each worth on average $400, thus

> the cost of the whole would be 600 millions of dollrs [*sic*]. These estimates are probably beyond the fact; and from the no. of slaves should be deducted 1. those whom their Masters would not part with. 2. those who may be gratuitously set free by their Masters. 3. those acquiring freedom under emancipating regulations of the States. 4. those preferring slavery where they are, to freedom in an African settlement.[70]

By 1860, the total number of enslaved persons had risen to four million and their average value had doubled since Madison wrote. After reviewing hundreds of transactions involving slave auctions in Arkansas, Orville Walters Taylor showed that values ranged from an average of $881 for a specific Arkansas plantation, to many thousands for highly skilled slaves, such as blacksmiths and field foremen.[71] He cited the 1860 census and suggested that the average Arkansas slave was worth "approximately as much as an eighty-acre farm, a city house, or a herd of a hundred cattle."[72]

The essential feature of slaves was that as chattels they had genuine investment and retail value. In a study of 15, 512 legal documents in

---

[70] 15 June 1819 *Writings* 8:439—47, http://press-pubs.uchicago.edu/founders/documents/v1ch15s65.html.

[71] Orville Walters Taylor, *Negro Slavery in Arkansas* (Durham, NC: Duke University Press, 1958), 78ff.

[72] Ibid., 79n9.

Southern county courts,[73] Loren Schweninger, an American historian, notes "the overwhelming evidence that slave owners considered their slaves primarily as property."[74] In addition, owners used "slaves as collateral for loans; to establish credit at mercantile establishments, auction houses, and grocery stores; and to trade for land, livestock, horses, machinery, supplies, and real estate. In many cases they used them as mortgages in the payment of their purchase price, signing promissory notes for part of the cost and using purchased slaves as collateral."[75] A pregnant female was more valuable than a non-pregnant female; the term *good breeders* appears in court documents.[76] Often heirs of slaveholders challenged the owner's wishes to free his or her slaves upon death: "family members tried to sell blacks who were slated to be manumitted."[77]

Richard Sutch summarized the average individual and net aggregate value of slaves from 1800 to 1862 by examining the history of the slave auction in New Orleans. The following are values per male field hand, according to three experts, U. B. Phillips, Stanley Engerman,

---

[73] The Race and Slavery Petitions Project Count Court Collection (RSPPCCC). https://library.uncg.edu/slavery/petitions/about.aspx. This project contains 3,000 petitions filed in Southern state legislatures in addition to 15,512 petitions filed in county courts. One can read detailed pleadings—by leading citizens—for compensation, for example to damages to their slaves by liquor salesmen, or by the very presence of free persons of color. In Nashville, in January 1860, citizens petitioned the state legislature: "To remove free people of color from the state. They believe that no slaves should be emancipated unless funds are provided for their immediate removal to Liberia. The free black population of Tennessee, the petitioners contend, is generally 'lazy, worthless, and engaged in trading with the slave race & thereby injuring their morals & *the property of the master.*'" PAR #: 11486001 (My emphasis.)

[74] Loren Schweninger, ed., *The Southern Debate Over Slavery, Volume 2: Petitions to Southern County Courts, 1775–1867* (Urbana, IL: University of Illinois Press, 2008), 12.

[75] Ibid.

[76] Ibid.

[77] Ibid., 14.

Laurence J. Kotlikoff.[78] Data have been extracted for 1820, 1840, and 1860, the year in which Lincoln was elected president and South Carolina seceded from the Union.

Year	1820	1840	1860
Phillips: fieldhand	970	1,020	1,080
Engerman: fieldhand	875	773	1,513
Kotlikoff: fieldhand	875	800	1,451
Avg. price all slaves	393	377	778
Slave population	1,538,022	2,487,355	3,953,760
Value of all slaves, $ millions	610	997	3,059

Gavin Wright observed that "the average slave owner held nearly two-thirds of his wealth in the form of slaves, and in many places the proportion was higher. In Harrison County, Texas, the typical slaveholding household had more than $10,000 in slave property, more than three times the value of its real property. In the antebellum South, wealth and wealth accumulation meant slaves, and land was distinctly secondary."[79] This imbalance meant that Southern states had few resources to build canals, railroads, roads, towns, cities, and educational centers. By 1860, for example, Massachusetts had 157 miles of railroad per 1,000 square miles; Virginia, by far the richest Southern state in rail resources, had 35 (Louisiana had 7).

These striking differences between the value of slaves and the much smaller value of real property meant that Southerners felt compelled to

---

[78] Richard Sutch, "Appendix: The Value of the Slave Population, 1805–1860," in Roger Ransom and Richard Sutch, "Capitalists without Capital: The Burden of Slavery and the Impact of Emancipation," *Agricultural History* 62 (3) (1988), Tables A.4, 155–6, and A.1, pp. 150–1; Roger Ransom and Richard Sutch, "Who Pays for Slavery?" in Richard F. America, ed., *The Wealth of Races: The Present Value of Benefits from Past Injustices* (Westport, CT: Greenwood Press, 1990), appendix tables A.1 and A.2, 47–50.

[79] Gavin Wright. *Old South, New South: Revolutions in the Southern Economy Since the Civil War* (New York: Basic Books, 1984), 19–20.

maintain the legality and market for slaves. That this compulsion contradicted their avowed values as Americans and as Christians meant that they faced an unsolvable problem.

CHAPTER 5

The Original Contradiction: Southern Rejoinders

The founders who championed slavery confronted logical and ethical contradictions.[1] They affirmed the principle of freedom that justified their rebellion from England while they denied freedom to their slaves and to their slaves' children. Because they were not moral imbeciles, they struggled with their consciences. They recognized, sometimes dimly, that slavery contradicted their religious beliefs. We might agree that under some circumstances a criminal should forfeit his liberty; we cannot agree that his children should also forfeit their freedom. No natural law or religious ethic justifies that claim. On the contrary, as Jewish and Christian scriptures made clear, crimes committed by fathers do not fall upon their sons, and crimes committed by sons do not fall upon their fathers. (Deuteronomy 24:16). That all human beings are born into sin, that is, fallen from original grace, means that all persons, not just slaves, are imperfect.

The justification for perpetual slavery is that it made owners rich.

---

[1] See Eugene D. Genovese, *The Slaveholders' Dilemma* (Columbia, SC: University of South Carolina Press, 1992). Owners did, indeed, have dilemmas; I focus upon the logical contradictions they faced.

It promised to make them even richer when the need for slaves increased with the conquest of new territories.

From the beginning, slavery proponents recognized this economic fact, and they did everything they could to prevent and retard restrictions on slavery. To secure ratification of the Constitution, proslavery and antislavery parties agreed to a compromise on the importation of slaves. The result was article I, section 9 of the 1787 Constitution: "The Migration or Importation of such Persons as any of the States now existing shall think proper to admit, shall not be prohibited by the Congress prior to the Year one thousand eight hundred and eight, but a Tax or duty may be imposed on such Importation, not exceeding ten dollars for each Person." This does not forbid the importation of slaves after 1808; it restricted antislavery legislators from making it illegal until 1808. This compromise did not signal a new liberality on the part of Southerners. The urge to celebrate the "miracle of the Constitution," as with all efforts to idealize the past, obscures the deep cost of these compromises that created an ethically compromised government. In Thurgood Marshall's words, it was "defective from the start, requiring several amendments, a civil war, and momentous social transformation to attain the system of constitutional government, and its respect for the individual freedoms and human rights, we hold as fundamental today."[2]

On the contrary, by accepting this prohibition upon further debate, slave owners, especially those with many slaves, gave themselves a protected, indigenous market and at least twenty years to build up their holdings. Through natural expansion their holdings would increase and they could sell excess progeny. If slavery were forbidden in new federal territories those sales could not occur. Forbidding the expansion of slavery would also depress the value of their current slaveholdings because it diminished their investment value. Worse,

---

[2] Thurgood Marshall, "The Constitution's Bicentennial: Commemorating the Wrong Document?" *Vanderbilt Law Review* (1987). See also Raymond T. Diamond, "No Call to Glory: Thurgood Marshall's Thesis on the Intent of a Pro-Slavery Constitution" *Vanderbilt Law Review* (1989)

new states would bring new congressmen who might restrict slavery even to the point of abolition. That would have destroyed most of the property in the slaveholding states.

If, as some historians argue, slaveholdings constituted between 60 and 90 percent of Southern wealth, then abolition would annihilate slaveholders' net worth by that amount. The rich and powerful owned the most slaves. They would shoulder the brunt of this reversal. Having enjoyed the pleasures and wealth that slavery afforded them for generations, owners were not going to consent to this form of economic downturn. With his usual acuity, Lincoln recognized these motives and argued for gradual emancipation and compensation to owners. However, radicals in his party refused to contemplate such compromises; radicals in the other party refused to countenance the disappearance of their "natural resources," as they called their slave population.

These logical and emotional contradictions required a response. Persons who claim either legal or philosophic coherence cannot admit that their reasoning rests upon contradictions. From the classical Greeks forward, authorities required coherent reasons to justify their actions. Walt Whitman could declare in "Song of Myself" that "Very well then I contradict myself" without consequences. No US senator or congressman could take this literary escape. When Southern authorities faced these internal contradictions and confronted a rising tide of antislavery forces, they needed to find rejoinders to the antislavery voices.

The Solution Space: the Range of Possible Southern Rejoinders

A solution space is a set of possible answers to a well-specified problem. For example, a client hires an architect to design a house with particular features on a particular piece of land for a specific price. The client's needs, the budget, the property, and similar constraints define the solution space available to the architect. Architects practicing in Honolulu confront different problems and offer different solutions than architects practicing in Minneapolis. They have different solution spaces. The struggle over the Constitution, its compromises, and the vast wealth that slavery afforded Southerners defined the solution space in which all parties acted.

Most importantly, owners and slaves were human beings. All the drama, vigor, beauty, cruelty, and multiplicity of life presented itself to both groups. Without slavery, each group would have developed its own solutions to the problems of living. With slavery, these experiments of cultural coexistence and experimentation could not occur. The logic of slavery is that either one controls what one owns or one's way of life is destroyed. All slaves (and their children) must remain in bondage. If some escape through illegal means, they must be pursued with hot vengeance lest their success inspire others. This impulse to control slave property is another consequence of affirming the contradiction "property in persons." As many noted, there was no "fugitive horse" clause in the Constitution; horses are not human beings with transcendental rights of which they are aware or can be made aware. Slaves do have such rights, and they do seek freedom when they are imprisoned. For that reason owners must be vigilant, suspicious, and dedicated to an eternal struggle between themselves and their property. That was Jefferson's poignant insight when he said that owners "held the wolf by its ears": they could not let go without suffering catastrophic losses.

Jefferson and other owners recognized that their slaves shared their wish for freedom. Out of that recognition—that moment of commonality between master and slave—came insights into perfecting the slave system, slave patrols, violence, and other means to control the slaves' minds and spirits. This required owners and their minions to plot relentlessly to crush the spirits of fellow humans. This was a great crime and a great sin. Owners needed to defend themselves against those moral truths and against the agony of deciding between justice and wealth. Every element of Jewish-Christian values favored the former; every element of self-interest favored the latter. Owners pursued defensive options available to anyone caught in a contradiction.

In informal terms, to affirm a contradiction between justice (a transcendental good) and self-interest (a mundane instinct) is to create a barrier within the self. This causes distress and emotional consequences of a contest, a struggle, within one's mind. Jefferson said it better than most because he was more skilled than most. But owners felt it and found themselves compelled to respond to these burdens. To do so they fabricated rejoinders. In strict legal parlance a rejoinder is "the pleading served by a defendant in answer to the plaintiff's reply (the pleading in answer to the defense)."[3] In a more general sense a rejoinder is a reply that is "intended as sharp or witty." The *Oxford English Dictionary* cites, for example, pamphlets and articles from the early sixteenth century through the nineteenth century entitled as rejoinders to contentious issues of the day.[4] Proslavery authors offered both kinds of rejoinder; some were legal, and others ranged across every possible intellectual field. Like John C. Calhoun, many began with a recitation of US laws, especially the history of the US Constitution.

We can arrange their rejoinders, their solutions to their ethical and emotional dilemmas, on a grid. It lays out four options that exhaust the solution space available to owners who confronted the contradiction "property in person." These four options are available to all thinking subjects, in varying degrees at various times. They are not fixed by personality or heritage. One might cycle through all of them in quick succession without altering one's personality or one's heritage. Confronting a contradiction we can:

1. Call the contradiction a paradox beyond human understanding.
2. Treat it as a puzzle that we will solve by clever inventions.
3. "Split" our consciousness into separate domains.
4. Acknowledge the contradiction, then resolve it by forfeiting one of its parts.

Contradictions one and two will be discussed in this chapter; the third in chapter 6, and the fourth in chapter 7.

---

[3] Bryan A. Garner, *A Dictionary of Modern Legal Usage* (New York: Oxford University Press, 1990).

[4] "rejoinder, n.". *OED* Online. March 2013. Oxford University Press.

Call the contradiction a paradox beyond human understanding.

If we affirm that slaves are *both* persons *and* property, we can reduce our distress by calling the contradiction a paradox. This places the conflict beyond our reach and into the realm of unsolvable problems. Paradoxes are the union of two statements, both valid, which contradict one another. For example, physicists tell us that light acts like a particle sometimes and like a wave at other times. Lay people ask, "So which is it?" The physicists reply that our notion of light is paradoxical: light is both particle and wave at the same time. Christian theology affirms the contradiction that Jesus was both fully human and fully divine—a paradox.

Even murkier paradoxes bedevil philosophy and theology. Philosophers want to know how the concept *truth* works in mathematics and logic, disciplines that are foundational to knowledge. From Aristotle forward, eminent philosophers have tried to explain the concept of truth; no one, so far, has been victorious. Barring a consensus, the problem remains unsolved. Empathy is neither required in these struggles nor in these attempted resolutions. We are not concerned with our experience of paradoxes (which produces vertigo in some and anger in others). There is little value in exploring our distress empathically. We recognize that our suffering is conceptual. It occurs within physics or within mathematics, for example. When we leave the classroom the paradox and our frustrations with it disappear.

Is the contradiction "property in persons" a paradox? No. Paradoxes are conceptual dilemmas. They reveal the limits of clear and distinct ideas, such as the word *truth* and the word *light*. The paradox of light—that it acts both as a particle and as a wave—reveals problems with our concepts *particle* and *wave*, not with nature, as Niels Bohr put it.[5] The problems with slavery are not conceptual; they are

---

[5] "Bohr had been particularly concerned with the problem of particle-wave duality, i.e. the problem that experimental evidence on the behaviour of both light and matter seemed to demand a wave picture in some cases, and a particle picture in others. Yet these pictures are mutually exclusive. Whereas a particle is

legal, psychological, and ethical. The contradiction of slavery, of property in persons, is not a paradox that resists logical solution. The contradiction is within the hearts and minds of owners who wanted two things: to remain rich and empowered (to retain their human property) and to feel themselves honorable Christians.

Treat it as a puzzle that we will solve by clever inventions.

The challenges that confront detectives and inventors seem, at first, to resemble paradoxes: two or more sentences seem both true, yet when added together produce a contradiction. Detectives and inventors succeed by dissolving these apparent (unsolvable) contradictions into (solvable) puzzles. By discovering the actual story of the crime or by dividing up an impossible engineering task into smaller, solvable parts, each bridges a seemingly unbridgeable gap. In doing so they do not use empathic investigation. Southern writers who defended slavery as a "positive good" used invention.

Detectives Face Contradictions

Detectives reverse engineer a murder the way that technicians reverse engineer competing technology. Starting from the final effect—the dead body—detectives reason backward to the hidden causes—motives, actions, and devices—that produced the lethal outcome. For example, in a TV mystery, Lt. Commander Pierce apparently commits suicide in a locked room on a submarine.[6] The ship's commander is outside Pierce's room when he and two witnesses hear a gunshot. Mr. Monk asks: "If someone murdered Pierce and made it appear to be suicide, who would benefit?" or *cui bono* to cite the Latin phrase. The commander becomes a suspect when Monk learns that

---

always localized, the very definition of the notions of wavelength and frequency requires an extension in space and in time." Jan Hilgevoord, "The Uncertainty Principle," in *Stanford Encyclopedia of Philosophy*, 2006. http://plato.stanford. edu/ entries/qt-uncertainty/#WavPar DuaCom.

[6] Monkophiliacs will recognize "Mr. Monk Is Underwater." *Monk*, Season 7, Episode 5. First aired: August 15, 2008.

the lieutenant commander had suppressed evidence of gross error by the commander in a lethal accident and Pierce was about to spill the beans. That establishes a motive and lets Monk reason: "If the commander killed Pierce, he did so before the alleged discovery by the witnesses." Hence, the "gunshot sound" reported by the witnesses did not coincide with the shot that killed Pierce. It follows that the commander devised a fake gunshot just before he and the two crewmates broke through Pierce's door. To solve the mystery, Monk must discover how the commander created the fake gunshot.

As ritual requires, Monk tells us what really happened: the commander had killed Pierce earlier and then rigged a firecracker—using a burning cigarette—to explode just before he burst through the door. All is clear. Did Mr. Monk use empathy to solve the case? He put himself in the mind of the killer and asked himself what facts about Lt. Commander Pierce would motivate murder. Yet, Monk works by algorithms and acute observations, not by empathy. Part of the show's irony is that Monk observes people but does not understand their inner workings. He's a brilliant observer of human actions, not a master psychologist. Everyone is distressed by the murder, but only Monk, with his nose for clues and memory of inconsistencies in narrative, understands it.

Inventors face similar conundrums

Mr. Monk resolved the (apparent) contradiction in the shipboard murder case by altering the temporal markers. Genrich Altshuller counts this among the methods inventors use to solve dilemmas. In his book *And Suddenly the Inventor Appeared*, this is "Method 28: Separation of contradictory requirements in time and/or space."[7] Altshuller describes this and another thirty methods that he derived from surveying thousands of patent applications in the Soviet Union in the 1950s through the 1970s. Used in various combinations, these

---

[7] Genrich Altshuller, *And Suddenly the Inventor Appeared, TRIZ, the Theory of Inventive Problem Solving* (Worcester, MA: Technical Innovation Center, 1996 [orig.1984]), 119.

techniques facilitate finding new solutions to engineering tasks (which are always puzzles.)[8]

Altshuller summarizes his method in four steps. Each step reduces the original problem—which was a contradiction—into noncontradictory propositions that eventuate in a statement about a physical puzzle. When we've solved that physical puzzle our work is done.

"Slavery as a Natural Good" and Other Inventions

We find similar efforts by Southern intellectuals, authors, and theologians to resolve the contradiction of American slavery. They invented novel ways to defend slavery against its critics, to justify it as a positive good, and to assuage their consciences.

In the 1830s, western Virginia legislators were galled by the fact that eastern Virginia slaveholders held political power incommensurate with their numbers. They proposed to base representation in the Virginia legislature on whites alone. Henry Wilson, who was vice president under Ulysses S. Grant, recounted these struggles in his history of the Confederacy, two volumes published during the war and one two years after.[9] In addition, slave rebellions terrified many whites who feared that they too could be victims of black retaliation. These legislative debates intensified in fall 1831 after the Nat Turner slave rebellion in August in South Hampton, Virginia. Shocked by the killing of white people, Virginia authorities feared that even larger and bloodier attacks against whites—slaveholders and non-slaveholders alike—might occur. To forestall those calamities, legislators debated whether or not to curtail or to abolish slavery in the state.

In these famous debates—and the literature that they spawned—we observe the inventive reasoning that proslavery theorists used to defend the institution. The strongest defense of slavery rested upon four claims: economic—that slaves constituted the dominant form of

---

[8] Ibid., 113. Because many problems are routine, Altshuller offers a recipe book of eighty (or more) standards that offer ready-made solutions.

[9] Henry Wilson, *History of the Rise and Fall of the Slave Power in America*, vol. 1 (Boston: J.R. Osgood & Co., vol. 1 & 2, 1872; vol. 3, 1877), 190.

Southern wealth; cultural—that thanks to slavery, Southern elites could enjoy the leisurely pursuit of art, literature, and contemplation; scientific—that Africans were a distinct and inferior race incapable of self-governance; and theological—that Christian doctrines did not support much less require abolition. While one may dispute each of these claims, they are not entirely specious. Among these defenses of slavery we do not find the flag-waving dogmatism of the postwar period; no strident proclamations of states' rights, for example, appear in these discussions.

Economic Arguments

James Gholson and other representatives in the Virginia House of Delegates from the slaveholding regions of Virginia emphasized that raising slaves was a lucrative business. Henry Wilson cited Gholson who had proclaimed that this reproductive increase "consists much of our wealth"[10] Thomas Dew, a young Southern scholar, quickly wrote a similar defense of slavery that was published in the *American Quarterly Review*. In his book, *Review of the Debate in the Virginia Legislature of 1831 and 1832*, Dew argued that raising and selling Virginia slaves "becomes an advantage to the State, and does not check [diminish] the black population as much as at first view we might imagine, because it furnishes every inducement to the master to attend to the negroes, to encourage breeding, and to cause the greatest number to be raised.... Virginia is in fact a negro-raising State for other States."[11]

In an 1832 debate in the Virginia House of Delegates, John Chandler of Norfolk criticized his fellow Virginians. By creating slavery they endangered all whites, he said. While everyone agreed that slaves were property, slave revolts endangered both owners and nonowners. Chandler did not deny that, "the master has property not merely in the female slave, but in the [her] issue AD INFINITUM."

[10] James Gholson, cited in Ibid., vol. 1, 100.
[11] Thomas Dew, *Review of the Debate in the Virginia Legislature of 1831 and 1832.* (repr. Applewood Books, Bedford, MA: n.d.), 49.

However, white, non-slaveholders had a higher right: that of their lives that were threatened by the slave rebellion in Southampton.[12]

Regarding the conundrum of property in persons, Chandler makes two telling points. First, Virginia slaves were either stolen from Africa or sold by Africans who took them as plunder in war. Second, slaves were once free men and "liberty, RIGHTFULLY cannot be converted into slavery, [therefore] may I not question whether the title of the master to the slave is absolute and unqualified, and beyond the disposal of the government?" While affirming, again that "slaves and their increase are property," Chandler insisted that they are "a species of property truly described as a curse to the land, and an increasing curse, which the legislature, not only by that law which is superior to all other laws—THE PUBLIC SAFETY—but by the provisions of the bill of rights, has the power to remove."

In response to these debates, Dew provided proslavery advocates speaking points with which to defend the institution. The first chapter in his book is "Abolition of Negro Slavery." It is a clever, passionate, and learned effort to argue against critics of slavery, including Southern whites who feared slave insurrections. Dew dismissed Chandler and others who painted terrifying scenes of destruction by rebelling slaves. Noting the superiority of weapons, tactics, and control available to the white masters and the corresponding poverty of weapons, leaders, and communication available to slaves, Dew took five pages to argue persuasively that the likelihood of successful rebellion in Southern states was nil. Unlike French radicals who imbibed the fantasy

---

[12] Speech of John A Chandler of Norfolk County, in the Virginia House of Delegates, on the Policy of the State with respect to Her Slave Population, January 17, 1832. Published: Richmond, Virginia, Thomas W. White, Printer, 1832. He adds: "Look at Southampton. The answer is written IN LETTERS OF BLOOD, upon the floors of that unhappy county. Under these circumstances, may we not inquire into the right of our ancestors to inflict this curse upon us, seeing that it has already interfered so essentially with the first article of the bill of rights?" (All capitalization and emphasis in the original.) https://archive.org/details/speechofjohnacha1832chan.

of universal brotherhood and freed tens of thousands of blacks, Southern leaders would do no such thing. Because French intellectuals emphasized the "Rights of Man," following the Revolution of 1789, by 1800 persons of color believed that they too had rights and that they could mount a successful revolt, which black Haitians did. The success of the insurrection in St. Domingo (Haiti) was, Dew said, a sin that "rests on the [French] National Assembly, and should be an awful warning to every legislature to beware of too much tampering with so deliberate and difficult a subject as the alteration of the fundamental relations of society."[13]

Regarding the alleged economic harm that slavery does to the South, Dew showed that slave labor produced great wealth as long as slaves were "worked in bodies under the eye of a superintendent [slave master], and are made to perform more labour than freemen" (ibid., 126). Because Southern climates made crops abundant, free natives had little incentive to work hard. Only with slavery—and the extraordinary drive that the master and overseer bring to cultivation—could these regions produce wealth: "We doubt whether the extreme south of the United States, and the West India islands, would ever have been cultivated to the same degree of perfection as now, by any other than slave labor" (ibid., 126). Dew sidestepped the unseemly question of asking how much persuasion the overseer had to bring upon slaves to make them work in regions that no one else would tolerate. The perfect cultivation of difficult terrain under harsh conditions requires the perfect cultivation of overwhelming force, brutalization, and threats of future punishment.

Dew argued that if Northern states had left it alone, Virginia

---

[13] Dew, *Review of the Debate in the Virginia Legislature, 115*. Other apologists rejected Dew's modest nod to the *seeming* contradiction of Christian slavery and, instead, cited hundreds of passages in the Hebrew Bible and the New Testament. Thornton Stringfellow, for example, argued that Christianity condoned slavery. See "A Brief Examination of Scripture Testimony on the Institution of Slavery" (1841) in Drew Gilpen Faust, ed., *The Ideology of Slavery* (repr. Baton Rouge: Louisiana State University Press, 1981), 136–67.

would have become wealthier. However, Northern manufacturing interests pushed through national tariffs and other federal laws that protected their industries and increased costs for agricultural regions of the country: "It is the action of the federal government which is ruining slave labor" (ibid., 128). Dew's argument reappeared in numerous contemporary defenses of the Old South. (It reappears in contemporary blogs and websites that defend the Old South and reinterpret the Civil War as a matter of Northern aggression.) Because it ignores moral arguments against slavery and imputes to the North venal motives masked under abolitionist concerns, this argument is emotionally appealing to nineteenth and even some twenty-first century Southerners.

The true story is more complex. In *Prelude to Civil War: the Nullification Controversy in South Carolina*, William Freehling a professor of American history, reviewed the historical and political context of Southern responses to early nineteenth century political events, especially those that touched on slavery.[14] Freehling sought to explain how Southern states, among them South Carolina, could move from "the enthusiastic nationalism of 1816 to the extreme sectionalism of 1836" (ibid., xiii). He examined the intellectual and political history of this twenty-year period and showed that it was the "acute anxieties surrounding the mere discussion of slavery" that helps explain the movement away from Union and toward the Civil War (ibid., xi). Contrary to Dew's calm reassurances, Freehling documented the widespread anxiety about slave revolts that any hint of abolitionism roused in South Carolinian slaveholders: "Abolition conjured up grotesque specters of plunder, rape, and murder. The slave, too barbaric and degraded to adjust peacefully to freedom, seemed certain to declare race war the moment he threw off his chains."[15]

---

[14] William Freehling, *Prelude to Civil War: the Nullification Controversy in South Carolina, 1816-1836* (New York, Harper & Row, 1966).

[15] Freehling cites the Vesey Conspiracy of 1822; a huge fire on Christmas Eve in Charleston in 1825; and another fire scare in 1826 in Charleston, (ibid., 61). The Vesey Conspiracy was an elaborate plot, developed over a

Cultural Arguments

Dew could not deny that slaves were often miserable (as Jefferson noted). While he agreed that in many ways the institution was "evil," he said that slavery was thrust upon the South. Dew asked rhetorically "Must we shrink from the charge which devolves upon us, and throw the slave in consequence into the hands of those who will have no scruples of conscience—those who will not perhaps treat him so kindly?"[16] In support of this claim, Dew celebrated Southern gentility: "Look to the slave-holding population of our country, and you everywhere find them characterized by noble and elevated sentiment, by humane and virtuous feelings."[17] He offered no evidence that humane and virtuous feelings were more prevalent in Richmond, say, than in Philadelphia. The systematic sexual misuse of slave women—admitted by many—does not suggest a surplus of noble feelings among male slave owners.

William Harper, a distinguished lawyer, former US senator, and a chancellor of South Carolina, wrote assiduously upon the benefits of slavery and against any constraints upon it. His *Memoir on Slavery* was an address he delivered in 1837; he revised it in 1838; it was reprinted in 1852.[18] Among the benefits of slavery, Harper asserted, was the bounty it bestowed on black women. Because they are, by nature, of loose moral substance, a slave woman has many sexual contacts and thus will produce children born out of wedlock. In a slaveholding

---

five-year period by a smart but erratic freed slave, Denmark Vesey, to rouse up battalions of slaves in Charleston and attack their masters. Thanks to turncoats and informers, rich whites escaped; yet, "The Lowcountry gentry would never again forget the possibility" of murderous revolt, (ibid., 59).

[16] Dew, *Review of the Debate in the Virginia Legislature*, 107.

[17] Ibid., 109.

[18] William Harper, *Memoir on Slavery*, Read before the Society for the Advancement of Learning of South Carolina, 1837 (Charleston, SC: James S. Burges, 1838). Repr. in Drew Gilpin Faust. *The Ideology of Slavery: Proslavery Thought in the Antebellum South, 1830–1860* (Baton Rouge: Louisiana State University Press, 1981), 78–135.

society this does not produce animus and difficulties for her: "She has not impaired her means of support [her slaveholder continues to feed her], not materially impaired her character, or lowered her station in society" (ibid., 106). Indeed, thanks to the wisdom of slavery, her immaturity and indiscretion yielded a bounty: "her offspring is not a burden, but an acquisition to her owner" (ibid.). We recall that Thomas Jefferson kept the six children he fathered by Sally Hemings, his slave mistress, as slaves at Monticello, though with favored status. Some he freed before his death and others in his will, the only slaves for whom he did these services.[19]

In a parallel way, Harper said because slave women provided ready sexual favors to all men (white and black), they make (white) prostitution almost unknown in Southern states. While some slave women marry, many do not and although unwed motherhood is unfortunate, it is a lesser evil than the (alleged) "70,000 prostitutes of London, or of Paris" and the ten thousand of New York and other Northern cities.[20] That some white men had sexual contact with black women is unfortunate, but "the intercourse is generally casual; he does not make her habitually an associate, and is less likely to receive any taint from her habits and manners" (ibid., 107). In contrast, Harper asserted, sex with a white prostitute endangers white men. They spent more time with white prostitutes and thus their "moral feelings are bewildered and the boundaries of virtue and vice are confused" (ibid.). Harper did not deny that sexual intercourse between the races produced children, but he added that children born of white-black sexual contact had a new, slightly higher caste than their mothers. (He did not visualize free-born white women might have sexual contact with enslaved men.)

---

[19] Douglas R. Egerton, "Jefferson, Thomas, On African Americans and Slavery" in *Encyclopedia of African American History, 1619–1895: From the Colonial Period to the Age of Frederick Douglass*, ed. Paul Finkelman (*Oxford African American Studies Center*, http://www.oxfordaasc.com.proxy.library.vanderbilt. edu/article/opr/t0004/e0311 [accessed March 12, 2011]).

[20] William Harper, "Memoir on Slavery," in Faust, *The Ideology of Slavery*, 105.

Harper cleverly mixed admissions of these unfortunate facts with an inventive notion that the elevation of some requires the degradation of others. Slavery and its associated institutions "would indeed be intolerable in the sight of God and man if, condemning one portion of society to hopeless ignorance and comparative degradation, they should make no atonements—if, besides degraded slaves, there should be ignorant, ignoble, and degraded freemen" (ibid., 116). Many Southern authors defended slavery by appealing to Greek and Roman parallels; Harper invented a mechanical model to justify the institution. Because slaves were permanently inferior, their masters must compensate all the more. In other words, slavery makes (free, white, educated) men nobler, more selfless, more honorable, and more successful than they would otherwise be. The "wise governor" of the universe would not tolerate slavery, Harper asserted, if free, white, educated men did not manifest superior intellectual and moral development "to which we are called and incited by our situation" (ibid., 117).

Harper extended this defense of slavery and assigned similar elevated virtues to white, elite, somewhat-educated women. Just as their white brothers, fathers, and sons were necessarily elevated by being slave owners, so also were elite white women elevated above Northern and European women. He uses the same model of compensatory balance: "It would indeed be intolerable, if, when one class of society is necessarily degraded in this respect, no compensation were made by the superior elevation and purity of the other" (ibid., 119). Harper's inventive solution rests upon five assertions:

- God governs the universe justly and seeks "balance."
- God permits American slavery to persist.
- Slavery is an admitted evil, or at least an unfortunate fact of American life.
- To retain balance, God requires that slaveholders be of sufficient superiority that their virtues outweigh both the evils of slavery—such as they are—and the vices of the slaves, which are numerous.

- Southern elites manifest these elevated virtues; their men are nobler, their women are more refined than their Northern and European counterparts.

Therefore, Harper concluded, slavery ought to continue as long as Southern elites retain their elevated cultural standings, their morals, and their refinement.

This inventive mechanism does three things. First, it paints a flattering portrait of Southern gentility. They who controlled the government, education, religion, publishing, and all other forms of power—including physical violence—were, Harper preached, made noble by their station and their actions. Second, it calls upon God as a witness for slavery arguing that by not destroying it, God sanctions it. Third, it assuages Southern guilt over the misery that slavery brought to millions. Without the misery of slaves (not worse, Harper claims, than that imposed on Northern millworkers) the greatness of Southern character could not emerge.

Thomas Dew: Slavery as a Positive Good

Adoration of the cultural goods of leisure and contemplation that slavery affords provided the glue for Dew's invention of the concept of "slavery as a positive good." "Aristotle, and the great men of antiquity, believed slavery necessary to keep alive the spirit of freedom."[21] Assertions that slave owners were, somehow, more humane than non-slave owners makes it puzzling that they would be terrified that their interactions with their charges might lead the latter to join roving bands of murderers intent upon their destruction. Dew attempted to address this conundrum by another round of applause such as: "We have no hesitation in affirming, that throughout the whole slave-holding country, the slaves of a good master are his warmest, most constant, and most devoted friends. . . ."[22] Dew declared that these close, faithful, obedient, and trusting relationships were poisoned by

---

[21] Dew, *Review of the Debate in the Virginia Legislature*, 112.
[22] Ibid., 110.

the "imprudent philanthropist" who interfered with this feudal order. These misguided persons give ideas to slaves, such as liberty, that render "the slave more intractable and unhappy."

Dew didn't address the question of why simpleminded, loving servants (slaves) would find abstract ideas offered by imprudent philanthropists of any interest when compared with the direct, concrete goods offered by masters. Nor did he question whether Africans could attend to foreign abstractions such as "liberty." However, thanks to slavery, he and others—white, rising bourgeoisie scholars—could exploit the time and comforts that slavery afforded them to lead lives devoted to the mind.

Dew and other Southern intellectuals sought to align themselves with Edmund Burke and other principled conservative Europeans who defended the ancient institutions of ordered classes, kingship, and commerce. Thus, when criticizing antislavery preachers and other imprudent philanthropists, Dew cited lines from Burke's *Reflections on the French Revolution* regarding mixing religious with political thought: "No sound ought to be heard in the church but the healing voice of Christian charity. The cause of civil liberty and civil government gains as little as that of religion by this confusion of duties."[23]

By citing Burke, who was universally admired, Dew insinuated that Burke shared Dew's opinion that antislavery preachers were imprudent and dangerous mischief-makers. This is precisely false. Burke was responding to a sermon delivered on November 4, 1789, by Dr. Richard Price, a mathematician and friend of the American Revolution. Price, a dissenting minister (later Unitarian) who preached against inherited monarchy, supported aspects of the French Revolution. Price's opinions about English government infuriated Burke. Burke did not favor American slavery; on the contrary he proposed a general plan of gradual abolition in his essay, "Sketch of the Negro Code." In Burke's words: "If the African Trade could be considered with regard to itself only, and as a single

---

[23] From Edmund Burke, *Reflections on the French Revolution* (Harvard Classics), 1909–14, para. 19.

object, I should think the utter abolition to be, on the whole, more advisable, than any scheme of regulation and reform. Rather than suffer it to continue as it is, I heartily wish it at an end."[24] He followed this with an eloquent attack upon the institution of slavery, because "the principles of true religion and morality, and to the rules of sound policy, [require us] to put an end to all traffick in the persons of men, and to the detention of their said persons in a state of slavery, as soon as the same may be effected without producing great inconveniences in the sudden change of practices of such long standing."[25]

Burke's "Code" contains some 7,832 words—all seemingly used to show how England might best undo the slave trade and slavery in all its dominions over time and with the least chance of chaos and political catastrophe.

Scientific Arguments: *De Bow's Review*

Harper's lengthy defense of slavery appeared in installments of *De Bow's Review*, edited by J. D. B. De Bow and published continuously in New Orleans between 1846 and 1884 except during the war years of 1862–1864. (De Bow has different spellings.) The *Review* was widely read in the South and was widely respected. Combining studies of population, economics, literature, history, geology, and the natural sciences, the *Review* also presented sophisticated analysis of topics relevant to educated elite Southern readers.

In the issue where part 3 of Harper's memoir appeared, its editors announced their common hopes:

Fellow-citizens, the age in which we live is one of great achievements in arts and sciences and in human progress. The nations of the world are engaged in the great race for position and for empire. It becomes our

---

[24] A Letter to the Right Hon. Henry Dundas, One of His Majesty's Principal Secretaries of State. [With the Sketch of a Negro Code] Easter–Monday Night [April 9], 1792. http://www.econlib.org/library/LFBooks/Burke/brkSWv4c7.html.
[25] Ibid.

country to aim high, and to realize as soon as may be that bright and glorious destiny for which God and nature seem to have reserved her.[26]

A typical table of contents is this from volume 20, issue: 3, March 1856. (The articles are enumerated here.).

1. Slavery in the Virginia Legislature of 1831–'32, Part III— Emancipation without Deportation
2. The Black Race in North America, No. III
3. Medical Topography of Florida, No. IV
4. Tropical Agriculture, Book II
5. Southern Convention at Richmond—Its Objects
6. Lumber and Naval Store Commerce of Alabama
7. Our Policy with the Indian Tribes
8. The National Post Office—Its Expenditures and Revenue
9. Where Does the South Stand?
10. The Army and the War Department
11. Our Controversies with England
12. State Aid to Railroads
13. University of Virginia—Statistics
14. University of North Carolina
15. The Loss of Our Trade with the North
16. Accidents by Railroads and Steamboats, and Losses by Fire, during the Year 1855
17. National Agricultural Society; List of Officers for 1856

Items 1, 2, 9, and 15 pertain to slavery, politics, and economic difficulties with Northern cities. The remaining thirteen items are studies of outcome measures, higher education, governmental policy, and economic development. All seventeen items share a rational and scientific tone. While tendentious and highly rhetorical, except in rare cases articles in the *Review* are scholarly and written to high standards of exposition. However, if one wished to believe in the inherent right to

---

[26] 1850, vol. 50, no. 3, 232.

own slaves, the *Review* offered a steady flow of discourses on the alleged inferiority of Africans, the value of slavery for the slaves themselves, and the history of American slavery that proved that the South had no special sins.

For example, in "The Origin, Progress and Prospects of Slavery," published in 1850, the editors recount their version of the history of slavery in the United States, examine United States census data from 1790 to 1840, and argue that "no State, or class of States, can be more responsible than another, for the introduction and extension of the institution of slavery in the Union."[27] Thus, Southern states are not responsible for the existence of slavery and have but little "responsibility for its continuance" (ibid., 15).

The latter sentence is false, of course. Southern states shaped the proslavery Constitution of 1787 and dominated the federal government up to 1860. The authors review the history of slavery in the ancient world, among Jews, and in the New World, among American Indians, Queen Elizabeth, and Yankees. Because those illustrious persons owned slaves it is unfair to criticize Southern owners. Suffering from severe amnesia, they end with a lament: "It is well known how the introduction of slavery was forced upon the South, and how long resisted" (ibid., 19).

The editors of *De Bow's Review* are more effective when they cite contemporary authorities on natural science and anthropology. There they need not falsify the historical record. Instead, they could draw upon scientists who seemed to demonstrate that the human race is not a unity and that we are not all of one common human family. As they argued in one article, the human race is diverse: "Now we begin to talk of races—their physical and psychical qualities—their fitness for certain forms of government—their capacities for moral and intellectual culture—their true positions in the social scale, &c."[28] By sifting through contending authorities on the unity of human beings, they argued that current evidence does not support a common human origin and therefore does not

---

[27] 1850, vol. 9, no. 1, 15.
[28] 1850, vol. 10, no. 2, 114.

support the ethical arguments made for the political and ethical equality of white and black persons. Of special importance is their attack on the criterion of interracial fertility.

Authors like professor John Bachman, who favored the idea of a single human race, held that because "all the races of mankind produce with each other fertile progeny... constitutes one of most powerful and undeniable arguments in favor of the unity of the races."[29] After some legalist parsing and personal attacks on Bachman, the authors asserted that human races do not lose their typical features, even after living for thousands of years in diverse environments. (They hold that Jews constitute a different race as well.) Those like professor Bachman who argued for the unity of the races speculated about a process that took many thousands of years. The *Review* authors dismissed Bachman's thoughts on the grounds that such speculations required life to have arisen in diverse parts of the world at the same time. And, the editors affirm, since the Book of Genesis says this is impossible, and Genesis is the revealed Word of God, Professor Bachman was wrong.

But, while Bachman held that human beings were of one race, he was not an enemy of slavery. On the contrary, Bachman held that rightly understood, Christian scriptures were compatible with the natural sciences, including anthropology. The Holy Scriptures recognized the permanent inferiority of Africans and for that reason enjoined masters to be kind:

> The fact that nature has stamped on the African race the permanent marks of inferiority—that we are taught by their whole past history the lesson of their incapacity for self-government, and the Scriptures point out the duties both of masters and servants, should be sufficient to dispel every improper motive in an unbiased search after truth alone.[30]

---

[29] Ibid., 122, citing John Bachman, *The Doctrine of the Unity of the Human Race Examined on the Principles of Science* (Charleston, SC: C. Canning, 1850), 119. LC control no. 05029882)

[30] John Bachman, *The Doctrine of the Unity of the Human Race Examined on the Principles of Science* (Charleston, SC: C. Canning, 1850), 8.

The editors of the *Review* attacked Bachman because in their minds if he were correct about the unity of the races, abolitionists gained leverage. Central to the abolitionists' argument was that because human beings are essentially alike and derive from a common family, they share an ethical unity. The striking motto of the English antislavery movement asked: "Am I not a man and a brother?" If we answer in the affirmative, it becomes difficult to champion slavery. While Bachman the theologian affirmed proslavery theology, Bachman the scientist undermined the scientific pretensions upon which the editors of the *Review* rested. For that offense the editors admonished him.

In the same vein the author of "Hybrid Races of Animals and Men," another article in the *Review*, argued that epidemiological evidence about the longevity of colored persons in Boston and other parts of New England suggests a decay among mixed-race persons: "It seems to me one of the necessary consequences of attempts to mix races—the hybrids cease to be prolific; the race must die out as mulatto; it must either keep black unmixed, or become extinct."[31]

In response to abolitionist efforts, the editors of the *Review* enthusiastically reviewed *Negro Mania*, a 549-page book by John Campbell. Campbell excerpted and republished many anti-black essays and added his own flavor of derision and contempt for Africans. The *Review* editors praised the book "as a necessary portion of the library of the statesman and scholar, giving, as it does, in a condensed form, the main points of an interesting study."[32] It was necessary as a source of arguments against human equality and therefore against emancipation at any time. Campbell cited James Cowles Prichard, a noted ethnologist, regarding physical and therefore spiritual and mental differences between whites and blacks. Like that of many scientific racial theorists, Prichard's research was designed to prove a thesis, the

---

[31] Unsigned. *De Bow's Review* 19, no. 5 (1855): 538.

[32] "Equality of the Races—Negro Mania," *De Bow's Review* 11, no. 6, (1851): 630–34. Review of John Campbell, *Negro Mania: Being An Examination of the Falsely Assumed Equality of the Various Races of Men* (Philadelphia: Campbell & Power, 1851).

inferiority of blacks. His title announces his thesis: "On the Extinction of some Varieties of the Human Race" (1839).

The editors of the *Review* were so impressed by Campbell's book they returned to it a year later and devoted more than ten thousand words to it. It was, they said, "a work of which it would be difficult to show all the merits in a review, for almost every line and word of it deserves to be paused upon."[33] It establishes as incontrovertible the fact that the different races are wholly distinctive, with differences that are "inalienable and unchangeable" (ibid., 508). For that reason the abolitionists' efforts to assert equality of black with white are "opposing the beautiful order of God's developed thought in creation" (ibid., 509).

Without slavery and its institutions the white and black races will comingle: "Abolition is the extinction of the one or the other" (ibid., 512). Without slavery and its enforcement regimens, civilized Americans will disappear and with them the dream of an American empire. The editors then excerpted whole sections from *Negro Mania* about black inferiority, and so forth. An odd feature of the *Review*, and of Campbell's book, is this persistent citation and recitation of the same slanders against blacks of all regions and all time periods. The mania that emerges in *Negro Mania* is the compulsion to proclaim continuously that blacks are radically, wholly, and permanently unlike whites—that even their hair is unlike the hair of white people. While the Egyptians are acknowledged to have created a great civilization by Campbell, he and the authorities he cites insist that Egyptians were not black but a mix of red and yellow race (to use Campbell's categories). Their hair proves it: "The hair of the Egyptians resembled in texture that of the fairest Europeans of the present day" (ibid., 515). Three years after this long article the *Review* editors published a note, "White Hair and Negro Wool" that described a Dr. Gibbs's comparison of hair from blacks, whites, and mulattoes.[34]

While the editors often evoked the Bible as an authority superior

---

[33] "Equality of the Races—Negro Mania," *De Bow's Review* 12, no. 5 (1852): 507.

[34] *De Bow's Review* 18, no. 1 (1855): 52.

to all others, they faced the danger that both the Hebrew Bible and the New Testament claim a singular creation for all human beings and a universal ethic of brotherly love. These theological principles animated—and many argued, justified—the religious rejection of slavery. To retain both their Christian identity and to defend slavery, the planters and their advocates needed theological rejoinders.

Theological Arguments

While Burke cited both religion and morality in his critique of slavery, Dew was not wrong to claim that one could be both Christian and a slaveholder. The struggle between abolitionists and proslavery authors turns not on the narrow basis of Christian (or Jewish) theology but on the presence or absence of empathy. Indeed, the arguments adduced by Southern theologians about the Bible's indifference to slavery are somewhat persuasive. Christian history and Christian scripture do not show Christian abhorrence of slavery. Christian doctrines derived from revelation, such as Resurrection, Immortality, and such, do not offer immediate grounds for rejecting slavery.

Many Christians, especially Quakers, found in their reading of the Bible grounds for pursuing abolition. While it took Southern Quakers longer to affirm this conclusion than it did those in the North, they did eventually join their Northern coreligionists. However, their rejection stems from an empathic solidarity with slaves as persons. While Quakers cited Jesus as a model of love and understanding, they could not deny that Jesus tolerated slavery and that Christian theologians provided no unequivocal support for abolition. Proslavery Christians could demonstrate that their religion did not require them to challenge the institution. Indeed, if one affirms the theological notion of eternal life gained only through baptism in a Christian church, then by bringing Christian doctrines to Africans, slaveholders did them an infinite service. After a life of work, Christianized slaves would receive eternal life in heaven while their African relatives suffered in hell or oblivion.

Empathy is an immediate perception and experience of connection between self and other; it is horizontal, one might say. Empathy is not derived from intellectual doctrines imposed upon one from above. Among the latter are theological constructs, such as the Christian doctrines of resurrection and eternal life. By definition, these point to realities beyond anyone's immediate experience. Gifted preachers might engender enthusiastic feelings about these possibilities, but they could not engender empathic understanding, unless they themselves had returned from the grave.

Another similar religious doctrine is the proclamation that a text, such as the Bible or the Qur'an, is divinely inspired and thus free from actual contradiction or limitation. Empathy is about this world, not the next. Hence, a divine text cannot evoke empathic recognition. If we stumble or find fault with the Bible, the source of error is within us, within our limitations, sinfulness, and incompleteness. A divine text requires authoritative interpreters, and both text and interpreters must be seen as superior to ordinary individuals and ordinary readers. Doctrines derive not from this world but from another world and thus they require ritual protection, ideally administered through political power, for their proper defense and elucidation.

Regarding the ethics of Christian slavery, Dew agreed that it appeared troublesome: "It is said slavery is wrong, in the abstract at least, and contrary to the spirit of Christianity."[35] And, "With regard to the assertion that slavery is against the spirit of Christianity, we are ready to admit the general assertion."[36] In response, Dew adduced a series of historical claims and unspoken assumptions that portray slavery as tolerable and—all things considered—the best solution to a bad circumstance. Taken together, these assertions, innuendoes, and slivers of facts was an invention. Using it, Dew resolved the problem of "Christian slavery" by celebrating Christian masters who brought African heathens to know Christ and so gain eternal life.

First, Dew argued that the Jews countenanced slavery, and Jesus

---

[35] Dew quoted in Ronald F. Reid and James F. Klumpp, *American Rhetorical Discourse*, 3rd ed. (Long Grove, IL: Waveland Press, 2004), 92. (Emphasis in original.)
[36] Ibid., 293.

and the Apostle Paul did not interfere with Roman slavery or any other earthly powers. He implied that by not attacking the institution, Jesus and Paul therefore sanctioned it two thousand years ago and would, somehow, sanction it in 1832, in republican America. This is persuasive if one believes that Jesus set the exemplar for all time and all institutions; that Roman law, for example regarding crucifixion for many offenses, ought to be respected for all time. Another point of Roman law of the classical period proscribed that if a master were murdered in his house by one of his servants or "even by an unknown assassin, all the slaves who were in the house at the time of the killing could be put to death."[37]

Both Jesus and Paul were Jewish preachers who teetered on the edge of respectability among their own people; it would have been disastrous to confront the Roman state and assail one of its core institutions. Indeed, both men were executed by the Roman state for far lesser crimes, as John the Baptist had been. Their crimes were advocating religious beliefs inimical to Roman politicians; they did not murder Roman citizens. Later, when Christians gained political power they did undo the barbarity of numerous Roman laws, among them crucifixion and gladiatorial combat.[38]

Some authorities argue that Stoic ethical reflection, such as Seneca's discussion in Moral Letters (No. 47) had more influence on moderating the treatment of slaves than did Christian teachings.[39] The strongest argument against slavery seems to derive not from transcendental teachings per se, but from an empathic engagement with slaves as persons. Seneca, a famous stoic philosopher and Roman politician (1 BCE–65 CE), berated slave owners whose immaturity made them enslaved to their passions, lusts, and fears.[40] Seneca said these

---

[37] George Mousourakis, *The Historical and Institutional Context of Roman Law* (Aldershot, England: Ashgate, 2003), 163n.32.

[38] Ibid., 378.

[39] Gad Heuman and Trevor Burnard, eds., *The Routledge History of Slavery* (London: Routledge 2010), 31–32.

[40] *Seneca: Ad Luclium, Epistulae Morales.* Trans. Richard M. Gummere (London:

slave owners used slaves to provide them ever greater gustatory, sexual, and diverse erotic pleasures: "With slaves like these the master cannot bear to dine; he would think it beneath his dignity to associate with his slave at the same table" (ibid., 305). However, he emphasized, "Because fortune can reward some and punish others, prudent persons do not assume that they will always be masters. Many free-born men have become slaves; you can also: 'Treat your inferiors as you would be treated by your betters'" (ibid., 307). We should value all persons, free born and slave, "according to their character, and not according to their duties" (ibid., 309).

The Apostle Paul might have confronted slavery, but he also avoided challenging the rights of owners. In his letter to Philemon, an affluent supporter of the Christian movement, Paul addressed slavery cautiously. Both antislavery and proslavery advocates found elements in this letter that seemed to support their position. The core of the letter is a petition to Philemon, a rich and powerful patron, to forgive his runaway slave, to see him as a brother, and to treat him accordingly.

As many learned Southern preachers argued, the Bible also does not show Jesus rebuking any slave masters: "Did he never give them to understand that, if they would be his disciples, they must set their slaves at liberty? No, Brethren, nothing of the kind occurs in his whole history.... He sought to reform the hearts and lives of men, and to fit them for Heaven; not to change their relative condition on earth."[41] However plausible this may be as church history, it does not address the ethical conflicts of American slaveholders. Being Christians, they received the Great Commission: "And Jesus came and

---

Heinemann, 1918), 301–13. http://www.archive.org/details/adluciliume pistu01 seneuoft. Seneca's biography remains contested, but his values are not. See Anna Lydia Motto, "Seneca on Trial: The Case of the Opulent Stoic," *The Classical Journal* 61, no. 6 (March 1966): 254–58.

[41] "Excerpts from George Freeman's The Rights and Duties of Slaveholders: Two Discourses Delivered on Sunday, November 27, 1836, in Christ Church, Raleigh, North-Carolina (1837). http://www.assumption.edu/users/lknoles /douglassproslaveryargs.html.

spake unto them, saying, All power is given unto me in heaven and in earth. Go ye therefore, and teach all nations, baptizing them in the name of the Father, and of the Son, and of the Holy Ghost." A version of this commandment, which is at the center of Protestant evangelical thought, appears at least five times in the New Testament.[42]

Obeying this commandment, some Southern and many Northern clergy excoriated the ways in which owners refused to preach the full Christian story to their slaves. Freehling cites the story of Francis Goulding, a young slaveholder, keen to bring Christian teachings to his slaves: "At first Goulding used pictures to illustrate key Biblical phrases. But the community, realizing that illustrated texts were used in teaching infants to read, soon demanded that other means be employed."[43] In response, Goulding gave scriptural passages to slave owners, which they were to read out loud to their slaves. However, slaves memorized the oral passages and connected them to written words, that is, they learned to read. Reading brought education and education brought power and with power slaves could mount resistance and rebellion. Even half-verbal, half-hallelujah exhortations by fervent preachers were dangerous because preachers tended to persuade slave listeners rather than to command them. This raised the grave danger that the preacher, and by extension other instructors, risked obscuring the clarity of absolute control unsullied by persuasion: "efficient slave management required the complete supremacy of the plantation supervisor."[44] To seek to persuade slaves meant that you respected their minds. To persuade is to acknowledge that the other has some degree of choice. To seek to persuade slaves is to affirm them as actors, as agents with internal worlds over which they had autonomy. Slavery depends upon terror, and terror does not abide autonomous subjects.

---

[42] Matthew 28:18–19. See also Mark 16:14–18; Luke 24:44–49; Acts 1:4–8; John 20:19–23.

[43] Freehling, *Prelude to Civil War: the Nullification Controversy in South Carolina, 1816-1836*, 74.

[44] Ibid., 76.

In Favor of Slavery: the Positive Good

Dew acknowledged that while slavery seemed un-Christian, its persistence is, on the whole, a positive good for both slaves and owners, and it cannot be abolished without certain disaster. He affirmed that slaves were property, at least one-half of the wealth of Virginia, and that as such they could not be freed without economic and social catastrophes.[45] The progress of some required the progress of all, but in the end the natural difference between the races would assert itself.[46] Freedom was, Dew and his followers argued, a great and natural good, but it could be won by and secured only by elites positioned in a natural hierarchy of master and servant, owner and slave.

Dew aligned himself with Athenian intellectuals of the classical Greece who also depended upon hordes of slaves. By celebrating Athens and idealizing the classical period, owners mirrored the ruling classes of Britain who fostered similar identifications of themselves with the great names of Greek and Roman antiquity. According to Freehling, "The planters' political ideal was the [English] House of Lords rather than the halls of Congress, and their political assumptions derived from the elitest cult of the English country gentry."[47]

Eugene Genovese, initially an avowed Marxist and later a Catholic historian, articulated Dew's analysis of the dilemma of increased

---

[45] Thomas Roderick Dew, "Abolition of Negro Slavery," *American Quarterly Review* 12 (1832): 189-265. Reprinted Thomas Dew, *Review of the Debate [on the abolition of Slavery] in the Virginia legislature of 1831 and 1832* (Richmond, VA: T. W. White, 1832). "We hope sincerely, that the intelligent sons of Virginia will ponder well before they move—before they enter into a scheme which will destroy more than half of Virginia's wealth" (ibid., 131).

[46] Ibid.

[47] Freehling, *Prelude to Civil War: the Nullification Controversy in South Carolina,* 89. By avoiding democratic practices, they retained power, as legislators, to appoint "all other state officials, from the governor to tax collectors, as well as United States senators and presidential electors" (ibid., 89–90).

freedom: that with it came the rise of free labor and the passion of its members for increased access to power and control.[48] This would lead, inevitably, Dew argued, to the dissolution of coherent government since, in his view, a coherent government required strict class divisions and rule by the elite not by the masses. Freeing American slaves would bring hordes of new citizens clamoring for their rights. That would impinge upon the rule of elites and produce atrocities against the ruling classes witnessed in the Terror that followed the French Revolution. In this way, freed slaves would "provoke anarchy and deprive the propertied classes of their power to rule."[49]

Dew could not affirm Jefferson's universalism. Proslavery inventions required one to deny continuity between the highest and the lowest persons. Antislavery theologians could argue the Jewish-Christian teachings required one to affirm a common human family. As the motto of the English antislavery league put it, "Are slaves not our brothers?" Proslavery theologians, however, could call upon religious texts and historical traditions that buttressed hierarchy: For did not God place husbands at the head of the family? So too, masters were ordained to rule (benevolently) those slaves who were among their children.

While Jefferson the man led a divided personal life, Jefferson the thinker remains undivided: human being forms a unity, a single, common species. That the man could not live up to his ideals does not invalidate the thinker. The latter truth produces trenchant and irrefutable arguments against slavery. For that reason, as with Calhoun, Dew and other apologists attacked Jefferson, a great son of Virginia, in order to make their invention work.

George Fitzhugh, a self-taught lawyer in Virginia, asserted in 1857 that because of its peculiar institutions and its unique history, the South needed to create its own literature, separate and distinct from those of Europe and the North.[50] For the latter seeded ideas and doctrines "at

---

[48] Genovese, *The Slaveholders' Dilemma*.

[49] Ibid., 160.

[50] George Fitzhugh, "Southern Thought," in Faust, *The Ideology of Slavery*, 272–99.

war with slavery, without expressly assailing the institution" (ibid., 278–79). Fitzhugh concluded all books in the moral sciences, if not written by proslavery men, are, by definition, dangerous for they "inculcate abolition either directly or indirectly" (ibid., 279). Even if these books were written by earlier Southern writers, they are likely to be "as dangerous as the Declaration of Independence, or the Virginia Bill of rights" (ibid., 279). The latter two documents are, of course, among Jefferson's legacies.[51]

Dew and other inventive defenders of slavery did not pretend that they could be both sons of Virginia, emulators of Jefferson and also defenders of perpetual slavery. Having staked their reputations upon the defense of slavery through every logical means available, they went all in. If being consistent required them to reject Jefferson's greatest legacies they did so directly. That freedom-loving Americans owned slaves was not, as they saw it, a contradiction or a paradox. It was a puzzle that their lengthy essays on anthropology and American history had resolved. They did not split their minds into separate divisions. That is the third option as we see in the next chapter.

---

[51] See also Mason I. Lowance, *A House Divided: The Antebellum Slavery Debates In America, 1776-1865* (Princeton: Princeton University Press, 2003). For a typical sermon that draws on the same arguments, see "Excerpts from George Freeman's The Rights and Duties of Slaveholders: Two Discourses Delivered on Sunday, November 27, 1836, in Christ Church, Raleigh, North-Carolina (1837). Freeman's text is Colossians 4:1: "Masters give unto your servants that which is just and equal, knowing that ye also have a master in heaven." Web version: http://www.assumption.edu/users /lknoles/douglassproslaveryargs.html.

PART THREE

CHAPTER 6

Response to Contradiction: Splitting

A third response to the problems posed by a contradiction is to affirm both of its propositions but at different times. The short name for this maneuver is *splitting*. The benefits of splitting are substantial: we are spared mental anguish and we can affirm either proposition when it suits us. On some occasions it is attractive to affirm one side; at others it is attractive to affirm the other side. Life is full of conflicts that require immediate choice. We do not enjoy the luxury of the philosophers who can puzzle over philosophical paradoxes. Pacifists who examine the morality of the death penalty, for example, hear two contradictory commands: defend life at all costs and defend freedom from terror and crime at all costs. In these circumstances splitting one's thoughts and feelings into two separate domains solves the dilemma. When facing the choice to either join the armed forces—and contemplate killing human beings—or to not join the battle against a dangerous enemy, pacifists face a crisis of conscience. Some remain true to their convictions: they do not split their minds and feelings into two regions, and they refuse to serve in wartime. If drafted they face prosecution and jail in the United States, jail and execution in some other nations. Others use some version of splitting: in one part of their minds they affirm the absolute requirement to not kill; in another part of their minds they affirm the absolute need to defend their families and nation.

Christian slaveholders did the same thing: in one part of their minds they affirmed their Christian identity; in another they affirmed the naturalness of perpetual bondage. To keep these contradictions from colliding within themselves they shored up the barriers between these divided parts of themselves. In church they felt passionately tied to Christian teachings. With each sermon, hymn, and prayer they affirmed their self-understanding as persons of God and bearers of Christ's teachings. This was their public face and their private self-portrait. Both were, however, in contradiction to the way they made their money and secured their fortunes: by owning the labor, bodies, and minds of other human beings. It is impossible both to love the poor, such as slaves bereft of everything, and to profit by their suffering at the same moment and in the same psychic space. Owners split their psychic space, their minds, into compartments: one labeled *Christian*, the other labeled *Master*. On Sundays owners luxuriated in their Christian identity, on all the other days they enjoyed the fruits of tyranny. While splitting is effective, it is not perfect. Every so often—through doubts, dreams, and moments of insight—people sense something wrong with this maneuver since the mind aims at unity, at knowing who we are fully. We yearn to be connected to our complete experience.

Within political groups splitting is common, if not universal. In small-scale groups, such as tribes, splitting produces witchcraft beliefs and various forms of witch hunts and witch killing. What our society calls *murder*, these societies call cleansing—evil ideas and people who carry them are destroyed, the social threat is eliminated, and social cohesion improves.[1]

---

[1] "One of the most important factors tribal members take into account in deciding whether a given act is deviant is how it affects other people." Robert A. Scott "Deviance, Sanctions, and Social Integration in Small-Scale Societies," *Social Forces* 54, no. 3 (1976): 610. If an act neither harms another person nor disrupts social relationships it is not deviant.

While different groups use different words to name witchcraft (such as sorcery, black magic, the evil eye, and such), they share a common belief: "evil thoughts" that appear in our minds are products of other minds that wish us harm.[2] Because there are no such things as demons, ghosts, the evil eye and other malevolent spirits, this common belief cannot be correct. Many people do evil things but that does not prove that they are possessed by evil spirits. On the contrary, the allure of witchcraft beliefs stems from splitting: we deny the all-too human origin of these evil actions. If one does not affirm belief in witchcraft, then we must affirm its opposite; that evil thoughts are within persons, within their minds. This leads to an even more distressing thought: we too might harbor evil thoughts and wishes. If the "evil" is within me how can I escape it? By splitting off our recognition that all persons are capable of evil thoughts and evil deeds, we safeguard ourselves from this distress. They, not we, are capable of terrible actions. In large-scale traditional groups, splitting is the mechanism by which religious and political leaders ascribe "evil" impulses to the devil or other imaginary beings. These non-self beings invade us; they infiltrate our minds against our will. They cannot be removed without spiritual warfare. Because splitting is a universal form of thinking, savvy political leaders use it when necessary to advance their agendas. In this sense, many politicians are canny. They recognize their subjects' anxieties and then exploit them to increase panic, anxiety, and regression to primitive solutions. As in cases of violence done against slaves, atrocious acts upon the body, especially skin and the genitals, rouse feelings that make reasoning—and therefore legal and ethical thinking—impossible. D. W. Griffith used these devices in *The Birth of a Nation*: once we believe that violence done against naked white flesh is actual, we feel a version of it within ourselves. Before cinema, rhetoricians had only words and metaphors; after cinema they had new, more powerful ways to induce ecstatic feelings, to shape conviction, to rouse action, and to

---

[2] P. J. Stewart and A. Strathern, *Witchcraft, Sorcery, Rumors and Gossip* (Cambridge, UK: Cambridge University Press, 2004)

diminish reflection.[3] Griffith's melodrama does not translate complicated problems from words to pictures; it simplified them into a
(literally) black-white story of evil (a rapacious black man) and good
(a noble white man who avenges the murder of his innocent white
sister.)

These devices are available to all people in all cultures in all
epochs. They are not distinct or confined to apologists for American
slavery. We find the same rhetorical devices in the Spanish Inquisition (the sixteenth century), in *Mein Kampf* (Adolph Hitler's
twentieth-century autobiography), and South African apartheid laws
(mid-twentieth century). They also appear in the speeches of many
Southern US politicians from 1780 to current times. These appeals to
group solidarity and to a mythic past are identical. In each instance, a
dominant group fears annihilation of its way of life and its identity
(or at least manufactures those anxieties in its subjects). The group's
leaders confront a contradiction: our deathless, indestructible, and
blessed group faces destruction. How could this happen when God
himself has decreed our way of life to be sacred and eternal? If God
be for us, as we are assured, who can be against us? The answer is only
evil persons operating in secret.

Spanish Inquisition: an Early Example

The Spanish Inquisition was established by King Ferdinand II of Ara-
gon and his wife Isabella I of Castile in 1478. Its mission was to
investigate heresies and to examine the loyalty of all those professing
to be Christians, especially former Jews who had converted to Christianity under threat of death in the previous one hundred or so years.

---

[3] "In *Birth*, as in *Intolerance* (1916), *Broken Blossoms* (1919), and *Way Down
East* (1922), Griffith defined the basic components of the melodramatic
modern movie: a light realistic touch combined with unfathomable pathos.
No genre is better able to translate myriad complicated and ultimately irre-
solvable problems into the chaotic swirl typical of personal relations." M.
Wallace, "The Good Lynching and *The Birth of a Nation*: Discourses and
Aesthetics of Jim Crow," *Cinema Journal* 43, no.1 (2003): 88.

So intense were these concerns about Jews and Muslims that the king issued decrees in 1492 and 1501 ordering them to convert or leave Spain. Adding, it appears, to the motives for these mass expulsions were anxieties about converted Jews who had attained significant political and economic power. Although in the popular press and movies the Spanish Inquisition appears to be unique, it was not. Other European powers, notably those associated with regions now identified as Italy and Portugal, established inquisitions in their own nations and in their colonies.[4]

Spanish Inquisition authorities ascribed evil acts to Marranos, Christians who had converted from Judaism.[5] Among their alleged crimes were secret plans to claim Christian identity, then work against "real" Christians and enslave them under Jewish dominion. The accusers' reasoning was that "those of them who asked to be baptized to Christianity were under no compulsion to do so; and thus they did it of their own free choice."[6] While making these charges, Spanish authorities had to deny that they had used intimidation and terror to force earlier conversions. For if they agreed to the historical facts—that thousands of Jews were violently deprived of their religious identity—the accusers could not also claim that the Marranos had voluntarily feigned conversion in order to sabotage Christians. For the conspiracy allegations to be plausible, the accusers had to argue that converts voluntarily made false conversions—that they *chose* to convert to Christianity. To account for the presence of former Jews among Spanish Christians they concluded that evil deeds had been performed.

---

[4] Robin Vose, "Beyond Spain: Inquisition History in a Global Context," *History Compass* 11, no. 4 (2013): 316–29. The Inquisition "was something of a global phenomenon by the end of the 16th century. Modern research has begun to show just how true this was, though still for the most part in piecemeal and unsystematic fashion and with serious gaps remaining all too evident" (ibid., 322).

[5] Benzion Netanyahu, *The Origins of the Inquisition In Fifteenth Century Spain* (New York: Random House, 1995).

[6] Ibid., 943.

In this way, an original act of splitting "real Spaniards" from "false Spaniards" developed into splitting "real Christians" from "false Christians." This devolved into the assertion that between the latter were two types: Jews forced to convert by force (and thus false Christians) and converted Jews who secretly retained their Jewish identity and plotted against the authentic (Spanish) Christians. So, they were false Christians as well. The oddity of these conspiracy allegations is that even if there were such a group of diabolical Jews intent upon subverting Spanish Christianity, by converting they would have destroyed their deepest bonds with Judaism. They would forfeit their authentic Jewish identity: "no Jew could be considered *faithful to the Law* and its *voluntary violator* at one and the same time."[7]

When examined logically, these Spanish authorities' accusations crumble unless one uses occult categories as explanations. That the Spanish authorities used such categories does not, again, prove that they believed what they said. Because splitting is ubiquitous and alluring, clever politicians have long employed it in their public appeals.[8]

Hitler and *Mein Kampf*

A similar move occurred in *Mein Kampf*, published in 1925, when Adolph Hitler described a contradiction: Aryans are superior to Jews, as the lion is superior to the rabbit, yet inferior Jews have trumped superior Aryans. Jews, he pronounced, were weak, the group least likely to survive the inexorable laws of nature. Yet, Jews have persisted for thousands of years and continued to threaten Aryan-Germans in the twentieth century. How could inferior, mendacious people harm those inherently superior to them in everything that matters, especially

---

[7] Ibid.

[8] See, for example, Norman Roth, *Conversos, Inquisition, and the Expulsion of the Jews from Spain* (Madison, WI: University of Wisconsin Press, 2002). He notes that anti-Jewish authorities in Spain could draw upon a long tradition of bizarre and false allegations against Jews, such as Jews betrayed Toledo to the invading Muslims in 711 CE (ibid., 91).

manly authority? In Hitler's parlance, "The mightiest counterpart [meaning *antithesis*] to the Aryan is represented by the Jew."[9]

As in witchcraft allegations, only occult powers can explain this uncanny outcome. Like witches, Jews used hidden means to deceive their superior hosts and to carry out multigenerational conspiracies:

> As long as the Jew has not become the master of the other peoples, he must speak their languages whether he likes it or not, but as soon as they became his slaves, they would all have to learn a universal language (Esperanto, for instance!), so that by this additional means the Jews could more easily dominate them![10]

Nuances and distinctions appeal only to intellectuals, Hitler asserted. When a nation is at war, propaganda must be focused, one-sided, and relentless: "When the nations on this planet fight for existence—when the question of destiny, 'to be or not to be,' cries out for a solution—then all considerations of humanitarianism or aesthetics crumble into nothingness" (ibid., 177–78). In World War I, the English knew this truth; the Germans did not. Their ignorance, Hitler said, contributed to Germany's humiliating defeat in 1918. English propagandists played continuously upon the theme of the "bloody Hun," while German propagandists used parodies and careful arguments. English propagandists appealed to the basest emotions; German propagandists aspired to create works of art. In the spirit of producing more effective propaganda, Hitler offered this poster idea: "With satanic joy in his face, the black-haired Jewish youth lurks in wait for the unsuspecting girl whom he defiles with his blood, thus stealing her from her people" (ibid., 325).

---

[9] Ralph Manheim, trans., *Mein Kampf,* (1925/26, Boston: Houghton Mifflin, 1971), 300.

[10] Ibid.,307. "To what an extent the whole existence of this people is based on a continuous lie is shown incomparably by the *Protocols of the Wise Men of Zion*, so infinitely hated by the Jews." He adds, "They [the *Protocols*] are based on a forgery, the *Frankfurter Zeitung* moans and screams once every week: the best proof that they are authentic"(ibid.).

Taking his own advice, throughout *Mein Kampf* Hitler pursued a simple story: Jewish ideas and Jewish blood have conquered a sleeping people, the Aryans. This occult truth explained the catastrophes of World War I and Germany's political crises: all were caused by the poisoning of German blood by Jews, by the replacement of German values with Jewish values. (At one point Hitler calls Jews vampires). The myth of blood and race unifies *Mein Kampf* and presages the split world of German propaganda:

> Only by examining and comparing all other problems of life in the light of this one question shall we see how absurdly petty they are by this standard. They are all limited in time—but the question of preserving or not preserving the purity of the blood will endure as long as there are men. (ibid., 328)

Or, as Hitler says eleven pages later, "The racial question gives the key not only to world history, but to all human culture" (ibid., 339). Alternating with lurid rape scenes are Hitler's relentless diatribes against German intellectuals, especially those impressed by Marxism. To counter them, Hitler proclaimed that Jews are a distinctive race of persons, rooted in blood kinship, who seduced and cajoled otherwise stronger peoples to tolerate them. From positions of authority Jews will seek to conquer and rule. In trade unions, universities, the press, politics, public opinion, indeed all areas of power, Jews, he said, sought to subjugate their betters.

An even sharper statement appears in volume 2, chapter 2, "The State." There, Hitler returns to the priority of race and blood (of *volkish* essences) over mere ideas. Blood is everlasting and essential. Education, a common language, and common values are not permanent; they cannot unify a nation. That power lies only "in the blood, we would be justified in speaking of a Germanization if by such a process we succeeded in transforming the blood of the subjected people. But this is impossible" (ibid., 389). By his evil genius, Hitler fostered a massive act of splitting of German memories ("We lost the Great War") from German wishes ("We are invincible").[11]

---

[11] Regarding race laws in the Third Reich, see Wolfgang Benz, *A Concise*

Germans who imbibed Hitler's solution imbibed his contradiction—a weaker people had conquered them, the superior in every way. He knew that his followers needed a device with which to unite themselves. That device was splitting.

The Christian Origins of Apartheid: a More Recent Example

We find the same drive to split one group from another, to base this division on "race" in the creation of apartheid in South Africa after World War II. Hermann Giliomee says that architects of apartheid emerged from the Dutch Reformed Church[12] and others who studied American race laws promulgated after the Civil War during the Jim Crow era.[13] They combined their study with zealous efforts to preserve Afrikaner identity.[14] Afrikaners are white European residents of South Africa who trace their ancestry to either Dutch or German or other European nationalities. Because the Dutch colonized South Africa early

---

History of the Third Reich, trans. Thomas Dunlap. (University of California Press, 2006), 142–43. Regarding the concept of "defilement of the race" (*rassenschande*), see Frank Caestecker, and David Fraser "The Extraterritorial Application of the Nuremberg Laws. *Rassenschande* and "Mixed" Marriages in European Liberal Democracies," *Journal of the History of International Law,* vol. 10, no. 1, (2008): 47.

[12] Hermann Giliomee, "The Making of the Apartheid Plan, 1929–1948," *Journal of Southern African Studies* 29, no. 2 (June 2003): 373–92.

[13] See, for example, Susan Rennie Ritner, "The Dutch Reformed Church and Apartheid," *Journal of Contemporary History* 2, no. 4 (1967): 17–37. The Church "did not rest content with the traditional *baasskap* [boss-ship or domination] principles on which South Africa had been run since 1652—the simple, pragmatic acceptance of the superiority of the white man to the 'natives' he dwelt among. It is the Church that has insisted upon progressively sterner definitions of 'separateness,' ending up with" Apartheid (ibid., 17).

[14] The major influences on H. F. Verwoerd, the so-called architect of apartheid, were American social science, both psychology and sociology, and American race laws. See Roberta B. Miller, "Science and Society in the Early Career of HF Verwoerd." *Journal of Southern African Studies* 19, no. 4 (December 1993), 634–66.

in the seventeenth century, their language, their church—Dutch Reformed—and their institutions dominated political life until the English encroached on their territories in the late 1870s. After two bloody wars, the English won and Afrikaners (also known as Boers) were absorbed into the British Empire. That defeat long resonated in the minds and hearts of Afrikaners who immediately created legends, myths, and stories about the heroism of their ancestors and the vast injustices done to them. This tradition persisted in scholarly books by white South African authors who wrote volume upon volume of narratives describing the valor of (white) South Africans who settled South Africa.[15]

Supporting the latter was a claim to Christian identity that required them to preach the gospel to all South Africans, white, colored, and black. Nationalists proclaimed that their goals were lofty and inspired: to show blacks and coloreds that they too could enjoy separate but equal security in their homelands. Afrikaners would grant to blacks the same rights that they granted to themselves. In this imaginary (delusional) future, "Africans would have their own schools, churches, residential areas, homelands and governments on which they could put their own cultural imprint. . . . It was within the context of an emphasis on culture that the ideology of Christian-National education developed."[16]

Giliomee notes that the authors of apartheid recast their history into sacred stories that became objects of worship: their origins and their Christian identity. The flower of Afrikaner intelligentsia, including esteemed churchmen and professors, took part in this national plan of salvation. To construct a modern platform for postwar South Africa a commission "sent out a circular, inviting opinions, to all elected representatives of the party, all chairmen and secretaries of

---

[15] Shula Marks, "African and Afrikaner History," review of *The Oxford History of South Africa. I. South Africa to 1870; 500 Years; A History of South Africa. The Journal of African History* 11, no. 3 (1970).

[16] Hermann Giliomee, "The Making of the Apartheid Plan, 1929–1948," *Journal of Southern African Studies* 29, no. 2 (2003): 385.

the party's district councils, all 'well-disposed' Afrikaner lecturers at universities and other 'knowledgeable experts and interested persons'" (ibid., 390). Completed in 1947, the Nationalist Party used the commission's report in the 1948 elections which they won and after which they instituted full-scale apartheid.

Distinguished professors of mission studies helped shape these reports and added their authority to them: "To justify the rejection of 'equal rights and opportunities,' the report used terminology very similar to that first employed in the Dutch Reformed Church during the 1930s: 'It was decreed by God that diverse races and volke [people] should survive and grow naturally as part of a Divine plan'" (ibid., 390). Beleaguered by the British and outnumbered by black Africans, Afrikaners told themselves a story of heroic resistance and divine protection at Blood River:

> A historical highlight of Afrikaner history was the Covenant of December 9, 1838, when the Afrikaners begged God for a victory over their enemies. They promised to commemorate their hoped-for victory and to build a church. On December 16, led by Andries Pretorius, some 500 Afrikaners fought ten to twelve thousand Zulu warriors. The Afrikaners won without a man killed and 3,000 Zulu dead.[17]

Looking backward, twentieth-century nationalists made this battle a foundation of South African heritage: through it Christianity and civilization were preserved in Africa.

It is difficult to reconcile a Christian God with the slaughter of three thousand Zulus—by cannons and high-powered rifles that could fire every five seconds—trying to protect their traditional lands against invaders.[18] Not content with mere narration, Afrikaner leaders under-

---

[17] Jack R. Van Der Slik, review of Hermann Giliomee, *The Afrikaners: Biography of a People* (Charlottesville, VA: University of Virginia Press, 2003). http://www.dordt.edu/publications/pro_rege/crcpi/115679.pdf.

[18] See S. P. Mackenzie. *A Revisionist Approach* (New York: Routledge, 1997), 75ff.

scored the validity of this account by creating an edifice, the Voortrekker Monument which uses twenty-seven gigantic panels to portray the founding myth of the Afrikaner peoples: "Conceived and completed during a period of feverish Afrikaner nationalism in the 1930s and 1940s, the portrayals make no concessions: black people are uniformly represented as barbaric savages standing in the way of brave and heroic Boers claiming to bring civilization to the interior in the nineteenth century."[19]

Feverish nationalism drove a large group of people, inspired by images of terror and destruction, to split the world into self versus enemy, a pure and noble people against mere savages. Similar moments of feverish nationalism animated American slaveholders in the early nineteenth century. They also saw themselves beleaguered by incessant Northern economic forces and incessant Northern abolitionists whose message threatened their way of life and, they felt, their very lives.

It is easy to condemn slave owners, Spanish Inquisitors, and Afrikaners because we are assured of their moral failings. It is more difficult to see the same errors in our stories, especially our claims to heritage.

Most, if not all, nations and groups tell stories about their origins in which historical facts are not welcome. These stories recount heritage not history. They are repeated endlessly. Each new generation of Boers learned about the Great Trek and visited the Voortrekker Monument. Feeling the same feelings and sharing the same myth of origins made each child a member of a distinctive group just as American children are schooled in stories of our "fore trekkers." American history classes are designed to instill a sense of American values and the trajectory of American people—our story. In our public rituals, such as inauguration day and the president's State of the Union address, we hear a simple narrative again and again. We seek communion with our imaginary past and future. David Lowenthal, an American historian, noted: "We are apt to call such communion

---

[19] Albert Grundlingh, "A Cultural Conundrum? Old Monuments and New Regimes: The Voortrekker Monument as Symbol of Afrikaner Power in a Postapartheid South Africa," *Radical History Review*, Issue 81 (Fall 2001): 96.

history, but it is actually heritage. The distinction is vital. History explores and explains the past grown more opaque over time; heritage clarifies the past so as to infuse them with present purposes."[20]

Why Splitting Persists

To compare prophecy against prophecy we compare narrative against narrative. As mandated in a court of law, we postpone judgment until both sides of the dispute have aired their cases—told their stories. This requires hard, patient work. When time is short and the dangers are great, splitting and action-discharge become attractive. Time was short for Southern leaders. They recognized that the fragile accords of the 1830s and 1840s that defended slavery as it existed could be overturned with westward expansion. Abolition was a dangerous idea. They did not underestimate its effect on non-owners who, like them were Christians but unlike them had no economic stake in the preservation of the institution. When faced with what felt like annihilation they acted with great force and conviction.

Fascist leaders disdain the very idea of "thinking"—what I have termed *integrative responsiveness*—about politics or any other event. When asked by socialist politicians to explain his position, Benito Mussolini—who saw himself as Hitler's mentor—replied, "The Socialists ask what is our program? Our program is to smash the skulls of the Socialists."[21] In "The Doctrine of Fascism" (1932), Mussolini used ten thousand words to describe the same solution.[22] Writing for

---

[20] David Lowenthal, *The Heritage Crusade and the Spoils of History* (Cambridge: Cambridge University Press, 1998), xv. See also David Lowenthal, "Fabricating Heritage," *History and Memory* 10 (1998): 1. Yet, Lowenthal notes, "The very notion of a universal legacy [heritage] is self-contradictory; confining possession to some while excluding others is the raison d'être of heritage" (ibid., 23).

[21] Walter Laqueur. *Fascism: Past, Present, Future* (New York: Oxford University Press, 1997), 50.

[22] Benito Mussolini, *The Doctrine of Fascism*, cowritten with Giovanni Gentile. All Mussolini citations are from this unpaged source. http://www.worldfuturefund .org/wffmaster/Reading/Germany/mussolini.htm.

the *Italian Encyclopedia*, Mussolini proclaimed that Fascism made philosophic reasoning (a type of integrative thinking) unnecessary: "Fascism is action and it is thought." Or, as he put it, Fascists are not violent men, though many do "belong to the restless but meditative class."

Mussolini blamed the catastrophe of World War I upon liberals and their false doctrines, especially the sanctity of the individual. The (Jewish, Christian) notion that individuals are ends in themselves is illusory and harmful: "the individual, by self-sacrifice, the renunciation of self-interest, by death itself, can achieve that purely spiritual existence in which his value as a man consists." The only liberty is, therefore, the liberty of the individual within the State. The "Fascist State—a synthesis and a unit inclusive of all values—interprets, develops, and potentiates the whole life of a people." Rejecting socialist dreams of universal peace, of the value of goodwill, Fascism "trains its guns on the whole block of democratic ideologies, and rejects their practical applications and implements."

Like Mussolini, American slave owners and the politicians and priests whom they controlled realized that their system of governance—domination of subjects who wished to be free—required them to react to abolitionism with as much force as necessary. Although he was brutal, Mussolini was not stupid. He traced the inefficiencies of European governments to struggles between political groups whose policies and philosophical differences made democracies sloppy and prone to stasis. Like all tyrants, Mussolini recognized that directives from a central authority bypassed the quagmires of squabbling parliaments. Searching for fair and just outcomes was foolish. No form of government can be judged *sub specie aeternitatis* (under the aspect or eye of eternity) he asserted. On the contrary, the "permanent and universal reality in which the transient dwells and has its being" of Fascism is that individuals are members of a spiritual calling. Individuals gain value when they are members "of the family, the social group, the nation, and in function of history to which all nations bring their contribution." Mussolini made himself perfectly clear: "Anti-individualistic, the Fascist conception of life stresses the importance of the State and accepts the individual only in so far as his interests coincide with those of the State, which stands for the conscience and the universal, will of man as a historic entity."[23]

American slaveholders and their defenders did not achieve a unified, fascist state. Southern states carried out democratic processes (for white voters). Numerous leaks in the barriers they erected against abhorrent ideas, like abolitionism and equality of black and white, prevented them from achieving a fascistic ideal. In addition, within their own minds the majority of American slave owners carried the ideals of the Declaration of Independence, even if those ideals festered there. However, the logic of ownership and the incessant pressures owners felt from Northern agitators and some four million slaves pushed Southern authorities closer and closer to fascism. For it alone promised a total, national police force and a unified spirit, as Mussolini put it.

The Law, Mob Violence, and Splitting

This appeal to a "unified spirit" is another name for mob violence.

---

[23] This dismissal was a direct attack on the values espoused by the Jewish-Dutch philosopher Baruch Spinoza (1632–1677). In his masterpiece, *Ethics*, written around 1677, and an earlier work, *Theological-Political Treatise*, written around 1670, Spinoza offers a rigorous defense of individual piety, reason, and autonomy against all other powers, especially the state and religious institutions. Spinoza said that individuals were the prime locus of rationality and values and as such individuals should be protected against the state. Mussolini correctly viewed them as his enemies. Spinoza defended individual conscience and individual choice. Mussolini rejected that and said that to create a new form of life and human consciousness, Fascism "enforces discipline and uses authority, entering into the soul and ruling with undisputed sway." In contrast to Kant's wish to articulate a program for perpetual peace (1795) for example, Mussolini declared that: "War alone keys up all human energies to their maximum tension and sets the seal of nobility on those peoples who have the courage to face it. See, Immanuel Kant, *Perpetual Peace: A Philosophical Sketch* (1795). For an English translation, see https://www.mtholyoke.edu/acad/intrel/kant/kant1.htm.

When a group feels that its way of life is threatened by forces that seem uncanny, it sets aside legal rules, especially the sanctity of individual rights. In so-called primitive societies, dangerous persons are labeled witches, with their deaths justified and their murders often mandated. In nineteenth-century America, dangerous persons were not labeled as witches, they were labeled as abolitionists or, worse, insurrectionists who threatened to incite a war of black against white. For example, W. E. Channing, although an early abolitionist, asserted, "Undoubtedly there may be crimes, so unnatural, so terrible to a community, that a people may be forgiven, if, deeming the usual forms of justice too slow, they assume the perilous office of inflicting speedy punishment."[24]

Such an instance occurred in St. Louis on April 28, 1836. Francis L. McIntosh, a free African American boatman, had, witnesses said, interfered with two officers attempting to arrest two other sailors. He killed one of the officers, the deputy sheriff, and wounded the other. A group of citizens pursued McIntosh and threw him in jail. When news of the events spread, a large crowd marched to the jail and dragged McIntosh into the street: "Unnamed persons chained him to a tree, stacked wood around him, and burned him to death."[25]

Judge Luke E. Lawless convened a grand jury to investigate this event. He asked them if the killing of McIntosh was an act of the few or of the many? If the few, then the grand jury should indict the defendants "without single exception." They should be tried for murder under the ordinary rules of criminal law. However, if these deeds were the product of "congregated thousands" of people "impelled by that mysterious, metaphysical, and almost electric frenzy, which, in

---

[24] Cited by James Elbert Cutler, *Lynch-law: An Investigation into the History of Lynching in the United States* (New York: Longmans, Green, 1905), 194. He refers to *Liberator*, April 19, 1839 (9:63). See also *The Complete Works of W.E. Channing,* 10th ed. (London: Routledge and Sons, 1884), 567.

[25] http://www.civilwarstlouis.com/Reviews/mcintoshlovejoy.htm. Excerpted from Louis S. Gerteis, *Civil War St. Louis* (Lawrence, KS: University Press of Kansas, 2001).

all ages and nations, has hurried on the infuriated multitude to deeds of death and destruction—then, I say, act not at all on the matter; the case then transcends your jurisdiction—it is beyond the reach of human law."[26]

Lawless then blamed abolitionists for McIntosh's actions, and he exonerated those who had killed him.[27] In other words, abolitionists had spread their dangerous ideas to free blacks like McIntosh. Their peculiar, evil, and uncanny ideas had caused McIntosh's crimes; in response to these horrific crimes (and the ideas which spawned them), white citizens fell into a "mysterious, metaphysical, and almost electric frenzy." That metaphysical power drove them to burn McIntosh alive. That power was transcendental, beyond ordinary, human law.

Many distinguished citizens agreed with Judge Lawless. Louis Gerteis writes,

[a] Whig newspaper, the *Bulletin*, . . . praised the wisdom of Judge Lawless's remarks. The Catholic weekly, the *Shepherd of the Valley*, similarly endorsed the judge's stance. Lawless's comments contained 'much sound wisdom and discretion,' wrote the Catholic editor, who then equated abolitionism with Protestantism and with revolt against all authority, spiritual and secular.[28]

Local politicians feared African American revolts; Catholic leaders

---

[26] Cited by James Elbert Cutler. *Lynch-law*, 109–10. He cites *Liberator*, June 25, 1836 (6:102). See also http://www.zoominfo.com/p/Luke-Lawless/13422379. (Accessed January 16, 2016).

[27] "Because a near insane frenzy gripped the mob responsible for McIntosh's death, Lawless instructed the jury not to single out specific people for being responsible. Try as they might, he said, the jury could never understand the mania which seized the masses that day." http://www.clevelandcivilwarroundtable.com /articles/biography/lovejoy.htm.

[28] Excerpted from Louis S. Gerteis. *Civil War St. Louis* (Lawrence, KS: Kansas, 2001), n.p. http://www.civilwarstlouis.com/Reviews/mcintoshlovejoy.htm.

in the region feared an upsurge in Protestant control and power. By locating the causes of the annihilation of McIntosh "beyond the reach of human law," Lawless made the lynching irreproachable. As he saw it, the Constitution pertained only to mundane matters: it had no say in "metaphysical" causes. It was not mere mortals who burned McIntosh to death; it was something beyond ascertainable actors, something mysterious and metaphysical.

By truncating the reach of law, Lawless engaged in splitting. When citizens went beyond the law they assumed, Channing said, "the perilous office of inflicting speedy punishment." Channing endorsed a contradiction when he elevated a mob to a superior office, which is an authority granted by law and executed according to due process, the very qualities that mobs lack.

White Citizens Councils and Other Spectacles

The Ku Klux Klan in the nineteenth century, White Citizens Councils, and other American paramilitary groups in the twentieth century mounted similar dramas.[29] Carrying out spectacular, usually unpunished, crimes against African Americans, they made it clear that it was safer to belong to their groups (or at least, not challenge them) than to resist them.[30] In psychological terms, lynching induced ecstatic lust in

---

[29] "The activities of the political police against 'enemies of the State' can be compared to a drama, the three acts of which are performed perpetually. Act I. Spotting the enemies, unearthing their plots and their organization. Act II. Chasing and catching them. Act III. Punishment and repression." Ernest Kohn Bramsted, *Dictatorship and Political Police: The Technique of Control by Fear* (London: K. Paul, Trench, Trubner, 1945. Repr. New York: Routledge, 2003), 23.

[30] Cf. Hannah Arendt: "The Nazis did not strike at prominent figures as had been done in the earlier wave of political crimes in Germany . . . instead, by killing small socialist functionaries of influential members of opposing parties, they attempted to prove to the population the dangers involved in mere membership." In Germany and other states controlled by Nazi authority, political crimes were brazen precisely because they "made clear to the population at large that the power of the Nazis was greater than that of the

the lynch mob and an altered state of consciousness and terror in the African Americans who were its audience.[31]

Because they were public spectacles, lynchings and the numerous people who attended them were photographed many times. Jacqueline Denise Goldsby notes that lynchings of African Americans were de-signed to be both dramatic and also pointless, as contextless spectacles: "Lynching would have us believe, through the sheer force of its viscerality, that African-American life was so expendable and white supremacy so incontestable that the possibilities of deriving meaning from the violence were both endless and pointless."[32] Spec-tacles are to be seen and marveled upon. They are designed to be unforgettable and, at the same time, unthinkable. By inducing shock and terror, spectacles make dissociation (a form of splitting) more likely. A divided self becomes even more divided; we can forget what the other part of us knows to be true.

Southern white authorities used terror to influence future choices of ordinary citizens (African Americans). Spectacular lynchings and other atrocities seared upon African American psyches the awful truth that at any time they or their sons or their fathers could be de-stroyed in this humiliating way. Resistance was futile and foolhardy. James Allen, a contemporary American scholar, scoured flea markets for photographs of lynchings in America. Concerning a postcard photo of a lynching of an unidentified African American male, around 1908, in Oxford, Georgia, Allen noted that it was done near a railroad track. There, hundreds of people could see the dangling corpse: "Publicizing their work was a priority for the mob that murdered this

---

authorities and that it was safer to be a member of a Nazi paramilitary organiza-tion than a loyal Republican." Hannah Arendt, *The Origins of Totalitarianism*, 2nd ed. (1951, New York: Houghton Mifflin Harcourt, 1973), 344.

[31] See also Walter White, *Thirty Years of Lynching in the United States, 1889-1913*. National Association for the Advancement of Colored People (1919, New York: Negro Universities Press, 1969).

[32] Jacqueline Denise Goldsby, *A Spectacular Secret: Lynching in American Life and Literature* (Chicago: University of Chicago Press, 2006), 218.

unidentified African American. A lighted telephone pole near rail-road tracks created a well-lit gallery for passing trains."[33]

Because they are atrocities, lynchings gain their power by induc-ing in viewers fascination and horror. Both these states of mind are painful and disorganizing. The fastest and most immediate response to them is splitting, to locate one's experience and memories in dif-ferent parts of the mind. One cannot easily grasp the pain that such treatment induced in the victim. It is also difficult to imagine the sa-distic pleasures that coursed through the people who did these things. With sufficient effort and moral courage some people during the heyday of slavery did grasp that pain and imagine those sadistic pleasures. They did so by way of spiritual identification with slaves and empathy for those who kept them enslaved.

---

[33] Gelatin silver print reproduced on a photo postcard. 3H x 5H" Pencil in-scription on reverse: "Oxford Georgia." James Allen et al., *Without Sanctuary* (Santa Fe, NM: Twin Palms, 1999). For an online version of its images, see http://www.withoutsanctuary.org/main.html.

CHAPTER 7

Response to Contradiction: Spirituality and Empathy

A fourth response to the problems posed by the contradiction of Christian slavery is to resolve it by denying one of the two affirmations. Christian slave owners could renounce their religion and its moral core. By forfeiting their claims to be observant Christians their dilemma is resolved. Or, they could affirm their Christian identity and renounce slavery. The first option seems to have been rare; the second did occur but not frequently. When it appeared, it stemmed from Jewish-Christian teachings about the commonality of human beings as fellow creatures. Because the heroes of the antislavery movement relied upon this solution, it is tempting to see it as sufficient. However much we identify with these sentiments and admire those courageous enough to embody it, a problem remains: the "brotherhood of man," to use the nineteenth-century formula, rests upon feelings, upon shared human convictions, and it rests upon religious sentiment.

In Jewish theology this teaching appears in the assertion that all persons are made in God's image. According to the book of Genesis, "So God created man in his own image, in the image of God created he him; male and female created he them" (1:27). Composed around the sixth century BCE, some 2,700 years ago, Genesis described the creation of human beings as the last act of God's activity; after that God instructs human beings in their role as caretakers of the earth and all its inhabitants. This role as caretaker corresponds to God's efforts to shape a world for human beings: "And to every beast of the earth, and to every fowl of the air, and to every thing that creepeth upon the earth, wherein there is life, I have given every green herb for meat: and it was so" (1:30). Explicit in this story is the unity of human beings as creatures who are essentially the same from the point of view of God's will. Although human beings differ in dramatic ways, by skin color, culture, talents, and another hundred ways, their origins are identical. More so, because they are created in God's image, they share some aspect of God's divinity.

How much they share is subject to cultural norms and theological judgment. For observant Jews, and later for observant Christians and Muslims, the creation story asserts the unity of human beings as a transcendental truth: it cannot be refuted by mere evidence of difference. Indeed, as a transcendental truth it cannot be refuted at all. Those who proclaim this spiritual truth as the antidote to societal ills, such as slavery in the nineteenth century and racism in the twentieth century, cannot demonstrate its unvarying truth. For example, traditional Islamic teachers affirm a version of the unity of persons. Abdul Aziz Said, a noted contemporary scholar, says that because God rules every aspect of human lives, human rights derive from human obligations to God. Those obligations are laid out in Islamic scriptures and commentaries: "Human rights are parts of one whole—a universal dialogue of a *unity of being* separated by time, environment and experience."[1] However, these rights depend upon right belief: the unforgivable sin is apostasy. While Islam proclaims the right to freedom of religion, "a Muslim cannot convert into another religion, nor can a Muslim woman marry a non-Muslim man." Because Islamic teachings derive from God's revelations, which are immutable and perfect, a person who has partaken of their truth and then rejects it has sinned against all that is

---

[1] Abdul Aziz Said, "Precept and Practice of Human Rights in Islam," *Universal Human Rights* 1 (1) (1979): 63. (Emphasis in original.)

good and productive for human beings.

In traditional Muslim countries, the punishment for apostasy, renouncing one's faith, is execution. From the first century forward, Christian leaders announced similar warnings against false prophets, those who had heard and then perverted the truth of Christian revelations and Christian scriptures. In the words of the Apostle Peter, "But there were false prophets also among the people, even as there shall be false teachers among you, who privily shall bring in damnable heresies, even denying the Lord that bought them, and bring upon themselves swift destruction" (2 Peter 2:1). The logic of swift and awful punishment for apostasy is that the disease of wrong thinking might infect others, endanger their immortal souls, and defile the community. In contemporary Muslim nations, the Western value of freedom of religion raises particular problems. This freedom is enshrined in Article 18 of the United Nations Declaration on Human Rights (UNDHR): "Everyone has the right to freedom of thought, conscience and religion; this right includes freedom to change his religion or belief, and freedom, either alone or in community with others and in public or private, to manifest his religion or belief in teaching, practice, worship and observance." According to theocratic principles, this alleged right amounts to defending the right of people to fall into mortal errors and to draw others away from the true faith. At a minimum, such sins require severe corporal punishment as is meted out in Saudi Arabia.[2]

Such terrible punishments were typical of European theocracy as well. R. C. Caenegem, a contemporary Dutch scholar, notes: "Apostasy was punished by death, as happened in 1222 when Archbishop Stephen Langton 'held a provincial council at Oxford, and there he degraded and handed over to the lay power a deacon who had turned Jew for the love of a Jewess. The apostate was delivered to the sheriff of Oxfordshire, who forthwith burnt him.'"[3]

---

[2] "UN Rights Chief Urges Saudi King to Halt Flogging of Blogger," *Reuters* US ed., Jan 15, 2015, http://www.reuters.com/article/us-saudi-rights-flogging -idUSKBN0KO25A20150115.

[3] R. C. Van Caenegem, "Historical reflections on Islam and the Occident,"

Similar to Jewish and Christian apologists for slavery, traditional Islamic teachers did not find reason to disavow legalized slavery. According to its sacred writings, "God hath ordained your brothers should be your slaves; Therefore, him whom God hath ordained to be the slave of his brother, his brother must give him of the food which he eateth himself, and not order him to do anything beyond his power."[4] In contrast, William Wilberforce, the great antislavery member of Parliament who championed the Slavery Abolition Act of 1833, based his efforts on other Hebrew Bible verses and their New Testament counterparts. Among his favorite New Testament passages were: "There is neither Greek nor Jew, circumcision nor uncircumcision, Barbarian, Scythian, bond nor free: but Christ is all, and in all. Put on therefore bowels of mercies, kindness." The identical thought appears in the New Testament book of Acts: "[God] hath made of one blood all nations of men, for to dwell on all the face of the earth."[5]

Although these are poetic and forceful pronouncements they are not more beautiful than similar pronouncements supporting other theocratic regimes. One may share Wilberforce's theology, but that sharing, one's commonality with him, does not prove that alternative theologies are thus disproven. The arts provide a parallel path to that offered by Wilberforce's theology. The arts offer access to the emotional worlds of both the slave and the slave owner. By treating slaves and owners as equally human and equally accessible to human understanding, artists look upon them as fellow creatures, as more alike than different. As we survey the solution space to the problem of slavery, we find that the empathic moment, seen in Harriet Beecher Stowe, Lincoln, and, of course, slaves and former slaves, offers one

---

European Review 20, no. 2 (2012): 204. He cites: F. Pollock and F.W. Maitland, *The History of English Law, II* (Cambridge: Cambridge University Press, 1968), 548.

[4] Ibid.

[5] Colossians 3:11–12; Acts 17:26, cited by William Wilberforce. *A Letter on the Abolition of the Slave Trade, Addressed to the Freeholders of Yorkshire* (London: Luke Hansard & Sons, 1807).

solution to the contradiction "property in persons." Empathic narrations seem crucial to waking up persons to the suffering of others, to their shared humanity. However, because they rely upon our feelings they are not objective, that is they do not logically require us to affirm them. Many groups and regimes we find distasteful, if not criminal, also evoked strong feelings and promoted ecstatic proclamations of unity.

Empathic Narrations

Harriet Beecher Stowe in *Uncle Tom's Cabin* and Carter Godwin Woodson in *The Mis-Education of the Negro* illustrate empathic expertise. Each portrays real persons and evokes emotional recognition in us. Empathy is the capacity to articulate to oneself how other persons experience their life worlds. By "life world" I mean the sense that Frederick Douglass, for example, had of the forces that impinged upon him from the outside (for example, the overseer, the weather, his body) and of those forces that impinged upon him from the "inside" (for example, his fears, thoughts, and hopes). To be empathic to Douglass is to grasp how he experienced himself in relation to these diverse realities.

Each life world includes a temporal map that charts a person's shifting sense of past, present, and future selves. The hope that Stowe gives to her Christian characters are for a future state in which injustices are made right and the Kingdom of God is realized. The conviction of the Kingdom, that it has come through the crucifixion and the resurrection of Christ, makes suffering in this world temporary compared to the certainty of redemption. In the paradoxical language of the Apostle Paul, the Kingdom of God has occurred and is occurring now even as it will occur later, at the end of time. We can comprehend the value of this faith by comparing it to its absence; to the despair that many people experience when they believe that their suffering is meaningless and endless. Seasoned psychotherapists know that when patients speak of "nothing to live for" or view their future as "stale, flat, and unprofitable," they should look for suicidal feelings. Suicide becomes attractive when we cannot envision a future in which our suffering stops and where it has a meaning for others. With no future to pull us forward and no sense that others will benefit from our lives, death seems to offer release, to let us rest in peace.

Empathy is a multidimensional concept. It names one end of a spectrum that begins with sharing a person's feelings and ends with understanding those feelings intellectually but not sharing them. To use the term correctly we must satisfy a triple demand: one is emotional, that we grasp how another being feels in its body—my dog quivering over his chew toy for example; the second is validity, that our reading of the other's experience is accurate; the third is conceptual, that we can distinguish the other person's feelings from our own.[6] To submerge ourselves into the other's feelings is sympathy, what suffering people do not need. A traumatized person cannot be helped by another equally traumatized person.

Variations along the sympathy-empathy spectrum occur daily. Parents who ache for anxious children, moviegoers entranced by a compelling film, and excited fans at a rock concert share the same sensations or good vibrations of another person's experience. That is sympathetic immersion. At the other end of this spectrum is the following illustration. It draws upon images of Greek women some 2,600 years ago who carried baskets on their heads. Through empathic genius Greek artists transformed inert stone columns for a building into nearly-living persons.[7]

---

[6] Jean Decety, a distinguished neuroscientist who studies empathy, puts it this way: "Despite the various definitions of empathy, there is broad agreement on three primary components: (a) an affective response to another person, which often, but not always, entails sharing that person's emotional state; (b) a cognitive capacity to take the perspective of the other person; and (c) emotion regulation." Jean Decety and Philip L. Jackson, "A Social-neuroscience Perspective on Empathy," *Current Directions in Psychological Science* 15, no. 2, (2006): 54. See also Jean Decety & Philip L. Jackson, "The Functional Architecture of Human Empathy," *Behavioral and Cognitive Neuroscience Reviews* 3, (2004): 71–100.

[7] From Forrest Wilson, *What It Feels Like to Be a Building* (Washington, D C: The Preservation Press, 1988). Some people prefer illustrated books by

This line drawing helps us understand how buildings remain upright. The weight of a roof presses down upon columns the way that these two figures press against each other. Through empathic recognition we recognize that these two opposed forces—the dark figure pressing down, the light figure pushing up—must be identical. Otherwise the upper figure would fall, or the lower figure would rise above the ground. Drawing upon that memory, we understand how a building's foundation strains to support its superstructure.

By finding the effective image, sound, and story, artists communicate

David Macaulay, such as *The New Way Things Work* (1998); *Mosque* (2003); and his first masterpiece, *Cathedral* (1973). Macaulay does not portray buildings as animals with muscles and he doesn't demonstrate the empathic dimension evident in Wilson's book. *Karyatides* were priestesses at the temple of Artemis at Karyai, the Peloponnesus. The caryatid porch on the Erechtheum (421–406 BCE) on the Acropolis of Athens is an example. Male counterparts are atlas figures who carry the world on their shoulders.

our inarticulate experiences to us. They cocreate those experiences in us. They show us what we felt but did not know. But they do so at a distance, a distance provided by the formal requirements of narrative, balance, economy, representation and other forms of discipline required by their arts. Artists observe how people act, think, and react. They do not hallucinate themselves into their subjects; they picture themselves into their subjects' life-worlds, including their self-understanding. They ask, "If I were you, how would I act?"—they remain conscious of the subjunctive mood.

What novelists and painters have always known—that we unconsciously shape our sense of the past and the future—cognitive scientists affirm: memory (and its numerous connections to our sense of self and group) is not a mechanical recollection of engrams, of coded storage that we access the same way our laptop accesses RAM and its hard drive. On the contrary, we now know that "to remember" is to reassemble a set of patterns that vary, sometimes dramatically, in each cycle. Freud stumbled upon this truth in the late 1890s when he tried to assess the validity of memories of adult-child sexual encounters relayed to him by his patients. A century later, the so-called memory wars of the 1990s in the United States centered upon two distinct facts: that some children are abused sexually (and deny it) and other children—and adults—can be cajoled into remembering abusive events that did not occur. In ordinary language, to remember is to recall actual occurrences. Contemporary scientific psychology proves that this is not true. Because memory is not a mechanical recording, numerous errors, biases, and unconscious distortions shape our seemingly valid sense of memory.

At the level of public recollection of national memory similar shaping and editing occurs. Literary critics, theologians, and others cocreate cultural works within specific discourses and specific cultural landscapes. During times of crisis religious leaders cite selected scriptural passages and reread them according to their sense of what their audiences require. The meaning of Hebrew Bible verses about the land of Israel, for example, differs for Jews who support the policies of the current government of Israel compared to Jews who do not. A culture that has a long history of texts, commentaries, and traditions can select among its memories particular narratives that justify one political action over another. For example, people who advocate for Zionist objectives cite one set of Jewish stories; those who oppose cite another.[8] The elaborate efforts Southern preachers used to defend slavery rested upon their reading of Christian scriptures, as did the counterarguments by Christian abolitionists.

Within public arts and popular culture, similar efforts to reshape memory and to draw upon selected narratives appear continuously. American novels, movies, and Broadway musicals, for example, are good to the degree that they illuminate the visible and invisible structures of contemporary American lives. These structures may be difficult to see and difficult to talk about. However, their illumination counts as valuable. In sharp contrast, paranoid fantasies reveal a person's ideas about the world, not knowledge of the world and the self. Paranoid wishes do not show us how to go forward, except suggesting that we build a time machine. In contrast, great art is structured and systematic—and beautiful—because the world is structured and systematic—and beautiful—even the world of suffering and loss. Artists may have intense beliefs that they wish to communicate to us and perhaps make us share. But those wishes are not part of the artistic object. Leni Riefenstahl's opinions about Nazi spectacles are separate from the genius of her film, *Triumph of the Will* (1935), which made Hitler godlike and which has influenced cinema ever since. Assessing the moral implication of art by Riefenstahl and Richard Wagner, the latter a notorious anti-Semite, is an ethical task. How can awful people produce great art and kind, loving people produce trivialities? These questions—and the emotional conflicts they create—deserve attention. But these tasks are distinct from the works themselves and from the task of art history. Philosophers do not discover truths hidden within works of

---

[8] See, for example, Yechiel Klar, "From 'Do not arouse or awaken love until it so desires' through 'Return to Zion' to 'Conquest of the Land': Paradigm Shifts and Sanctified Reenactments in Building the Jewish State." *International Journal of Intercultural Relations* 43 (2014): 87–99

art; that is a form of conspiracy theory. They can, though, begin with the work of art and reflect upon their experiences of it. Their resonances with the work and their associations to it may provoke important questions of personal, social, and political meaning.[9]

Artists do not see deeper into us the way that biologists peer deeper into the hidden parts of the cell. We call James Joyce and Jane Austen "deep" as ways to honor them. But this metaphor of depth is misleading. Austen, Joyce, and Susan Sontag are exacting naturalists; they explore the texture of lived experience, the mere surface. Yet the surface is where we live. We may say that a dream is from the unconscious, but that is just a way of talking: a dream is one among numerous subtle features of intense, conscious experience. We need art to amplify unspoken, nonverbal parts of ourselves into larger, spoken, and complete wholes. When successful, artists and humanist critics help make visible what was invisible.[10]

The Milgram and Zimbardo Experiments

This unity of persons includes our potential unity with the minds of the slaveholders, not just those who opposed them. Politically, emotionally, and ethically there are many reasons for activists to stress the evilness of slavery and to denounce its proponents. Looking back to the beginning of the Civil War and its aftermath we know which side was morally right. However, we should also look inside ourselves. Within us slumbers a similar capacity to take part in and defend slavery. To deny this is tantamount to splitting ourselves off from this part of our nature, what I have called "the pleasures of owning persons."

We cannot understand slavery if we demonize its practitioners and deny our potential to do and think as they did in their contexts. To challenge our own tendency toward splitting we should conceive of how the slavery dilemma could exist within us, within our psyches.

---

[9] For example, see Susan Sontag, *On Photography* (New York: Farrar, Straus and Giroux, 1977).

[10] From Volney Gay, *Progress in the Humanities* (New York: Columbia University Press, 2009).

A rough analogy comes from the famous "prison" experiment that Philip Zimbardo, a social psychologist, conducted at Stanford University in 1971.[11] As Zimbardo described it, he would study prison life with normal, healthy, young men from an elite institution. Flipping a coin, he assigned one half the group to be prisoners and the other half to be guards. In this clever way "there were no differences between boys assigned to be a prisoner and boys assigned to be a guard."[12]

Zimbardo and his colleagues soon observed that the guard-students became increasingly effective, that is, brutal toward the prisoner-students. With advice from former inmates and experienced jailors, the experimenters subjected the prisoner-students to disorientation, threat, and other forms of psychological pressure such as stripping them naked; "delousing" (which implies that they were—suddenly—dirty and suspicious); shaving their heads (by requiring them to wear stocking caps); and assigning them prison ID numbers. Following a "rebellion" by the inmates, the guards spontaneously evolved even more coercive ways to control the prisoners. Just as slave owners were terrified of slave uprisings, the guards became worried about their own security, fearing that the prisoners would overpower them.

Zimbardo described his role as superintendant and his anger when he heard of plans for a mass "jailbreak." To maintain control he appealed to the Palo Alto Police Department and asked them to place his pretend-prisoners in their real jail. Not sharing Zimbardo's delusion, the police refused. Zimbardo "left angry and *disgusted* at this lack of cooperation between *our* correctional facilities."[13]

---

[11] C. Haney, W. C. Banks, and P. G. Zimbardo, "Study of Prisoners and Guards in a Simulated Prison." *Naval Research Reviews*, 9, (1973): 1–17. Washington, DC: Office of Naval Research. On the experiment itself, see http://www.prisonexp.org/ Zimbardo reflected upon the ensuing controversy in *The Lucifer Effect: Understanding How Good People Turn Evil* (New York: Random House, 2007).

[12] http://www.prisonexp.org/psychology/4.

[13] http://www.prisonexp.org/psychology/26. (My emphasis.) Following Stanley Milgram, who conducted similar experiments in 1961 shortly after the trial of

Zimbardo cited earlier, famous experiments by Stanley Milgram at Yale begun in 1961. To assess the willingness of ordinary people to follow orders, even if it meant harming others, Milgram asked his subjects to "punish" an actor who got the wrong answers on a fake memory quiz. The subjects administered shocks to the actors using a fake "shock generator" with thirty switches named "Slight Shock" to "Danger: Severe Shock." These dramatic experiments have provoked fifty years of commentary, including fictional adaptations. There are different ways to explain these findings. But they remain troubling, for example, between 50 and 67 percent of all subjects in the Milgram experiment willingly gave "450-volt" shocks—clearly marked "severe"— to subjects when an authority pressured them to do so.

Zimbardo summarized Milgram's findings (which have been replicated many times in many different contexts) in ten maxims. Those relevant to the institution of slavery are:[14]

- Employ an ideology that justifies using any means to achieve the goal. (We have seen that the entire structure of Southern education, including religious training, justified slavery.)[15]
- Create contractual obligations, verbal or written. (The 1787 Constitution, numerous state and local statutes, such as those that required service on slave patrols, and public opinion shaped in sermons, editorials, and other forms of control created legal and interpersonal obligations.)

Nazi war criminal, Adolph Eichmann, Zimbardo generalized from his experiment to explain the ubiquity of evil and our ability to fall into roles that might make otherwise good people do bad things. See Stanley Milgram, "Behavioral Study of Obedience." *Journal of Abnormal and Social Psychology* 67 (1963): 371–78. doi:10.1037/h0040525. PMID 14049516. http://content.apa.org/journals/abn/67/4/371.Full-text PDF.

[14] Zimbardo, *The Lucifer Effect*, 23–24. (Phrasing modified.)

[15] He cites S. T. Fiske, T. E. Harris, and A. J. C. Cuddy, "Why Ordinary People Torture Enemy Prisoners." *Science* 306 (2006): 1482–83.

- Give participants roles to play (teacher, student) that carry positive values and give them well-defined powers. (All relevant roles in Southern education, from the nursery schools to law schools and universities, carried high esteem and were organized to defend slavery.)

- Create ways to diffuse responsibility for negative outcomes. (Washington did not need to demean himself and whip his slaves; his overseers did that for him. Thus, he was a good master. Lincoln noted that Southern elites did not permit overseers into their front parlors.)

- Make the "exit costs" from the institution high; allow verbal dissent (that lets people feel good about themselves), but insist on behavioral compliance. (Southern authorities permitted people to talk about ameliorating the scandalous aspects of slavery. Stonewall Jackson and other Southerners spoke of their Christian duty to their slaves. The latter meant instilling in slaves proper beliefs about their personal conduct.)

To return to the antebellum South, slaveholders and the participants in the Yale and Stanford experiments acted in similar ways to one another. However, the environmental pressures upon Southern whites, especially slave owners, were far greater than those imposed upon the student-guards in Zimbardo's experiment. His normal, middle-class American students (like other test subjects in other countries where the experiment was repeated) knew that they were taking part in an experiment at a prestigious university. Their livelihoods, social standing, and futures were not at stake. The psychology experiment would end soon and they would return to the safety and security of their everyday lives. Even in these benign circumstances the majority of subjects obeyed authorities or became authoritarian. Were these aberrations? Prior to publicizing his findings, Milgram asked forty psychiatrists to predict the number of normal persons who would give the maximum shock of 450-volts. Their average guess was 1 percent (versus the 67 percent that Milgram found.) In other words, aberrant subjects were those who refused to push the dial all the way to the "danger" reading. Most of the American psychiatrists were grossly inaccurate in estimating the autonomous function of individuals. They nourished an illusion that individuals surely would be immune from irrational beliefs and engaging in unfair actions. This illusion persisted even though each of them had just come through World War II and had learned the awful facts of nearly universal refusal to defend European Jews.

In contrast to American college students doing psychology experiments in the 1960s, slaveholders and their families in 1860 knew that their financial, political, and perhaps personal security rested upon defending slavery. In Jefferson's famous expression cited earlier, slave owners "have the wolf by the ears, and we can neither hold him, nor safely let him go. Justice is in one scale, and self-preservation in the other."[16] This is a telling metaphor. It names both the owners' terror (that they could be destroyed by their captives) and their existential conflict: they wished to be just but they also wished to preserve their fortunes and their heritage.

An honest man, Jefferson knew that to maintain slavery he needed access to overwhelming force and multiple threats of force. We saw how Presidents Washington and Jackson responded to insubordination by their slaves. While each man wished to appear and to act justly, neither could afford to let slave resistance or worse, slave rebellion, go unpunished. For these reasons the Southern framers of the 1787 Constitution wrote the fugitive slave clause into the laws governing all American states.[17] Otherwise, Northern states would be too

---

[16] Thomas Jefferson to John Holmes, (discussing slavery and the Missouri question), Monticello, April 22, 1820. Jefferson used the phrase on at least two other occasions. See Monticello, https://www.monticello.org/site/jefferson/wolf-ear.

[17] Article 4, section 2: "No person held to service or labour in one state, under the laws thereof, escaping into another, shall, in consequence of any law or regulation therein, be discharged from such service or labour, but shall be delivered up on claim of the party to whom such service or labour may be due."

attractive for slaves wishing to escape servitude in Southern and border states. While the South alone held slaves, both North and South would defend the institution at the national level. This made the protection of slavery a national policy applicable in all the states.

Slaveholders feared slave rebellions and so they created elaborate police efforts to prevent them. They also took emotional comfort in stories about the "good plantation"; their intellectual, political, and religious elites elaborated complex (and confusing) narratives about the naturalness of slavery. Most slaveholders and their families identified themselves as good Christian stewards; very few identified themselves as sociopaths or sadists. Most likely very few of their overseers were sadistic as well. Sociopaths are untrustworthy and dangerous to everyone, not just to slaves and other kinds of inmates. In the agricultural journals devoted to slave management, overseers strained to be effective stewards of their employers' property, not malignant actors who harmed that property.[18]

Narrative reflection that names and represents cultural depths requires empathy, humility, and reconciliation—values that we admire and that religions laud. Compared to splitting evident in propaganda, narrative reflection is preferable. Indeed, it dominates creative literature, mature religion, and psychotherapy. Integrative narratives confront contradictory elements within personal and collective stories and shape them into visions of a future state. This retelling does

---

[18] Speaking of research findings on studies of Brazilian guards who engaged in violent torture (which he calls violence workers), Zimbardo notes: "Sadists are selected out of the training process by trainers because they are not controllable, get off on the pleasure of inflicting pain and thus do not sustain the focus on the goal of confession extraction. From all the evidence we could muster, [these violence workers] were not unusual or deviant in any way prior to practicing their new roles, nor were there any persisting deviant tendencies or pathologies among any of them in the years following their work as torturers and executioners" (Zimbardo, *The Lucifer Effect*). See also M. Huggins, M. Haritos-Fatouros, and P. G. Zimbardo, *Violence Workers: Police Torturers and Murderers Reconstruct Brazilian Atrocities* (Berkeley, CA: University of California Press, 2002).

not solve contradictions now, in the present. The antitheses remain. However, narratives provide immediate benefit. By preventing untoward actions, integrative narratives prevent reactive crimes. They offer non-paranoid narratives of the future. The rule of law, empathic reflection, critical engagement, "deep" readings of a culture, and similar instances of integrative thinking take time to create and to absorb. That alone makes them valuable: they inhibit the impulse to attack based on fantasies about the other. The Western legal value of due process does not guarantee justice, but it does guarantee that lynching and similar impulsive crimes will not occur without consequences if enough people pursue the truth. The long battle to stop lynching began in the late nineteenth century, and it succeeded in the late twentieth century.

If integrative thinking is superior to splitting and other reactive forms of thought, then why is it not the norm? On analogy with other technological advances, a superior solution should win out over time. Some 5,000 years ago iron replaced bronze that replaced copper that replaced stone.[19] About twenty years ago microcomputers displaced minicomputers; ten years ago flat-screen monitors replaced CRTs. Surely, urbane, nuanced, and empathic reflection evidenced 2,700 years ago in Western and Hindu traditions (among others) should, by now, have replaced splitting as a mode of thought.

This has not occurred for at least two reasons. Integrative thinking, as demonstrated in narrative literature like *Uncle Tom's Cabin* is not a fully realized solution. It is not a technology that once in place provides a reliable answer to all subsequent questions. The problems that integrative thinking takes on are not reducible to scientific puzzles. If they were they would yield to scientific examination.[20] At its

---

[19] Bronze became important because it was the first metal used to shape other metals. See Ian McNeil, ed., *Encyclopedia of the History of Technology* (New York: Routledge, 2002), 388.

[20] Reflecting upon a lifelong effort to understand language, J. J. Katz, an important American linguist, reports that he had shared the conviction of many Anglo American philosophers that at least some of the central problems of

best integrative thinking creates open-ended narratives. It offers heuristics, helpful devices, that help us generate stories about a future in which our maladies are cured and our conflicts are resolved: "Every valley shall be exalted, and every mountain and hill shall be made low: and the crooked shall be made straight, and the rough places plain" affirmed Isaiah in the Hebrew Bible (40:4). Demagogues also offer visions of the past and the future. Both the Hebrew Bible and *Mein Kampf* tell stories about who we were and who we should become. Our task is to judge which of these prophetic visions is valid and which is false. To do that we must keep honest accounts and we must tolerate the possibility that we might be wrong, that our initial fantasies about the best answer—our story—might lead us astray. To tolerate this psychic tension we have to rely upon institutions (the university, the courts, and free inquiry) to defend us from the pressure of immediate needs.

Integrative thinking addresses the paranoid attitude evident in propagandistic group actions. Psychiatric patients come to their paranoia, we might say, with justification: they have been hurt; they are in panic; they fear that they will be hurt again. Propagandists have no such excuses. Their slogans, posters, and TV ads are designed to instill fear and provoke action. Propagandists and con artists are always in a hurry: we must invest in this stupendous opportunity; we must go to war right now. Because it detoxifies paranoid thinking and defies propaganda, integrative thinking typifies the work of theologians, philosophers, and psychotherapists. However, even these narratives

---

philosophy stemmed from faulty theories of language. Solve those problems, he thought, and the philosophic conundrums associated with them should disappear. Having offered a rigorous theory of semantics earlier in his career, Katz changed his mind: "It now seems to me that, although certain aspects of any philosophical question may be illuminated by some of the ideas that linguistics has to offer or will have to offer, the truly important questions of explication in philosophy are questions about *broad* concepts for which philosophical theories are needed." J. J. Katz, *Semantic Theory* (New York: Harper & Row, 1972), 452. (His emphasis).

do not offer solutions. Often they prevent us from taking the wrong medicine but they do not offer cure.

Thinking about Thinking: Mentalization

Around late adolescence many young people realize with a shock that they can think about their minds. They realize that they had been thinking one way (as a child) and that they can now think another way (as an adult). That they can entertain different thoughts. Adding to this shock is the realization that their parents no longer speak with the authority of gods. Parents, priests, rabbis, schoolteachers, and politicians, for example, also think one way but could think another way. This is both liberating and terrifying. The liberating part is that young persons learn that the world is suddenly larger than it seemed in childhood. Obedience to authorities suddenly ceases to be automatic. Young people may start to demand why they should act or believe one way when other ways seem just as valid.

The terrifying part is that the adolescent may perceive the world of childhood and its security were illusory. In intelligent people this provokes intense agony. If they give up the security of childhood for the freedom of adult choices, they lose the assurances of attachment and a place in the world. If they remain childish they lose the pleasures and rewards of independent thought. In Western literature, Hamlet, the Prince of Denmark in Shakespeare's play, exemplifies the brilliant adolescent who comes to understand himself, his ability to think, just as he is thrust into terrifying duties. Wrenched out of his philosophical studies, he goes home to bury his beloved father and attend his mother's wedding, and he discovers treachery. People, including his mother, are not what they said they were. If Hamlet had remained childish, that is not learned to perceive duplicity and fraud, he would not be tormented by his mother's marriage. He would be spared his destiny, to settle a wrong done against his father. As Hamlet says when he confronts former friends who spy upon him, "There is nothing either good or bad but thinking makes it so" (Hamlet, Act II, scene 2). That painful truth is not available to young children. It comes only by recognizing the variability of thought and conviction.

Peter Fonagy, a contemporary psychologist, uses the term *mentalization* to designate this ability. When present this ability produces resilient children. Some children raised in chaotic homes by belligerent and harmful parents do not model themselves on their parents.[21] We know that (typically) parents pass on to their children patterns of abuse, sometimes for generations. What was done unto them, damaged children do to their children and sometimes to their grandchildren. Yet, some persons raised in horrible circumstances do not abuse their children. What makes these kids resilient and able to become good parents when they become adults? Fonagy says that fortunate children, even when raised in brutal circumstances, can think about their own minds. They can reflect on their experience; they can remember their past actions and compare them against a possible future.[22]

What allows a child to not identify with an abusive parent? Fonagy and other researchers have shown that successful children

---

[21] Peter Fonagy, "Thinking about Thinking: Some Clinical and Theoretical Considerations in the Treatment of a Borderline Patient," *International Journal of Psychoanalysis* 72 (1991): 639–56; "Psychoanalytic and Empirical Approaches to Developmental Psychopathology: An Object-relations Perspective." *Journal of American Psychoanalytic Association* 41 (Supplement): 245–60; Peter Fonagy et al., "Measuring the Ghost in the Nursery: an Empirical Study of the Relation between Parents' Mental Representations of Childhood Experiences and Their Infants' Security of Attachment," *Journal of American Psychoanalytic Association* 41 (1993): 957–89.

[22] "What particularly distinguishes resilient individuals from those who remain damaged and damaging is a *capacity to reflect on mental experience,* perhaps allowing the child to modify negative working models in later relationships. In other cases, the capacity may be inhibited as a way of defending the developing self against the impact of malevolence and abuse. The phenomena of borderline personality disorder may be rooted in a distortion of this reflective capacity." "Psychoanalytic and Empirical Approaches to Developmental Psychopathology: an Object-relations Perspective." *Journal of the American Psychoanalytic Association* 41 (Supplement 1993): 245. (My emphasis.)

discover benign people—such as teachers or coaches or a friend's parents—who think before acting. By modeling themselves upon these mature adults, resilient children learn how to live with other people—which their parents could not do. Successful children reject their parents' paranoid worldview. They learn to tolerate diverse, even conflicting realities and to reject the urge to attack (or submit) to other people. To mentalize is to recall the past (such as "I was abused") and to imagine a novel future ("I will not always be abused"). It is the ability to think about thinking. This permits the child to conceive of a future that does not repeat the past. In other words, mentalization represents a kind of freedom: my destiny is not determined by my past experiences.

Self-Reflection: *Heart of Darkness*

A well-known instance of self-reflection concerns English racism and the plunder of Africa. In *Heart of Darkness*, published in 1902 at the height of British imperial power, Joseph Conrad exemplified reflective thinking. The novel opens in the harbor of the Thames, adjacent to London. The narrator looks out across the river as a ship, the *Nellie*, prepares to sail. After giving a luscious description of the tides, the sky, and the lazy-relaxed mood of the sailors, Conrad ascribes a semi-hallucination to Marlow, the book's narrator. Marlow reflects upon the ironic duality of the harbor's history: English vessels, dedicated to colonial dominance, prepare to leave a harbor where a few millennia earlier Roman vessels had entered, dedicated to Roman dominance of British tribes. Marlow describes his mental state:

> I was *thinking* of very old times, when the Romans first came here, nineteen hundred years ago —the other day.... <u>*Imagine*</u> the feelings of a commander of a fine—what d'ye call 'em?—trireme in the Mediterranean, ordered suddenly to the north run overland across the Gauls in a hurry; put in charge of one of these craft the legionaries—a wonderful lot of handy men they must have been, too—used to build, apparently by the hundred, in a month or two, if we may believe what we read. *Imagine* him here—the very end of the world, a sea the colour of lead, a sky

the colour of smoke, a kind of ship about as rigid as a concertina—and going up this river with stores, or orders, or what you like.[23]

I cite this passage because it shows Conrad exhorting the reader to imagine the mind of Roman sailors who entered that harbor two thousand years earlier. In other words, Conrad exhorts us to empathic engagement. Earlier in the novel Conrad described the setting sun and lights on the shore: "a great stir of lights going up and going down." London, a gigantic city of light and commerce had "been one of the dark places of the earth" to the gallant Romans who saw only dark gray sky against dark gray water. Marlow asks us to imagine a Roman who, from his perspective, has come to the end of the civilized world. Who "has to live in the midst of the incomprehensible, which is also detestable. And it has a fascination too that goes to work upon him. The fascination of the abomination—you know, imagine the growing regrets, the longing to escape, the powerless disgust, the surrender, the hate."[24]

First-century Rome was to Britain as nineteenth-century Britain is to Africa. England was dark to the Romans, as Africa seemed dark to the English. And because the unknown is "detestable," both groups of men generated disgust, then hatred for the unknown savages. However, the Romans imported no ideology of salvation. They made no pretense of improving the lot of British savages: "They were conquerors, and for that you want only brute force—nothing to boast of, when you have it, since your strength is just an accident arising from the weakness of others. They grabbed what they could get for the sake of what was to be got."[25] In contrast, the European conquerors of the dark continent told themselves that they represented something noble: they brought civilization to the uncivilized and Christianity to heathens.[26]

---

[23] Ross C. Murfin, ed., *Heart of Darkness and Essays from Five Contemporary Critical Perspectives* (New York: Macmillan, 1996), 20. (My emphasis.)

[24] Ibid., n.p.

[25] Ibid., n.p.

[26] On Conrad's view of Africans, see Tim Dean, "The Germs of Empires: Heart of Darkness, Colonial Trauma, and the Historiography of AIDS" in

Conrad knew better. That is why he documented the Englishmen's terror of a new world and their surge of hatred toward its natives. Using our terms, faced with an otherwise uncontrollable terror, Roman and British colonial soldiers relied upon the defense of splitting. They had traveled to the end of the known (and secure) world. They confronted an unknown place that promised gloom and degradation—the darkness. To stave off their terror they bifurcated the world; the Romans were strong and manly, the English were manly and Christian; the savages lurking near the Thames and the Congo were weak, but fascinating creatures.

Self-Reflection and the Centrality of Story

Novels like *Uncle Tom's Cabin* and *Heart of Darkness* offer a single, coherent narrative about contradictions and puzzles in our emotional lives. Effective propaganda does the same thing. So, our question becomes how can we decide which effective story to call our own? A key measure is the degree to which a story asks us to reflect on our failures, our mistakes, our anxious moments. As we will see in the next chapter, this distinguishes clever books about the Civil War and the defense of the Lost Cause from valid books about that event. The

---

The Psychoanalysis of Race, ed. Christopher Lane (Columbia University Press, 1998), 308–09. Chinua Achebe, a renowned African novelist, decried the way Conrad described Africans: after reading *Heart of Darkness,* "I realized that I was one of those savages jumping up and down on the beach." In contrast, Edward Said, a respected writer on colonialism, praised Conrad's exquisite self-consciousness and his ability to describe the duality of the artist who lives in exile (and who therefore can see and say things that remain invisible or unsayable to the natives). See his *Joseph Conrad and the Fiction of Autobiography* (Cambridge, MA: Harvard University Press, 1966). Said later reported, "I used Conrad as an example of someone whose life and work seemed to typify the fate of the wanderer who becomes an accomplished writer in an acquired language, but can never shake off his sense of alienation from his new—that is, acquired—and, in Conrad's rather special case, admired home." *The London Review of Books,* 7 May 1998, http://www.lrb.co.uk/v20/n09/said01_.html.

former celebrate revenge and warriors; the latter articulate tragedy and the errors of revenge.

Self-reflection, thinking about thinking, is superior to splitting because it increases the amount of information available for reflection. With more information come better chances to employ mature solutions, from diplomacy to humor to arts, which preclude the rush to violence. However, because self-reflection, even in the most refined of novelists and theologians, emerges out of specific cultures and evokes specific feelings it cannot demonstrate to skeptics that the causes it champions, even antislavery, are inherently better than its competitors. Our particular experiences, including our personalities and our capacities for empathy, are by nature particular. This subjective dimension cannot be the ground of ethical reflection. That ground must exist outside our subjective experiences and it must be available universally to all persons. Jewish, Christian, and Islamic theologians addressed this demand for universality through their traditions of divinely revealed truths from a transcendent person, God, and were given to us. According to each tradition's teaching, this requires us to bind ourselves to its revealed truths and to the orthodoxy in which each thrives. These are deeply subtle traditions that appeal to the majority of people in the contemporary world. Their historical importance and their appeal do not prove that they can offer a universal ethic independent of revelation and orthodoxy.

CHAPTER 8

Response to Contradiction: Narrative Fiction

Are *Uncle Tom's Cabin, Heart of Darkness*, and *To Kill a Mockingbird* better stories than those offered by the apologists for Southern slavery? After all, none is scientific; none provides an irrefutable demonstration of its truths. Are we not left with mere differences of taste, mere differences of opinion? Some might argue that because the North won the Civil War, it has dominated public opinion and so told its stories with more authority than equally good stories offered by defenders of the Old South and its traditions. If the South had won, according to this view, then its views of the war would have prevailed with the same force. Its stories would enjoy the stature afforded the antiracist novels named above.

We can defend these novels on three grounds. First, they are accurate portraits of divided selves. Conrad's insight into the English feelings about Africans echoes his insight into the same feelings that the Roman sailors felt upon first seeing England's foreign shores. Through empathic reconstruction, Conrad united two seemingly disparate peoples. More radically, he united nineteenth-century English whites with black Africans whom they reviled, whom they judged as radically separate. The English, Conrad reminds us, were themselves once primitive tribes whom the Romans despised in part because they feared them. The "heart of darkness" in both nations' narratives lies within the breasts of the conquerors. First the Romans and later the English recognized, indirectly, that their savage attacks upon indigenous people stemmed from their hidden anxieties about these strange people. By being different they threatened the "superior" race's sense of singularity. Dimly aware of their ignoble origins, novel languages and novel cultures threatened to expose that arbitrariness, the fabrications that made up Roman and English claims to greatness. By being victims upon whom the Romans and the English exercised their lust for power, natives provoked brief moments of guilt and despair. Bloody, thrilling violence against poorly armed natives quelled these momentary anxieties. As empires always affirm, might makes right. However, splitting is not a perfect answer; those thoughts and feelings we split off and ascribe to others, were part of ourselves. No matter how dim this recognition may be, it cannot be extinguished.

Second, proslavery inventions increase splitting; these novels decrease it. In place of splitting us from our own capacity for selfishness, these novels substitute accurate, empathic accounts of the inner lives of all of the actors, the good and the bad. Even when Stowe presents Simon Legree as an example of brutality, she counterbalances him with portraits of good owners who taught their slaves reading and religion. Confronting this historical fact, she has a visitor remark,

> In my opinion, it is you considerate, humane men, that are responsible for all the brutality and outrage wrought by these wretches; because, if it were not for your sanction and influence, the whole system could not keep foothold for an hour. If there were no planters except such as that one," said he, pointing with his finger to Legree, who stood with his back to them, "the whole thing would go down like a mill-stone. It is your respectability and humanity that licenses and protects his brutality.[1]

---

[1] Harriet Beecher Stowe, *Uncle Tom's Cabin* (New York: Penguin Books, 1986), 486. All citations from this edition.

In contrast, proslavery preachers told stories in which the differences between masters and slaves were permanent, decreed by God to be everlasting, and in which the owners alone manifested self-consciousness. To ward off tremors of guilt for the pleasure of ownership—and for stealing the bread that others earned—proslavery authors struggled against themselves. Braver ones, among them Thomas Jefferson, shared their struggles in writing and in person with friends; less brave ones, the majority it appears, found ways to deny what they knew to be true. They shunned simple truths—of universal human sympathy, for example—by splitting, by constantly reminding themselves of their permanent superiority, of the "burdens of ownership," and of their Christian mission, just as the white authors of apartheid did in South Africa a century later.

These maneuvers required psychic energy and demanded constant upkeep. For that reason, the walls that proslavery writers erected within themselves appear formidable but were, in fact, fragile. A hundred years after *Uncle Tom's Cabin*, African Americans confronted Jim Crow laws in the United States and asked to be treated with civility. In a famous confrontation on April 19, 1960, with Ben West, the mayor of Nashville at the time, Diane Nash, then a student at Fisk University, asked him: "Do *you* feel it is wrong to discriminate against a person solely on the basis of their race or color?" The mayor paused and then said softly, yes, he did think it was wrong. West later said, "They asked me some pretty soul-searching questions—and one that was addressed to me as a man."[2] Nash's courage and her calmness, in face-to-face confrontation with the inner feelings of the oppressor, and hundreds of similar instances, helped breach walls of legal oppression that seemed solid and everlasting.

Earlier efforts to effect desegregation resulted in the landmark legal cases of the 1950s and the civil rights laws of the 1960s. Bayard Rustin, an early civil rights leader and one of the architects of the 1963 March on Washington, noted that in Southern hotels and lunch

---

[2] Quoted in Lynne Olson, *Freedom's Daughters: the Unsung Heroines of the Civil Rights Movement from 1830 to 1970* (New York: Scribner, 2001), 159.

counters Jim Crow impeded commerce. It was a nuisance "in a society on the move (and on the make). Not surprisingly, therefore, it was the most mobility-conscious and relatively liberated groups in the Negro community—lower middle class college students—who launched the attacks that brought down the imposing but hollow structure."[3] Those structures were relatively weak compared to economic and political institutions that resisted passionate stories about visible unfairness.

Yet, those passionate stories were important, as was *Uncle Tom's Cabin*, in mobilizing empathy for young people especially and sympathy for the movement that created anxiety about "Black Power." The latter may have been vital to certain political agendas, but its stories would, if not tempered, evoke white dread and provoke retaliation: "These spokesmen [for Black Power] are often described as the radicals of the movement, but they are really its moralists. They seek to change the white hearts—by traumatizing them."[4] Moralists do not seek to persuade and to reason; they seek to shock and bully.

Third, proslavery inventions decreased our collective repertoire of human understanding. Like all propaganda, these inventions provoked anxieties, in this case images of hordes of slaves bent upon revenge against their white owners. Those anxieties provoked, in turn, reactive responses in many Southerners. *Uncle Tom's Cabin*, *Heart of Darkness*, and *To Kill a Mockingbird* reflect human beings in their complexity. Each novel expands our inventory of self-understanding. They exemplify humane solutions; they circumvent occult and irrational solutions. By reading *Heart of Darkness* (1902) and Toni Morrison's celebrated novel, *Beloved* (1987) and responding to them, we become less divided. We are better able to resolve conflicts and to avoid both mystification which requires one to forgo understanding. An interviewer asked Toni Morrison how she under-

---

[3] Bayard Rustin: "From Protest to Politics" (1965). *The American Mosaic: The African American Experience.* ABC-CLIO, 2011. June 19, 2011. (web page).
[4] Ibid.

stood the fact that her house burned down shortly after she had won the Nobel Prize in Literature in 1993: "Did the fire seem like some kind of mystical leveling for flying too high?" To this notion of "mystic leveling," Morrison responded, no, the prize was a bright spot in an otherwise difficult period: "So I regard the fact that my house burned down after I won the Nobel Prize to be better than having my house burn down without having won the Nobel Prize. Most people's houses just burn down. Period."[5] Regarding splitting and propaganda, Morrison said that: "powerful, sharp, incisive, critical, bloody, dramatic, theatrical language is not dependent on injurious language, on curses. Or hierarchy."[6] Language that is sharp, incisive, and critical is powerful because it increases the store of facts about a human tragedy, such as slavery: "You're not stripping language by requiring people to be sensitive to other people's pain. I can't just go around saying, 'Kill whitey.' What does that mean? It may satisfy something, but there's no information there."[7] In our terms, there is no accurate description there. While understandable and satisfying in the short run, these responses are reactive and harmful in the long run.

Portraits of the Divided Mind: Odysseus Predicts Temptation

Odysseus was a Greek warrior who fought for the Greeks in their ten-year war against the Trojans, a war that occurred around 1250 BCE. Written some four hundred years later, *The Odyssey* is the rollicking adventure story of his trials, tribulations, and triumphs as he struggled to return to his home and his beloved wife, Penelope, in Ithaca, Greece. During that ten-year epic, Odysseus encountered gods, goddesses, beasts, and monsters with whom he struggled. Among the semidivine beings who stood in his way were the Sirens. They appear in Book 12. These were women whose voices and songs were irresistible

---

[5] Claudia Dreifus, http://www.en.utexas.edu/amlit/amlitprivate/texts/morrison1.html.

[6] Ibid.

[7] Ibid.

to mortals; once hearing them sailors could not turn away, they would join the heap of dead men whose bones still had flesh on them warned the goddess Circe.

> So they spoke, sending forth their beautiful voice, and my heart was fain to listen, and I bade my comrades loose me, nodding to them with my brows; but they fell to their oars and rowed on. But when they had rowed past the Sirens, and we could no more hear their voice or their song, then straightway my trusty comrades took away the wax with which I had anointed their ears and loosed me from my bonds.[8]

Predicting that he will be tempted by the Sirens' voices and crash his ships on the coastal rocks, Odysseus followed the goddess Circe's advice: "Me alone she bade to listen to their voice; but do ye bind me with grievous bonds, that I may abide fast where I am, upright in the step of the mast" (line 155). This seems not quite honest since Odysseus could also have stuffed his ears with wax. We realize that he wished to both hear the Sirens' alluring song and to stay alive. Being clever, Odysseus knew that his mind could be divided; he rationally predicted a future state of irrationality. He would be the lone drunk and his men would all be designated drivers. Homeric heroes are divided souls; a wise person mimics Odysseus and plans ahead.

Some 2,700 years later, Sigmund Freud made the same point. He also noted that the mind is divided into parts that struggle against other parts. Freud labeled these parts the ego, id, and super-ego (the "I," the "it," and the "overseeing-I.") These correspond to a self-conscious, active and alert self; a libidinal, often nonconscious self; and an active and nonconscious observer self that judges the conscious self. "Ego-id" conflicts refer to struggles between the conscious self and urges and impulses that seem to come from below. (Folk

---

[8] A. T. Murray, *The Odyssey with an English Translation* (Cambridge, MA: Harvard University Press, 1919), 447. See also Bruno Snell, *The Discovery of the Mind*. Cambridge, MA: Harvard, 1953), chap. 1, "Homer's View of Man."

Christians call these struggles between our rational nature and our animal nature.) "Ego-superego" conflicts refer to the human capacity to judge oneself as if we were another person and to punish ourselves, sometimes lethally. (Often Christians call these struggles between our fallen nature and our angelic nature.)

Scientific Studies of the Divided Mind: Talking to Ourselves

More recently, Daniel T. Gilbert and Timothy D. Wilson, contemporary American psychologists, summarized psychological studies that support Homer's insight. This divided-self makes judgment and planning possible. Because we can visualize diverse futures with diverse consequences we can choose one action over another. We present a story about the future to our self and then we gauge our feelings to that story *as if* it were occurring. (Gilbert and Wilson term these feelings "pre-motions" meaning emotions aroused in anticipation of a future state.) "Organisms remember the past so that they can predict the future."[9] Using terms from K. E. Stanovich, a Canadian cognitive scientist, they label these parts system 1 and system 2.[10]

Gilbert and Wilson confine their discussion to cognitive events, the show-and-tell that occurs between system 1 and system 2.[11] System 2 generates scenarios of the consequences of choices; system 1 reacts emotionally to those scenarios: "We know which future events

---

[9] Daniel T. Gilbert and Timothy D. Wilson, "Why the Brain Talks to Itself: Sources of Error in Emotional Prediction," *Philosophical Transactions of the Royal Society* 364 (2009): 1335.

[10] K. E. Stanovich, *Who Is Rational? Studies of Individual Differences in Reasoning* (Mahwah, NJ: Erlbaum, 1999).

[11] They cite contemporary authors; they could also cite William James who struggled with these issues one hundred years ago. See Lecture VIII, "The Divided Self, and The Process of Its Unification" in *The Varieties of Religious Experience* (New York: Longmans, Green, and Co., 1902). See also George Santayana, *Character & Opinion in the United States: with Reminiscences of William James and Josiah Royce* (New York: Scribner and Sons, 1921), 64–96.

will feel good and which will feel bad because we feel good or bad when we simulate them."[12] This kind of premonition is a conditioned response: having learned that thunderclouds mean possible tornadoes, people living in Oklahoma worry when they see thunderclouds on the horizon. In more complex situations, one part of the mind, system 2, tells a narrative about a future state of affairs and shows that narrative to system 1. System 1 reacts to this story as if it were happening in reality. System 1 generates emotional responses to that imagined reality. These emotional responses help us learn what we feel but cannot yet say: "We evolved to have emotional reactions to events in the present, and thus, to find out how we will react to events in the future, *we simply pretend those events are happening now.*"[13]

Circe told Odysseus a story about the exciting but dangerous Sirens and so became system 2 for Odysseus. In response to these exciting images, Odysseus's system 1 generated two feelings, anxiety and lust. These conflicted with each other: the first says "Flee!" the second says, "Stay!" Thanks to Circe, Odysseus resolved the conflict with stout ropes, beeswax, and an obedient crew.

While essential to human survival, this system can cause problems. Its virtues—speedy access to earlier experience, quick responses, and comparison of present with past images—are also its limits. Because it is designed to help us decide quickly, this system impedes reflective and integrative thinking. Splitting one's thoughts and feelings into separate, watertight compartments makes it impossible to communicate between parts of the self.[14] I cannot know why I fear black people if my fear and the images that produced it occur instantaneously, beyond my awareness. In its finest moments, imaginative literature about slavery makes us feel what we wish to avoid. We are taken in by the power of narration and we grasp, for a time, the emotional horror of slavery and its contradictions. For example, Toni Morrison brings us to the central crisis in her novel, *Beloved.* Sethe, an escaped slave

---

[12] Gilbert and Wilson, "Why the Brain Talks to Itself," 1335.

[13] Ibid., 1339. (My emphasis.)

[14] Ibid., 1339–40.

and a young mother, flees with her children. She is about to be recaptured by her slave-master. To avoid that fate, she kills her baby daughter, Beloved: "Her humanity had been so violated by this man, and by her entire experience as a slave-woman, that she kills her daughter to save her from a similar fate; she kills her to save her from psychic death."[15]

If our history is dominated by suffering, then we automatically assume dire consequences, especially of novel choices. (In psychotherapy parlance we have emotional biases or "transferences.") If a girl's history is shaped by an abusive father, for example, she will anticipate harm from male authorities. New male teachers, coaches, doctors, and therapists—among others—will evoke dread. Dread drives her to search for signs of hidden danger. If she finds none, she will challenge him, testing his real feelings for her. Caught in these struggles, she discounts benevolent encounters as false negatives. If I believe that there's a terrorist onboard my flight, finding 300 persons to be safe does not decrease my dread if the plane holds 301. The absence of attack only proves that it could or will occur later. In moments of terror we *are* in pain; we *are* in a waking nightmare; the past *is* present.

When slave owners heard about John Brown's raid on Harper's Ferry in December 1859, they visualized themselves being attacked by their slaves as they read the accounts. That which owners had feared before the creation of the United States, and had feared regularly since, had truly come to pass: slave rebellion. In countless sermons, discussions, and editorials, officials announced that these violent actions were the fruition of abolitionist ideas.[16] In contrast,

---

[15] Barbara Schapiro "The Bonds of Love and the Boundaries of Self in Toni Morrison's "'Beloved,'" *Contemporary Literature* 32, no. 2 (Summer, 1991): 200.

[16] "The Harper's Ferry raid helped set the stage for Civil War because it terrorized Southern whites, forcing many into the conviction that "the abolitionists were translating their hated theories into direct action, and that the Brown raid heralded the opening of the abolitionist offensive."

Europeans idealized Brown. Victor Hugo, the great French novelist and provocateur, designed a much-publicized image of John Brown on the gallows, a shaft of light from heaven falls on the body, beneath the engraving are the words, "*Christo—Sicut Christus*, John Brown" ("for Christ, just as Christ, John Brown").[17] Henry David Thoreau made the same point as did many Northern preachers who "saw nothing blasphemous about the comparison."[18]

Second, encounters between system 2 and system 1 depend upon stories, upon narratives about the future. Gilbert and Wilson discuss simple incidents in which people imagine their future response to tasty foods or to receiving small amounts of cash. These are thin plots, we might say. In more complex incidents involving a person's safety or emotional security, the scenarios become stories about oneself and about those who perpetuate one's suffering. These are not stories about chocolate; they are stories about a person—a boyfriend, a boss, a rebellious slave—whose every action portends life or death.

To be terrified of others is to affirm Sartre's insight in *No Exit* that "hell is other people."[19] Sartre composed *No Exit* during the Nazi control of Paris in World War II. It portrays that world of depredation and horror with exactness. Forty years earlier across the Atlantic, William James proclaimed his version of spiritual, scientific, open-minded Americanism. The difference between these two visions emerges from each man's circumstance. Sartre envisioned a postwar

---

Armstead L. Robinson, "In the Shadow of Old John Brown: Insurrection Anxiety and Confederate Mobilization, 1861–1863," *The Journal of Negro History* 65, no. 4 (Autumn, 1980): 279. He cites Ollinger Crenshaw, "The Psychological Background of the Election of 1860," *North Carolina Historical Review* 19 (1942): 260.

[17] Seymour Drescher. "Servile Insurrection and John Brown's Body in Europe," *The Journal of American History* 80, no. 2 (September 1993): 499.

[18] John Staufer and Zoe Trodd, "Meteor of War," in *The Afterlife of John Brown*, ed. Andrew Taylor and Eldrid Herrington (New York: Macmillan, 2005), 132.

[19] Says Garcin in *No Exit* (*Huis clos* [1944]).

Europe of collapse, strife, and possibly a third world war. James envisioned a better, more open (American) world of constantly expanding horizons. In the words of George Santayana, a distinguished American philosopher, "Like most Americans, however, only more lyrically, James felt the call of the future and assurance that it could be made far better, totally other, than the past."[20] Religious stories could be mined, James asserted, for their pragmatic benefits; less mystery and more value would emerge: "Faith was needed to bring about the reform of faith itself, as well as other reforms."[21]

We think about our future in narratives generated from our past and our current horizons, as James illustrates in his typically American optimism. Yet, the future is not here and logically we can prove nothing about it. The laws of science might cease. It's possible that gravity, for example, will disappear and the world will fly apart. But that idea, a staple of both science fiction and psychotic delusions, generates intolerable anxiety. Emotions, it appears, develop out of concrete experiences of dangers and opportunities; thus, concrete emotional understanding trumps abstract reasoning. (A depressed psychiatrist, for example, cannot be reasoned out of his or her despair.)

Emotional premonitions share the complex organization of other emotions that have evolved alongside the human brain. John Tooby and Leda Cosmides, two contemporary evolutionary psychologists, argue that emotions "behave functionally according to evolutionary standards, the mind's many subprograms need to be orchestrated so that their joint product at any given time is functionally coordinated; rather than cacophonous and self-defeating."[22] If we combine their portrait of emotions with Gilbert and Wilson's portrait of how system

---

[20] George Santayana, *Character & Opinion in the United States: with Reminiscences of William James and Josiah Royce* (New York: Scribner and Sons, 1921), 88.

[21] Ibid., 88.

[22] John Tooby and Leda Cosmides "Conceptual Foundations of Evolutionary Psychology," *Handbook of Evolutionary Psychology*, ed. David M. Buss (New York: Wiley, 2005), 52.

2 generates stories to which system 1 responds, we gain a multidimensional view of why emotions are essential to adaptation. They coordinate our feelings and our actions; they orchestrate our memories and expectations; and they do this quickly and invisibly.

Because emotions occur nonconsciously, we do not know ahead of time what feelings and impulses might be set free. If strong emotions have provoked painful consequences, such as punishment, children learn to suppress them. More so, emotions are complex products of our minds, our experience, and our mammalian heritage. If we view emotions as collections of feelings, impulses, and idiosyncratic beliefs about the self, no single concept and no single explanation is sufficient to explain them: "An emotion is not reducible to any one category of effects."[23]

This means that we cannot reduce emotions to simple, easily defined objects. For example, the emotion of "shame" is a body-based experience, an idea, a kind of interpersonal action, and a set of ideas about one's public face. Each of these factors is conditioned by training and cultural contexts.[24]

Because emotional processing occurs faster than deliberative reasoning and is nonconscious, we must discover what we feel *post facto*, after we've observed ourselves. Pushed by automatic feelings, we act or speak. Later, upon reflection, we realize that strong emotions drove us to act in ways we may not understand or may abhor. As Paul says in his letter to the Romans, "I do not understand what I do. For what I want to do I do not do, but what I hate I do."[25] Being part of scripture,

---

[23] Ibid., 53.

[24] For example regarding Western versus Eastern notions of shame, see Olwen Bedford and Kwang-Kuo Hwang. "Guilt and Shame in Chinese Culture: A Cross-cultural Framework from the Perspective of Morality and Identity," *Journal for the Theory of Social Behaviour* 33:2 (2003): 127–44.

[25] Romans 7:15 New International Version. Compare the King James Version, "For that which I do I allow not: for what I would, that do I not; but what I hate, that do I" and The New American Bible, "What I do, I do not understand. For I do not do what I want, but I do what I hate."

these sentences cannot be reduced to a single proposition, to a simple meaning. Who we are and how we understand the Book of Romans, its relationship to other Pauline epistles, to other New Testament texts, and to Judaism, shape our interpretation of this passage. Yet, we cannot deny that Paul refers to a universal human experience of dividedness, of feeling split between our intentions and our actions. Without help, this split yields misery, "Miserable one that I am! Who will deliver me from this mortal body?" Paul asks (Romans 7:24).

Paul offers a theological account of this divided self. However to be noted is that the emotional state Paul calls "miserable" (Greek *talaipwōros*) refers to a state of turmoil, of hard labor that one must endure, unsure of relief. Its antithesis is *tala-kardis* meaning stout-hearted, optimistic, of good cheer. The painful state begins in a narrative in which one's future is of unending toil; the opposite state begins in a narrative of sure and reliable relief.[26] Paul says that we are a mystery to ourselves. We need, therefore, to rely upon others—parents, authorities, and seers—to tell us what we felt and what it means. Religious authorities have always stood ready to help us distinguish the good from the bad. Yet, they can get it wrong and their authority and clarity stems, in part, from their denial of alternate, equally valid readings of the past. Each new form of Christian thinking, for example, requires new readings of Paul's letters.

The evolutionary advantage of these premonitions is that they drive us to act decisively when a few seconds may determine life or death. The disadvantage is that when we try to reason about our emotional life we are always looking backward to feelings and the dramatic scenarios that occurred almost instantaneously. Great novelists and great authors, among them Abraham Lincoln, are essential to our well-being because they articulate ways to tell us *what* we feel. This, we note, is another narrative or representational event: authors help shape the story that we henceforth tell ourselves. They slow down the reactive process; we give ourselves over to them and risk, therefore, being changed.

---

[26] Romans 7:24. See http://www.greekbible.com/index.php.

The Adaptive Advantages of Narratives

Some authorities on evolution assert that adaptations, not genes, are the basic units of evolution: "Natural selection produces well-engineered structures called *adaptations* that effectively and efficiently solve the numerous reproductive problems posed by the environment."[27] If we accept this handy definition, then we can retain our loyalty to Darwin—that human behavior evolves according to the same rules as anatomical evolution—and not be confined to seeking the single gene for short stories versus the gene for novellas. Short stories, novellas, TV sitcoms, and Icelandic sagas are instances of complex behavior—storytelling—that is adaptive. This engineered product—the narrative—solves numerous human needs for memory, recollection, identity, group solidarity, and so on.

W. H. Calvin, a contemporary neuroscientist, notes that: "After many generations, only those stories of timeless relevance are left alongside the likely-ephemeral contemporary ones."[28] At first glance, this seems circular: stories that have persisted must have timeless relevance because they have persisted. We can break this circle if we can specify what "timeless relevance" means.

"Timeless relevance" means that a story offers us emotional utility, a connection between our sense of who we are and our future, and that it appeals to generations of readers. In addition, it should have these characteristics:

- Not too local, not too rooted to specific times and places.
- Not refutable, that is, not dependent upon factual claims.
- Easily narrated and remembered.

---

[27] Edward M. Hagen, "Controversial Issues in Evolutionary Psychology" in *Handbook of Evolutionary Psychology,* ed. David M. Buss (Hoboken, NJ: Wiley, 2005), 147. (His emphasis.)

[28] W. H. Calvin, "The Six Essentials? Minimal requirements for the Darwinian Bootstrapping of Quality," *Journal of Memetics—Evolutionary Models of Information Transmission* (1997): 1. See also his book, *How Brains Think* (New York: Basic Books, 1996).

- Evocative but not too sensual.
- Hierarchical and redundant.
- Relevant to universal struggles within the self and between self and others.

Important messages, when one wants to go to war or to purchase a bride or to declare peace, for example, are redundant.[29] When the message is crucial and evokes strong resistances, the sender must increase redundancy or risk failing to convince the viewer.

To increase redundancy we use many images to convey the same message, each one reinforcing the other. Part of the genius of the early civil rights leaders was their insight that white Americans would respond to the plight of African American college students and schoolchildren more quickly than they would to the unfair treatment of adult African Americans. The four girls who died in the bombing of the 16th Street Baptist Church in Birmingham in September 1963 and other young victims were *perfectly* innocent. We can imagine that adults have made bad choices that explain their wretched state, but eight-year-olds cannot be blamed.

Effective literature and effective cinema are redundant, each building upon a set of images that reinforce the same message. Harriet Beecher Stowe began *Uncle Tom's Cabin* with a declaratory chapter, "In Which the Reader Is Introduced to a Man of Humanity." She portrays Uncle Tom, an unusually fine person, and Harry, a charming and beautiful child. Tom, we learn "is a good, steady, sensible, pious fellow" who got religion four years earlier. Harry is a lovely young Negro boy. Eliza, his mother, has "the same rich, full, dark eye, with its long lashes; the same ripples of silky black hair" as her son.

In contrast to these attractive people, we meet two rich, shallow white men, who use poor grammar. One is Haley, a slave trader, who says that he avoids, when possible, separating slave women from their

---

[29] Roy Rappaport, "Ritual, Sanctity, and Cybernetics," *American Anthropologist* 73 (1971): 59–76, and *Pigs for the Ancestors: Ritual in the Ecology of a New Guinea People* (New Haven, CT: Yale University Press, 1968).

infants because the mothers may die of grief, thus ruining one's investment: "And the trader leaned back in his chair, and folded his arm, with an air of virtuous decision, apparently considering himself a second Wilberforce."[30]

This conversation prefigures the novel's central themes: the destruction of the slave family, the sale of Tom and Harry, Eliza's despair, her flight, and Uncle Tom's decision to abide by the sale in order to secure the finances of his original owners who might otherwise sell all their slaves and so destroy the community. Tom's initial sacrifice prefigures his later Christ-like actions on behalf of slaves whom Simon Legree is working to death on his plantation. Each of these initial scenes helps us to grasp the novel's theme, to be moved by its characters, and to absorb the fervor of abolitionist feelings.

In a similar way directors guide us into the emotional world of a movie in the first seconds of the film. Its titles, music, color, camera movement, lighting, and other visual elements frame and shape our experience before we meet the main characters or discover the plot. Each of these preliminary elements forms a redundant, multilayered introduction to the emotions and to the conflicts that constitute the movie's drama.

Integrative Thinking versus Splitting:
Lord Jim versus Jesse James

> *The vilest scramble for loot that ever disfigured the history of human conquest and geographical exploration.* —Joseph Conrad[31]

When Conrad imagined the minds of Roman sailors in *Heart of Darkness* he did not draw on social scientific studies. He was not a sociologist. Roman sailors left no firsthand accounts of their feelings

---

[30] Beecher Stowe, *Uncle Tom's Cabin*, 46–47.

[31] Joseph Conrad, "Geography and Some Explorers," *National Geographic*, March 1924. Also in "Geography and Some Explorers" in *Last Essays*, ed. Richard Curle (London: J. M. Dent & Sons, 1926), 10–17.

as they approached the coast of Britannia in the first century of the modern era. Lacking that resource, Conrad drew upon his maritime memories and his imagination. He wrote from firsthand experience of twenty years at sea. From his immersion in that world, he imagined how sailors two thousand years earlier would have experienced the dark harbor where unknown savages waited to attack them.

In Conrad's time, English apologists argued that the English must appear as gods to the Africans. This split between English demigods and African savages could not persist. Having ascribed all human failures to natives, colonial experts first struck a pose of noble concern.

Kurtz's essay on his African subjects evokes, Marlow says, images of "an exotic Immensity ruled by an august Benevolence."[32] But this maneuver—a combination of denial of European greed, sentimentality, and religious zeal—fails. Kurtz's high-flown efforts to soar above the tawdry facts of his profession dissolve into murderous rage. Kurtz's rage appears in his report on how to handle African natives: "He began with the argument that we whites, from the point of development we had arrived at, 'must necessarily appear to them [Africans] in the nature of supernatural beings—we approach them with the might of a deity,' and so on, and so on" (ibid.). This inflated sense of English power generated an inflated sense of themselves; as deities they could use their immense powers for justice and good works: "By the simple exercise of our will we can exert a power for good practically unbounded, etc., etc." (ibid.). Marlow describes Kurtz's soaring rhetoric and a magnificent conclusion, "though difficult to remember, you know" (ibid.). Kurtz's words showed an "unbounded power of eloquence—of words—of burning noble words. There were no practical hints to interrupt the magic current of phrases" (ibid.). However, there was a handwritten note at the end of Kurtz's document: "It was very simple, and at the end of that moving appeal to every altruistic sentiment it blazed at you, luminous and terrifying, like a flash of lightning in a serene sky: 'Exterminate all the brutes!'" (ibid.)

Conrad modeled Kurtz on men he had met on another voyage in

---

[32] Joseph Conrad, *Heart of Darkness*.

1890. In that year, he took a mate's position on a river ship for the *Societe Anonyme pour le Commerce du Haut-Congo (SAB)*.[33] One of many competing companies, the SAB was organized in 1888 to help King Leopold II of Belgium plunder the ivory and rubber reserves of the Congo Free State which was, effectively, Leopold's private estate. Lauded in his home country, Leopold opened up the Congo River's vast reserves to all parties willing to help him exploit the river basin. When rubber became one of the world's most valuable commodities and too few laborers were available, Belgian agents used violence and intimidation to force local peoples into compulsory labor, especially portage. Between 1888 and 1905 the value of the rubber trade increased 168 times (about 17,000 percent). In what became infamous atrocities, the members of the company's police, *Force Publique*, were rewarded for the amount of rubber they forced natives to extract; penalties failing to meet these standards were violent reprisals, among them severing hands. The severed hands were presented to the company commanders as evidence of effective management: one history of the Congo states that "This happened so much that human hands took on a value of their own, becoming a sort of currency."[34] By some estimates the Congo's population declined from 20 million to 8.5 million between 1891 and 1911.[35]

When Conrad sailed up the Congo in 1890, on a ship similar to the one described in *Heart of Darkness*, he recorded observations that later appeared in that novel. The narrator's reflections on the oddity of that voyage and the bizarre world created by the intrusion of Europeans into Africa are Conrad's. He does not pretend that that voyage and the numerous atrocities against Africans committed by (Christian) Europeans can be enumerated like a grocery list—or reduced to accounts of rubber and ivory taken through terror. Those awful stories provoke

---

[33] http://www.victorianweb.org/authors/conrad/chron.html.

[34] Didier Gondola. *The History of the Congo* (Westport, CT: Greenwood Press, 2002), 67–68.

[35] Martin Ewans, *European Atrocity, African Catastrophe: Leopold II, the Congo Free State and its Aftermath* (London: RoutledgeCurzon, 2002).

dissociations, dream-like states, in persons who attempt to comprehend them, to keep their minds undivided, to avoid splitting. When
Conrad tried to comprehend, to absorb the full story of the crimes he
witnessed (and heard about), he faltered, like most of us would, in understanding these terrible scenes. It was like trying to capture a dream,

> that commingling of absurdity, surprise, and bewilderment in a tremor
> of struggling revolt, that notion of being captured by the incredible
> which is the very essence of dreams . . . no, it is impossible; it is impossi-
> ble to convey the life-sensation of any given epoch of one's existence—
> that which makes its truth, its meaning—its subtle and penetrating es-
> sence.[36]

Knowing these truths and seeing firsthand the cruelty of Europeans in Africa, Conrad rejected the self-praise Europeans heaped upon
their "missionary" work on the continent. Exactly how model Englishmen and other European elites could turn savage against a
helpless population, was a question that tormented Conrad. A similar
question torments us when we visit the Thomas Jefferson Memorial
in Washington, DC, and then tour Jefferson's slave estate in Charlottesville. How is this union of brilliant political thinking and a
crime against humanity possible?

In addition to witnessing the brutality of Leopold's agents in the
Congo, Conrad had earlier taken part in an act that jeopardized the
lives of a thousand Muslims (non-Christians and "non-whites" in nineteenth-century European categories.) Nineteen years before he wrote
Heart of Darkness, Conrad was part of an English crew on the *Jeddah*, a
ship that was carrying one thousand Muslim pilgrims to the holy city
of Mecca. In early August 1880, during a heavy storm, the ship's captain, Lucas Clark, evacuated his crew, his wife, and himself to lifeboats
leaving the thousand Muslims to drown in the ocean near the Arabian
Peninsula. In a telegram, Captain Clark said that the ship had been

---

[36] Citation from http://www.pagebypagebooks.com/Joseph_Conrad/Heart
_of_Darkness/Chapter_I_p2.html.

sinking, that the boiler had become unmoored, and that it had punched a gaping hole in the ship. He added that the Muslim passengers were murderous and uncontrollable. A second telegram from a second source reported that another vessel had towed the *Jeddah* safely into port. At an extensive inquiry, Captain Clark said that one of the reasons he had abandoned ship was that his (white) wife had been threatened by the (dark-skinned) passengers. English officials confirmed, "This allegation is specially dealt with by the Court of Inquiry, and according to their report there is no truth in it."[37] Captain Clark reverted to the racist ideology that ascribed lust for white women to all dark-skinned men. However, in this case, it did not save him.

An inquiry was struck to investigate this betrayal of maritime duty, with focus on Captain Clark's explanation for the apparent crime. One newspaper declared that while many pilgrim ships were sailed by cowardly men, "We sincerely trust that no Englishman was amongst the boatload of cowards who left the *Jeddah* and her thousand passengers to shift for themselves."[38] In contrast to Captain Clark, the captain of a French vessel, the *Antenor*, discovered the foundering ship, boarded her, and by enlisting the help of its Muslim passengers, pumped enough water out of the ship to keep her afloat until she reached port three days later. As the *Antenor's* chief mate put it, by working together his crew and the Muslim men on board showed "the hearty good-will with which the sailors were conducting their operations, and how likely it would be that they would reanimate, by their coolness and determination, the failing spirits and flagging energies of the pilgrims."[39] It is a scene worthy of Steven Spielberg: a

---

[37] Gene M. Moore, "Newspaper Accounts of the 'Jeddah Affair,'" *The Conradian* 25, no. 1, "Lord Jim:" Centennial Essays. (Spring 2000): 104–39. Citing: Proceedings of the Legislative Council of Singapore, 14 September 1880, as recorded in the *Straits Times Overland Journal* 20 (September 1880): 2–3.

[38] *Daily Chronicle*, cited by Moore, "Newspaper Accounts of the 'Jeddah Affair.'"

[39] Moore, "Newspaper Accounts of the 'Jeddah Affair.'"

multiracial and multiethnic group comes together under catastrophic circumstances to man the pumps for three days running, thereby saving the lives of a thousand people, among them many women and children.

Conrad's shame at this world-famous failure generated another great novel, *Lord Jim* (1889/1890), which in Conrad's words is a story about the "acute consciousness of lost honour."[40] Jim, a perfectly decent young man, cannot understand the evil ways of other men. He dreams of glory and valor on the high seas. He sees himself "saving people from sinking ships, cutting away masts in a hurricane, swimming through a surf with a line" (ibid.). These dreams evaporate when he and his crewmates abandon a pilgrim vessel, like the *Jeddah*, headed toward Mecca. And as in that story, there is an official inquiry into what appears to be dereliction of duty. Through the wise, world-weary language of Marlow, Conrad says that trying to discover why such events occur is like trying to solve an impossible puzzle. The investigators and the crowd listening to the evidence expect "some essential disclosure as to the strength, the power, the horror, of human emotions." But this cannot and did not occur. Attempting to pressure Jim to explain himself and the actions of his shipmates "was as instructive as the tapping with a hammer on an iron box, were [*sic*] the object to find out what's inside" (ibid.). In this beautiful metaphor, Jim is the iron box and the inquisitors are banging on him, as he bangs on himself. Jim's shame and his internal struggles drive the rest of the novel, and they predict his final act of self-sacrifice and contrition. Early in the novel, Marlow says, "It was for me, with all the sympathy of which I was capable, to seek fit words for his meaning. He was 'one of us'" (ibid.).

Drawing upon his shame, Conrad makes Jim's story and Jim's agony apparent to us. Like Conrad and Jim, we have earned our share of shame. This act of synthesis, of bringing Jim to remember his wishes alongside his failures, elevates Jim out of the category of comic-book

---

[40] Joseph Conrad, *Lord Jim* (1889/1890) *in Blackwood's Magazine,* author's note, n.p.

heroes and gives him unity. Jim does not split his mind in two parts; one warring against the other. Nor does Conrad attempt to solve the puzzle of Jim's less-than-ideal actions. The impulses and fears that drove Jim to do the wrong thing remain inside the iron box. Jim and we know that that box is within him, within a dark heart, and within that lies the mystery. The sources of Jim's errors are not outside himself; they do not reside in demonic others who forced him to act against his will. Jim's guilt, his shame, and his suffering are his alone. That act of containment, of acknowledging the duality within him, is part of the nobility of Jim's character. It is why Conrad and we love him. That is a second aspect of Conrad's synthesis; by loving Jim we share, at least for a moment, Jim's unity of self. We recognize that we also might have acted as he had (and as Conrad had). As Conrad said about himself, he was not impressed by superficial finery, by a man's linen, as he put it. Rather, he had a "democratic quality of vision" with which he looked at all persons.

Heart of Darkness and *Lord Jim* focus upon persons whose motives are complex, hidden from themselves, and sources of internal doubts. Their agonies are between one part of themselves and another part. They wrestle with guilt and shame, locating the source of each within themselves.

At the crux of the American civil rights movement, in *To Kill a Mockingbird*, Harper Lee portrayed the dilemmas of American racism and located its fault lines between conscious and unconscious actors. In the film version, released in 1962, Atticus Finch, the heroic attorney, is played by Gregory Peck.[41] He confronts a mob ready to lynch Tom Robinson, an innocent black man accused of raping a white woman. The mob represents people at their most regressed, dominated by splitting. American racism (fueled by images of sexual violence) comes alive in their lust to attack and destroy a black body. A divided psyche demands a divided world and a cartoon script: Tom, a lustful black man penetrated an innocent, passive white woman. (Just as Jefferson Davis said in his memoirs and as D. W. Griffith portrayed in

---

[41] Directed by Robert Mulligan, Universal, 1962.

The Birth of Nation.) Having imagined these forbidden (and longed-for) sexual scenes, the mob's members are driven to enact a fitting, mechanical response. Lynchings are, of course, not accidental events. Their history and cultural logic merit reflection long denied them before Ida B. Wells documented the spectacles surrounding lynch mobs that acted freely in the American South (and sometimes in the far West and Middle West).[42]

When *To Kill a Mockingbird* appeared in 1962—a year before the March on Washington—the political context had shifted. Middle America was willing to conceive of Southerners (at least if they were Southern white men who resembled Gregory Peck) who could confront ecstatic forms of blood lust and spectacle. At the height of his illustrious career, Peck's screen personae embodied American virtues—he had defended America in *Days of Glory* (1944), *Twelve O'Clock High* (1949), *On the Beach* (1959), and *The Guns of Navarone* (1961). He stood up against anti-Semitism in *Gentleman's Agreement* (1947).[43] A man of unusual good looks and liberal commitments, Peck was Atticus Finch before he took the role. Confirming the uncanny melding of actor and character, the American Film Institute named Atticus Finch the top film hero of all time.[44]

In her novel, Harper Lee focused upon a white family and white responsibility through her two heroes, Atticus, a distinguished attorney, and his daughter, the irascible and lovable Scout (Jean Louise). In the movie's most frightening scene, Atticus places himself between a

---

[42] See "Ida B. Wells-Barnett, 1862–1931," *Crusade for Justice; the Autobiography of Ida B. Wells*, ed. Alfreda M. Duster (Chicago: University of Chicago Press, 1970).

[43] That it took an iconic white, non-Jewish, all-American movie star to portray a sympathetic Jew is a measure of the anxiety that the studios felt about this subject. In addition, the anti-Semites in the film are rich New Yorkers for whom the majority of Americans had little sympathy. See Vincent P. Franklin et al., *African Americans and Jews in the Twentieth Century* (Columbia, MO: University of Missouri Press, 1998), 91–93.

[44] http://www.afi.com/100Years/handv.aspx.

white mob and the jailed Tom who knows his fate at their hands. Mirroring her father's bravery, Scout comes between her father and the lynch mob. She addresses Mr. Cunningham, one of its leaders, who owes her father an entailment (a debt) for past legal services. We doubt that Scout would fail to see that her beloved father faced a threatening mob and we doubt that a child would confront a mob's ringleaders with her poignant questions. Yet, we love Scout in her ideal form. She manifests integrative thinking as antidote to the lynch mob (and splitting):[45]

"I said 'Hey, Mr. Cunningham. How's your entailment getting along?'"

Scout wakes him out of his stupor. She forces him to comprehend the duality of his mind: that there are three, distinct temporal periods. There is the *past*, with its entailments and social debts between him and her father. There is the *present*, in which he is threatening to harm the same man. There is the immediate *future* over which Cunningham now has control; he and his mob do not have to fall into a "mysterious, metaphysical, and almost electric frenzy" of killing Tom and perhaps Atticus.

In the past, Mr. Cunningham's feelings were civil and balanced—a present good was given in exchange for a promised future good; in the present there is only the imperious excitement of blood lust. Cunningham blinks, he has awakened. He recalls that past conversation and its social fabric, his debt, and his previous feelings toward this little girl. By walking closer to him, Scout presses upon him, driving home her insistence.

"Don't you remember me, Mr. Cunningham? I'm Jean Louise Finch."

Scout brings him back, to recall social and economic entailments, the civic bond that had linked the three of them together.

"You brought us some hickory nuts early one morning, remember?"

---

[45] Horton Foote, *To Kill a Mockingbird; Tender Mercies; and The Trip to Bountiful: Three Screenplays by Horton Foote* (New York: Grove Press, 1989), 51.

[She repeats her exhortation: Remember!] "We had a talk. I went and got my daddy to come out and thank you." [There was a rational, symmetrical process between them: she remembered to fetch her father so that he could witness Mr. Cunningham's goodwill and affirmation of their communal agreement.] "I go to school with your boy. He's a nice boy." [Mr. Cunningham is a father and he will have to explain himself to his "nice boy."] "Tell him 'hey' for me, won't you?" [She commands Cunningham to fix in memory this new encounter, to keep his son and Scout in mind and to conceive of a future in which he will communicate her message to his child.] "You know something, Mr. Cunningham, entailments are bad."

Scout increases pressure upon Cunningham to remember. She asks him to realize who she is and to remember and so recall his feelings about his own child. She gives Cunningham an assignment: remember to recall *her* remembrance of his son to the boy: a triple instance of integrative thinking. Scout disarms Mr. Cunningham by making him remember his responsibilities to her and to other children. Having been awakened, he leads the group away from its original intention. She also awakens in him ancient lessons he learned in Sunday school and in his civics class.

Righteous Retaliation

In a diametrically opposite manner to the three novels described above, much of the pro-Confederate literature that flourished after 1865 portrayed unblemished, heroic warriors who acted always in self-defense or righteous retaliation. For example, John Newman Edwards was a notably brave Confederate officer who rode with Major General Joseph O. Shelby, an illustrious CSA leader in Missouri and Western environs. Edwards chronicled Shelby's exploits in *Shelby and His Men* (1867), an exhaustive history of Shelby's Civil War campaigns. In 461 pages, Edwards gives precise, if exaggerated, details of skirmishes, major battles, and strategy.[46] Without difficulty we forgive

---

[46] Edwards's work shows a "journalist's exaggerations. Edwards should always be corroborated with other contemporary accounts," according to Mark K.

Edwards's language when he writes in the preface about the "Confederate War" and the "grand panorama of heroic endurance and devoted courage." Just two years from the War's cessation, and immersed in Victorian literary style, his sentiments are understandable. We are less forgiving about another book he published, *Noted Guerrillas or, The Warfare of the Border.*[47] In that book Edwards celebrated and defended actions by non-Confederate fighters, including outright sociopaths like Bill Anderson and Jesse James. James, Edwards said, "blended the ferocity of a savage with the tenderness of a woman." Edwards wrote rapidly and skillfully, but his portraits of Jesse and Frank James as Robin Hoods who took from greedy, vicious bankers and gave to the poor are fanciful. The James brothers stole from whom they could and no evidence exists to show them giving to the poor. Like many men on the frontier, they were skilled, cunning, and brave to the point of recklessness. Unlike his accounts in *Shelby and His Men*, Edwards's stories about the James brothers and similar pro-Confederate gangs in *Noted Guerrillas* are embellished, often to the point of fantasy.[48]

Regarding Jesse James and other guerrillas, Edwards explains: "What they did in self-defense any Anglo-Saxon would have done who did not have in his veins the blood of a slave. The peaceful pursuits of life were denied to them."[49] According to this story, men whose first inclination was peace found themselves barred from those pursuits by evil Unionists who wrought atrocities upon their people. In response, they became heroic avengers seeking reparation for crimes

---

Christ, Arkansas Civil War Sesquicentennial Commission. http://www.encycl opediaofarkansas.net/encyclopedia/entry-detail.aspx?entryID=7017.

[47] John N. Edwards, *Noted Guerrillas or, The Warfare of the Border* (Saint Louis, MO: Bryan, Brand, 1867).

[48] Jesse's "robberies, his murders, his letters to newspapers, and his starring role in Edward's columns all played a part in the Confederate effort to achieve wartime goals by political means." T. J. Stiles, *Jesse James: Last Rebel of the Civil War* (New York: Vintage, 2002), preface.

[49] Edwards, *Noted Guerrillas or, The Warfare of the Border*, 456.

committed against family and friends. They became guerrillas "because the home they had left had been given to the flames, or a gray-haired father shot upon his own hearth-stone. They wanted to avoid the uncertainty of regular battle and know by actual results how many died as a propitiation or a sacrifice" (ibid., 22–23).

To drive home this morality tale, Edwards describes villains, most of them antislavery men from Kansas, such as, Emmet Goss, a Jayhawker, and a menace to innocents: "He boasted of having kindled the flames in fifty-two houses, of having made fifty-two families homeless and shelterless, and of having killed, as he declared, until he was tired of killing" (ibid.). Confronting this evil killing machine was Jesse James, the hero of Edwards's story: "Death was to come to him at last by the hand of Jesse James" (ibid.,153–54). Jesse is described with loving details: his face was "as smooth and as innocent as the face of a school girl. The blue eyes very clear and penetrating. . . . His form tall and finely moulded was capable of great effort and great endurance" (ibid.,167). Jesse is gallant, courtly, caring. He evokes images of Errol Flynn in *The Adventures of Robin Hood* or *The Sea Hawk*: "On his lips there was always a smile, and for every comrade a pleasant word or a compliment" (ibid., 168).

Jesse's feminine demeanor serves him well when he is disguised, "arrayed in coquettish female apparel, with his smooth face, blue eyes, and blooming cheeks, [he] looked the image of a bashful country girl, not yet acquainted with vice" (ibid., 172). While Jesse kills enemy men, he is scrupulous about not killing women, and obeying their wishes. When a beautiful young woman petitions him to save the life of an enemy combatant, he relents. Once, while about to kill a Federal official, he heard "an exceedingly soft and penetrating voice called out to him: 'Don't kill him, for my sake.'" James looked and saw a young girl. Taken in by her beauty and courage, he remembered his sister and his mother who had "always instilled into his mind lessons of mercy and charity. He lowered his weapon and announced to the young woman: 'Take him, he is yours. I would not harm a hair in his head for the State of Kansas'" (ibid., 194).

Those "lessons of mercy and charity" did not pertain to enemies who dared to fight back or who were cunning. According to Edwards, those were wicked and dispatched quickly. For example, a Union man feigned death, then rose up to shoot one of Jesse's men: "Almost before he had touched the ground Jesse James avenged him, firing twice into the head of the militiaman as he stood over him with his horse" (ibid., 287). Edwards had a flexible ethic. When Jesse or another guerrilla uses trickery, it is a source of amusement. Edwards described six incidents that he labels "shameful." Each is an instance of Union soldiers and antislavery militiamen. In one account, a disguised guerilla fools a Union man who accosts the "old lady" to his shame. In another, Union soldiers are sexually loose; in another, Jayhawkers (pro-Union guerrillas) are rapacious and cruel; in another, Union soldiers shamefully abandon one of their officers. In a fifth, a Union officer is fooled by Quantrell; and in a sixth, so desperate are Union men to arrest and punish a guerrilla, they shamefully convict an innocent man.[50]

---

[50] The word *shame* or a version of it appears six times in *Noted Guerrillas*. [1] A guerrilla disguised as an old woman approaches a Union picket. Edwards adds some theatrical intrigue and clever exchanges: "Where the reserve post was, the sergeant on duty took her horse by the bridle, and peered up under her bonnet and into her face. "Were you younger and prettier I might kiss you," he said. "Were I younger and prettier," the old lady replied, "I might box your ears for your impudence." "Oh! ho! you old she-wolf, what claws you have for scratching!" and the rude soldier took her hand with an oath and looked at it sneeringly. She drew it away with such a quick motion and started her horse so rapidly ahead that he did not have time to examine it. In a moment he was probably *ashamed* of himself, and so let her ride on uninterrupted" (96). On the ride back, the guerrilla, still in disguise, kills men who pursue him. [2] Union soldiers are sexually loose: "Four miles from Independence, and back a little from the road leading to Kansas City, a house stood occupied by several women light of love. Thither regularly went Federal soldiers from the Independence garrison, and the drinking was deep and the orgies *shameful*. Gregg set a trap to catch a few of the comers and goers" (172). [3] Jayhawkers who opposed the proslavery guerrillas are rapacious and cruel. A Union officer was only obeying the

Edwards wrote for Southerners who felt betrayed by the Union victory. What had begun as their fierce battle for "Independence," faltered after two years and became a slugfest with a superior foe and in defense of an institution, slavery, that was ignoble and not worth dying for. Rather than confront that shameful fact, and suffer the pain of remorse and guilt, Edwards helped Southerners reinforce their illusions. He and they believed that the South could not have been wrong and its soldiers could not have been defeated by lesser men, men from the North. Having wedded themselves to this tale, they yearned for stories that reinforced it. At its core this myth was the claim that a surplus of perfidy, of vast conspiracies, of unfairness—not a lack of Southern "grit and steel"—made the right outcome, the South's triumph, impossible. Contemporary versions of this myth adorn numerous websites, among them The League of the South. It advocates secession from the United States, which some of its members consider an occupier of Southern states.[51]

---

shameful order No. 11 from St. Louis Headquarters. It ordered the removal of all persons "living in Jackson, Cass, Bates, and northern Vernon counties Missouri to be removed from their present places of residence." [4] Union men abandon an officer: "When Leonard fell his men *shamefully* abandoned him and dashed away, as Steinmetz's men had done, without drawing rein, until they too reached Fayette, panic-stricken and exhausted" (305-06). [5] A Union Lieutenant seems to have cornered Captain William C. Quantrell. Quantrell denies that he is the infamous guerrilla. The Lieutenant is confused: "Not entirely convinced, and yet more than half way *ashamed* of the part he was playing, the Lieutenant stepped away from the door several feet and bade Quantrell call his orderly sergeant, keeping him still covered with the gaping muzzle of the Mississippi rifle." He is fooled as well (400). [6] Desperate to arrest and punish a guerrilla, Union officers convict an innocent man: "The charge upon which he was convicted was a charge *shamefully* false. Infuriated at the escape of men so notoriously desperate as were these Guerrillas of Quantrell, the Federal authorities at Louisville needed a victim. George Roberson was found. Any evidence was sufficient for conviction. No evidence at all would have answered just as well" (419).

[51] Although they deny racists beliefs, they make the natural hierarchy of the

Edwards rode this wave of rage and humiliation by feeding his readers endless, repeated accounts of Jesse James and other Confederate heroes who defied Union troops and their allies. Each account was a breathless story about a small group of Southerners facing overwhelming odds. In each, former Confederate soldiers or guerrillas achieved extraordinary success through cunning, bravery, and manly superiority. The simplicity of Edward's stories in *Noted Guerrillas* is not accidental. Because Edwards crafted them to satisfy a hunger for immediate relief from shame, they were short, bite-sized daydreams of derring-do and justified slaughter of the enemy. (Action stories use the same device—the hero slays with a magical device. Sometimes this is Samson's jawbone of a donkey in Judges 15:15 in the Bible; King Arthur's sword in *Excalibur*, or the Bride's sword in *Kill Bill*.)

After reading dozens of Edwards's stories, we get the point: the cause of Jesse's battles was the same thing that caused the South to lose the war. Their failures were not in themselves but in others—CSA leaders, Yankees who fashioned a strangling blockade of Southern ports, Jayhawkers and other criminals who wantonly destroyed innocent civilians. When that rage declined, so did Edwards's audience. However, the same devices remain available to anyone who wishes to avoid integrative thinking and who craves the luxury of revenge fantasies or deeds.

The Attack on Immutable Characteristics

In our times, this craving has reappeared in hate groups investigated by the FBI and catalogued by the Southern Poverty Law Center (SPLC). Their definition of hate group includes the criterion, "All hate groups have beliefs or practices that attack or malign an entire class of people, typically for their immutable characteristics."[52] These

---

South clear: "We, as Anglo-Celtic Southerners, have a duty to protect that which our ancestors bequeathed to us. If we do not promote our interests then no one will do it for us." http://dixienet.org/rights/2013/faq_frequently_asked_questions .php

[52] "The Southern Poverty Law Center counted 939 active hate groups in the

immutable characteristics include gender, race, ethnic origins, sexual orientation, and original religious identity. For example, Jewish heritage makes one a Jew (and therefore worthy of hatred) in the same way that the Spanish Inquisition made it impossible for Jews to be anything other than Jewish. The psychological rationale for these claims is identical to the rationale behind identity groups: each is based on blood. In more refined and less visceral ways, heritage groups, such as the Sons of Confederate Veterans (SCV), demand that applicants show blood kinship with a soldier from the CSA. The SCV's founding motto, penned by a Confederate officer in 1906, makes its mission clear. It is to support "the vindication of the Cause for which we fought; to your strength will be given the defense of the Confederate soldier's good name, the guardianship of his history, the emulation of his virtues, the perpetuation of those principles he loved and which made him glorious and which you also cherish."[53]

Seeking to replicate their glowing image of long-dead Confederate soldiers, members of the group organize themselves into camps, each with a commander, lieutenant commander, and so on. This playacting requires some substance that makes these wishes for union with an idealized past actual; that actual substance is blood. As in any drive to prove continuity between self and the ancestors, this requires tangible proof. For that reason, the SCV requires applicants to prove blood connections: "Application for membership in the Sons of Confederate Veterans is

---

United States in 2013. Only organizations and their chapters known to be active during 2013 are included. All hate groups have beliefs or practices that attack or malign an entire class of people, typically for their immutable characteristics. This list was compiled using hate group publications and websites, citizen and law enforcement reports, field sources and news reports. Hate group activities can include criminal acts, marches, rallies, speeches, meetings, leafleting or publishing. Websites appearing to be merely the work of a single individual, rather than the publication of a group, are not included in this list. Listing here does not imply a group advocates or engages in violence or other criminal activity." http://www.splcenter.org/get-informed/hate-map.

[53] Lt. Gen. Stephen D. Lee, CSA, Commander, United Confederate Veterans, 1906. http://tennessee-scv.org/index.html.

based upon identification and establishment of your relationship to your Confederate ancestor. You will need his name, unit, state of service, and information as to his honorable service [killed / wounded / captured / discharged]."[54]

The United Daughters of the Confederacy (UDC) requires both blood relationships and devotion to the Southern Cause.[55] Membership is for women sixteen or older "who are lineal or collateral *blood descendants of men and women* who served honorably in the Army, Navy, or Civil Service of the Confederate States of America, or who gave Material Aid to the Cause." The latter clause means that descendants of men like Jesse James and other guerrillas who gave material aid to the Cause are eligible for membership. The bloodline is essential: "Women who were adopted are eligible only through the *bloodline of the biological parent.* Also eligible are those women who are *lineal or collateral blood* descendants of members or former members of UDC." Lineal descendants share a direct line to a Confederate ancestor; collateral descendants share a more remote ancestor.

The crucial element is, again, blood. The UDC adds a political criterion as well: "No Confederate ancestor who took the Oath of Allegiance before April 9, 1865, shall be eligible to be used for application for membership." April 9, 1865, is the date of Lee's surrender to Grant at Appomattox Court House, Virginia. By taking an Oath of Allegiance to the United States before Lee's surrender, Confederate soldiers acted dishonorably, in the eyes of the UDC. Hence, their heirs cannot claim membership in the organization. If, however, a Confederate ancestor took the oath before April 9, 1865, and *then later recanted by his actions,* this nullified the oath. In that case, his descendants can apply for membership: "If proof of further Confederate service is available, *thereby nullifying the Oath of Allegiance,* the

---

[54] "The more you know about your ancestor, the more likely you are to find his records and supporting information. You will very likely find the search is easier than you think, and it will be a most rewarding and moving personal experience." http://tennessee-scv.org/membership.htm.

[55] All UDC citations from: http://www.hqudc.org/membership/.

ancestor shall be considered for approval." (My emphasis.)

To put this more nakedly, if an ancestor gave a (sacred) oath to the United States government, then broke it to take up arms against the United States, his Confederate service is honorable. On that basis, his descendants may become members of the UDC.[56]

Edwards, and other defenders of the Lost Cause, did not pretend to offer well-rounded, thoughtful accounts of complex experiences. They offered immediate, satisfying stories of revenge, self-justification, and idealization of ancestors. Affinity and blood-based alliances offer the same analgesic: the distressing question *Who am I?* is answered: I am like my (blood) ancestors who were extraordinary men and women, worthy of idealization. By joining a group, adopting its rituals, and invoking stories of the ancestors, I share their values, their heroism; their deathless valor. Those values made them great. Through my link to them I shall become great as well. The Lost Cause is not lost.

Are There Universal Narratives and Universal Needs?

Distinctive cultures develop distinctive languages that are intelligible only to their members. Yet, each distinctive form of speech is an instance of language, each is intertranslatable, and each is learnable in principle by any human speaker. In the same way, we can acknowledge that Africans kidnapped from their homes—over a 250-year history—were strange to Europeans and Americans. We can acknowledge that these dark-skinned, half-clothed natives did not resemble white Americans, but we can assert that underneath these visible differences is an invisible, common essence that can be discovered. And now we can believe that enslaved Africans shared an essential kinship with their owners.[57]

---

[56] See Karen L. Cox, *Dixie's Daughters: The United Daughters of the Confederacy and the Preservation of Confederate Culture* (Gainesville: University Press of Florida, 2003).

[57] Lovejoy estimates a total of ten million taken from Africa between 1650 and 1900. See by Paul E. Lovejoy, *Transformations in Slavery*. (Cambridge:

This claim of shared kinship is based on the conviction that to be human is to be of one species, one race. Racist ideologues always deny this claim; antiracists always affirm it, and the struggle between the two groups begins again. These struggles are political, ethical, and legal. To what degree can we speak of universal values such as human rights if legal rights exist only in particular instances, defended by particular nation states? We may agree that all languages are intertranslatable. But we do not and cannot speak language. We speak a particular language, not the abstract, hidden code that links our language to all other languages. We may wish to affirm Jefferson's stirring words about universal equality, but on what reasonable grounds, other than wishing it were so, can we tell that story?

In contrast to Edwards, jurists and other legal authorities were held to higher standards. Many years of training and the tradition of legal decorum require them to rise above narrow self-concerns and strident advocacy. They were required to provide legal reasons for or against opinions, even when those opinions are not in accord with their emotions. At their best, jurists should manifest the same complexity and affirmation of unity evident in Conrad or any other honest author.

How some Southern jurists struggled with that task regarding the laws of slavery is our next topic. Because they could not solve the contradiction of "thinking property," they failed. From those failures we move on to consider how two remarkable Southern women succeeded.

Cambridge University Press, 2000). For more recent estimates, see See D. Eltis and D. Richardson, *Extending the Frontiers: Essays on the New Transatlantic Slave Trade Database.* (New Haven, CN: Yale University Press, 2008).

CHAPTER 9

Response to Contradiction: Exposing Legal Fiction

Endless Cycles

Some forms of legal reasoning show integrative thinking and therefore share commonalities with Conrad's novels and similar forms of reflection. When a novel or similar work captures internal psychological conflicts of a distinctive period of time containing its diverse and contradictory parts, it shapes how later generations understand that epoch. For Southerners and other Americans, *Gone with the Wind* and *The Birth of a Nation* achieved that form of dominance. For others, *Lord Jim, Heart of Darkness*, Faulkner's novels, *The Color Purple* by Alice Walker, and similar novels have done the same. Once this elevation has occurred, subsequent writers and thinkers must locate themselves against their ancestors, the dominant authors who set the terms and named the conflicts with which they must contend. By the time of the Greeks, some 2,500 years ago, each generation of writers and philosophers had to locate themselves against their illustrious forbears. For example, Aristotle placed himself at the end of a tradition beginning with the pre-Socratics in the early sixth century BCE, through his mentor, Plato, to himself in the late fourth century BCE. While he admired Plato, he also wrestled with him as an antagonist, as someone he respected but also as his opponent.

Integrative thinking is the attempt to understand how human beings think about themselves in all their particularities. This requires us to take a stand outside ourselves, to examine our minds using our abilities to remember honestly, and to keep every side of our feelings within our mind at the same time. In addition, we must try to reason. Reasoning requires us to be consistent, to follow out a line of thought without regard to its end point. Integrative reasoning about justice, for example, may lead to conclusions that violate the interests of the stronger party. If this were not so, the idea of justice would dissolve into the calculation of power: those with the stronger army, those with more control determine what is just. While this may occur all too commonly, we cannot agree that the concept of justice is reducible to this cynical conclusion.

This consequential feature of integrative thinking emerged in reviews of freedom suits and other actions brought on behalf of enslaved persons in the United States. A "preference for freedom"—rooted in the language of the Declaration of Independence—complicated the task of proslavery authors. Once the notion of universal rights, especially Jefferson's Declaration, entered into American discourse it slowly dissolved arbitrary distinctions. That blacks were not social equals was guaranteed by the laws and violence used to subjugate them. Yet, as Lincoln recorded, even slaveholders admitted that slaves were human beings and that unlike other kinds of chattel, slaves had some rights, however obscure those rights appeared to the majority of whites. State and municipal laws regarding slavery depended upon the murky categories of "race" and "color" and upon vague or nonexistent records of the color of a person's parents and grandparents. As one writer stated:

> By the late seventeenth century, what had been chiefly a psychological category had become a major legal and economic category in the colonies, black slavery. And for most of the time from the seventeenth century through the American Civil War, the notion that African-Americans were different and inferior served as the cornerstone of American slavery and seemed to need no elaboration.[1]

---

[1] Jonathan Bush, "Free to Enslave: The Foundations of Colonial American

It fell to judges to discern which persons counted as "slave property" and which did not. In ambiguous cases some judges expressed a preference for freedom over property rights when they assessed freedom suits brought by slaves and Indians, wrote one author: "Decisions in favour of freedom which the court gave in these and other cases were not based simply upon precedent but were freely argued on each occasion."[2] This preference for freedom worried slave owners who perceived that, if pursued, these legal principles would lead to the dangerous idea of "the emancipation of all slaves."[3]

Slaveholders had every right to fear such thinking. When jurists followed the reasoning that supported slavery, they deduced its corollaries: that if slaves were nothing more than chattel property, a legal owner of a slave could do with that slave whatever the owner wished, even to the point of murder. By beginning with the contradiction of having property in persons, defenders of slavery were committed to denying (logically) the category of "murder" to the destruction of one's own slaves. (If one chooses to slaughter his beef cattle, he is not charged with a crime, much less homicide.) Officials in numerous towns and municipalities refused to be that consistent and in egregious cases they brought charges against slave owners who harmed or killed a slave. As we saw earlier, Daniel Ruffin, the North Carolinian judge, clarified why slavery requires terror and lawlessness.

The English legal argument against slavery was laid down by the influential English jurist William Blackstone (1723–1780). In his *Commentaries on the Laws of England*, which Lincoln studied in preparation for the bar examination, Blackstone denied the legal possibility of slavery in all forms (by conquest, by sale, and by birth): "If neither captivity, nor the sale of oneself, can by the law of nature and reason, reduce the parent to slavery, much less can it reduce the off-

---

Slave Law," *Yale Journal of Law and the Humanities* 5: no. 2, (1993): article 7, 20.

[2] Duncan J. MacLeod, *Slavery, Race, and the American Revolution* (New York: Cambridge, 1974), 115.

[3] Ibid., 116.

spring." Thus, he concludes: "And now it is laid down, that a slave or negro, the instant he lands in England, becomes a freeman; that is, the law will protect him in the enjoyment of his person, his liberty, and his property."[4] If slavery has no legal basis it persists only by virtue of positive laws promulgated by municipalities and tolerated by states. To use the language of this book, because slavery depends upon the contradictory claim that persons can be things, its proponents were caught in endless cycles of illogical and self-contradictory rhetoric. To return to Lincoln's homely insight: if slavery was a "good," as John C. Calhoun and numerous Southern preachers held, it was a good that none of them chose for himself or for his children.

A Mystery to Myself: Higher Self versus Lower Self

Humanist virtues appeared in the works of Greek and Roman authors. These include self-conscious awareness of cultural arbitrariness (Plato), *Phronesis* or practical wisdom (Aristotle), naturalism, balance, modesty (Seneca), and civic service. In the later Roman state "virtue" was replaced by luxury and entertainment. The latter, Edward Gibbon argued, were dangerous because they impeded the proper functioning of the state. In his massive effort to describe why the Roman Empire collapsed, Gibbon traced the decline to the loss of public service and the contract between patricians and plebeians joined under a constitution. In this contract were united the freedom of popular assemblies with the authority and wisdom of a senate and the executive powers of a regal magistrate. When the consul displayed the standard of the republic, each citizen bound himself, by the obligation of an oath, to draw his sword in the cause of his country till he had discharged the *sacred duty* by a military service of ten years. This wise institution continually poured into the field the rising generations of freemen and soldiers.[5]

---

[4] *Commentaries on the Laws of England: A Facsimile of the First Edition of 1765–1769* (Chicago: University of Chicago Press, 1979): 1:411–13.

[5] Edward Gibbon, *The History of the Decline and Fall of the Roman Empire* (1776–1788), vol. 4 (Paris: A. and W. Galignani, 1840), 342. (My emphasis.)

This Roman idea of virtue is that individual men and women consciously and deliberately vowed to serve their country. This personal commitment evoked, Gibbon said, a sense of sacred duty. By taking such an oath, Roman citizens united in themselves their interior lives with their civic duty. When he displayed the emblem of the Republic, the consul called forth this union of the private self with the public self. From that union, Gibbon said, flowed the strength of the Republic. When that union disappeared in the later years of the empire, the strength of the Republic diminished.

We have divided minds. This makes judgment, planning, and neuroses possible. Because we can conceive of diverse futures with diverse consequences we choose one action over another. To predict consequences, we tell a story about the future and then gauge our feelings to this scene. To be neurotic is to tell (paranoid) stories that preclude learning; therapists supplant our stories—our solution to the mystery of being a person—with better stories that make learning possible. Going a long way back in human thought, we find that every tradition distinguishes two parts to the self; a higher self, dominated by language, and a lower self, dominated by passion and impulsiveness. The first is *higher* in terms of cognitive processes, not necessarily regarding ethics or empathy. In *To Kill a Mockingbird*, Scout's goodwill, her ability to remember a coherent, mutual exchange between her father and Mr. Cunningham, defuses a crime in the making. Scout's feelings for her father and her memory of Mr. Cunningham were from her lower self. As I suggested earlier, Lincoln's defense of human equality and his hatred of slavery were not deduced; they emerged from his empathy for unrequited labor.

The higher self includes the capacity for reason, language, self-reflection, and patience. The lower self includes the capacity for impulses and the passions, for the immediacy of feelings. It is wordless, that is, it does not generate nor immediately respond to language. For that reason, while some psychologists and others speak about the "language of the body" this is a weak metaphor. Myriad ailments of the flesh may coincide with verbalized feelings—heartache, for example—but these rare occurrences do not demonstrate that the body uses linguistic codes to express itself. A headache tells us that something is wrong, not what caused it and how to resolve it. Poetry, humor, theater, and cinema use language in its more figurative, that is, scenic and evocative modes to evoke feelings originating in the lower self.

To cross the gap between the two selves, physicians, shamans, and medicine experts must generate a set of exploratory devices, stories, and actions that use language to explain nonlanguage. This requires *hermeneutics*, rules that permit one to interpret a sacred text or a sacred action. Hermeneutics are codes of interpretation. However, because the lower self is nonverbal (or a-linguistic) it does not generate social communication, that is, propositions intelligible to all. We cannot prove that any particular reading of a set of feelings, or a text or novel or film that generates emotional responses is exhaustive and complete.

For that reason, Lincoln's feelings about slavery, based on his empathic genius, did not, in themselves, generate legal arguments against it. Indeed, one of the most powerful forces that shaped abolitionist sentiment was Harriet Beecher Stowe's evocation of loss and degradation in *Uncle Tom's Cabin, or Life Among the Lowly*, which was written in response to the Fugitive Slave Law.[6]

To defend one code against another, cultural elites, those who tell us what is good and bad, must protect the sanctity of their hermeneutic system. Because these systems are based on more or less arbitrary decisions, this defense cannot rest upon plausibility and empirical demonstrations. The former are subject to dispute and argumentation and the latter are hard to come by. I may worship on Sundays and drive on the right hand side of the road; if most of us agree, both actions become codified as "the way things are." To disguise the arbitrariness of these codes, those who protect them invoke mystical confirmation and, when necessary, violence. Since ancient times, philosophers and theologians have used symbolic discourses to bridge the gaps that separate

---

[6] Regarding the novel's reception and critical standing, see Cindy Weinstein, ed., *The Cambridge Companion to Harriet Beecher Stowe* (New York: Cambridge University Press, 2004), 3–5.

the parts of the self. I noted earlier in chapter 8 Gilbert and Wilson's notion of the divided self as composed of two systems.[7]

Lacking markers of difference, to naïve persons a "premonition" of danger—as when Barack Obama, a black man, was elected president of the United States—feels identical to an emotional experience: our way of life, denoted 160 years ago by John C. Calhoun as the "natural superiority" of whites over blacks, is ended. The very idea of a black president provokes a never-ceasing anxiety that the world of propriety and class stability is ending; the worst thing has occurred. Unless one rises up in righteous anger and strikes against agents of sedition and revolution, a sacred way of life will be extinguished. Facing that danger, men must defend themselves and, when needed, use violence to enforce codes that have kept the world sane and stable.

Anxiety and Rage in the Story of Emmett Till

Thanks to 250 years of relentless sermonizing and propaganda, up through our time, white Americans believed that blacks were structurally inferior to whites. Challenges to that propaganda evoke instantaneous emotional responses in some whites. The first emotion is fear; it lasts for a microsecond before it provokes anger, then rage, then actions. Anger, rage, and action mask that initial fear: we are not afraid of blacks; we despise them. This sequence of emotional triggers occurs in the time it takes to feel enraged over a perceived insult.

In Southern states in the 1950s black boys and men who talked inappropriately to white women risked massive retaliation. On August 24, 1955—three months after the Supreme Court directed integration of Southern schools—Emmett Till, a fourteen-year-old African American kid from Chicago, visiting family in Leflore County, Mississippi, whistled at Carolyn Bryant, a white woman exiting a store in Money, Mississippi. Till's relatives knew that this could trigger violence from white men when they learned of it.

---

[7] Daniel T. Gilbert and Timothy D. Wilson, "Why the Brain Talks to Itself: Sources of Error in Emotional Prediction." *Philosophical Transactions of the Royal Society, B* (2009), 1335–41.

Four days later, on August 28, around 2:30 a.m., Roy Bryant, Carolyn's husband, Roy's half-brother J. W. Milam, and a third person appeared at the home of Mose Wright, Emmett's great-uncle. They abducted Emmett and then tortured the boy, finally shooting him and dumping his body, wired to a seventy-pound fan, into the Tallahatchie River.[8] Shortly after the boy's body was discovered, Bryant and Milam were arrested on charges of murder. After a four-day trial in the Circuit Court, Second Judicial District of Tallahatchie County, the case concluded. The jury, all white men, adjourned at 2:34 p.m. to deliberate and returned sixty-eight minutes later to deliver its verdict of not guilty.[9] Six weeks later, on November 8, 1955, a grand jury in Leflore County convened to consider kidnapping charges against Milam and Bryant. The grand jury did not issue an indictment.

In January 1956, *Look* magazine published the confessions of Bryant and Milam.[10] Although the FBI report noted some problems with the timelines cited in the *Look* article, the basic facts are uncontested: Emmett was killed because two white men, enflamed by local and state officials who were enraged by the Supreme Court's school integration decision, enforced the tradition of black subservience using white violence. According to one witness of the torture and killing: "During the beating Till was never respectful to the [white] men and did not say 'yes sir' and 'no sir.' Things got out of hand and Till stated something to the effect of 'he was as good as they are.'"[11]

As in other notorious cases, the police and judicial system perpetrated

---

[8] All citations are from the FBI's retroactive, 464-page report on the case published on February 9, 2006. It is accessible at: http://foia.fbi.gov/till/till.pdf

[9] A transcript of the trial of J. W. Milam and Roy Bryant of September 1955 appears as appendix A, 112–462, of the FBI report. See also Christopher Metress, ed., *The Lynching of Emmett Till: A Documentary Narrative* (Charlottesville, VA: University of Virginia Press, 2002).

[10] "The Shocking Story of Approved Killing in Mississippi," written by William Bradford Huie. See http://www.pbs.org/wgbh/amex/till/sfeature/sf_look_confession.html.

[11] FBI report, 90. Also Paul Theroux *Deep South: Four Seasons on Back Roads* (New York: Houghton Mifflin Harcourt, 2015), 200.

violent crimes against dark-skinned people. For that reason, Bryant and Milam had little to fear when they murdered Emmett Till.[12] While Bryant's wife may have elaborated a quasi-rape scenario to him, Bryant's instantaneous rage, similar to the instantaneous anxiety Till's relatives felt after his error, were instances of the lower self telling a story to the higher self. The same story evoked rage in whites and anxiety in blacks. Scenes of black-white sexual contact dominated Bryant and Milam (both ex-soldiers). Till had broken the code of black-white conduct. The code was built around the irrational claim of white superiority, and it perpetuated that illusory pleasure. As John C. Calhoun noted as far back as the 1840s, it was a point of pride of poor white men in the South that at least they were not black. Violations of the code threatened that form of pleasure. They required swift punishment analogous to the "up to 300 lashes" that Andrew Jackson advocated in the ad for his runaway slave. Those who murdered Emmett Till felt themselves justified in doing so.

These interactions between the storytelling part and the emotional-responsive part of the self occur so rapidly that the "upper self," the self that is capable of language, reason, postponement, and reflection, cannot intervene. (In psychoanalytic terms, the negative transference emerges prior to self-reflection.)

It's conceivable that when Bryant and Milam kidnapped Emmett from his uncle's house, they planned to intimidate him, whipping him if necessary, until he showed them proper respect. When Emmett refused, their sense of honor and the logic of a Jim Crow regime required them to increase their corrections just as George Washington felt compelled to sell his disobedient slave, Tom, into labor on the sugar islands.

---

[12] The FBI report lists, for example, the case of Elmer O. Kimbrell, a white man, who in December 1955 killed Clinton Melton, a black employee at a service station after Melton had filled his gas tank when Kimbrell had asked for only $3 worth. Enraged, Kimbrell left the station, got his gun, and killed Melton. Kimbrell, who was friendly with J. W. Milam, was acquitted of the murder and died thirty years later (26).

Sentimentality, Delusion, Mystification:
Products of Dissociation

Discussed in chapter 6 was Jacqueline Denise Goldsby's conclusion that lynchings were *both* spectacular and thus unforgettable to viewers, especially blacks, *and* forgettable, that is, not reflected upon after the horror passed.[13] This peculiar quality of atrocity images means that their effects are insidious and long-lasting. Insidious because one cannot forget them and long-lasting because they continue to affect one. Until they are exorcised, atrocity images misshape the minds of those who witnessed them and those who discern that they too might become victims of the same attacks. "This could be you" is the lesson inscribed on the minds of onlookers. Brutality like whippings and lynchings are expensive. They require significant resources, must be organized and ritualized for maximum effect, and they damage or destroy valuable property.

Mimicking brutal parents everywhere, slaveholders used bribes when they were cheap. They offered praise, "love," and attention that emphasized the hierarchy of master and obedient child when these devices proved useful. They alternated these inducements with threats to use punishment whenever the master felt it was warranted. Such parents and slave owners learned that they could concentrate the subject's mind upon the master with reminders of the club and the whip. In more subtle ways, masters control subjects by first reminding them of the possibilities of pain, then in a demonstration of alleged kindness, forgo punishment. The physical relief that floods through a terrified person can, sometimes, generate feelings of relief and love for the master: "I was not harmed. He saved me." That, in turn, rewards the master, increases the pleasure of evoking terror, and makes terror more likely.

George Orwell explored identical devices throughout *Nineteen Eighty-Four*: compulsory hating ceremonies, martial music, evocation

---

[13] Jacqueline Goldsby, *A Spectacular Secret: Lynching in American Life and Literature* (Chicago: University of Chicago Press, 2006).

of danger and dread from bombs, threats of reprisals and discovery punctuate the novel. In his original draft, Orwell outlined the frenzied passion that scenes of atrocities induce in movie audiences. He described a propaganda film showing a passenger ship full of enemy civilians being chased by the military: "Audience much amused by shots of an old fat Jew trying to swim away with a helicopter after him. First you saw him wallowing along in the waves, like a porpoise, then you saw through the helicopter's gun sights, then the sea round him turned pink and he suddenly sank as though the bullet holes had let in the water. Audience shouting with laughter."[14]

While Orwell excised many of these atrocity scenes from the novel's final version, his insight persists: terror makes coherent thinking, for example, deducing that 2 plus 2 = 4, impossible. With the destruction of coherent thinking, people can affirm contradictions and remain oblivious to their incoherence.[15]

Overcoming Mystification; Undoing Dissociation

The stupor, the sense of impossible complexity that terror induces in victims is debilitating. In psychological terms, stupor, confusion, and mystification are all instances of dissociation. Apologists for terror, such as proslavery advocates before the war, and the defenders of the Confederacy after the war, perpetuate these dissociative moments by sentimentality, obfuscation, and endless mythmaking. The effect of the latter is to drown critics in trivialities, which, if not observed exactly, make one ineligible to comment. A person whose intrinsic sense of self is unified is less likely to dissociate and more likely to act

---

[14] George Orwell, *Nineteen Eighty-Four: the Facsimile of the Extant Manuscript*, ed. Peter Davison (San Diego: Harcourt, Brace, Jovanovich, 1984), 28.

[15] "Nationalism is power-hunger tempered by self-deception. Every nationalist is capable of the most flagrant dishonesty, but he is also—since he is conscious of serving something bigger than himself—unshakably certain of being in the right." George Orwell, "Notes on Nationalism," (May 1945. Repr. *England Your England and Other Essays*. London: Secker and Warburg, 1953). http://orwell.ru/library/essays/nationalism/english/e_nat.

in ways that others, not sharing that unity, find courageous. This appears vividly in the story of two women from South Carolina who abandoned their slave-owning families and joined the Quaker resistance to slavery.

The Unity of the Spirit:
Quakerism and the Resistance to Slavery

One way to understand the minds of slave owners is to examine how some persons who benefited by the institution and were immersed in its pleasures rejected both. Among the few that did so and left a record of their thoughts were Quakers, as noted earlier. The foundation to the Quakers' resistance to slavery was their insistence that authentic religion emerged when the Holy Spirit showed individuals how to live properly. George Fox (1624–1691), the founder, preached disdain for social hierarchies, titles, and other signs of presumed superiority. Because the Spirit trumped all human authorities, including clergymen and other alleged superiors, individuals could—and should—examine themselves, to hear what their deepest selves felt in response to the Spirit's promptings. We see these principles articulated in Robert Barclay's influential treatise, *Apology for the True Christian Divinity,* published in 1676 and reprinted through the eighteenth and nineteenth centuries.[16]

> The testimony of the Spirit is that alone by which the true knowledge of God hath been, is, and can be only revealed.
>
> All true revelations to all persons come through the Spirit. It is the same testimony even if presented in different languages and forms.
>
> Because the Spirit generated scripture and all other instances of religious teachings, it is superior to them all. Spirit is the first and principal leader.
>
> While Jesus Christ was (and is) one with the Spirit, persons who do not know Christ are nevertheless saved by Him. "Christ hath tasted death for

---

[16] Originally published in 1676 as *Theologiæ Vere Christianæ Apologia.* Translated by Barclay into English, http://www.qhpress.org/books/apology.html.

every man"—persons living in Africa, for example, who had no access to Christianity are, nevertheless, saved and worthy of inclusion in the totality of a single, human race made in God's image.

The central teaching of the Spirit, through Jewish and Christian expression, is that everyone shall "learn to *do to others as they would be done by;* in which Christ himself affirms all to be included."

All true and acceptable worship to God is offered in the inward and immediate moving and drawing of his own Spirit. Because God sends "secret inspirations of his Spirit in our hearts," we alone can know directly how we are to act and think.

Rituals that were once coextensive with the presence of the Spirit, such as Communion, washing of feet, and the like are now "but the shadows of better things, they cease in such as have obtained the substance."

Because God alone, acting through the Spirit, can touch personal conscience, all uses of force, threat, violence, and other devices to command obedience are false and contrary to the Spirit.

The goal of human life is to sidestep vanity, find redemption, and seek "inward communion with God." Therefore all salutations of pomp, hierarchy, titles, and the like are degenerate as are frivolous recreations, sports, games, and so on.

This last point is crucial to Barclay. He gives explicit directions or six propositions as he put it, regarding proper actions between persons. Titles such as "Your Holiness," "Your Majesty," and all flattering words are forbidden because they encourage vanity and impede modesty. So too, display and "superfluities in apparel, as are of no use save for ornament and vanity." Finally, the use of violence, including war is prohibited: "The last thing to be considered is revenge and war, an evil as opposite and contrary to the Spirit and doctrine of Christ as Light to darkness."

These teachings animated an important Quaker treatise on slavery. In 1754, John Woolman, a learned American Quaker, published a twelve-page tract arguing that ownership was not compatible with

Quaker principles. His pamphlet was much cited and helped shape the thinking of Quakers who followed him, among them, Sarah and Angelina Grimké. Woolman extended Barclay's core ideas and applied them directly to American slavery. His pamphlet, *Considerations on the Keeping of Negroes: recommended to the Professors of Christianity of Every Denomination,* has as its motto Jesus's admonition: "Verily I say unto you, Inasmuch as ye have done it unto one of the least of these my brethren, ye have done it unto me" (Matthew 25:40). In other words, because the Spirit resides in all persons, harm done to one person, no matter how lowly and socially unimportant, is harm done to Jesus.[17]

Echoing the sermons of George Fox and the theology of Robert Barclay, Woolman begins by emphasizing that inward, spiritual truths are granted to all. They are made available through interior reflection—not training, not instruction, not by learning. By attending to that inward voice and reflection we see that we are limited, mortal, identical in origins, of one blood, essentially the same. Among things we share is our all-too-human desire for the pleasures of rank, hierarchy, and demarcations of distinction. We are "filled with fond notions of superiority." Persons in high ranks tend toward corruption and degeneration; they forget these interior truths. To wish for a world in which one group is favored over another (as many whites thought of themselves) and to denigrate others, "supposes a darkness in the understanding." God's love is universal and "so where the mind is sufficiently influenced by it, it begets a likeness of itself, and the heart is enlarged towards all men."

To guard against the error of denigrating persons, like African slaves, who seem lesser, we must imagine that "our ancestors and we had been exposed to constant servitude"; destitute of education; like Africans, our labor stolen from us; and that we "had generally been treated as a contemptible, ignorant part of mankind." In that case, should we, "be less abject than they now are?" By asking us to imagine ourselves as others, particularly as despised others, Woolman asks

---

[17] John Woolman (Philadelphia, 1754). The following quotes are from Woolman.

us to see them face-to-face, as persons with inner lives, wishes, and selves like our own. Hierarchy, rank, and assumed superiority make this kind of imagination impossible.[18]

Self-love and the pleasures of dominating others, which form the core of slavery, poison the mind: "The mind becomes reconciled with it, and the judgment itself infected," Woolman wrote. When we see this clearly, and are humble and perceive the error of self-love, "we shall then consider mankind as brethren." All persons are "the sons and daughters of one father." The best criterion is "Whatsoever ye would that men should do unto you, do ye even so to them." Or, to put it another way, "How should I approve of this conduct, were I in their circumstance, and they in mine?" Negroes were taken from their homes and they deserve the kindness due all strangers: "If a stranger sojourn with thee in your land, ye shall not vex him. But the stranger that dwelleth with you shall be unto you as one born among you, and thou shalt love him as thyself" (Leviticus 19:33–34).

The urge to leave a large estate, to create vast wealth, to give our children fortunes is to ignore the goal of life which is "to walk in the path of the just, our case will be truly happy." The task for human beings, especially those who own human property, is to achieve a "true renovation of mind." Wealth breeds self-love and pleasures of lording it over others. This is especially harmful to children in slave-owning families: "being masters of men in their childhood, how can we expect otherwise than that their tender minds will be possessed with thoughts too high for them; which gaining strength by continuance, will prove like a slow current, gradually separating them from or keeping from acquaintance with that humility and meekness in which alone lasting happiness can be enjoyed."

---

[18] Writing about whites in apartheid-era South Africa, Nadine Gordimer said that the minority whites lived among the majority blacks "as people live in a forest among trees." Trees are living entities but we do not expect them to have personalities, ideas, and even proper names. Cited in *New York Times*, "Books," July 14, 2014. See also Ronald Suresh Roberts, *No Cold Kitchen: A Biography of Nadine Gordimer* (Johannesburg: STE, 2005), 20.

By this rule, the mania to achieve lives of leisure, to become masters of others, to use others for those ends is an error. It creates a perverted mind: persons ensnared in this illusion live with "counterfeit joys." In contrast, the goal is to become persons who have "come to the unity of the Spirit, and the fellowship of the saints." Having achieved genuine happiness, "ease, liberty, and, many times, of life itself" become secondary. Ownership of fine things, such as houses, clothing, carriages—and slaves—because they are admired by the world makes true happiness impossible, especially for children raised in those homes. For Woolman, for that reason and because it violates the essential truths evidenced in scripture (the Hebrew Bible and the New Testament), slavery is antithetical to true Christian witness.

Coming to Grips with Ownership: Sarah and Angelina Grimké

Few owners freed their slave property; those who did and who joined the fight against slavery were remarkable people. Among them were two sisters, Sarah Grimké (1792–1873) and Angelina Grimké (1805–1879). They hailed from a distinguished South Carolina family, made rich by plantation ownership, brilliance, and political connections. Their father, John F. Grimké, through his mother (Mary Faucheraud), descended from Huguenots, French Protestants, who left France after the persecutions of the seventeenth century. Through his father he descended from German merchants. John studied law in London and was among those who petitioned King George III to respect colonial rights. When the Revolution commenced, he served as captain, later as major in the Continental Army. After the war he served in high offices in South Carolina and was a member of the Convention in 1788 that approved the US Constitution. Other honors and distinctions followed.[19]

In their teens, both girls questioned their parents' political and religious beliefs. When they became young adults, Sarah first, then

---

[19] Order Book of John Faucheraud Grimké. August 1778 to May 1780. *The South Carolina Historical and Genealogical Magazine* 13, no. 1 (January 1912): 42–55.

Angelina rejected their parents' beliefs, abjured the family fortune, and joined Northern abolitionists. (Angelina later became a major leader of the women's movement.) Their rejection of slavery and their campaigns on behalf of the abolitionist movement were crucial to the antislavery movement. First, they brought immediate, firsthand witness to the everyday world of slavery in the American South. Second, they wrote well. With great self-control they described hundreds of atrocities they had witnessed or had been witnessed by reliable second parties. Third, their accounts were about elite whites in South Carolina, not about easily dismissed "crackers" whose low status might explain their brutality toward slaves. Fourth, and most important, they acknowledged that they had been beneficiaries of slavery.

For example, in *American Slavery As It Is: Testimony of a Thousand Witnesses* (see note 23), they wrote: "Self-justification is human nature; self-condemnation is a sublime triumph over it, and as rare as sublime." Self-justification and elaborate self-deception dominated Southern authorities on slavery before the war; after the war, the same people systematically distorted their motives and the realities of slavery. As we have seen, Jefferson Davis got the machine going with his autobiography; the Sons of Confederate Veterans, The United Daughters of the Confederacy, and many others followed his lead. They expended ferocious energy on revising the history of the Confederacy and aggrandizing the Lost Cause. Most people of the Grimké's class lent their energies to self-justification, precisely in the service of "elaborate self-deception." How, then, did the Grimké sisters manage this sublime feat when most people of their class, and millions more who supported slavery, could not?

A partial answer is that they knew well the institution of slavery in South Carolina and that knowledge appalled them from an early age. They were also unusually intelligent, disciplined, and independent thinkers. They were raised in a three-story mansion in Charleston with a slave servant for each child. Severe in her standards and committed to her social role as an elite, their mother, Mary Grimké was a devout Episcopalian in her fashion. Their father, Judge John Grimké, was wealthy thanks to his large plantation, Belmont, which was up-country near Union County, South Carolina. Older by twelve years, Sarah Grimké insisted on being the godmother to her infant sister, Angelina. In her diary and in letters to her sister, Angelina sometimes called Sarah "Mother." As a girl, Angelina expressed doubts about her Episcopal confirmation. Both women kept diaries with heartfelt entries about their circumstances. They recorded daily the brutality exercised against slaves, sometimes by their brother, even in their refined home. A typical entry is this by Angelina, "Mother is perfectly blind to how miserably she had brought us up. . . . She rules slaves and children with a rod of fear!"[20]

Sarah became familiar with Quakers when she traveled with her father to Philadelphia to consult a Quaker physician. Following her father's death, Sarah entered a phase of concentrated religious reflection. After a year of intense study, mixed with melancholia, she studied Quaker writings. In 1821, at age twenty-nine, Sarah moved to Philadelphia, joined the Quaker sect, and lived according to its dictates. After many years of struggle with her mother, Angelina converted to Quakerism by 1828. Deeply immersed in the New Testament and its principles, the sisters commanded respect as thinkers when most women had neither public voice nor presence.

Angelina was a gifted writer and a brilliant observer of herself. For example, in 1835 she sent a famous letter to William Lloyd Garrison, founder and editor of *The Liberator*. In it, she astutely assessed how men in power exploited mob violence against reformers all the while seeming to rise above it. Having grown up among slaveholders, and knowing their sentiments about their human property, Angelina explained why their attachments to slavery were adamantine: "If we call upon the slaveholder to suffer the loss of what he calls his property, then let us show him we make this demand from a deep sense of duty,

---

[20] Katherine DuPre Lumpkin. *The Emancipation of Angelina Grimke* (Chapel Hill, NC: University of North Carolina Press, 1974). See also Gerda Lerner, The *Grimké Sisters from South Carolina: Pioneers for Women's Rights and Abolition* (Chapel Hill, NC: University of North Carolina Press, 2004).

by being willing to suffer the loss of character, property—yea, life it-self, in what we believe to be the cause of bleeding humanity."[21] This was both brave, because she marked herself as a renegade and a target of vitriol from her class, and accurate: owners had staked their wealth and their social lives on slavery. They did perceive any criticism of the institution as an attack on themselves and their families. They would fight for slavery and against abolition with all the force they could muster.

In 1836, Angelina Grimké published *An Appeal to the Christian Women of the South.* In some twenty thousand words she presented a systematic exposition and refutation of proslavery authorities. With lawyerly precision and scholarly expertise she examined, then refuted theological arguments used by Southern pastors to defend slavery. For example, she showed that servants in the Hebrew Bible were not chattel property; in contrast to Southern laws and traditions, they were defended as persons. More so, even elite leaders labored: "Look at Sarah [Abraham's wife], that princess as her name signifies, baking cakes upon the hearth. If the servants they had were like Southern slaves, would they have performed such comparatively menial offices for themselves?"

Naïvely, Angelina had hoped her status among Charleston's great families would help her gain Southern readers. However, "Charleston's postmaster gave the Appeal the same treatment he gave all abolitionist literature: he ordered it publicly burned."[22] She began the *Appeal* with a passage about Esther, the great heroine of the Hebrew Bible who risked her queenly status—and her life—to plead for her Jewish people. Esther's famous speech, "If I perish, I perish," (Esther 4:13–16), was, of course directed by Angelina to herself and to her women readers. As would Lincoln, Angelina asks her readers to consider the Golden Rule and asked: "Why not place *your* children in the way

---

[21] Published September 19, 1835, from Larry Ceplair, ed. *The Public Years of Sarah and Angelina Grimké* (New York: Columbia University Press, 1989), 150.

[22] http://historyengine.richmond.edu/episodes/view/1012.

of being supported without your having the trouble to provide for them, or they for themselves? Do you not perceive that as soon as this golden rule of action is applied to *yourselves* that you involuntarily shrink from the test; as soon as *your* actions are weighed in *this* balance of the sanctuary that *you* are found wanting."

Because they knew the financial and political leaders of South Carolina, all members of the so-called best families, the Grimké Sisters helped demolish the excuse that well-educated Southern gentry were appalled by the unfortunate excesses of overseers and similar low-class workers. With Sarah and her husband, Theodore Weld, Angelina collected firsthand reports about the treatment of American slaves and published them in 1839 in *American Slavery As It Is: Testimony of a Thousand Witnesses.*[23]

Their summaries are searing, sober, and lucid. Their methods were to document precise accounts, with names, dates, locations, and witnesses of how slaves were actually treated as opposed to the relentless campaign by Southerners to portray it as benign: "Well-weighed testimony and well-authenticated facts with a responsible name, the Committee earnestly desire and call for."[24] For example, they wrote about William Smith, a congressional senator from South Carolina from 1816 to 1823 and afterwards from 1826 to 1831. As was common to many owners, Smith did not pay for help from physicians when slaves on his plantations needed care. In one plantation, near Huntsville, Alabama, people there reported that "If the medical skill of the overseer, or of the slaves themselves, can contend successfully with the disease, they live, if not, they die."[25] These behaviors did not impede Smith's rapid political ascent. President Andrew Jackson appointed Smith twice, in 1829 and 1836, to the US Supreme Court but Smith declined.[26]

---

[23] Theodore D. Weld, ed., *American Slavery As It Is: Testimony of a Thousand Witnesses* (New York: The American Anti-Slavery Society, 1839). http://docsouth.unc.edu/neh/weld/menu.html.

[24] Ibid.

[25] Ibid.

[26] "Declined the appointment of Associate Justice of the Supreme Court of

Their pleas to end slavery were based on common human feelings, on extensive evidence, and on Christian duty. They presented voluminous proof against owners who claimed that they were kind to their slave property. They did not shirk from strong words: "Despots always insist that they are merciful. The greatest tyrants that ever dripped with blood have assumed the titles of 'most gracious,' 'most clement,' 'most merciful.'"[27]

Beginning with Themselves: Sarah and Angelina

Part of the sisters' effectiveness lay in their origins among Southern gentry and in their gender and brilliance. However, the most persuasive part of their analyses was their comprehension of the rewards and pleasures of ownership. These rewards and pleasures depended upon fearful obedience by slaves and required violence and threats of violence. Those facts they knew firsthand as children who grew up with a personal slave and through countless observations of life in the genteel homes in Charleston. Sarah wrote, for example, about an esteemed Christian woman who in frustration with an eighteen-year-old woman who had run away had the young woman flogged, then a heavy spiked collar placed on her neck, and then "a strong and sound front tooth was extracted, to serve as a mark to describe her, in case of escape." Another wealthy and highly esteemed female acquaintance in Charleston told Sarah that she had ordered "the ears of her waiting maid slit for some petty theft. This she told me in the presence of the girl, who was standing in the room." This woman was from one of the first families in Charleston.

From the view of worldly actors, all visible differences between classes, races, the sexes, and similar demarcations are essential; superficial differences denote profound, unalterable differences. Within Quaker teachings and Angelina's theological reflections on them, all persons capable of moral reflection were essentially the same. The Unity of

---

the United States tendered by President Andrew Jackson in 1829 and 1836." http://bioguide.congress.gov/scripts/biodisplay.pl?index=s000628.

[27] Weld, *American Slavery As It Is*, 8.

Persons meant, as she understood it, that Northerners shared in the crimes of slavery as much as Southerners: Northern racism, which was endemic to antislavery groups, and the universal dismissal of women were instances of the same error. White Northern "pity" for Africans was a similar form of disdain: they "regarded the colored man as an *unfortunate inferior*, rather than as an outraged and *insulted equal*."[28]

For that reason, with Garrison and others Angelina argued against the American Colonization Society, a movement to send free blacks and newly emancipated slaves back to Africa, particularly Liberia. Colonization appealed to many Northerners, especially those who believed that black inferiority was biologically rooted and unalterable. Convinced both that slavery was wrong and that Africans would never equal whites, it appears that a majority of Northern whites favored expelling blacks. Abraham Lincoln and his Republican allies strongly favored colonization. Northern newspapers made the rationale clear. In gentler words than many used, one editor wrote: "We think we have a proper estimate of the character of the negro, and our feelings towards the race are of the most kindly character. We would elevate them, but not at the expense of the white man. We have no idea of sinking our own race, in order to raise up the inferior African."[29] Not having to win (white, male) votes and placate the majority of white Americans who were convinced of black inferiority, Angelina and others probed the depth of American racism. It permeated North and South; the so-called free states and the slave states. Northern states and cities regularly enforced black codes that restricted voting, home ownership, freedom to move at will. Some Northern communities required free blacks to post $500 bond to guarantee "good behavior."[30] With customary zeal and precision, Angelina criticized the "colonizationists

---

[28] Ceplair, *The Public Years of Sarah and Angelina Grimké*, 171.

[29] Douglas Harper, "Slavery in the North," http://slavenorth.com/colonize.htm.

[30] Harper, "Slavery in the North," http://slavenorth.com/exclusion.htm, quoting Leon F. Litwack, *North of Slavery: The Negro in the Free States, 1790-1860* (Chicago: University of Chicago, 1961), 72.

[who] held up the colored man to public view, as a being who can not rise in his own native America to a level with his white brother," who must be shunned. In doing so they hallowed mere prejudice and violated the Golden Rule, the command of Christ.[31]

Because Northerners, including pious ministers, were imbued with racist beliefs, Angelina argued that the abolition movement should begin in the North. Northerners who felt superior to Southerners should examine themselves and the hundred slights and wounds they inflicted on darker-skinned people in their churches, even in abolitionist meetings. By numerous compromises and outright complicity in the rewards of slavery "the *North was guilty*."[32] As she came to articulate the then-radical ideal of female equality, she drew upon her long experience with both Northern and Southern forms of division, of splitting persons into hierarchical groups and of splitting one's mind into separate compartments. The single, unifying principle was that because all persons have the same nature, which is fundamentally moral, they all have the same rights: "These rights may be wrested from the slave, but they cannot be alienated; his title to himself is perfect *now*."[33] In the same way, the mere circumstance of sex does not give men higher rights than women. Grimké's championing of abolition evoked outrage from the South and censure from some in the North; championing of female equality had no less an effect on her readers.

Angelina speaks directly to our task of understanding the heart and minds of slave owners. Unlike many persons who rejected slavery on grounds of piety alone, she added a lucid psychological appraisal of the pleasures of slavery. In a letter on "Prejudice," written in 1837, Angelina counters the demand that abolitionists should sugarcoat their message, to be unassuming, humble, and show pity and sympathy for slave owners. On the contrary she said if she and others did so they would be copying the servile behavior demanded of slaves (indeed all

---

[31] Ceplair, *The Public Years of Sarah and Angelina Grimké*, 122.
[32] Ibid., 186. (Emphasis in original.)
[33] Ibid., 191.

colored persons): they "are taught to be '*very humble*' and '*unassuming*,' '*gentle*' and '*meek*,' and then the '*pity* and generosity' of their fellow citizens are appealed to." Owners demanded these forms of deference because each display added to their emotional pleasures. An owner feels kindly to slaves who show proper obedience: "He feels kindly toward the individual, *because* [the slave] is an *instrument* of his enjoyment, a mere *means* to promote his wishes."[34]

Integrative thinking, the ability to register differences and contradictions, cannot occur in dissociative states. Slaveholders struggled to placate slaves whom they needed to remain productive, but they could not forgo punishment and the constant threat of punishment. William Cooper and Thomas Terril, American historians, cite a North Carolina slaveholder: "It is a pity that agreeable to the nature of things Slavery and Tyranny must go together and that there is no such thing as having an obedient and useful Slave, without the painful exercise of undo [*sic*] and tyrannical authority."[35]

The cost of this system, which depended upon threat and violence at every level, weighed also on the minds of slaveholders and the South in general. Trying to justify an unjustifiable deed, Southern politicians, clergy, and other elites deluded themselves and their audiences. They could not square this circle.

---

[34] Both citations from ibid., 169.

[35] William J. Cooper, Jr. and Thomas E. Terril. *The American South: A History*, vol. 1 (New York: Rowman & Littlefield, 2008), 236.

CHAPTER 10

Mother Ann, Kant, Lincoln: the Unity of Human Being

We end by reflecting upon a sketch by John Downman, an English artist, of a young black man, above. The sketch was done around 1815. His face is beaming and he looks healthy, well-fed, and well-treated. His smile and inner glow are appealing. He was, most likely, a servant. Being a servant did not place him outside the boundaries of full-fledged human being. We see no essential differences between his spirit and ours. He is one of us; we'd like to get to know him. Photographs of American slaves do not show people who look like this young man; they are not lighter or darker, handsomer or less, but their eyes are different. Most were not as well dressed as he. However, many house slaves were clothed in uniforms and finery, at least when important guests were present. The difference between slaves and this young man is that they—and their parents and their children, and sometimes their children's children—were brutalized and he was not. We should try to reflect on this fact. It is hard enough to imagine being flogged for a petty "error." It is much more difficult to imagine seeing one's father or mother or child being brutalized. (We recall that owners forced slaves to watch others being tortured.) To see one's daughter, for example, reduced to slavery, knowing her fate, knowing that she will be crushed is too much to bear. Murderous rage and a life devoted to avenging this crime make perfect sense. Each of the four million American slaves living in the South in 1860 had to endure this profound humiliation, mostly in silence.

English house servants worked hard; miners, farmers, milkmaids, dustmen, smiths, and stevedores—among hundreds of occupations—worked hard too. Many had to endure financial hardships. Accidents happened frequently; employers were not always fair; life could be short and difficult. However laborious and awful these jobs were, those who held them did not experience the catastrophic knowledge of slave families: that they had failed to protect their children from soul murder. For American slave owners, it was a small step from employing servants, mimicking the style of wealthy English families, to owning slaves. Many proclaimed that their slaves had more security than factory workers in the North. Thomas Jefferson said that because he kept slave families together his slaves had comforts not available to English laborers.[1] Using this rationalization, owners could

---

[1] Lucia Stanton, *Slavery at Monticello* (The Thomas Jefferson Memorial

enjoy both ownership and a conviction of their moral superiority. In 1853, leaders of an English antislavery group sent a petition, signed by some 562,448 English and Scottish women to Harriet Beecher Stowe, author of *Uncle Tom's Cabin*. Composed and championed by the Duchess of Sutherland, the petition begged the women of the United States to understand that the gradual emancipation of Southern slaves was their Christian duty. Julia Gardiner Tyler, the wife of former President John Tyler (1841–1845), denounced the petition. Mrs. Tyler attacked English women, especially the duchess for intruding on American practices. They should look to their own country and observe that English working people were worse off than American slaves, she said. Slaves, she proclaimed, lived well compared to the poor whites of London. The slave she insisted, is "clothed warmly in winter, and has his meat twice daily, without stint of bread."[2]

These rationalizations were not a perfect defense against moral doubts, however. We recall that the framers of the 1787 Constitution did not use the word *slave* in that document. In a similar way, slave owners who traveled in Northern states and abroad referred to their slaves as servants. These verbal niceties disappeared in documents of secession drafted by the states that were to constitute the Confederate States of America. In those documents, proponents called slavery and slaves by their real names. They also defended the South as a distinctive culture. The South was a civilization like classical Rome; both achieved greatness by virtue of the leisure that slavery afforded its elite citizens. The greatness that the South achieved was, in this way, a counterbalance to the unfortunate costs of slavery. Was this pragmatic argument for slavery persuasive? Was it ethical? On what grounds could we refute it?

Foundation), 14.

[2] Evelyn L. Pugh, "Women and Slavery: Julia Gardiner Tyler and the Duchess of Sutherland," *The Virginia Magazine of History and Biography* 88, no. 2 (April, 1980): 193–94. The quotation is from the *Richmond Enquirer*, January 28, 1853.

Toward a Universal Ethic

Southern apologists asserted both that slavery was protected in the US Constitution and that it rewarded owners (who became culturally sophisticated) and rewarded slaves (who became Christians). Who, other than the slaves, is to say that they were wrong? Can we find grounds for a universal ethic that transcends opinions, cultures, and traditions that are inconsistent with one another?

Although colonial-era planters had tried to enslave Native Americans, by the early 1800s the word *slave* meant *black* to most Americans.[3] This union of deeply embedded racial hierarchy and the denigration of slaves fomented ill treatment of all black persons, enslaved and free. We saw earlier that the Shakers, like Quakers and members of similar orders, refused to abide by these racial laws. Their fellow Christians, including the majority of mainline denominations in the South, had no such problem. On the contrary, Southern Christians pointed to the Bible, both the Jewish and Christian scriptures, where they found toleration of slavery. As we have also seen, learned men like John C. Calhoun and leaders of the Society for the Propagation of the Gospels, cited scriptural passages supporting the duty to bring Christianity to Africans who would have forfeited its benefits if they had remained heathens. Bishop Leonidas Polk, one of the founders of the University of the South, was a resolute Confederate officer. His special calling was to attend to the spiritual needs of planters who had a large number of slaves, as he did. How might we understand the difference between the two groups of Christians, between the Quakers and Shakers, on the one side and Bishop Polk, on the other?

Fervent Prayers

In *Gone with the Wind,* we saw that Scarlett's parents held nightly fervent prayers with the family. Their slaves watched the white family

---

[3] See Larry Eugene Rivers, *Slavery in Florida* (Gainesville, FL: University Press of Florida, 2000).

and hummed along with the service. These meetings were, according to the author, a special time for the family's slaves. Although, "The old and colorful phrases of the litany with its Oriental imagery meant little to them," it satisfied them emotionally.[4] According to this account, black minds could not grasp the subtlety of Jewish-Christian ideas (Oriental images and teachings); they could only chant the refrains. That semi-articulate form of speech satisfied them. They enjoyed, the book says, the privilege of standing outside the circle, beaming at their beloved white family at the circle's center.

Among subtle teachings of the New Testament was Jesus's admonition to the rich young man who asked how he might inherit eternal life. The young man said that he had kept the proper laws; what more need he do? Jesus replied, go and sell all that you have, give to the poor, and you will have treasure in heaven. This disheartened the young man: "And he was sad at that saying, and went away grieved: for he had great possessions" (Mark 10:22). Most commentators do not infer that Jesus was saying sacrifice everything, rather surrender your love of luxury and pleasures. By challenging the young man, Jesus showed him that "he is attached to his riches, and burns with covetousness," as John Calvin put it in the early seventeenth century. Owners who had sunk their family fortunes into slaves and into land maintained by slaves owned valuable, perhaps irreplaceable property. Contemplating losing that property, through any means, caused them much sadness and grief as well.

The insight into the love of wealth and luxury drove the Quakers to denounce extravagance and self-importance. Both are normal wishes and both are sources of pleasure; both elicit genuine goods, such as esteem, social standing, and, in the case of slavery, wealth. Once wedded to these goods, maintaining and expanding these sources of pleasure becomes paramount among all wishes. Like the rich young man, the idea of losing them causes much anxiety. Owners had these normal concerns and the additional knowledge that ownership had turned their "servants" into potentially lethal enemies.

---

[4] Margaret Mitchell, *Gone with the Wind* (New York: Macmillan, 1936), 68.

The wolf they held by the ears, to use Jefferson's words again, was inside *their* homes; bathing *their* children; preparing *their* meals; using knives—and perhaps deadly plants—in *their* kitchens.

We recall Sarah Grimké's account of the Charleston matron who inflicted severe punishments on her eighteen-year-old housemaid. How did that happen? What thoughts and feelings drove this highly respected woman to these actions, about which she had no shame? In contrast, how did Sarah and Angelina, two other highly respected women from the same city and from the same class with the same training, abandon their privileges and take up the cause for slaves, even when it cost them social standing, friendship, and other deprivations?

The matron was not possessed by a demonic "other" that made her act contrary to her Christian conscience. She reasoned and reacted as many owners did in her circumstances. Numerous reports in *Slavery As It Is* documented similar punishments demanded by men and women of the highest rank, all of them professing Christians, many of them leading members of their congregations. Others were future governors, financial leaders, and esteemed members of the judiciary. Our initial shock at these accounts stems from our naïve belief that high rank requires unusual talents and high moral values. The first is often true; the second is not. On the contrary, high rank required conformity with social norms and socially approved religious observances. To be highly esteemed in slaveholder society required one to mirror its expressed values, Christian piety, its accommodation of slavery, and to affirm them in solemn ceremonies at home and at "high church" functions in public. Donations of church organs, pews, silver, and fine furnishings for the church building—or the church building itself—were public displays that magnified their Christian standing and their Christian credentials.

The Charleston matron valued propriety, reputation, and conformity with her community's feelings about "thinking property": slaves were necessary to Southern greatness, hers and her family's, but they were dangerous, liable to conspire against their owners' best interests. According to these rules, by running away the young woman was a thief. She had stolen a valuable object—herself—from her mistress. Through her actions, which she well knew were forbidden, the slave threatened the wealth and therefore the foundation of civilized society in South Carolina. In addition to the dangerous precedent her escape would set for other slaves, she would shame the matron for running such a lax household. All these burdens fell on the matron. They made her slave's actions outrageous and when continued after proper warnings, infuriating. When lesser punishments proved ineffective, and as her frustrations increased, the matron required stronger devices. By scarring the young woman's mouth, the matron made her young slave a permanent, living sign of the costs of flight: all infractions must be countermanded with violence; the larger the threat the greater the violence it provoked.

In addition, the large, distinctive gap in the young woman's front teeth would make it easier to identify her if she should escape again. In numerous reward notices of escaped slaves, published everywhere, owners highlighted identifying scars: an ear cut off (or burnt off) or severed ligaments in the foot signaled prior punishment for earlier escapes. Crippled legs; missing eyes; burns, scars, and brands on faces; ears sliced or notched; toes cut off; missing front teeth, and an endless variety of scars created by whips and other devices provided clues for eager bounty hunters. The bounties ranged from $5 to more than a $500; some were for "dead or alive." Bounties, paying for night patrols, hiring overseers and such were the cost of doing business as owners. Those costs are trivial compared to the money generated by exploiting slave labor, slave offspring, and leasing slaves to others. The political and legal protection that the federal government, Southern states, and Southern cities gave to slavery made owning and leasing slaves a lucrative and prudent investment. Members of the emerging middle class as well as the more established gentry could make their fortunes in a stable market protected from abolitionist forces.[5]

---

[5] "Because Southern political and social institutions protected slavery and tied it to the very fabric of society, it was a wise investment." L. Diane

To maintain a docile workforce required physical and psychic scars; the first were indelible warnings to the young woman and those who saw her; the second were essential to maintaining a high, constant level of anxiety and through it, subservience. However, these were uneasy compromises; owners were not stupid. They knew that having used relentless violence, in every mode that proved effective, they created grudging obedience. If they decreased their vigilance, dangers of a "servile insurrection," increased. When Martha Washington, the president's wife, freed her slaves soon after the president's death she did so because the president's will promised them freedom after her death. Martha and her friends, among them, Abigail Adams, feared that her malcontent slaves, smelling freedom, might hasten that event. A mysterious fire had been set at Mount Vernon, for example. Martha and her family were concerned that this was the act of disgruntled slaves and a portent of imminent disasters.[6]

The higher one's professional rank and the more property one owned, the greater was the cost of pursuing actions contrary to the interests of owners. It may be difficult to grasp this burden of wealth, particularly wealth in slaves. Most people do not have vast wealth, and it is hard to understand the anxieties of the very rich when we see that their lives are filled with things—luxuries and pleasures—we wish to have. If some money is good, then a ton of money—and prestige, fame, and such— must be better. However, within the world of the rich (and the very rich) every step up the ladders of fortune and prestige makes the cost and dangers of falling all the greater. Like the rich man who addressed Jesus, it's a long way down from life at the top to "life among the lowly" (to cite the subtitle of *Uncle Tom's Cabin*).

Inherited wealth and other forms of unearned wealth, such as proceeds from lotteries, have the paradoxical effect of making one less

---

Barnes, Brian Schoen, Frank Towers, eds., *The Old South's Modern Worlds: Slavery, Region, and Nation in the Age of Progress* (New York: Oxford University Press, 2011), 193.

[6] Helen Bryan. *Martha Washington: First Lady of Liberty* (Hoboken, NJ: John Wiley and Sons, 2002), 377–78.

secure than if one had earned it through one's skills and determination. The psychological truth of the Quakers' admonitions about the nobility of work is that by earning our daily bread we feel a bodily connection between our exertions and the rewards and pleasures that follow. Inherited wealth makes this discovery less likely; in the case of slavery, it makes it almost impossible. The management of house servants, which typically fell to the mother of the family, required her to train her children to manage the help. That is one reason why children were given personal slaves: they needed to acquire these skills early. (If a room were cold, one learned to order a slave to secure a shawl, rather than fetch it for oneself.) As they learned the types and uses of punishment, for example thrashing and whipping house slaves, children learned how to be masters of men, as the Quakers put it.

In a display of documents from a large Tennessee plantation, Wessyngton about thirty-five miles northwest of Nashville, the Tennessee State Museum displayed a handwritten list of to-do items written by the plantation's mistress, Jane Washington in the 1850s. With fastidious attention Mrs. Washington noted various errors by her house slaves and the punishments each was to receive, usually "whipping." In an 1852 letter to her husband, George, she described a squabble among three of her slaves that she settled; the three of them "being whipped, the chastisement brought down their tempers, and all is calm now."[7]

By taking that road, Mrs. Washington and others honored ideals of their family and their class. They assumed roles that their church and family told them were their destiny and through which they would contribute to the greatness of the South. By taking those roles it became impossible to conceive of the minds of their slaves, those whom they managed, the people they owned and disciplined. Empathy for someone whose flesh you have just ordered to be flayed, for example, or her front tooth wrenched from her mouth, or her son sold away, is not possible. Empathy would make such necessary (and

---

[7] John Baker Jr. *The Washingtons of Wessyngton Plantation: Stories of My Family's Journey to Freedom* (New York: Atria Books, 2009), 151.

prudent) punishments or sales impossible. Then actual punishments and the threat of future punishments that slavery required would be impossible to carry out. Empathy for the slave would deprive owners of essential devices they needed to maintain the institution. It would ruin slavery. Yet, slavery supported the enterprise of Southern aristocracy, its rewards and pleasures, its grand estates, and its social ranks. By extension, literature and Christian texts that broached this arena became suspect for they had the pernicious effect of dissolving boundaries between rulers and the ruled, between owners and their property.

An additional ideological support, much used as we have seen, was the alleged biological fact of racial hierarchy. That the white owners' slaves were black meant that the gulf between them and their servants was *existential* and *ontological*. It was *existential*, meaning that the happenstance of the period—and the accident of their birth compared to their servants' situation—made them winners and their servants losers in that particular lottery. In this sense, the English gentry had Irish servants and not vice versa, because English weapons and English militaries subdued Irish lords who had contended for domination for hundreds of years. If the Irish had won, no doubt many of their servants would have been English. However, with blacks the story was different. The gulf between white owners and black slaves appeared to be *ontological*, meaning that it was rooted in the "being" (*ontos*) of the two groups. It was rooted, according to their doctrines, in the biological essence of whiteness, superior, and the biological essence of blackness, inferior. When this natural order was respected, all was peaceful; when it was disturbed by "abolitionist fanatics," all was chaotic danger. Hundreds, if not thousands of years of European conviction about race shaped Northern and Southern views of the "black problem." Many Northerners disliked slavery; very few wished to have free blacks join their communities, especially in large numbers. Sarah and Angelina Grimké discovered this fact when they presumed that African Americans would be welcomed to abolitionists meetings in the North. Regarding Northern women in the abolitionist movement, Angelina noted that "on account of their strong aristorcratical [*sic*] feeling," members of the Ladies Society were "exceedingly inefficient."[8] The same ladies refused to have colored women join their group; Angelina proposed to disband the "aristocratic" group and merge her work with that done by colored women.

Rescue of Jews: Heroic or Consistent?

The Grimké sisters acted in ways that seem heroic to us. In their teen years, each had been given a slave girl. By governing their individual servants they would learn the nature and rules of commanding obedience. The young woman given to Sarah died shortly; the girl given to Angelina made her uncomfortable and she was returned "to the donor" (I assume this was their mother.) After she became an abolitionist, Angelina sought out the young woman who had been sold away. She begged the new owner to accept any amount of money for the woman's freedom. The owner refused.[9] In their letters to intimate friends, Sarah and Angelina wrote about losing their family's love and their place, their location in their home and community. However, once they became Quakers most of their trepidations disappeared. How did that happen? One answer is to consider the Quakers' insistence upon the identity between the voice of authentic self and God's will. Persons with paranoid ideas also believe that they are merged with God; the difference is that paranoid people feel aggrandized and inflated by this merger; the Grimkés felt humbled and called to love others more, not less. With their form of religious certitude came increased clarity and therefore increased security. That security gave them the strength to make choices that might cost them everything, including property, public stature, and even life itself. Once Sarah and Angelina had achieved that form of clarity, their choices no longer required courage as we might define it. Angelina noted many times in her letters and her public speeches, once she realized that abolition was a cause

---

[8] Larry Ceplair, ed. *The Public Years of Sarah and Angelina Grimké The Public Years* (New York: Columbia University Press), 129.
[9] Ibid., 295.

worth dying for, her mind became clear, her feelings resolute, her anxiety disappeared.

Similar to the Grimké sisters, many of those who rescued Jews during the World War II did not believe that they acted heroically. They did not have to overcome terror and then act; they acted immediately. In *We Only Know Men,* Patrick Henry reviewed studies of the Nazi occupation of the South of France and French responses to it. He summarized the efforts of historians, social scientists, and religionists to understand how some people risked everything to save the lives of strangers.[10] Thanks to the work of clergy and laypersons in the plateau region, some 5,000 persons were rescued from certain death, among them 3,500 Jews, many of whom were children.[11] This story provokes at least two questions. Would we have been among those who acted heroically? What motivated these ordinary farmers and townsfolk to risk so much for strangers, most of them from different cultures, who observed a different religion?

To the first question, the odds tell us that we, like the majority, would have feared reprisals and would have obeyed German and local authorities. This does not make us moral idiots. During the crisis presented by the German occupation, outright resistance could provoke horrific retaliation against oneself and against one's family. The challenge was to find ways to preserve one's life without promoting the Nazi cause. Most of us would have acted like most of the citizens of the South of France and thought of ourselves and our families. In the same way, most whites in the slaveholding areas of antebellum America supported the institution of slavery.

To the second question, researchers found a cluster of childhood experiences, parental influences, and empathic sensibility that typified the

---

[10] Patrick G. Henry, *We Only Know Men: the Rescue of Jews in France During the Holocaust* (Washington, DC: Catholic University of America Press, 2007). The title comes from the refusal of Pastor André Trocmé to distinguish Jews from other persons (men) in the village.

[11] Henry focused upon the village of Le Chambon-sur-Lignon in the *Massif Central* region of south-central France.

rescuers. Important is the speed by which rescuers made their decision to expose themselves to danger: the majority did not calculate the risk-reward of their actions. While they were not suicidal, neither were they deliberative. They did not run through various cost-benefit scenarios, assigning weights to each one. That these life and death decisions were made quickly suggests that the rescuers were preconditioned to altruism and solidarity. Their "lower selves" in this sense, that is their emotional centers that drive immediate actions, were organized along the lines of empathic engagement. Numerous interviews with rescuers, done over many years, show consistently that when they saw a desperate human being they felt their duty instantaneously.

Magda Trocmé, the wife of Pastor André Trocmé, a distinguished figure in the rescue efforts, was among the earliest to receive the Jews. The choice to rescue was not complicated, she said: "We had no time to think. When a problem came, we had to solve it immediately. Sometimes people ask me, 'How did you make a decision?' There was no decision to make." There was no decision because the ontological question had been answered: "The issue was: Do you think we are all brothers or not?"[12] Henry reported that significant studies of the res-cuers showed this again and again: their impulse to help persons caught in need was "spontaneous, as though there were no other course of action available to them."[13]

Carefully done interviews and studies of more than a one thou-sand rescuers showed a cluster of personality traits that distinguish those who rescued from those who did not. Chief among these traits were independence of thought and action; a family member who modeled empathy; deep and sustained relationships with others; and the ability to see Jews as human beings identical to themselves.[14]

---

[12] Henry cited Carol Rittner and Sondra Myers, eds., *The Courage to Care: Rescuers of Jews during the Holocaust* (New York: New York University Press, 1986), 102.

[13] Henry, *We Only Know Men*, 156.

[14] See Gay Block and Malka Drucker, *Rescuers: Portraits of Moral Courage in the Holocaust* (New York: Holmes & Meier Publishers, 1992); Eva Fogelman,

Of particular interest is the finding that parents of rescuers were light on physical discipline and heavy on reasoning with their children: rather than insist on obedience, they explained to their children why actions that harmed others were wrong. Using the terms of this book, by reasoning with their children, these parents united the child's verbal "higher-self" capacities with the child's feelings and emotionality—the child's "lower-self." Skills and identities acquired in adult life, professional and social status, belief in the afterlife, education, and political affiliation did *not* predict rescue behavior. What mattered, in other words, was early family life in which children acquired empathic skills by absorbing the values of loving parents and other adults.[15]

By avoiding corporal punishment, these parents made it less likely that their children would dissociate between their higher and lower selves. In exactly the opposite mode, Southern parents who owned house slaves, who were comparatively better treated than field hands, demonstrated to their children that minor differences of skin color, social status, and the like created two classes of human beings: the master's white family (destined to rule) and their black slaves (destined to be ruled). To maintain this allegedly natural order, corporal punishment of slaves was necessary, the punishment increasing in proportion to the slave's failure to learn his or her place. The young slave woman whose front tooth was yanked out had vexed her owner a number of times. Like most owners, the matron used disciplinary methods that ranged from reprimands, to deprivation of food, to threats to separate families, to whipping and other forms of violence, and finally to deportation to even worse environments. Each of these

---

Conscience and Courage: Rescuers of Jews During the Holocaust (New York: Doubleday, 1994); and Nechama Tec, *When Light Pierced the Darkness: Christian Rescue of Jews in Nazi-Occupied Poland* (New York: Oxford University Press, 1986).

[15] Henry, *We Only Know Men*, 153, citing Fogelman, *Conscience and Courage*, 263, says that 89 percent of rescuers reported a parent or adult who acted as an altruistic role model.

devices evolved to exert maximum control of slaves' behavior and domination of their minds.

Pain and threats of additional pain make the target prone to dissociate, that is, to separate higher level from lower level mental functioning. Persons held in prisons and children subjected to sexual abuse or to extreme deprivation learn how to create altered states of consciousness. According to psychiatrist and researcher Judith Lewis Herman, "They learn to alter an unbearable reality. Prisoners frequently instruct one another in the induction of trance states. These methods are consciously applied to withstand hunger, cold, and pain."[16]

The punishment and systematic degradation of slaves also affected the owner's children. First, as noted earlier, they absorbed their parents' lessons that there was a radical, species-like division between themselves and their dark-skinned slaves. Second, they molded their minds around their parents' minds: they learned to feel both unusually important and disconnected from the suffering required to provide them their abundant rewards and pleasures. Third, they absorbed the pleasures of domination and mastery. Once entrenched, these pleasures require that mastered object to perform as demanded. A balky car is frustrating; a TV set that works intermittently becomes irritating; a computer that crashes just when you need it evokes anger. Failure in each instance evokes annoyance. However, if the faulty object is a *person*, one's thinking property, disobedience evokes rage. I feel foolish, I look like a failure; I am humiliated by an inferior whose will is countermanding mine. The offender must pay an immediate and costly price. Angelina Grimké in *American Slavery As It Is* summarized the necessity of ruthless correction:

> So in every case of disobedience, neglect, stubbornness, unfaithfulness, indolence, insolence, theft, feigned sickness, when his directions are forgotten, or slighted, or supposed to be, or his wishes crossed, or his

---

[16] Judith Lewis Herman, "Complex PTSD: A Syndrome in Survivors of Prolonged and Repeated Trauma," *Journal of Traumatic Stress* 5, no. 3 (1992): 381.

property injured, or left exposed, or his work ill-executed, the master is tempted to inflict cruelties, not merely to wreak his own vengeance upon him, and to make the slave more circumspect in future, but to sustain his authority over the other slaves, to restrain them from like practices, and to preserve his own property.[17]

An honest man reported to the Grimkés that when he was fourteen or fifteen years old he tried to "correct" (that is strike) an older, larger male slave. In self-defense, the slave restrained the young master. Considering this "the height of insolence," the boy cried for help, his parents ran to his rescue: "My father stripped and tied him, and took him into the orchard, where switches were plenty, and directed me to whip him; when one switch wore out he supplied me with others." When the slave was whipped into submission and begged forgiveness, the boy "kicked him in the face."[18]

By perpetuating visions of themselves as "loving Christians," Southern elites so fully split their wishes from their observations that they could not see themselves as other than doting masters. In *Gone with the Wind*, Margaret Mitchell used brilliant storytelling to underscore this fantasy numerous times. Rather than acknowledge—and mourn—the actuality of whites who owned slaves in "body and soul," she ascribes these wishes to a slave woman, Mammy: "Mammy felt that she owned the O'Haras, body and soul, that their secrets were her secrets; and even a hint of a mystery was enough to set her upon the trail as relentlessly as a bloodhound."[19] This may have been a deliberate echo of the famous speech in *Uncle Tom's Cabin* when Tom responds to Simon Legree, the brutal master, that Legree only owns Tom's body, not his soul.[20] Regardless, the

---

[17] Theodore D. Weld, ed., *American Slavery As It Is: Testimony of a Thousand Witnesses* (New York: The American Anti-Slavery Society, 1839), 111–12, http://docsouth.unc.edu/neh/weld/menu.html.

[18] Ibid., 52.

[19] Mitchell, *Gone with the Wind*, 21.

[20] Harriet Beecher Stowe, *Uncle Tom's Cabin* (New York: Penguin Books, 1986), chap. 33.

effect of this passage is to transform actual ownership, the iron law of the plantation, into whimsical ownership. Mammy's concern for her white family is a kind of loving, protecting ownership. Indeed, Mammy was "devoted to her last drop of blood to the O'Haras"[21]

Affluent Southern Christians favored slavery; the poor and those who chose a life of radical equality, like the Quakers, did not. This should not be surprising. Slavery is a device for extracting cheap labor and enhancing the return on one's investment; those who could afford to own slaves and for whom it made economic sense, did so. Poor people could not afford such expensive modes of production.

The Shakers and Slavery

Similar to the Quakers, but more radical, the Shakers rejected class hierarchy. The principle source of the Shakers' rejection of slavery was their founder's original vision. Mother Ann Lee (1736–1784) was born in Manchester, England, was forced into an unwanted marriage, gave birth to four children, each of whom died in infancy, and came to experience visions and ecstatic religious experiences that motivated her to abandon her Quaker meetings to found her own group, the United Society of Believers in Christ's Second Appearing. They were also called the Shaking Quakers of Manchester because of their ecstatic dancing.[22] Organized into small, communitarian groups they abandoned sexuality because, Mother Ann taught, it brought sin into the world. She preached the rejection of worldly goods, social hierarchy, male domination, and class discrimination, including slavery. Her religious zeal enabled her to bring a handful of followers from England to New England in 1774, and then into Indiana and Kentucky. Although she was illiterate, Mother Ann's followers compiled her precepts and taught them to new believers.[23]

---

[21] Mitchell, *Gone with the Wind*, 23.

[22] Stephen Stein, *The Shaker Experience in America* (New Haven: CT: Yale, 1992), 2–7.

[23] Jean M. Humez ,"Ye Are My Epistles": The Construction of Ann Lee Imagery in Early Shaker Sacred Literature," *Journal of Feminist Studies in Religion* 8, no. 1 (Spring, 1992), 83.

Based on her ecstatic visions, Mother Ann taught that Christ had returned as promised in Christian scripture. Many other visionaries in England and New England said the same thing; Mother Ann added the revolutionary idea that Christ had returned in female form: through Mother Ann the Second Coming was made clear. In some versions Mother Ann was merged with Christ; in others she was the Queen of Heaven.[24] To grasp this momentous truth and to feel its consequences one had to confess publicly, forsake sin, and try to emulate the "perfectly sinless life of Christ."[25] Shaker dances, which shocked and sometimes titillated onlookers, were designed to give members access to their internal visions in the tradition earlier advocated by George Fox and the Quakers. These ecstatic moments helped the dancers feel these spiritual truths in their bodies. Naturally, dancing was exciting in many ways, among them no doubt sexually, but the Shakers danced to feel themselves closer to the Spirit, not to be aroused sexually. (However, every so often a Shaker woman got pregnant while in residence.)

In Mother Lee's language, these truths were sent by God and were revealed in her ecstatic visions. For Mother Ann, slavery is wrong because it denies that slaves can grasp the gospel and therefore merit God's and our love. Mother Lee taught that because Christ had returned we are living in the end times when ordinary structures of the world, as she put it, would dissolve and false differences, including gender, class, and race, would disappear. From the Shakers' point of view, the end of history and the beginning of Christ's reign on earth had begun; all would soon be judged as immortal souls are judged, naked and without earthly distinctions. One woman reported that Mother Ann told them to "live together, every day as though it was the last day you had to live in this world."[26]

---

[24] Stein, *The Shaker Experience in America*, 16.

[25] Humez ,"Ye Are My Epistles," 84. On the early history of the Shakers, see Stephen J. Stein, *The Shaker Experience in America: a History of the United Society of Believers* (New Haven: CT: Yale, 1992).

[26] Stein, *The Shaker Experience in America*, 27.

Because Mother Ann wrote nothing, we are left with posthumous accounts of her sayings gathered by her followers. Historians correctly view these stories with much skepticism, especially reports of miraculous cures, predictions, and premonitions. However, because Shakers rejected the world's hierarchies, including the racist core of English and American clergy, they achieved moral clarity where others did not. We see this in a story from the Shaker community in South Union, Kentucky.

Social Scorn and Shame

Shakers accorded dignity to all persons, including non-whites. While Shakers evoked scorn and anxiety from some of their neighbors, they also gave their neighbors a place to send family members who had violated racial and caste barriers. A letter from Molly in South Union, Kentucky, to the elders in Mount Lebanon, written on November 30, 1816, describes one such drama. They had welcomed to the community two new members. The first was a seventy-seven-year-old woman who had traveled six or seven hundred miles. The second was a newborn girl whose mother, Juliet, had joined the community when she was pregnant by a dark-skinned man. Juliet's parents gladly let their daughter flee to the Shakers "in order to escape the dishonor that it would bring on them."[27] Because they lived seventy miles from the community they believed that their neighbors would never learn about their daughter's condition. Molly noted that these parents were "counted as honorable People in the world." Because Juliet had wished to join the community two years before her pregnancy—a wish that her parents refused to grant—the Believers welcomed her, heard her confession, and helped deliver her baby. Juliet died three weeks later, leaving her daughter, "a little yellow papoos [*sic*] behind." Having discerned the nature of Juliet's parents, the Sisters raised the baby, whom they named Juliet to honor her mother. Ten months later, the grandmother heard

---

[27] All citations from Western Reserve Historical Society (WRHS). Section IV—Correspondence. Part A—Items: Folder—South Union, KY: 1801–1920. WRHS, IV:A-60.

about the infant and told the Sisters that, "if they brought the child there [to live with her] she would kick it out of doors as quick as she would a rattle snake." Molly added, "this same woman has faith and so has all the family."

Although the grandparents were Christians and were esteemed in polite society, they could not welcome their dead daughter's child into their lives. The reasons for this seem to derive from two facts: Juliet was not married and her child was of mixed race. Assuming that Juliet's parents were not moral imbeciles, we realize that they feared social scorn and the shame that would fall on them if their mixed-race grandchild returned to their home. A rattlesnake is dangerous; its bite will cause disfigurement, if not death. Although these are cruel words, they are honest, and they help us measure the grandmother's anxiety. She was caught up in the rules of the world of Kentucky in the early nineteenth century. Those rules required her to reject her pregnant daughter, to be apart from her at her death, and to never see her grandchild.

Immanuel Kant and the Ground of Ethics

Being illiterate, Mother Ann had not read the philosopher Immanuel Kant. However, Mother Ann's values prompted her followers to defend a helpless infant, and they resonated with Kant's ethical teachings. Kant was born in 1724, eighteen years after Benjamin Franklin, and a few years before George Washington (1732), John Adams (1735), and Thomas Jefferson (1743). His home city of Königsberg was a busy German port, the capital of Prussia until 1701, with a university. Kant's parents were from the skilled trades and though not highly educated were kind, devout Christians. They required the young boy to study the Bible, engage in intense introspection, and to pray. A gifted student, Kant absorbed the advanced thought of his day. In college, he read both natural science, especially the revolutionary works of Isaac Newton, and philosophy, with special emphasis upon John Locke, the philosopher who animated Jefferson's reflections on liberty.

Kant presented his ethics in *Groundwork of the Metaphysics of Morals,* which he published in 1785, while the Americans were writing the

US Constitution. The *Groundwork* provided, he said, a method for distinguishing valid from invalid ethical principles. Central to Kant's method is the assumption that human beings of every racial category are essentially the same. Similar to Jefferson who shared these ideals, Kant argues that persons share a common moral dignity. Kant affirmed a common, shared, and unitary ground to human beings. Kant's Lutheran education declared that all humans are created in God's image and are, therefore, kin. Because God is one, creatures made in his image are also one, at least in an abstract sense. John Bachman, the esteemed American naturalist, shared this theological principle and argued that scientifically speaking black and white persons were of one race. However, affirming that abstract notion of commonality—and affirming his devotion to Christian teachings— did not preclude Bachman from affirming the rightness of slavery.

The theological truism of the shared creation of all persons and his own rigorous demonstration of the unity of the races did not prevent Bachman from imbibing the prejudices of his day. Neither was it sufficient to inoculate Kant from the nearly universal racism of white European authors.[28] In 1787, the year that he revised his book on the limits of science, *The Critique of Pure Reason*, Kant also pronounced that the native people in Africa, India, and North America, among other dark-skinned persons, would never reach the heights of civilization that white Europeans alone had mastered.[29] Not knowing any of these persons, Kant based his deductions on reports from white travelers, missionaries, and colonial masters. Within that thought

---

[28] Charles Mills, *Blackness Visible: Essays on Philosophy and Race* (Itaca, NY: Cornell University Press, 1998). See also Emmanuel Chukwudi Eze, *Achieving our Humanity: The Idea of the Postracial Future* (New York: Routledge, 2001). See also Bernasconi, Robert. "Who Invented the Concept of Race? Kant's Role in the Enlightenment Construction of Race," *Race* (2001): 11–36, and Elden, Stuart. "Reassessing Kant's Geography," *Journal of Historical Geography* 35.1 (2009): 3–25.

[29] Pauline Kleingeld,, "Kant's Second Thoughts on Race," *The Philosophical Quarterly* 57.229 (2007): 573.

world, which mimics the self-congratulatory logic of American owners, blacks and others like them were destined to unending subordination. To put this in Kant's later language, accidental physical characteristics determined moral and intellectual characteristics as well. Forgetting his own principles of reasoning, Kant did not perceive his emotions, the pleasure of feeling himself to be among the so-called highest race animated his conclusions. As Thomas Hill and Bernard Boxill noted, Kant's "confidence that reason can overcome any assault from our sensuous nature may have fostered overconfidence."[30] This is perhaps a too generous reading of Kant's "sensuous" pleasures in affirming that he and his clan were the top of God's creation, superior to other human beings. Some scholars hold that by the 1790s, following the French Revolution and its rejection of hierarchies, Kant disowned his racist views. He denounced them and slavery, their natural consequence.[31] Evidence for this claim is that he also denounced European colonialism in favor of universal rights.

What Mother Ann saw immediately, that slavery in any form violates universal ethics, Kant had to deduce from first principles. In Kant's terms, we must treat persons as ends in themselves, not as a means to an end. No religious text and no religious intuition can trump this requirement. Kant recognized that persons have different life circumstances and different abilities. Stemming from his essay on the limits of the natural sciences, Kant argued that we have a dual nature; we live in two different worlds. Human beings belong to the world of strict causation: we are among the objects driven by natural causes that operate according to unchangeable laws discovered by natural scientists. In this world (which he calls the *phenomenal* world) the principles of the natural and biological sciences hold sway. Human beings are subject to the explanatory laws that govern all natural things.[32] Human beings also belong to a second

---

[30] Thomas Hill Jr., and Bernard Boxill, "Kant and Race," in *Race and Racism*, ed. Bernard R. Boxill (New York: Oxford University Press, 2001), 451.

[31] Pauline Kleingeld, "Kant's Second Thoughts on Race," *The Philosophical Quarterly* 57.229 (2007): 586–92.

[32] In his *Universal Natural History* (1755), Kant followed Isaac Newton's

world, a world of freedom (which Kant calls the *noumenal* world). We know that world by our deepest experience that our will is ours, not the product of mere chance. Echoes of this world appear in aesthetic experiences. For example, when we look at the stars on a clear night, we feel an intense pleasure, an experience of the "stillness of nature and the tranquillity [*sic*] of the mind, the immortal soul's hidden capacity to know speaks an unnamable language and provides inchoate [unformed] ideas which are certainly felt but are incapable of being described."[33]

While this is poetic, it does not tell us how to live. If something is unnamable we cannot reason about it and we cannot use it in public discourse. How can we reason ethically about the myriad decisions we must make in our ordinary, *phenomenal* lives? Kant's solution to this problem appeared in his *Groundwork of the Metaphysics of Morals* (1785) and was refined in *The Metaphysics of Morals* (1797).[34] In both works he showed that we cannot extract timeless, universal moral laws from empirical investigations. For example, slavery is a common feature of both small and large cultures. At various times, Jews, Christians, and Muslims owned slaves and participated in the slave trade. Was it acceptable then but not now? If the ethical status of slavery varies by culture and public opinion there is no reason it could not reappear later when public opinion shifts. We can discover interesting facts by surveying the history and sociology of slavery. But we cannot discover *laws* that govern the moral deliberations of all rational beings everywhere and for all time. If the majority of citizens

---

methods and proposed a strictly causal, non-deistic, theory of creation. All citations from Immanuel Kant, *Universal Natural History and Theory of the Heavens or An Essay on the Constitution and the Mechanical Origin of the Entire Structure of the Universe Based on Newtonian Principles.* (1755), trans. Ian Johnston, Vancouver Island University. Based on Georg Reimer's German edition of the complete works of Immanuel Kant (1905).

[33] Ibid., conclusion.

[34] Immanuel Kant, *Groundwork of the Metaphysics of Morals* (1785), trans. H. J. Paton (New York: HarperCollins, 1964), 123. All citations from the *Groundwork*, unless noted, are from this text.

of a democracy opt for slavery, as did the states of the Confederacy in 1861, who are we to oppose the will of the people?

In contrast to using opinion polls and democratic elections, Kant says that moral reasoning requires a foundation that is the same for all time, for all persons, and in all cultures. We need a way to assess ethical rules, guidelines, commandments, maxims, and the like. This "rule of rules" cannot be a generalization. For example, many, if not most, traditional cultures mistreat women: Is that a universally good thing to affirm? Is this tradition, which is similar to the rules that govern slavery, ethical? If we generalized from sociological reports, we would not like the results. Kant said that we should search for a rule that is not the mere summation of human customs and traditions. It must be like the rules of geometry that say that spheres are *perfectly* round, not almost round.[35] The ideas of "perfection" and "infinite" are valid in the realm of geometry, which is within the realm of thought. They are not valid in the realm of experience, of actual spheres in the phenomenal world of unchangeable laws.

With the Grimkés and Mother Ann, Kant affirmed the Golden Rule, to do unto others as we wish them to do unto us. Aside from piety, what recommends this rule above competing moral guidelines? Can we show through reason alone that it is the core principle and should guide all ethical reasoning? Responding to this question, Kant said that we need a way, a test with which we can evaluate competing rules and guidelines. That test is to imagine the guideline applied to everyone, in every nation, universally. We must picture, Kant said, that our rule guides how we treat others and how they treat us. More than that, Kant says that we must want this rule to guide everyone; we cannot merely accept it. We must wish the rule to become so dominant that by our choice it becomes universal, applying to us and all others.[36]

---

[35] Euclid, *Elements*. "Def. 14. *When a semicircle with fixed diameter is carried round and restored again to the same position from which it began to be moved, the figure so comprehended is a* sphere." http://aleph0.clarku.edu /~djoyce/java/elements/bookXI/defXI14.html.

[36] *Groundwork of the Metaphysics of Morals*, 89. "*Act as if the maxim of your*

As ultimate rulers and lawgivers, what would occur if the world ran according to *our* rules and those rules applied to us and our children? We might call this a supreme instance of integrative thinking: we are asked to place ourselves into a world where we legislate for all rational actors, for slaves as well as for owners. This requirement pulls us out of our specific experience and forces us to conceive of (to mentalize) a world under our dominion now and for all time. Kant argued that once articulated, this rule (the Categorical Imperative, as he named it) has far-reaching consequences, especially with regard to the status of humans and other rational beings. For rational beings are, he asserts, something *"whose existence* has *in itself* an absolute value, something which as *an end in itself* could be a ground for determinate law."[37] We cannot treat other human beings as merely means to an end, as entities whose wishes and self-understanding we can ignore. The reason for this is that human beings are capable of understanding themselves both as creatures, subject to natural forces, and as actors who can imagine themselves acting upon principle. To put this another way, human beings are capable of grasping the Golden Rule (assuming that they are not psychiatrically impaired or are too limited intellectually.) The moral intuition of the Golden Rule appeared in diverse religious traditions thousands of years ago. The rational argument appeared, Kant said, in his defense of its universality.

Because the Golden Rule and its philosophic version, the Categorical Imperative, forbid using persons as things, no form of slavery is ethically tolerable. Even so-called good owners systematically treated human beings as means, as devices that made them richer (often) and aggrandized (always). As rational creatures who live within a community of individuals we are each masters (but not owners) of ourselves. We cannot ethically reduce ourselves to objects, to slavery,

---

action were to become through your will a universal law of nature." (Emphasis in original.)

[37] Ibid., 95. Emphasis in original. Kant scholars debate whether this famous formula is a logical consequence of the categorical imperative, or it derives from Kant's Christian values. See Robert Johnson. "Kant's Moral Philosophy," *Stanford Encyclopedia of Philosophy,* http://plato.stanford.edu/entries/kant-moral/.

to commodities, even if we believe that such trade is legal and proper. As human beings, persons cannot undo their special status and so they cannot sell themselves (or anyone else) into slavery. Because of their criminal actions, citizens of a state might forfeit their equality with other persons. But they cannot do so by economic transactions even if they chose that. As rational beings, persons can have no master other than themselves. A man, Kant says, "cannot become like a domestic animal to be employed in any chosen capacity and retained therein without consent for any desired period, even with the reservation that he may not be maimed or killed."[38] For the same reason human beings cannot ethically subordinate their wills to others, to the Supreme Spiritual Leader, for example.[39]

Kant argued that our yearning to do that which we ought to do justifies our conviction that we can conceive of a world of freedom. Although we cannot know freedom, we can think it.[40] Ecstatic religious experiences of the kind Mother Ann had do not prove that the Golden Rule is better than other rules; for example, the tyrannical rule that "might makes right." However, we can ask ourselves if we would like our children to live in such a world. Because the answer is negative, the tyrannical rule fails. In contrast Kant says we may not be able to know freedom scientifically, but we can organize our ethics around the Categorical Imperative.[41] This is an instance of integrative

---

[38] Hans S. Reiss, ed., *Kant: Political Writings by Immanuel Kant,* (Cambridge: Cambridge University Press, 1991), "On the common saying: 'This may be true in theory, but does not apply in practice,'" [1793], 76.

[39] Thomas Mertens, "Arendt's Judgement [*sic*] and Eichmann's Evil," *Redescriptions: Political Thought, Conceptual History and Feminist Theory* 2.1 (1998): 58–89.

[40] "The moral 'I ought' is thus an 'I will' for man as a member of the intelligible world; and it is conceived by him as an 'I ought' only in so far as he considers himself at the same time to be a member of the sensible world" in Kant, *Groundwork of the Metaphysics of Morals,* 123.

[41] "While we do not comprehend the practical unconditioned necessity of the moral imperative, we do comprehend its *incomprehensibility*" in Kant, *Groundwork of the Metaphysics of Morals,* 131. (His emphasis)

thinking: it affirms our existential anguish as creatures who know that our yearning for certain knowledge cannot be granted.

Mother Ann called upon her religious experiences to create Shaker communities where distinctions of gender, race, and class disappeared and all persons were identical in God's eyes. Thanks to their adherence to the rules of Shaker belief, members of the South Union community of Kentucky overcame the embedded racism of the South and rescued a stranded infant.[42] In their community the racial and

---

[42] Because the goodwill is the only uncontestable good, persons who possess it count as rational and therefore they are "ends in themselves." To defend this formula, which seems intuitively valid, Kant must defend the possibility of free will. If human beings are among the furniture of the universe shaped by Newtonian forces, the idea of free will makes no sense. We may feel that we choose one action over another, but if everything, including our sense of self and choice, is caused by natural forces, this an illusion. All versions of naturalism preclude the possibility of free will and thus, it seems, the possibility of ethics since moral reasoning presupposes that actors can choose between alternatives. Most courts, for example, will not find a person guilty of first-degree murder if the defendant is proven to be deluded, to be under the sway of insane delusions that made it impossible to choose among actual possibilities. In British and American law the most famous statement on this principle occurred in 1843 in response to the trial of Daniel M'Naghten who had killed a man he believed was the prime minister. In his reflections on this case, Lord Chief Justice Tindal wrote that if the jurors believed that M'Naghten knew what he was doing, that it was a wicked act, they should convict. However, "If the jurors should be of opinion that the prisoner was not sensible, at the time he committed it, that he was violating the laws both of God and man, then he would be entitled to a verdict in his favour." If none of us have free will, and therefore free choice, then we are all variations on Mr. M'Naghten: we *believe* that we are making free choices but actually we are merely carrying out actions caused by forces beyond our understanding. If we affirm this extreme version of naturalism, then ethical judgment and ethical criticisms are irrational exercises in self- delusion. Kant agreed that as actors in the natural world we are subject to its inescapable laws. However, he argues, human beings also belong to the "intelligible world" (what Kant calls the *noumenal* world) whose members can grasp the *idea* of

class distinctions that terrified the grandmother of the mixed-race infant, Juliet, had disappeared. If the grandmother had affirmed Shaker teachings she would have shared their response to her grand-daughter's predicament, the orphan of her deceased daughter. That would have helped everyone involved; the amount of hatred in the world would have decreased and the grandmother could have mourned the loss of her daughter.

Kant did not create a community of believers. Instead, he asked us to imagine a world of "as if." Think and act as if we were others, per-haps of different color or sex or intellectual endowment. To slave owners he demanded that they imagine themselves as slaves. The ground of Kant's reflection is human feeling. We are human beings, he said, because we share the "universal *feeling of sympathy,* and . . . the faculty of being able to *communicate* universally our inmost feel-ings."[43] Our inmost feelings are what Mother Ann championed, what the Grimké sisters articulated, what slavery destroyed both in the en-slaved and in the owners. That desecration of the human spirit is what animated Abraham Lincoln's rejection of slavery.

Lincoln and Dred Scott

The Grimké Sisters, Mother Ann, and Immanuel Kant laid out the requirement for ethical advance: reflect upon our common human feelings; examine ourselves (not others); ask if we can tolerate a world where we wished our children to be bought and sold. As a young man, Abraham Lincoln felt in his bones that slavery was wrong. In his adult years he laid out the historical and legal case in the concrete in-stance of American slavery. We see this emerge in Lincoln's debates with Stephen A. Douglas in the 1858 race for US Senator from Illinois.

---

freedom. Our wish to act freely and to do the right thing, this instinctive feature of human beings who reflect upon right action, is an instance of the good will. That I *want* to be good means that I have "moral feelings," a will to do the right thing.

[43] *Kant's Critique of Judgement,* trans. J. H. Bernard 2nd ed. (London: Mac-millan, 1914), appendix: Of the method of Taste: section 625, 254.

Each man responded to the Supreme Court's 1857 decision of the Dred Scott case.[44] with a distinctive reading of its relationship to the principles of justice, its implications for the Senate election, and for the looming 1860 Presidential Election.[45]

The direct question regarding Dred Scott, an enslaved African American who sued for his freedom was, according to Chief Justice Roger Taney, could Scott, whose parents were enslaved, become a citizen of the United States. If so, Scott would be "entitled to all the rights, and privileges, and immunities, guarantied [sic] by [the Constitution]."[46] The larger questions were: did the Constitution permit slave owners to treat slaves as chattel property and could Congress control the spread of slavery into new US states and territories? Taney and the majority of the Court answered yes on the first question and no on the second. In other words, owners were absolutely protected and the political compromises between pro and antislavery groups eked out for fifty years were dissolved. Taney's sweeping defense of slavery, the dismissal of already enacted federal laws inhibiting its spread, and the threat of subsequent proslavery rulings enraged Lincoln. It denied personhood to African Americans and it reversed the tide of federal efforts to control and eventually eliminate slavery.[47]

---

[44] *Dred Scott v. Sanford*, 60 US393–Supreme Court 1857.

[45] Edwin E. Parks, ed., *The Lincoln-Douglas Debates* (Chicago: Hall & McCreary, F. A. Owen. 1918), http://www.archive.org/stream/lincolndouglasde00link/lincolndouglasde00link_djvu.txt.

[46] "Can a negro whose ancestors were imported into this country and sold as slaves become a member of the political community formed and brought into existence by the Constitution of the United States, and as such become entitled to all the rights, and privileges, and immunities, guarantied [sic] by that instrument to the citizen, one of which rights is the privilege of suing in a court of the United States in the cases specified in the Constitution?" http://www.law.cornell.edu/supct/html/historics/USSC_CR_0060_0393_ZO.html.

[47] "In effect, the Court ruled that slaves had no claim to freedom; they were property and not citizens; they could not bring suit in federal court; and because slaves were private property, the federal government could not revoke a white slave owner's right to own a slave based on where he lived, thus nullifying the

Even before the founding of the nation in 1787, legislatures in slave states faced painful contradictions. George Mason, Thomas Jefferson, George Washington, Henry Lee, and Patrick Henry, each a famous Virginian, could not reconcile their ethical aversion to slavery with entrenched economic interests. Erik Root, an American historian, recorded efforts by the House of Burgesses in Virginia to tax, control, and eventually eliminate the slave trade only to be countermanded by the British Crown that defended the lucrative practice.[48] Among these efforts were Jefferson's attempts to restrict the slave trade and enact a law whereby any person born in Virginia after December 31, 1800, would be declared free.[49]

In addition, there was no uniform slave law that extended throughout the South. This meant that proslavery legislators in Southern states had to manufacture *ad hoc* justifications for their state alone. More pointedly, "common to the law" of slavery in its many forms was the second clash of mutually incompatible legal principles—that of the slave as person and that of the slave as property. And it was here that the "freedom suit" posed such a challenge to the system, because it occupied an anomalous position between these two, blurring a distinction that many saw as essential to the maintenance of slavery."[50] The mundane fact is that slaves were a form of wealth and while some Virginia planters lamented the evils of slavery, they would not forfeit the wealth it afforded them.[51] In

---

essence of the Missouri Compromise. Taney, speaking for the majority, also ruled that since Scott was an object of private property, he was subject to the Fifth Amendment to the United States Constitution which prohibits taking property from its owner 'without due process'." John S. Vishneski, III. "What the Court Decided in *Dred Scott v. Sandford.*" *The American Journal of Legal History* 32, no. 4 (Oct., 1988), 390. http://www.jstor.org/stable/845743.

[48] Erik S. Root, *All Honor to Jefferson? The Virginia Slavery Debates and the Positive Good Thesis* (Lanham, MD: Lexington Books, 2008), especially 13–20.

[49] Ibid., 19.

[50] David Thomas Konig, "The Long Road to *Dred Scott:* Personhood and the Rule of Law in the Trial Court Records of St. Louis Slave Freedom Suits." *University of Missouri-Kansas City Law Review* 75 (Fall 2006): 58–59.

[51] James Madison, another Virginian, "could not escape his dependence on

addition, even Northern opponents of slavery, including the young Benjamin Franklin, enjoyed the pleasures of having persons in bondage serve them. Franklin, we learn, kept a few slaves in his later years, ran ads for slave sales, and sometimes traded in them.[52]

Looking backward to the long history of American slavery, Douglas and Lincoln recognized that the Constitution—dedicated to liberty—acknowledged the legal realities of slavery. The difference between the two was that Douglas found an easy, nonlegal, nonphilosophic, and irrational solution to ethical contradictions and Lincoln did not. Nor did Justice John McLean, who dissented. McLean cited English rulings that an enslaved person brought to England, whose laws recognized no right to own slaves, was therefore free. The same held true for other European nations.[53] (This was the situation Jefferson faced when he brought his slaves, Sally and James Hemings, to Paris with him. Under French law, they had every right to sue for their freedom and they would have won it.) Throughout his 16,500-word dissent McLean said that because it is abhorrent to common law and human dignity, slavery can exist only by "positive law," that is, by explicit legislation which protects it within a limited domain. He added that by permitting an owner to retain slave property in a free state, the court's opinion effectively trumped the rights of that state's citizens to declare slavery illegal within its borders. If one owner can bring his slave property to a free state and exercise dominion over his human property, one hundred thousand additional owners

---

slavery, whatever his private qualms, and told his father during his last year in Congress that unless the delegates got a pay raise, 'I shall be under the necessity of selling a Negro.'" Ron Chernow, *Alexander Hamilton* (New York: Penguin, 2004), 175. See also: *The Writings of James Madison*, vol. 1 (*Correspondence 1769-1783*) > TO JAMES MADISON. mad. mss. > paragraph 592. http://oll.libertyfund.org/titles/madison-the-writings-vol-1-1769-1783.

[52] Ron Chernow, *Alexander Hamilton*, 212; see also 211, 214, 306.

[53] "The slave is held to be free where there is no treaty obligation, or compact in some other form, to return him to his master." Justice Mclean, Dissenting Opinion, *Scott v. Sandford*. http://www.law.cornell.edu/supct/html/historics/USSC _CR_0060_0393_ZD .html.

could do the same. In effect, the court's ruling made every US state, including those that had never countenanced the institution, open to slavery.

In his lengthy debates with Lincoln, Douglas avoided legal reasoning, which is a form of integrative thinking. Instead he resorted to race-baiting the Illinois crowd: "Do you desire to turn this beautiful State into a free negro colony, in order that when Missouri abolishes slavery she can send one hundred thousand emancipated slaves into Illinois, to become citizens and voters, on an equality with yourselves?"[54] He concluded by calling Lincoln and his supporters, "Black Republicans." Later, when a Republican stalwart yelled from the crowd, "Couldn't you at least call us *Brown* Republicans?" Douglas thundered back he would not: it was the Republican's "affection for African Americans that made them black."[55]

In contrast, Lincoln used legal reasoning, historical review, and empathic imagination to present his case. While he acknowledged common feelings of white supremacy, Lincoln denied that accidents of birth or circumstance alter moral principles (an ethical claim). His empathic core emerges in his definition of democracy: "As I would not be a slave, so I would not be a master. This expresses my idea of democracy."[56] As he was to do in his Address at Cooper Institute in 1860, Lincoln reviewed the history of earlier efforts to

---

[54] "If you desire negro citizenship, if you desire to allow them to come into the State and settle with the white man, if you desire them to vote on an equality with yourselves, and to make them eligible to office, to serve on juries, and to adjudge your rights, then support Mr. Lincoln and the Black Republican party, who are in favor of the citizenship of the negro." Parks, *The Lincoln-Douglas Debates*, 26.

[55] William Lee Miller, *Lincoln's Virtues* (New York: Knopf, 2002), 353. See also chap. 5 in Harry V. Jaffa. *A New Birth of Freedom: Abraham Lincoln and the Coming of the Civil War* (New York: Rowman & Littlefield, 2000).

[56] From August 1, 1858, according to Roy P. Balser. Mario Matthew Cuomo, and G. S. Boritt eds., *Lincoln on Democracy* (Bronx, NY: Fordham University Press, 2004), 121.

control slavery.[57] Federal laws forbidding the importation of slaves, going back to those passed in 1794, prefigured the Republican party's proposal to forbid the importation of slaves to new territories. Both laws are just and both derive from the ethical fact that slaves are *persons*, a term used explicitly in the 1787 Constitution.[58] As persons, Lincoln argued, slaves are "entitled to all the natural rights numerated in the Declaration of Independence—the right to life, liberty, and the pursuit of happiness."[59] Although Lincoln had no training in philosophy, his core insight is Kantian: that persons have an inherent dignity in themselves, as persons.[60]

Lincoln did not deny personhood to slaves; he puzzled over how

---

[57] Delivered on February 27, 1860. Source: Roy P. Basler, ed., *Collected Works of Abraham Lincoln* (Piscataway, NJ: Rutgers University Press, 1953), vol. 3, 522–50.

[58] (article I, section 2; article 1, section 9; article 4, section 2).

[59] Basler, *Collected Works of Abraham Lincoln*, vol. 3, 16. For example, article 1, section 9, clause 1, regarding the slave trade: "The Migration or Importation of such Persons as any of the States now existing shall think proper to admit, shall not be prohibited by the Congress prior to the Year one thousand eight hundred and eight, but a tax or duty may be imposed on such Importation, not exceeding ten dollars for each Person." In the Address at the Cooper Institute, Lincoln argued that "wherever in that instrument the slave is alluded to, he is called a 'person;'—and wherever his master's legal right in relation to him is alluded to, it is spoken of as 'service or labor which may be due,'—as a debt payable in service or labor. Also, it would be open to show, by contemporaneous history, that this mode of alluding to slaves and slavery, instead of speaking of them, was employed on purpose to exclude from the Constitution the idea that there could be property in man." (ibid., 545).

[60] Christopher Bracey, a contemporary American law professor, put it, "To have personal dignity is to appreciate oneself sufficiently that one would withstand pressures to lower one's self esteem. A strong sense of perspective on self-worth often has the effect of revealing the spuriousness of assaults on dignity." "Dred Scott, Human Dignity, and the Quest for a Culture of Equality," in *The Dred Scott Case: Historical and Contemporary Perspectives on Race and Law*, ed. David Thomas Konig, Paul Finkelman, Christopher Alan Bracey (Athens, OH: Ohio University Press, 2010), 125.

best to curtail and eventually to eliminate slavery; he recognized the dangers of secession and civil war.[61] However, in ways that seem unusual for a Northern politician, Lincoln did not castigate the South. He recognized the anxiety that Southern (and many Northern) whites had about an influx of newly freed African Americans: "A universal feeling, whether well or ill-founded, cannot be safely disregarded."[62] Lincoln did not escape the pervasive racism of American culture. However, Lincoln's empathy for the South should help us locate him in his time and recognize his moral courage. This may not be easy. We are tempted to idealize Lincoln. We want him, therefore, to represent our sense of our best selves—as not racist, for example. Or, we reduce him to just another politician whose fine language masked his ambition. In Lincoln's words, we ought to show him more charity. Lincoln helped recalibrate the thought-world of nineteenth-century Americans.[63] Lincoln's capacity to recast the American past, which undergirds all of his speeches, is matched by his capacity to envision the nation free of slavery.

---

[61] He cites Jefferson's 1821 comments, "It is still in our power to direct the process of emancipation, and deportation, peaceably, and in such slow degrees, as that the evil will wear off insensibly; and their places be, pari passu, filled up by free white laborers. If, on the contrary, it is left to force itself on, human nature must shudder at the prospect held up." Entry 7977: *The Jeffersonian Cyclopedia* (New York: Funk & Wagnalls, 1900), 816.

[62] Basler, *Collected Works of Abraham Lincoln*, vol. 3, 15.

[63] "Humans have a far larger set of evolved specializations that we call *recalibrational releasing engines* that involve situation-detecting algorithms and whose function is to trigger appropriate recalibrations, including affective recalibrations, when certain evolutionarily recognizable situations are encountered. By coordinating the mental contents of individuals in the same situation (because both intuitively know that, e.g., the loss of your mother is, as a default, experienced as a sad and painful event), these programs also facilitate communication and culture learning, both of which depend on a shared frame of reference." John Tooby and Leda Cosmides, "Conceptual Foundations of Evolutionary Psychology," in *Handbook of Evolutionary Psychology*, ed. David M. Buss (New York: Wiley, 2005), 60.

This is another aspect of integrative thinking: we are required to reflect upon the past and try to understand its meaning, its trajectory. Lincoln *hoped* to reveal the intentions of the founders; he *wished* to identify their best selves with himself; he *sought* to visualize their promises fulfilled.[64] Prior to these wishes, however, was his devotion to legal reasoning. In his Address at Cooper Union in February 1860, Lincoln assessed the reasoning that the American founders employed when they framed the Constitution of 1787 and in subsequent legislative acts. His old Illinois opponent, Stephen A. Douglas, had argued that the framers of the Constitution knew exactly what they thought about slavery and that the question had been settled by them in 1787. Lincoln sought to refute this static, timeless reading of the founders' intentions. The debate focused on the question: Were all issues regarding the control of slavery resolved in 1787 such that future legislatures could not control slavery in new federal territories? Douglas said they were, Lincoln said they were not.

In a brilliant speech of some 7,700 words, Lincoln recounted the history of the Constitution and the debates that led to its framing. It is a compelling performance marked by legal arguments and historical recitation. After documenting explicit votes taken on issues of slavery between 1784 and 1820, he shows that twenty-one of the thirty-nine original signers voted to give the federal government control over slavery at different times.[65] Hence, the majority of the founders did vote to control slavery in ways not specified in the 1787 Constitution. At the end of

---

[64] As Garry Wills put it. *Lincoln at Gettysburg: The Words that Remade America* (New York: Simon & Schuster, 1992), 148–76.

[65] "The sum of the whole is, that of our thirty-nine fathers who framed the original Constitution, twenty-one—a clear majority of the whole—certainly understood that no proper division of local from federal authority, nor any part of the Constitution, forbade the Federal Government to control slavery in the federal territories; while all the rest probably had the same understanding. Such, unquestionably, was the understanding of our fathers who framed the original Constitution; and the text affirms that they understood the question 'better than we.'" http://showcase.netins.net/web/creative/lincoln/speeches/cooper.htm.

the speech he addresses his Southern audience: "We know we hold to no doctrine, and make no declaration, which were not held to and made by 'our fathers who framed the Government under which we live.'" Because those fathers themselves took part in the control of slavery, he said, it is not revolutionary to propose a similar control on the expansion of slavery into new territories: "The Federal Government, however, as we insist, has the power of restraining the extension of the institution—the power to insure that a slave insurrection shall never occur on any American soil which is now free from slavery."

Lincoln's final thoughts on slavery and the causes of the Civil War appeared in his Second Inaugural Address delivered on March 4, 1865. The Gettysburg Address and the Second Inaugural are American prose poems that provoke numerous readings.[66] Having been shaped by both speeches, we bring to them scriptural intensity conditioned by our sense of the variable moral status of the United States.[67]

The Second Inaugural: Confronting the Divided Mind

The text of the Second Inaugural is twenty-six sentences, comprising

---

[66] Seventeen years after its erection, the Lincoln Memorial and the two texts it enshrines had become icons of American self-consciousness. It dominates Frank Capra's hymn to American values in *Mr. Smith Goes to Washington* (1939). It reappears in the science-fiction classic about the Cold War, *The Day the Earth Stood Still* (1951), by Edmund H. North, produced by Julian Blaustein and directed by Robert Wise. In the latter, Klaatu, a god-like alien ponders whether humans are worth saving. He visits the Lincoln Memorial and reads Lincoln's texts: KLAATU (visibly impressed): "Those are great words." (With an air of discovery). "He must have been a great man." In 1860 Lincoln saved the Union, in 1951 he saved the earth. (Revised final draft, February 21, 1951, http://www.scifiscripts.com/scripts/TheDayTheEarthStoodSTill.html.

[67] Perry Anderson and others who are wary of American nationalism cast a skeptical eye on Lincoln: "But Lincoln, of course, did not fight the Civil War to free slaves, whose emancipation was an instrumental by-blow of the struggle. He waged it to preserve the Union, a standard nationalist objective." Perry Anderson, "Arms and Rights: Rawls, Habermas and Bobbio in an Age of War," *New Left Review* 31 (January-February 2005): 14.

seven hundred words. Lincoln delivered it on March 4, 1865, five weeks before he was assassinated. As many have noted, a lesser commander in chief might have made a triumphal speech, denigrated the South, praised his own wisdom, and claimed that the North's impending victory demonstrated divine sanction for his policies. No self-praise emerged. Instead Lincoln recounted stark facts about the war that, Lincoln says, "came," without ascribing blame to either side.

Of these twenty-six sentences, nineteen are both factual and empathic; one is factual; six are theological reflections. The factual statement is, "One-eighth of the whole population were colored slaves, not distributed generally over the Union, but localized in the southern part of it." This is followed by two humble propositions that are deeply empathic to Southern concerns:

These slaves constituted a peculiar and powerful interest.
All knew that this interest was somehow the cause of the war.

The first proposition notes the oddity of American slavery (which should be acknowledged by all thinking persons) and the economic interest Southern planters had vested in it. As we have seen, the economic value of slaves was enormous: no amount of moralizing sermons by abolitionists could undo this fact. Very few people would find it easy to sacrifice half or more of their net worth, the effect of global emancipation on slaveholders. In addition, forthright Southerners had affirmed Lincoln's proposition. Some eighty years earlier, in 1788, Rawlins Lowndes, of South Carolina, made the same point: slaves are natural resources. Debating the provision to stop the African slave trade twenty years hence Lowndes said that without slaves South Carolina would degenerate into swamps. Only slavery made it salvageable: "*Negroes were our wealth, our only natural resource*; yet behold how our kind friends in the north were determined soon to tie up our hands, and drain us of what we had!"[68]

---

[68] Document 10, Debate in South Carolina House of Representatives. 16–17 Jan. 1788. Elliot 4:272–73, 285–86. (My emphasis.) *The Founders' Constitution*

Another South Carolinian, Charles Pinckney, one of the founders, fiercely defended slavery during the Constitutional Convention in 1787. In 1820, Pinckney looked back to these debates and re-articulated his understanding of the compromises of 1787. As he saw it, Congress had explicitly avoided challenging Southern traditions and practices regarding slavery. In his words, Congress recognized that "*the property of the southern states in slaves* was to be as sacredly preserved, and protected to them, as that of land, or any other kind of property in the eastern states was to be to their citizens."[69] This takes the question of slavery out of subtle disputes and legal quibbles. Just as New York had its great ports and Massachusetts had fishing and whaling and Maine had lumber, South Carolina had slaves.

In 1821, Pinckney debated the Missouri Compromise (which admitted Missouri as a slave state and Maine as a free state) and the fugitive slave clause (article 4, section 2 of the Constitution). The debate turned on what the Constitution meant by the term *citizen*. Who merited inclusion in that special category? Who did not? Pinckney found it absurd to include blacks in that category. He "perfectly knew that there did not then exist such a thing in the Union as a black or colored citizen, nor could I then have conceived it possible such a thing could have ever existed in it; nor, notwithstanding all that has been said on the subject, do I now believe one does exist in it."[70]

Vol., Article 1, Section 9, Clause 1, Document 10, http://press-pubs.uchicago.edu/founders/documents/a1_9_1s10.html. Citing Jonathan Elliot, ed., *The Debates in the Several State Conventions on the Adoption of the Federal Constitution as Recommended by the General Convention at Philadelphia in 1787,* 5 vols. 2nd ed. 1888 (New York: Burt Franklin, n.d.).

[69] Marty D. Matthews, *Forgotten Founder: The Life and Times of Charles Pinckney* (Columbia, SC: University of South Carolina Press, 2004), 132, citing Pinckney's speech in the House of Representatives on 24 February 1820. (My emphasis.)

[70] Charles Pinckney, Admission of Missouri, House of Representatives. 13 Feb. 1821. *Annals* 37:1129, 1134. *The Founders' Constitution.* Volume 4, Article 4, Section 2, Clause 1, Document 15. http://press-pubs.uchicago.edu/founders/documents/a4_2_1s15.html. (The University of Chicago Press.) (My emphasis.)

Pinckney came from an illustrious family woven into the governance in South Carolina and the nation. We can see how Pinckney's reasoning proceeds:

1. As the author of the article he should control its meaning.
2. He intended that the label *citizen* apply only to Caucasian persons.
3. Black and colored persons are not Caucasians.
4. Hence, they can never be considered citizens.

We may grant Pinckney the truth of propositions [2] and [3]: most likely he did wish to exclude non-Caucasians from full citizenship and, by definition, non-Caucasians are not Caucasians. We resist, though, assenting to propositions [1] and [4]. Even modern tyrants cannot control the semantic depth and reach of a shared language (though they try). Assuming the rights of ownership, Pinckney presumes the right to control the words *citizen* and *person*. If used in a too-free manner, these words threatened to extend the mantle of dignity to non-Caucasians and that would make slavery unseemly for men who claimed to be Christian defenders of liberty. To prevent that internal, painful conflict, Pinckney—and numerous others since his time—curtailed titles that grant equal dignity to blacks.[71]

---

[71] In the appendix to *Nineteen Eighty-Four*, George Orwell described how the "Ministry of Truth" (Minitrue) denuded English of its semantic richness: "All ambiguities and shades of meaning were eliminated from words. Each word was assigned only one clear meaning, and no other. Words were stripped of all associated connections with any other thoughts. All secondary meanings were eliminated. In addition, the number of words was progressively reduced to the barest possible minimum necessary for communication." This is another instance of splitting; the goal is to sever mental linkages; to make new associations and new semantic discoveries impossible; to prevent spontaneous and original thought. As Orwell noted in an essay published shortly before *Nineteen Eighty-Four*, "All nationalists [people who idealize a nation] have the power of not seeing resemblances between similar sets of facts. A British Tory will defend self-determination

Pinckney did not invent the English language. He did not patent the word *citizen*, nor did he craft the article in question by himself. The matter was debated and other voices made equally persuasive counter arguments about the term's meaning. The term *citizen* was as contentious in 1787 as it was in 1821 and as it is now. The grandiose aspect of Pinckney's claim is that as the author of the clause in question he had eternal control and ownership over its future meanings. This dictatorial claim emerged out of a divided mind: having denied full humanity to slaves (and other non-Caucasians), Pinckney cannot permit himself to conceive of a future in which they would merit the status of citizens. Nor does he imagine himself as dark skinned, deprived of dignity, and as a target of his laws and of his own maxims.

Pinckney's assertions mirror the calamity of American slavery. They emerged from his divided mind, and his divided mind emerged from the contradictory forces that shaped American politics for hundreds of years. Pinckney's speech illustrates the disease; Lincoln's speech illustrates the antidote. The answer to Pinckney's assertion appears in the final paragraph of the Second Inaugural. In response to a war that cost seven hundred thousand lives and for which many blamed him, Lincoln articulated his devotion to the value of unity (of the Union; of continuity with the founders' wishes to solve the original contradiction; of the shared sacrifice of the war; of a common human family). The poetry of the speech crystalizes in its vision of a future Union, grounded on unity, forgiveness, and empathy: "With malice toward none, with charity for all." Lincoln reached back to the King James Bible, to American history, and to Jefferson's ideals (not his actions). Using those resources, he foresaw a future nation reunited with its founding ideals, its citizens completing the task begun in

---

in Europe and oppose it in India with no feeling of inconsistency." This ability to not see patterns, to not see parallels is fueled by the pleasure of merging with the idealized other, the Band of Brothers, the Corp, the Ancestors, etc., and hating what is outside the self. United in righteous, dissociative anger, we cannot be wrong and we savor this opportunity to hate. When James Bond kills the evil mastermind we share Bond's smirk.

1776. His deep metaphor of brokenness and repair began with wounded bodies, minds, and communities and extended to the broken nation and to a broken world.

When it is used to punish, enslave, and exploit others—which was the lifeblood and mission of the South—power is corrupted. To retain power of this type, rulers must instill in those who control the weapons and the courts and the prisons a horrific fear of those whom they have made enemies. Having wagered all their wealth and self-esteem on the defense of slavery in 1861, Southern elites had no factual or rational basis to defend the South when it was defeated in 1865. In response to that defeat came the maniacal defense of the Lost Cause, the zealotry of the United Daughters of the Confederacy and similar groups, and the relentless drive to recast the history of slavery and the war. All these and many other devices are resistant to insight; witness the continued battles over displaying the flags of the Confederacy and compulsive actions to deny the facts of slavery.

Southern patriots cannot let themselves grasp *why* the South fought: to defend the economic rewards of slavery and its diverse pleasures. Instead, they have spent immense energy to tell illusory stories that mask, but do not resolve, Southern shame and desolation. This drive has had tragic consequences for North and South and most especially for African Americans.

About the Author

Volney Gay is Professor of Religion, Professor of Anthropology, and Professor of Psychiatry at Vanderbilt University in Nashville, Tennessee. He is also Supervising and Training Analyst at the St. Louis Psychoanalytic Institute. He was Chair of Religious Studies, the College of Arts and Sciences at Vanderbilt for twelve years; Director of the Center for the Study of Religion and Culture at Vanderbilt for eight years; Director of Psychotherapy Training, Department of Psychiatry, Vanderbilt Medicine for three years; and Director of the PhD program in Religion, Psychology, and Culture at intervals for twenty-five years. He has directed thirty PhD dissertations.

Dr. Gay and his wife, Barbara, have two adult children. In 2010, he endowed the "Barbara Gay Lecture in Child Psychiatry" at Vanderbilt University to honor his wife's twenty-five-year commitment to the emotional needs of Nashville's schoolchildren. This is his ninth published book.

Index